Baseball's Most
Baffling MVP Ballots

Baseball's Most Baffling MVP Ballots

Jeremy Lehrman

McFarland & Company, Inc., Publishers
Jefferson, North Carolina

LIBRARY OF CONGRESS CATALOGUING-IN-PUBLICATION DATA

Names: Lehrman, Jeremy, 1971– author.
Title: Baseball's most baffling MVP ballots / Jeremy Lehrman.
Other titles: Baseball's most baffling Most Valuable Player [Award] ballots
Description: Jefferson, North Carolina : McFarland & Company, Inc., Publishers, 2016 | Includes bibliographical references and index.
Identifiers: LCCN 2016036389 | ISBN 9781476666754 (softcover : acid free paper) ∞
Subjects: LCSH: Most Valuable Player Award (Baseball)—History. | Baseball—United States—Statistics. | Baseball players—Rating of.
Classification: LCC GV877 .L35 2016 | DDC 796.357/64—dc23
LC record available at https://lccn.loc.gov/2016036389

BRITISH LIBRARY CATALOGUING DATA ARE AVAILABLE

ISBN (print) 978-1-4766-6675-4
ISBN (ebook) 978-1-4766-2613-0

© 2016 Jeremy Lehrman. All rights reserved

No part of this book may be reproduced or transmitted in any form or by any means, electronic or mechanical, including photocopying or recording, or by any information storage and retrieval system, without permission in writing from the publisher.

On the front cover: 1941 American League MVP award; background photograph © 2016 Gualberto Becerra

Printed in the United States of America

McFarland & Company, Inc., Publishers
 Box 611, Jefferson, North Carolina 28640
 www.mcfarlandpub.com

For you, Dad.

Acknowledgments

Andy Sobel is a wonderful reader and a better friend—any acknowledgment of his support and generosity as it relates to this project is inadequate, so instead I offer my sincere gratitude.

Thanks must be tendered to a trio of talented and accomplished sportswriters who took the time to reply to an email from some guy "writing a book": Joe Posnanski, Jerry Crasnick, and Dave Schoenfield—they had no earthly reason to respond to my emails, but I'm so glad they did. The same can be said for James L. Gates, Jr., Library Director at the National Baseball Hall of Fame and Museum. I would also like to thank Keith Allison for the use of his wonderful photos, and Dr. Sheryll Casuga for taking the time to answer my questions and offer her perspective.

Does it make sense to thank a website? How about the people behind the website—people I've never met? Well, thank you, Baseball-Reference.com, and thanks to the team who make it run. It was invaluable as a research tool.

Mike Rodriguez was kind enough to read portions of this book in its earliest form. We've been talking baseball for more than 30 years, and it never gets old.

Table of Contents

Acknowledgments	vi
Preface: A Few Things to Know	1
Introduction: "What does a man have to do to win this thing?"	5
1. A Firm Believer in Advertising: The History of the MVP Award	7
2. The Crab Performs Miracles in Boston	16
3. Establishing a Pecking Order	24
4. Out by a Mile	35
5. Revisionist History 101	50
6. Black Mike and the Triple Crown	74
7. The Octopus	84
8. Sticking It to the Splinter: Most Career MVP Snubs	94
9. The Gym Teacher Who Came in from the Cold	103
10. Curiouser and Curiouser	107
11. "What are we going to do? Break it in half?"	119
12. MVP Mosts (and Leasts)	124
13. A Certain Kind of Logic	130
14. Out of Character: MVP Flukes	141
15. Meet the Mets, Greet the … Team That Has Never Had an MVP	150
16. The Greatest Season That Never Was	158
17. Never Mind, Juan Gone—It's the 90s	164
18. Are MVP Voters Racist?	173

19. Fun with Arbitrary Endpoints: MVPs of the Decade	180
20. The Wonderful Argument	191
21. The Last Worst MVP: The Future of the Award	197
Appendix: The List, 1911–2015	209
Chapter Notes	215
Bibliography	231
Index	239

Preface:
A Few Things to Know

You'll find lots of numbers throughout these pages. *Lots* of numbers. That won't intimidate you. If you're reading this book, you're probably a serious fan of the game—and if you're a serious fan, you probably love to immerse yourself in statistics. But just in case you're a casual fan, or decide to give this book as a gift, or use it as supporting evidence to win a bet, here are a few things to keep in mind.

Wins Above Replacement (WAR)

Developed by Sean Smith, Wins Above Replacement (WAR) is used as a baseline statistic throughout this book. WAR estimates how many wins a player was worth to his team as compared to a replacement-level player.

If you're not familiar with WAR, the basic premise is this: Every action or reaction on the field is geared toward scoring more runs than your opponent. Every pitch, every catch, every hit, every walk, every *everything* is in service to accumulating or preventing runs.

Obviously, if a team creates more runs than it allows, it wins. So WAR calculates how many runs a player created (or cost) his team with his hitting and base running, and how many runs a player saved (or cost) his team with his defense. WAR then compares those contributions to the theoretical contributions of a "replacement-level" player. Think of a replacement-level player as a generic player called up from the minors. Playing under the same conditions, a major leaguer should contribute more runs—and hence, more *wins*—to his team than a replacement from the minor leagues.

And there you have it: WAR estimates the number of wins contributed by a player *above* what could be expected of a replacement player. According to MLB.com, the official website of Major League Baseball, "a player with a WAR of zero is essentially a replaceable piece, while a player with a WAR of about eight should almost always be an MVP candidate."

A player with a WAR of 10 is, well, Willie Mays.

Pitchers have their own version of WAR (pWAR), but the premise is essentially the same: By calculating the number of runs a pitcher allows as compared with the *expected* number of runs allowed by a theoretical replacement, pWAR calculates how many wins a major league pitcher contributes as compared with a minor-league call-up (don't concern yourself with pitcher won-loss records here; we're referring to *team* wins).

There is more than one formula to calculate WAR—we use Baseball-Reference.com's numbers for reasons that will become obvious in a few paragraphs.

Leading the league in WAR doesn't necessarily mean one should be handed the MVP award. WAR is just one supporting pillar in the broader MVP argument. Like any holistic stat, it allows room for interpretation (and WAR certainly has its share of detractors). Some fans prefer Wins Above Average (WAA), Runs [saved] Above Replacement (RAR), weighted on-base average (wOBA), or Win Shares. That's fine. Those are fine measurements. We don't use them (see Chapter 3 for more on WAR).

There are hundreds of other stats throughout, almost all of which will be familiar to you. Here are two that are central to the experience of reading this book.

- *On-base + Slugging Plus (OPS+), also called Adjusted Production.* This statistic compares the sum of a player's on-base and slugging percentages (OPS) against the league average while accounting for playing conditions. Here's how it works: League-average OPS+ is always given a value of 100. If a player generates an 80 OPS+ in a given season, that means his OPS production was 20% *below* league average. If a player generates a 120 OPS+ in a given season, his OPS production was 20% *above* league average. Ted Williams compiled a career 190 OPS+; Williams, by this measure, was 90% more productive than a league-average hitter over the course of his career.

    OPS+ is a much more useful metric than OPS, which merely combines a player's on-base and slugging percentages. Two players can generate very similar OPS, but significantly different OPS+, depending on where they play their games. One of many examples is Ellis Burks and Ken Caminiti, 1996.

1996	**OBP**	**SLG**	**OPS**	**OPS+**
Burks	.408	.639	1.047	149
Caminiti	.408	.621	1.029	174

Burks and Caminiti had virtually identical on-base and slugging percentages, but Burks compiled his numbers in the offensive twilight zone that was Colorado's Coors Field, while San Diego's Caminiti plied his trade at sea level, in a pitcher's park. OPS+ reveals that Caminiti was the significantly more productive hitter, relative to the league.

Another reason OPS+ is useful is that it allows us to compare offensive production across *eras* (by accounting for the playing conditions of the time). For example: Chuck Klein in 1930 hit .386/.436/.687, with 40 HR and 170 RBI; Willie McCovey in 1967 hit .276/.378/.535., with 31 HR and 91 RBI.

At first glance, it appears Klein had the far superior season—but McCovey was just as good a hitter *relative* to his time and place. Klein (159 OPS+) played his home games in the Baker Bowl (an extreme hitter's park), during the highest-scoring season on record; McCovey (the same 159 OPS+) had to ply his trade when pitching dominated the game. OPS+ takes these playing conditions into account and provides a more accurate picture of their relative production (it should be noted that OPS+ does not include base running, so it is not a complete picture of a player's offensive production).

- *Adjusted ERA (ERA+)*. Works like OPS+, except it is used for pitchers. It compares a pitcher's earned run average (ERA), adjusted for where he pitched, against the league ERA. So if two pitchers have the same ERA, but one pitches in a hitter-friendly park (think Fenway Park), and the other pitches in a pitcher-friendly park (think Dodgers Stadium), their ERA+ reflects their respective pitching environments.

  Here's an example of how it works: Felix Hernandez of the Seattle Mariners led the American League with a 2.14 ERA in 2014; Chris Sale of the Chicago White Sox was runner-up at 2.17. However, Sale's ERA+ was better than Hernandez' (178 to 170), because Sale pitched his home games at U.S. Cellular Field, a great hitter's park, while Hernandez took the mound at Safeco Field, a park that helps pitchers.

  If a pitcher has an 85 ERA+ in a given season, his ERA was 15% *worse* than league average. If he had a 115 ERA+ in a given season, his ERA was 15% *better* than league average (so, unlike ERA, *higher* is better).

  ERA+ also allows us to compare (to a reasonable extent) pitchers from different eras. Pedro Martinez pitched to a 1.74 ERA in 2000, which was the 87th best mark since 1900. But Martinez pitched his home games at Fenway Park, during one of the highest-scoring seasons in American League history. His *adjusted* ERA that season was *291*—the best mark ever recorded. As measured by ERA+, Pedro's 1.74 ERA in 2000 is superior to Bob Gibson's 1.12 ERA in 1968 (the third-lowest scoring season of the 20th century).

When in the course of the book we come across a number that may seem less than intuitive, an explanation will be provided.

Speaking of Numbers...

Every one of the thousands of numbers you'll find throughout was found using Baseball-Reference.com. It's simply the best baseball research tool in the world.

How to Approach the Text

This book is organized, for the most part, in chronological order—beginning in the early years of the 20th century and continuing through to the present day (and beyond). Don't worry if you're the non-linear type—you can dive in at any point in the narrative. Most chapters focus on a specific MVP vote from a specific year, but as you'll see, some sections are organized around a particular theme (e.g., baseball's Triple Crown) or question (e.g., has racial bias played a role in MVP voting?). The book doesn't attempt to deconstruct *every* MVP ballot cast over the last 100 years—only the most controversial, contentious, or confounding. In all, you'll find extended analysis or brief commentary on dozens of votes (as well as an annotated list of every Most Valuable Player winner since 1911). For more on the letter and spirit of the book, see the introduction.

A Note on Notes

You'll find copious notes throughout. Lots of people skip the notes. You shouldn't. There's lots of stuff in there to amuse, illuminate, and offend.

Introduction: "What does a man have to do to *win this thing*?"

Fred Lieb, a long-time dean of American sportswriters, used to recall with gusto a brief conversation he had with St. Louis Cardinals owner Sam Breadon in the fall of 1924. The topic at hand was the election of Dazzy Vance, Brooklyn's overwhelming ace, as National League MVP.

"Sam Breadon, Cardinal owner, nearly burned out the wires when he telephoned me from St. Louis," wrote Lieb. "Without a word of greeting, Breadon sizzled into his mouthpiece, 'What does a man have to do to *win this thing*? Hornsby not getting it is a [blasted] outrage!'"

1924	WAR	G	AB	R	H	2B	3B	HR	RBI	SB	CS	BB	K	BA	OBP	SLG	OPS	OPS+
Hornsby	**11.5**	143	536	**121**	**227**	**43**	14	25	94	5	12	**89**	32	**.424**	**.507**	**.696**	**1.203**	**222**

***Bold** indicates player led league*

Lieb was doubtlessly exercising editorial discretion in his recounting of the conversation; it's a certainty that Breadon wasn't so polite. At the time of the call, Lieb was chairman of the NL's Most Valuable Player committee, responsible for selecting the eight writers—one from each NL city—who voted on the league's top individual honor. The 1924 vote had special significance as it was the first "official" MVP award sponsored by the NL, and the league's first individual player honor of any kind since 1914, when auto magnate Hugh Chalmers discontinued his annual awarding of a new car to the "player deemed most useful to his club."

1924	pWAR	W	L	W%	ERA	G	GS	CG	SHO	IP	H	R	ER	BB	K	ERA+	WHIP	K/BB
Vance	**10.4**	**28**	6	**.824**	**2.16**	35	34	**30**	3	308.1	238	89	74	77	**262**	**174**	1.022	3.40

The 1924 award was seen as a two-horse race between Vance and the formidable Rogers Hornsby, who batted an NL-record .424 for the St. Louis Cardinals. The Cardinals were terrible that year, finishing in sixth place. Still, .424. The stuff of which MVPs are made.

The voters had other ideas—with one writer unable to find room on his 10-man ballot for the Cardinals' second baseman.

The result was met with peals of outrage in the Gateway City. Hornsby's snub became a bigger story than Vance's victory, and a cherished baseball tradition was born: The annual MVP controversy.

Breadon spoke for every 1924 Cardinals fan (and every 1986 Yankees fan, every 2012 Angels fan, every 1965 Giants fan) when he bellowed: "What does a man have to do to *win this thing*?" It's a question we as fans ask ourselves every time our favorite player gets passed over for an individual honor.

◆ ◆ ◆

Now, let's be clear: Vance's designation as most valuable was about the least controversial choice the writers could make (more on Vance in Chapter 1). But this wasn't the case in 1925 … or 1947 … or 1962 … or 1984 … or 1996 … or dozens of other seasons when the award went to a player who didn't deserve it. Some of these votes defy common sense; others defy belief. These "worst-of-the-worst" ballots are also some of the most fascinating in the history of the award, and provide an illuminating (and confounding) snapshot of the most prestigious and contentious individual award in sports.

Which brings us to the aim of this book.

These "scandalous" MVP votes deserve to be revisited and reconstructed (and, at times, defended or further vilified) because they tell us so much about the game and its times. Which of the so-called "worst MVP selections of all time" can hold up to contemporary statistical analysis (and the game's contemporary mores)? How many of these ballots wither under scrutiny, and how many, as it turns out, weren't so bad? Who *really* deserved the MVP in a given year?

We'll attempt in these pages to answer these questions, right some wrongs, convert some non-believers, and provide some fodder for your next fantasy-league drinking night. We'll dig deep to uncover the stories behind some of the names you see on those "worst MVP" lists. We'll take some detours, provide some context, unravel some threads, and look at familiar faces in different ways. We may not settle every argument, but we'll have fun in trying.

1

A Firm Believer in Advertising: The History of the MVP Award

Hugh Chalmers (b. 1873) was that most authentic American construct: The brazen, huckster industrialist. Part Henry Ford, part P.T. Barnum, the self-made Chalmers began his career at the age of 14 as an office boy at the National Cash Register Company; by the time he was 35, he owned an eponymous automobile manufacturer, the Chalmers Motor Company, renowned for building "medium-priced" cars aimed at a burgeoning and aspirant middle class.[1]

The charismatic Chalmers was a born salesman who saturated newspapers with ads for his cars (*"Not how large but how good"* was a tagline). He sponsored road races and exhibitions to showcase his merchandise, and became something of an authority on marketing and promotion. He was a popular speaker on the Chamber of Commerce circuit, giving countless talks on the art of selling, which he described as "simply influencing the human mind." His speeches were reprinted in newspapers, advertising books, and educational pamphlets—required reading, it seemed, for industrious young men. In a chapter he contributed to *Advertising Methods and Mediums* (1910), Chalmers wrote: "The relation of salesmanship to advertising is the closest relationship known. Closer than friends; closer than a team under a single yoke; closer than brothers; closer than man and wife, as there can never be separation and divorce."

Which is to say, Chalmers gave a lot of thought—a *lot* of thought—to how he might sell his cars to people who might not have known they wanted one. He came to an inescapable conclusion: "The automobile business more than any I know lends itself to advertising," he wrote in the *New York Times*. "I … sincerely believe that the business owes much of its … prosperity to newspaper publicity."

The automobile man was also a baseball fan, and keenly aware of the sport's immense and growing popularity in the early years of the 20th century (he was fond of peppering his speeches with baseball metaphors and imagery). In 1910, he hatched a marketing campaign that would dominate the summer headlines and become the progenitor of the modern MVP award: "Fans all over the country are turning their attention to the battle which is being waged between the leading batters of the big leagues for a motor car, which has been offered for the batting championship this season" (*Milwaukee Journal*, August 25, 1910).

The motor car on offer was a Chalmers-Detroit Model 30. The man doing the offering was Hugh Chalmers.

The Chalmers Trophy (1910–1914)

Outside of the world's heavyweight boxing title, the batting championship was probably the most prestigious individual accomplishment in professional sport during the first decades of the 20th century. With home runs few and far between prior to the live-ball era, the annual batting races were followed with keen interest by the sporting populace—an interest heightened in 1910 by a glamorous new prize. Prior to the start of the season, Chalmers had announced he would award a Model 30 of the player's choice (the car was made in both hard-top and convertible versions) to the "champion batsmen of the National and American leagues for the season." The batting titlist would be a star, and that star would be the de facto brand ambassador of Chalmers-Detroit.[2] For the cost of some parts and labor, the Chalmers Motor Company was guaranteed annual and protracted visibility with American sports fans.

The 1910 AL batting race turned out to be a spirited affair between Napoleon Lajoie, the popular and admired second baseman for Cleveland, and Ty Cobb, the popular and maligned centerfielder for Detroit. Chalmers couldn't have scripted it better himself: Baseball's two biggest names vying for the most glamorous prize ever offered a player. Between them, they had logged seven batting titles and two Triple Crowns. Cobb was anything but circumspect in his desire for the car. "I would much rather win an automobile than any other prize," he said. What followed became the most famous, contentious, and absurd batting race in baseball history.

Lajoie sprinted to a sizable early season lead, but gradually surrendered his advantage to Cobb as the summer wore on. Cobb finally surged ahead on the strength of a late–September hot streak, setting up a highly anticipated showdown for the season's final weekend. A showdown the Georgia Peach decided to avoid.

Cobb benched himself for the final two games of the season, a prudent if not especially honorable approach to securing that new car. In order to catch Cobb, Lajoie would need a finish for the ages. Entering the season's final day with 219 hits in 583 at bats (.376), he trailed Cobb by six or seven points in average (the leagues didn't provide daily statistics in those days, so the newspapers of the time had to make their best guess based on their own running tallies). Lajoie was a baseball immortal, but even gods don't go eight-for-eight without some help. Turns out, help was on the way.

Cleveland closed its season with a double header against the St. Louis Browns, managed by Jack O'Connor. In his first at-bat, Lajoie hit a fly ball that was played into a triple by the Browns' centerfielder. On his next trip to the plate, Lajoie spied Browns third baseman Red Corriden playing out of position (O'Connor stationed him in short left field). One of the best bunters of his or any day, it was little effort for Lajoie to lay one down the third-base line and trot to first.

Third at-bat, more of the same: Corriden played a hybrid third base–left field, Lajoie deadened one down the line for a "hit." This pattern would repeat itself for the rest of the day: Corriden gave Lajoie acres of space, and Lajoie took it. At the conclusion of the doubleheader, Lajoie had collected eight hits in eight at-bats, with a ninth plate appearance recorded as a sacrifice (it was later revealed that Browns scout Harry Howell attempted to bribe the official scorer into changing the sacrifice to a base hit, giving Lajoie a nine-for-nine day; the scorer refused).

Even with his dubious eight-for-eight day, it wasn't clear if Lajoie had overtaken Cobb for the batting title. Some sources had Lajoie edging Cobb by a point; others had Cobb edging Lajoie by the slimmest of margins. As noted, record-keeping in those days, like Jack O'Connor's ethics, was inexact and unreliable. It was often months before the official league numbers were released.

Word of the travesty in St. Louis quickly spread, and the press covered the scandal with a vigor and relish usually reserved for affairs of state. Chalmers was surely delighted at the controversy and its prominent placement on the front page of every newspaper in America. As drama it had everything: outsized personalities; intrigue; deception; conspiratorial scheming. And at the center of the storm, mentioned in every story, sermon, and summary, was Chalmers' American-made, 30-horsepower, $1500 object of desire.

The imbroglio made Chalmers a celebrity, and his opinions on the matter were treated as serious news (he conceded that there was something funny going on in St. Louis, but publicly held Lajoie beyond reproach). After a brief "investigation" (see notes for more), AL President Ban Johnson declared Cobb the official winner of the batting championship. On Johnson's orders, Browns

President Robert Lee Hedges fired O'Connor and Howell; neither worked in the game again. Red Corriden, presumably because he was merely following O'Connor's orders, was absolved of wrongdoing. Lajoie, it was determined, knew nothing of the plan beforehand, and thus escaped punishment.[3]

With customary promotional flair, Chalmers gave cars to both Cobb and Lajoie—an act of largesse that fueled additional press coverage.[4] While the press (and countless fans) decried the collapse of integrity and sportsmanship, Chalmers considered the award a smashing success as his automobile company was now known to every sports fan in the country. For a few bucks worth of merchandise, Chalmers received *millions* of dollars in publicity. In terms of return on investment, it's probably unmatched in the annals of sports advertising.

Of course, any publicity is good publicity ... until it's not. A well-timed scandal was priceless, but Chalmers understood that for the award to have any credibility moving forward, he would have to avoid a repeat of the 1910 batting-race fiasco.[5] The following season, he broadened the parameters of the award and empaneled a "Chalmers Commission" (comprising baseball writers from each major league city) to choose the player deemed "most useful to his club."

The MVP award was born.

Now given to a player based on his entire body of work for the season, Cobb was the easy AL pick in 1911, leading the league in batting (.420), runs, hits, doubles, triples, RBI, stolen bases and slugging; Chicago's Frank Schulte was named the inaugural winner in the National League, pacing the senior circuit in home runs, RBI, and slugging.

Lacking a tabloid-ready controversy, Chalmers was never able to replicate the frenzy generated by the 1910 batting race, and his trophy failed to recapture the attention or the imagination of the public.[6] Chalmers continued giving away cars for another three years, but he recognized a moribund campaign when he saw one. He ended the program after the 1914 season with a short letter to the Chalmers Commission: "With the presentation this year of the Chalmers trophy to Eddie Collins and John Evers, the work of the commission comes to an end. It seems unlikely now and undesirable also that we should continue these awards."

And that was that. His marketing campaign had run its course, and it was on to the next project for Chalmers.[7] It would be nearly a decade before one of the major leagues resuscitated an award for individual player achievement.

Hugh Chalmers died of pneumonia in 1932, at the age of 58. Obituaries at the time focused on his days as an auto man, accurately describing him as an industry pioneer and visionary. Scant mention is made of his short-lived foray into baseball. His impact, however, is undeniable: He is the architect of the modern MVP award. The Chalmers Trophy established baseball writers as the arbiter of player value; it used a weighted point system to rank players (first-place votes were worth ten points, second-place votes nine points, third-place votes eight points, etc.); and in decoupling the prize from statistical benchmarks (such as a batting title), it clearly established that value was a *judgment* call.

The League Awards (1922–1929)

Eight seasons had passed since Hugh Chalmers discontinued his annual prize, and AL President Ban Johnson thought it high time the AL introduced some form of recognition for individual accomplishment.

A skilled executive, accomplished orator, and overwhelming physical presence, Johnson attended the 1922 Owners Meetings with two grand proposals for a new award: (1) The player deemed most valuable would have a bronze bust placed in the Smithsonian Institution; or (2) The league would erect a monument to itself in Potomac Park, Washington, D.C., with the name of the annual MVP inscribed on a continuously evolving tableau.[8]

Credit Johnson with thinking big—but in the end, the owners decided to go with a more modest approach: Players received a "championship button" (and later, a diploma of sorts) citing their accomplishment.

And that wasn't the least underwhelming aspect of this ill-conceived award, which never attained a veneer of legitimacy. Blame the voting rules and eligibility requirements: As with the Chalmers Trophy, the league's most valuable player would be determined by a vote from select baseball writers in each AL city. Writers were permitted to vote for only one player per team; a player could only win the award once over the course of his career; player-managers were not eligible.

These restrictions meant that from an available talent pool of more than 200 players, only a handful would realistically be considered for the award in a given year—and if you were good enough or lucky enough to capture the award once, you were never again nominated for the distinction (this also meant, among other things, that Babe Ruth would claim a single MVP despite being the best player in baseball a dozen times). After a few years, the award was regarded as desultory at best.

The National League introduced its own version of an MVP award in 1924, determined to avoid the mistakes made by the junior circuit: *All* players were eligible; there was no restriction on the number of awards a player could capture over the course of his career; the writers could vote for more than one player from the same team; and to sweeten the pot, the player deemed most valuable would receive $1000 in gold coins. As with the AL award, two writers from each NL city would cast a ballot.

Brooklyn Robins ace Dazzy Vance (28–6, 2.16 ERA, 262 K) was the inaugural recipient, and his selection generated immediate controversy. Writer Jack Ryder, a recalcitrant sort from Cincinnati, couldn't find space on his 10-player ballot for the Cardinals' Rogers Hornsby, the NL's biggest star and best player. Explaining his snub of the St. Louis icon, Ryder is alleged to have said, "Hornsby is a valuable player to himself, but not a valuable player to his team."

The Vance selection generated discussion and debate—and kindled fan interest—long after the season ended. It also prompted, for the first time, the now perpetual argument over whether a pitcher should be considered for the award (the creation of a separate "Most Valuable Pitcher" award was suggested as early as 1925; it would be 31 years before the Cy Young award was introduced to recognize pitching excellence).

The AL award lurched along for seven seasons, generating little in the way of acclaim or outrage, before it was abruptly cancelled in 1929. AL ownership claimed that the award failed to capture the interest of the fans (which was partially true—the award was tantamount to taking your cousin to the dance), and "was not in the best interests of baseball because it tended to create jealousies and disappointments" among players.

News stories of the day cited another reason for the award's demise: The owners nixed the MVP because the winners had the audacity to cite their performance when negotiating next year's contract (which in turn emboldened other players to cite their own MVP-caliber performance when it came time to haggle). The American League owners would have *none of that*, and terminated the award. The National League followed suit a year later, with the press rolling their eyes at the absurdity of it all: "Of course, now that the award was abolished," wrote John Kieran of the *New York Times*, "the players will have no way of knowing how valuable they are, and they won't be able to ask for higher salaries. Clever people, those [owners]."

Filling a Void (1929–1930)

In the absence of a legitimate league award, *The Sporting News* offered an ersatz MVP for the American League in 1929, and both leagues in 1930. The award, based on an informal poll of baseball writers, was strictly honorary, and never caught on with the players or the fans. Philadelphia's Al Simmons and Washington's Joe Cronin took AL honors in 1929–30, respectively; New York's Bill Terry was named the honorary NL standard-bearer in 1930.

The *Sporting News* wasn't the only media outlet looking to appropriate the award: The Associated Press also commissioned a poll of "a committee of baseball writers representing each city in the circuit." Cleveland's Lew Fonseca took 1929 AL "MVP" honors in this vote (he was a *terrible* choice for the award, so it's probably best for all involved that it's been stricken from history). Cronin was named AL MVP in 1930, with Chicago's Hack Wilson taking NL honors.

If you're counting, that's five MVPs in two years—none of which are recognized as "official."

The Modern MVP (1931–Present)

Despite the owner's objections to the contrary, there was clearly an interest on the part of the fans and the press in recognizing a league's most valuable player in a given year. Informal polls by competing media outlets had little claim to legitimacy, so in 1931, with the blessing of Commissioner Kenesaw Mountain Landis, the Baseball Writers Association of America became the official stewards of the award.[9]

The BBWAA modeled its voting system on the National League award of 1924–29 (without the $1000 bonus); in 1944, the MVP was officially renamed the Kenesaw Mountain Landis Memorial Baseball Award, in honor of baseball's first and most powerful commissioner.

The first modern MVP vote was also the very first "What were they thinking?" vote.[10] Philadelphia's Lefty Grove was a sound choice in the American League (31–4, 2.06 ERA, 175 K), but things were a bit muddled in the senior circuit, with St. Louis second baseman Frankie Frisch claiming the honor over statistically superior candidates Chuck Klein, Bill Terry, and Frisch teammate Chick Hafey (in a voting oddity never since repeated, no player on the ballot received more than a single first-place vote).

1931	WAR	G	AB	R	H	2B	3B	HR	RBI	SB	CS	BB	K	BA	OBP	SLG	OPS	OPS+
Klein	4.8	148	594	*121*	200	34	10	*31*	*121*	7	–	59	49	.337	.398	**.584**	.982	152
Terry	6.1	153	611	*121*	213	43	*20*	9	112	8	–	47	36	.349	.397	.529	.926	149
Hafey	4.2	122	450	94	157	35	8	16	95	11	–	39	43	*.349*	.404	.569	.973	154
Frisch	3.7	131	518	96	161	24	4	4	82	*28*	–	45	13	.311	.368	.396	.764	101

Frisch in 1931 wasn't one of the ten best players in the league; he probably wasn't one of the three or four most valuable players on his own team. But the St. Louis captain was a star, a "leader" with a well-deserved reputation for defensive excellence and quick thinking. And, importantly, he played on the best team in the league.

The Frisch appointment as most valuable established the precedent that the MVP was as much a team award as an individual honor. Over the first decade of ballots, 13 of 20 MVPs (65 percent) came from championship clubs; 100 percent of MVP winners played for winning teams. The "champion bias" would only intensify over ensuing decades.

- 81 percent of MVP winners since 1931 have come from pennant-winning or playoff teams; it seems certain that this percentage will only increase with the expanded playoff format introduced in 2012.
- 97 percent of MVPs have come from winning teams, with almost all of these from serious contenders. Of 169 total awards granted since 1931, only *five* have gone to a player from a losing team.[11]

Over the years, the prominence and preeminence of the award grew. Baseball's MVP remains the most prestigious single-season individual honor in all of sport, and the BBWAA awards program has expanded to include the Jackie Robinson Award for outstanding rookie of the year (1947), the Cy Young Award for pitching excellence (1956), and the Manager of the Year Award (1983).

The full text of the BBWAA MVP ballot instructions reads as follows on the BBWAA'S website.

Dear Voter:
There is no clear-cut definition of what Most Valuable means. It is up to the individual voter to decide who was the Most Valuable Player in each league to his team. The MVP need not come from a division winner or other playoff qualifier.
The rules of the voting remain the same as they were written on the first ballot in 1931: Actual value of a player to his team, that is, strength of offense and defense.
1. Number of games played.
2. General character, disposition, loyalty and effort.
3. Former winners are eligible.
4. Members of the committee may vote for more than one member of a team.

You are also urged to give serious consideration to all your selections, from 1 to 10. A 10th-place vote can influence the outcome of an election. You must fill in all 10 places on your ballot. Only regular-season performances are to be taken into consideration.
Keep in mind that all players are eligible for MVP, including pitchers and designated hitters.

Award parameters and voting process have remained essentially unchanged since 1931, with one major exception: In 2012, the BBWAA announced that players with contractual bonuses tied to awards would no longer be eligible to participate in MVP, CY Young, or Rookie of the Year voting. "When we first started giving out these awards it was just to honor somebody. You got a trophy, there was no monetary reward that went with it," said BBWAA Secretary-Treasurer Jack O'Connell. "I honestly don't think people vote with that in mind.

But the attachment of a bonus to these awards creates a perception that we're trying to make these guys rich."

With the average major league salary exceeding $4 million in 2015, it's doubtful that players will miss the bonus clauses—but the days of honoring a player with a simple trophy are long gone. Major League Baseball's "awards season" is now an annual promotional event generating massive media coverage.

The MVP debates (via social and traditional media) usually commence in early September, a juicy storyline attendant to what is now a frantic, multi-team scramble for a chance to enter the post-season tournament to crown a world champion. "The MVP will likely be decided over the final month of the season as Team X and Team Y jockey for position" is an autumn theme as reliable as turning leaves.

The rhetoric and speculation ramp up after the final out of the World Series, reaching a fever pitch in early November: In the days before the awards are announced, the three "finalists" (simply the top-three vote-getters) for each of the awards are revealed. The awards are then announced, one per day, with a televised press conference, starting with the Rookie of the Year. The grand prize, the MVP, is announced last. Official presentation of the awards—in days past, a phone call to the winner from the head of the BBWAA—is now a televised event on the Major League Baseball network, with live streaming over the MLB.com website and mobile app. Immediately following the announcement of the awards, the annual second-guessing of the selections commences, with (seemingly) every media outlet questioning the sanity and sapience of the voters.

Hugh Chalmers would delight in the spectacle. A century after he introduced his most valuable player award, baseball is taking a page out of the great promoter's book with an annual media blitzkrieg beyond anything even he could envision or imagine.[12]

2

The Crab Performs Miracles in Boston

There is, of course, the poem. The eight-line trifle that became the most iconic lines of verse or prose ever written about the game, the trifle that would immortalize three very-good-if-unspectacular players. The poem is the reason we remember them today; the poem is the reason all three were later enshrined in the Hall of Fame.

So we acknowledge "Baseball's Sad Lexicon," by Franklin Pierce Adams, and those "saddest of possible words": "Tinker to Evers to Chance." And we remember its three principals—the leading lights of the Chicago Cubs, baseball's best team at the dawn of the 20th century.

- **Joe Tinker, shortstop**. If statistics are to be believed, Tinker was one of the greatest defensive players *ever*.[1] He was recognized, along with Honus Wagner, as the best glove man of his day, and his defensive WAR totals are breathtaking (fifth in career defensive value, behind Ozzie Smith, Mark Belanger, Brooks Robinson and Cal Ripken Jr.) He wasn't much of a hitter.[2]
- **Johnny Evers, second base**. Like Tinker, considered among the best defensive players of his time. Evers was famous for his quick temper, nervous energy, and unmatched baseball intelligence. An excellent baserunner and bunter in an era when these were essential skills.
- **Frank Chance, first base and manager**. Perhaps the most respected man in the game, Chance was known, without irony, as "The Peerless Leader," helming baseball's greatest ship: The 1906–10 Chicago Cubs.[3] Far-and-away the best hitter of the famed trio, Chance holds an obscure-but-fun record that will likely stand forever: His 67 stolen bases in 1903 is the single-season record for first basemen. He also

holds the career SB mark for the position with 376 (403 total SB, some coming as a catcher and outfielder). His game wasn't just speed: Chance owns a fine .394 OBP, and an adjusted OPS of 135.

Tinker to Evers to Chance.[4] That's the last time we'll reference the poem, because it's the least interesting thing about 1914 Most Valuable Player Johnny Evers.

❖ ❖ ❖

Known as "The Crab" or "The Human Splinter" in his playing days, Johnny Evers wasn't a very popular guy. At 5'9", 125 pounds, he assiduously subscribed to the maxim "It's not the size of the dog in the fight, it's the size of the fight in the dog."

Because Evers *fought*—physically, verbally, and psychologically—every time he stepped onto the field. He fought for every hit, every stolen base, and every deftly turned double play. He fought with opponents, with teammates, and especially with umpires. A live wire of frayed nerves and inexhaustible energy, Evers was more than willing to instigate mayhem to gain an advantage on the field. He could start a bench-clearing brawl with a gesture, and these

John Evers had the metabolism of a hummingbird, the temper of a wolverine, and an obsessive need to win (Bain Collection, Library of Congress, Prints and Photographs Division).

weren't the choreographed slow dances that pass for on-field brawls today; these could be brutal scraps fought with intent. He was constantly ejected from games, and regularly suspended.

When he wasn't fighting, he was whining and moaning and complaining and cajoling. It seemed like he argued every called strike, every play on the bases. He *detested* umpires, whom he viewed as a confederacy of arrogant dunces with a collective axe to grind (you could hardly blame the umps if they *were* out to get him; Evers once told the *New York Herald*, "My favorite umpire is a dead one"). He constantly jawed at opposing players. "Scrappy" and "dogged" and "pugnacious" were some of the euphemisms employed by the polite newspapermen of the day, but the more accurate description would fall somewhere between "infuriating" and an appellation unfit for print in these pages. The October 1915 *Baseball Magazine* stated, "Evers is one of the gamest fighters in baseball. He works to the last ounce of his strength to win. And when that strength is gone he works on his nerve. In the heat of a contest in which he is exhausting the last ounce of his strength to pull through a victory, is it to be wondered at that the quick-spoken, frail-built, nerve-worn Evers should show that belligerent attitude which is foreign to his nature."

When he wasn't fighting or complaining or playing, Evers was studying and thinking. Studying the game, studying opponents, studying and refining and honing technique. When his teammates hit the town after a game, Evers retreated to his room to analyze the MLB rulebook (and to eat mountains of candy in an attempt to keep some weight on). Anything to gain the slightest advantage in the season-long war of attrition.

In addition to fighting, complaining, and studying, Evers did something else: He won—or more accurately, his teams won. A *lot*. And Evers, while fairly detested as a person, was also respected as a player throughout the league.

Evers was a troubled man, unable to quiet his mind or his body. The relentless pressure he put on himself resulted in what was diagnosed as a "nervous breakdown" during the 1911 season. He also broke down in 1915, missing most of the season with what was likely nervous exhaustion. We can't say with any certainty that his approach helped his career, but we can say with some certainty that Johnny Evers wrung every drop of success he could out of his skeletal frame. It brought him fame, some degree of fortune, three world championships, and the 1914 National League MVP. We don't know if it brought him any measure of happiness.

◆ ◆ ◆

The Boston Braves were a bad team.
And not in the good sense of the word. Not *bad*, like Dick Allen was *bad*.

Just really, *really* bad at baseball. From 1900 to 1913, when they were known at various times as the Beaneaters, the Doves, the Rustlers, and finally the Braves, Boston finished an average of 43 games out of first place. Their 69–82 record in 1913 was their *best* finish in a decade.

So it must have been something of an adjustment for Johnny Evers, a key pillar on the best team in baseball for a decade, to join this motley collection of mostly anonymous cast-offs.

Evers had been dispatched from Chicago by Cubs owner Charles Murphy. Their contentious and convoluted split captured public imagination and made national headlines: Murphy had installed Evers as manager of the team (in addition to his playing duties) after the 1912 season, signing the Cubs' stalwart to a five-year contract.[5] Murphy fired Evers after one season, but claimed Evers had resigned from the club—a ridiculous charge, given Evers' well-known love for the Cubs and outright obsession with the game. "After Murphy had dismissed me," said Evers, "he claimed I had resigned. I must have been unconscious at the time as I have no recollection of it."

His canard revealed, Murphy then tried to trade Evers to Boston. Evers, having essentially been slandered by Murphy, rightfully refused to report, and the intrigue compounded from there: The newly established Federal League (launched in 1914 as an alternative to the existing major leagues) had been poaching talent from NL and AL rosters, and rumor had it that Evers was offered upwards of $30,000 (an enormous sum of money at the time) to defect.[6]

Joe Tinker, Evers' former double-play partner, had been the first high-profile star to make the leap to the "Outlaw League," as it was known (signing with the Federal League's Chicago franchise, no less), and MLB owners were terrified of a talent drain that could lead to true competitive parity with their existing monopoly. Signing Evers would help confer legitimacy on the Federals while establishing a new salary structure that made the MLB oligarchy nauseous.[7]

Recognizing what was at stake over the Evers affair, the NL owners quickly nixed the trade and granted Evers his release from the Cubs in the hopes that he would stay in the National League (it didn't hurt that Murphy was the most despised owner in the league, and that public sentiment was squarely with Evers). Evers signed with Boston of his own accord for $25,000, citing his admiration for manager George Stallings (they were two peas in a pod—Stallings was a demanding taskmaster with a notorious temper).

The media attention given the Evers affair was considerable, and he was among the most famous players in the game at the time of his signing. If nothing else, he would be a drawing card for the pathetic Braves, who had shown little inclination to do anything else but show up for their daily mauling at the hands of the rest of the league.

Evers would have none of it. Named team captain, he employed his abrasive and abusive leadership style to whip the squad into fighting shape. Living up to his reputation, he constantly badgered and cajoled teammates before, during, and after games (to say nothing of his perpetual clashing with opponents and umpires). Said shortstop Rabbit Maranville, "He'd make you want to punch him, but you knew Johnny was thinking only of the team."

Evers had an immediate and dramatic impact on the fortunes of the Braves, who emulated the scrappy play of their new second baseman and took the league by storm.

Well ... not exactly. At least not right away.

Despite the entreaties of their new captain, the team's record stood at 12–28 after 40 games. New team name, new star, same old Boston. By July 4, they were 15 games out of first place. But then something out of the ordinary happened. They won. And then it happened again. And again.

And it *kept* happening: The Braves went 68–19 (.780 winning percentage) over the second half of the season, taking the pennant by 10.5 games and sweeping the heavily favored Philadelphia Athletics in the World Series. It was an astounding turnaround for the perennial losers, who had finished 31 games out of contention the season prior. The team took its place in baseball lore as "The Miracle Braves."

Evers got much of the credit, and among the many honors and tributes received by the man (who was probably unable to enjoy them, given his temperament and disposition) was a brand-new Chalmers automobile, awarded to the "most important and useful player to the club and to the league."

1914	WAR	G	PA	AB	R	H	2B	3B	HR	RBI	SB	BB	K	BA	OBP	SLG	OPS	OPS+
Evers	4.9	139	612	491	81	137	20	3	1	40	12	87	26	.279	.390	.338	.728	113

Viewed through the prism of modern statistical analysis, Evers was a dubious choice for the honor. With the benefit of hindsight, it's easy to say the Chalmers Committee got it wrong—but the Evers selection does offer a fascinating glimpse into how the game was played in its early days.

◆ ◆ ◆

Boston dominated the 1914 Chalmers vote, with the top-three spots going to Evers, Maranville (undeserving of his runner-up status) and second-year pitching sensation Bill James. James was the clear choice for the award as he was one of the two best hurlers in the league (with the immortal Grover Cleveland Alexander, who finished 10th in the voting).[8] Boston teammate Dick

2. The Crab Performs Miracles in Boston

Ace of the 1914 "Miracle Braves," Bill James should have claimed the Chalmers award over teammate John Evers (Bain Collection, Library of Congress, Prints and Photographs Division).

Rudolph was also superb, and both played a much larger role in the Braves' stunning run than Johnny Evers (James went 23–3 with a 1.84 ERA from June 11; Rudolph 24–3, 2.04 over the same period).

1914	pWAR	W	L	ERA	GS	CG	SHO	IP	H	BB	K	ERA+	FIP	WHIP
Alexander	**8.9**	**27**	15	2.38	39	**32**	6	**355.0**	327	76	**214**	123	**2.26**	1.135
James	8.7	26	7	1.90	37	30	4	332.1	261	118	156	**150**	2.95	1.140
Rudolph	6.3	26	10	2.35	36	31	6	336.1	288	61	138	121	2.54	**1.038**

As great as this trio was, it can't be disputed that *everybody* pitched in those days: The league as a whole in 1914 hit .251/.317/.334. Teams scored an average of 3.84 runs per game, and the long ball was a rarity: Combined, the eight NL teams hit 267 *total* HR, or about as many as the 1997 Seattle Mariners.

Given this environment, Evers' modest batting line is more impressive than it might seem at first glance. So we grant that Evers wasn't helpless at the plate. Still, it's pretty clear he doesn't belong in the company of the league's best hitters.

1914	WAR	G	AB	R	H	2B	3B	HR	RBI	SB	BB	BA	OBP	SLG	OPS	OPS+
Burns	**6.4**	154	561	**100**	170	35	10	3	60	62	89	**.303**	**.403**	.417	.820	147
Magee	4.8	146	544	96	**171**	**39**	11	15	**103**	25	55	.314	.380	**.509**	.890	157
Cravath	3.9	149	499	76	149	27	8	**19**	100	14	83	.299	.402	.499	**.901**	**161**
Evers	4.9	139	491	81	137	20	3	1	40	12	87	.279	.390	.338	.728	113

New York's George Burns (fourth in the voting) was probably the best position player in the league, leading in WAR, runs, and stolen bases, while finishing second in on-base percentage to Charles Dillon Stengel (who later found some success managing the Yankees). Philadelphia's Sherry Magee (seventh) led in hits, doubles, RBI, and slugging, while his teammate Gavvy Cravath (23rd) captured the second of five home run titles. The best hitter on the Braves was Joe Connolly, who contributed a fine .306/.393/.494 line (Connolly only appeared in 120 games, and received no MVP support).

The Evers selection often makes the "Worst MVP" lists, but if he wasn't the right choice, he was a *reasonable* choice given the standards of the day. Evers was an excellent defender in an age where defense—especially infield defense—was paramount. Batters rarely struck out and rarely lifted the ball; fielders were using primitive equipment on poorly maintained (by today's surgical standards) fields; defensive positioning was rudimentary at best; infielders often had to handle dark, slick (with saliva and other effluvia), misshapen baseballs, while shortstops and second baseman put their health at risk every time they turned a double play (spiking was practically sanctioned). It was a different game, a *more dangerous* game, and middle-infielders were its toughest, most vulnerable, and, aside from star pitchers, most valuable commodities.

Because this was a game played one base at a time, attributes like base running, bat control, and tactical execution (think hit-and-runs, sacrifices, stolen bases) were prized—again, areas where Evers excelled. There were no three-run home runs on reserve to bail out a team's mistakes. With most games low-scoring affairs, playing "smart" was critical. Among the highest compliments a player could receive was to be called "heady," meaning thoughtful and resourceful. Evers obviously fit this bill.

This all changed, of course, with the advent of the "live-ball era" in 1920. The attributes that garnered Evers his trophy were rendered obsolete once the power game took shape. Let's use 2014—the lowest scoring season in 20 years—as an example: NL teams in 2014 plated 3.95 runs per game, scoring at essentially the same rate as the 1914 (3.84 R/G) version of the league. *How* they scored was another matter entirely.

Year	R/G	HR/G	K/G	SB/G	BA	OBP	SLG
1914	3.84	.021	3.72	1.15	.251	.317	.334
2014	3.95	.083	7.90	.56	.249	.312	.383

Today's players hit four times as many home runs, steal half as many bases, and strike out more than twice as often. Defense is highly calibrated, pitching is highly specialized, and teams use advanced statistical analysis to uncover the smallest advantages. The heady "Johnny Evers–type" is an anachronism in today's game.[9]

But not in 1914. In 1914, players like Johnny Evers were stars. Was he the best player in the league? No. Was he the most valuable player in the league? No. He wasn't the most valuable player on his own club. But he was to some degree the embodiment of what many voters considered the platonic ideal of a "ballplayer," and it garnered him the MVP.

3
Establishing a Pecking Order

No MVP season has been a *bad* season, per se. Some of them weren't anything to write home about, but none of them were poor by most accepted measures.

By "poor," we mean a season of below-average production as compared with the league average for a given position. Using WAR as our measure, we'll call any season of two (or less) a poor season. For context, think of WAR on a sliding scale from zero to 10. Per Baseball-Reference.com, a role player or substitute will contribute 0–2 WAR per season; an average starter, 2–3 WAR. Once a player gets into the 5-WAR range, he's in all-star territory; above 8 WAR, a player should be expected to garner serious MVP consideration.

A season that rates 10 or more WAR is exceptional, bordering on historic: Since 1901, position players have crossed the 10 WAR threshold only 55 times; pitchers have accomplished the feat 51 times.[1] It is possible for a player to generate a *negative* WAR value; these players don't usually keep their jobs very long.

As noted, the MVP has never been awarded to a player who had a lousy year—but Washington shortstop Roger Peckinpaugh came close in 1925, with what is probably the worst on-field performance of any winner. Peckinpaugh's 2.6 WAR essentially ties Willie Stargell (2.5) for the lowest of any MVP recipient.

How did an aging, hamstrung, feeble-hitting shortstop—one who missed more than a month of the season due to age and injuries—take the most prestigious individual honor in the sport over a formidable slate of superstar competition? We might thank the "Peerless Leader" Frank Chance for a recommendation he made more than a decade earlier.

◆ ◆ ◆

Roger Peckinpaugh was well-liked, well-respected, and, for more than a decade, the best defensive shortstop in the American League. He was never much of a hitter, but shortstops weren't *expected* to hit in those days. The prevailing wisdom (a thought that would hold for decades) was that competence in the field outweighed incompetence at the plate. Shortstops just didn't hit (Honus Wagner representing a singularity in the baseball universe).

Peckinpaugh fit this archetype to a "T," failing to reach even league-average standards for offensive production (as measured by OPS+) in all but three of his 18 seasons in the game. In 1925, Peckinpaugh produced one of his stronger (relatively speaking) years: In a plum season for offense, his .294 BA and .367 OBP were almost exactly league average; his .379 SLG was below league average.[2] On an adjusted basis, Peckinpaugh contributed 10 percent less offense than an average hitter—which is perfectly acceptable for an accomplished shortstop, as they are rightfully held to a different set of criteria when determining value. Defensive geniuses don't need to be much better than a league average hitter to generate MVP-level production.

But in 1925, his 15th season in the majors, Peckinpaugh was hardly the defensive alchemist of his youth. His glove was still adequate, but certainly not enough to make up for 272 points of on-base and slugging percentage—the difference in raw offensive production between Peckinpaugh and MVP runner-up Al Simmons of the Philadelphia Athletics.

◆ ◆ ◆

His family knew him as Aloysius Harry Szymanski; the press called him "Bucketfoot Al" (for his distinct batting stance). By any name, Al Simmons was one of baseball's best hitters for a decade.[3] His run of excellence began in 1925, the year Peckinpaugh claimed his MVP. It's not a fair fight.

1925	WAR	G	AB	R	H	2B	3B	HR	RBI	SB	CS	BB	K	BA	OBP	SLG	OPS	OPS+
Simmons	6.5	153	654	122	**253**	43	12	24	129	7	14	35	41	.387	.419	**.599**	1.018	149
Peckinpaugh	2.6	126	422	67	124	16	4	4	64	13	4	49	23	.294	.367	.379	.746	91

Simmons wasn't ignored by voters—he garnered 41 voting points to Peckinpaugh's 45—but his 1925 campaign became one of the first in a long, *long* line of outstanding efforts to be trumped on the ballot by an inferior performance from a player on a better team.

Peckinpaugh himself expressed a measure of regret that Simmons was passed over for the honor. "I'm sorry Al didn't get it," he said. "He's been a great help to his team and has had a fine season. But he has a better chance to get it later than I would have had, being a younger man." Unfortunately for Simmons, Peckinpaugh failed to prove prescient: Despite putting up gaudy numbers for years, the Philadelphia slugger never did claim an MVP.[4]

For all of his slugging prowess, you'll note that Simmons didn't claim a

Roger Peckinpaugh's unfortunate performance in the 1925 World Series led to a change in MVP voting (Bain Collection, Library of Congress, Prints and Photographs Division).

batting title with that .387 average. Despite his gaudy numbers, he wasn't the best hitter in the league that year. Detroit Tigers outfielder Harry Heilmann was at least his equal.[5]

Heilmann is of course famous for hitting over .390 four times in the 1920s (winning batting titles in alternate years). A mere dusting of additional hits spread over the course of those four seasons, and "Slug," as he was known, would have been the only man to ever bat .400 four times.[6] While it's worth noting that Heilmann plied his trade in an inflated offensive environment, the man could *hit* in any era.

Heilmann	WAR	G	AB	R	H	2B	3B	HR	RBI	BB	K	BA	OBP	SLG	OPS	OPS+	MVP
1921	6.8	149	602	114	237	43	14	19	139	53	37	**.394**	.444	.606	1.051	167	–
1923	9.3	144	524	121	211	44	11	18	115	74	40	**.403**	.481	.632	1.113	194	3
1925	**6.9**	150	573	97	225	40	11	13	134	67	27	**.393**	.457	.569	1.026	161	4
1927	7.2	141	505	106	201	50	9	14	120	72	16	**.398**	.475	.616	1.091	180	2

So how *does* a guy hit .390+ four times and not win an MVP? Really, it was just poor timing.

- In 1921, there was no award given in the American League (and Ruth would have run away with it had the award existed).
- The award was re-established by 1923, and Harry had his finest season. But…. Ruth. And his .393/.545/.764 slash line. One wonders if Harry gained a small measure of satisfaction by denying the Babe a shot at his only Triple Crown (the Babe finished second in batting average to Heilmann).
- As mentioned earlier, Heilmann had a case in 1925 as he led the league in WAR and hitting. But Heilmann's Tigers finished in fourth place, 16.5 games behind the flag-bearing Senators. Fair or not, he had no shot at the award.
- And in 1927, well, you might have read a thing or two about those Yankees and their star first baseman. Gehrig's .373/.474/.765 slash line includes 117 extra-base hits.

A career .342 hitter, there are two notable omissions on Heilmann's superb resume: He never appeared in a post-season game, and he never claimed an MVP. These "failings" can't be laid at Heilmann's feet: He was a superb player who toiled for subpar teams.

Back to the 1925 AL MVP ballot, which takes its place among the worst of all time. The 1925 Senators had successfully defended their AL pennant, pacing the second-place Athletics by 8.5 games. While the team's success was driven by a tight-fisted pitching staff that included an ancient-but-still-excellent

Walter Johnson and a slightly-less-ancient-but-even-better Stan Covaleski, voters chose to bestow the award on a shortstop in decline.[7] "Peck" was likely the fifth or sixth most valuable player on his own team; The Senators' best player, 24-year-old Goose Goslin, generated an MVP-worthy campaign (.334/.394/.547, 6.6 WAR), while 35-year-old Sam Rice produced one of the strongest seasons of his Hall of Fame career (.350/.388/.442, 4.5 WAR).[8]

Goslin's non-showing on the ballot is particularly vexing. Under the voting rules of the time, the writers were allowed to cast their ballot for only *one* player per team. Given this restriction, Goslin was the clear choice to represent the Senators. Even the most cursory glance at the rudimentary statistical records of the day made it clear that he was the Senators' most useful and important player.

The Goslin slight wasn't lost on Pittsburgh catcher Earl Smith. A notorious needler, Smith throughout the 1925 World Series between the Senators and the Pirates made sure to remind Goslin about the MVP snub every time the Senators' outfielder stepped to the plate. The baiting didn't seem to work, as Goslin had a fantastic series, hitting .350/.379/.692 with three home runs.

By contrast, Peckinpaugh had just about the worst seven games of his entire life, effectively handing the 1925 Championship to the Pirates. Peckinpaugh—as noted earlier, a truly great defensive player in his prime—had a dismal series, committing a record eight errors (including two in the deciding Game Seven). Hobbled by an ankle injury that cost him the last two weeks of the regular season, he really didn't have any business being on the field. Peckinpaugh's performance was so poor it led to a change in the American League's MVP protocol: From 1922 to 1925, the AL had announced its award prior to the start of the World Series; after the Peckinpaugh debacle, the league announced that the season's most valuable player would be revealed *after* the conclusion of the Series, to "lessen the burden of a player so named who must also perform in that event."

Underscoring the absurdity of Peckinpaugh's selection, Senators president Clark Griffith announced after the season that his reigning MVP shortstop would be benched in favor of youth and speed. Griffith was blunt when explaining his decision: "I think in [Buddy] Myer we have a better player than Peck."[9]

Slightly better than helpless at the plate, just about average in the field. How *did* Peckinpaugh take home the hardware over vastly more deserving candidates?

◆ ◆ ◆

"Frank Chance stands forth as the biggest individual failure in the history of the American League," said Ban Johnson, the bombastic founder and president of the league. "I think any other man would have made a success of the venture. Surely, no one could have done any worse."

It was November of 1914, and Johnson was eviscerating Frank Chance, famed leader of the 1906–10 Chicago Cubs and recent manager of the New York Yankees, for the benefit of *The Sporting Life*, the preeminent sports journal of the day.[10]

Chance, one of the game's biggest stars and legendary characters, had abruptly resigned as manager of the Yankees with three weeks left in the season. Holding court two months later with *The Sporting Life* (November 28, 1914), Johnson clearly felt the time for politesse had passed. He took the Chance resignation as a personal insult and a grievous slight against his league wrote the *Sporting Life*, "President Johnson had great hopes of Chance moulding [sic] a winner in New York, and when, after almost two years as the leader of the New Yorks, he quit a dismal failure, the blow all but floored Ban for the count. The American League has ALWAYS PLAYED SECOND FIDDLE [emphasis theirs] to the Giants in New York, and Ban and other American Leaguers figured that Chance was the man to bring about a change in the condition of affairs."

"Of all the players that were on the New York roster in 1913 and 1914—and there were any number of likely-looking recruits—Chance failed to develop even one man of class," raged Johnson. "Why, it was an outrage." (This was patently ridiculous; the 1913–15 Yankees had very little talent—and they played like it.)

Of course, there was more to the story.

The catalyst for Chance's departure—doubtlessly known to Johnson but ignored in his re-telling of events—was a dispute with star pitcher Ray Caldwell, a hard-drinking, skirt-chasing, curfew-ignoring type who clashed with the disciplinarian approach of the Peerless Leader. After multiple transgressions against team rules, the young right hander was fined several hundred dollars by Chance; Caldwell in turn left the team and signed with the Buffalo Blues of the Federal League.

"Good riddance," thought Chance. But Yankees ownership had other ideas. Team President Frank Farrell overruled his manager, rescinded the fines leveled against Caldwell, and welcomed him back to the team with open arms.[11] Undermined and humiliated, the proud Chance essentially quit on the spot. While his timing may have caught the team by surprise, it was long known that Chance was frustrated with management's refusal to pay for talent (and the scouting department's inability to *identify* talent); the Caldwell incident was the proverbial straw. After two dismal seasons (the Yankees finished seventh in the eight-team league in both 1913 and 1914), Chance, who won two out of every three games he managed as a Cub, was no longer able to stomach losing and what he saw as a clear lack of support from ownership.

After a brief tit-for-tat in the press, the Yankees and Chance parted ways on what was reported as amicable terms (the Yankees issued a statement praising Chance as an all-time great, and Farrell and Chance "parted best of friends," according to the obliging press of the day). But it was the worst-kept secret in baseball that the two sides despised each other.

In a somewhat shocking maneuver, Farrell and co-owner Bill Devery named young shortstop (and Frank Chance favorite) Roger Peckinpaugh to replace the departed manager. Peckinpaugh, age 23 and with all of 300 or so major league games on his resume, would guide the team for the remainder of the 1914 season. It seems unthinkable today, and even by the standards of Peckinpaugh's time, when player-managers were somewhat common, it was an extraordinary appointment. Sixty years later, Peckinpaugh revealed how it came about for Marty Appel's *Baseball's Best*: "In September [Chance] came to me and said he'd had a run-in with the owners and he was going to quit and go home…. Chance says he was going to recommend me to run the club for the rest of the season. 'Maybe you can get a little extra dough out of it,' he told me. The next day, Farrell says, 'We want you to take charge of the team for the rest of the season.' So I say, 'Yeah? What's in it for me?' So they offered me a little extra dough. And that's how I became the youngest manager in the big leagues at 23."

And how did Ban Johnson view the Peckinpaugh appointment? As another opportunity to pile on Frank Chance for the benefit of *The Sporting Life*: "Roger Peckinpaugh, youth though he is, displayed far more class as manager of the New Yorks in the short time he was at the helm than Frank Chance ever did."

And so, at the age of 23, Peckinpaugh's die was cast, his character affirmed: Thoughtful leader of men. Brainy student of the game. *The classy young man who succeeded Frank Chance as manager of the Yankees.* It was a reputation he carried for the rest of his career, and in all likelihood this reputation secured him the MVP 11 seasons later, an MVP that served no purpose other than to recognize an old hand for his years of distinguished service.

Peckinpaugh was universally respected within the game, had, in his youth, been acknowledged as the best shortstop in the league, and had, since the moment he stepped onto the poorly groomed diamonds of the day, been praised for his baseball acumen and leadership.[12]

Today, the sports media call these things "intangibles," and they earned Peckinpaugh the 1925 American League MVP. He was an awful choice.

Most Replaceable Player

Roger Peckinpaugh (2.6) and Willie Stargell (2.5) hold the ignoble distinction for lowest WAR by an MVP. WAR reveals how two very different players, playing in very different environments, can take very different paths to the same overall result.

Here are their traditional stat lines from their respective MVP campaigns (each among the very worst in the history of the award; for more on Stargell, see Chapter 11).

Player	WAR	G	AB	R	H	2B	3B	HR	RBI	SB	CS	BB	K	BA	OBP	SLG	OPS	OPS+
Peckinpaugh	2.6	126	422	67	124	16	4	4	64	13	4	49	23	.294	.367	.379	.746	91
Stargell	2.5	126	424	60	119	19	0	32	82	0	1	47	105	.281	.352	.552	.904	139

On an adjusted basis, Stargell is about 50 percent more productive than Peckinpaugh in the batter's box. He's a vastly superior hitter. So why does WAR rate them as essentially equals?

Player WAR as calculated by Baseball-Reference.com is based on six components.[13]

- **Batting Runs (Rbat)**, or what a player contributes with his hitting;
- **Base running Runs (Rbaser)**, which measures stolen bases and caught stealing, advancing on passed balls, wild pitches, errors, and sacrifices; taking the extra base; tagging up, etc.
- **Grounding into Double Plays (Rdp)**, which calculates runs added or lost due to grounding into (or avoiding) double plays in DP situations. If it seems somewhat esoteric, it's not: The most valuable commodity in baseball is the out—a team only gets 27 of them per game. If a player is grounding into a lot of DPs, he's using up a lot of outs (and eliminating a lot of base runners);
- **Fielding Runs (Rfield)**, which estimates how many runs a player saved or cost his team on defense;
- **Positional Adjustment Runs (Rpos)**, i.e., recognizing the degree of difficulty involved with playing a certain position. Catchers, shortstops, and centerfielders will gain extra runs of credit, while corner outfielders and first baseman will lose runs of credit;
- **Replacement-level Runs (RAR)** estimates how many runs a player contributed above (or below) a theoretical replacement player.

Using these six components, we can make broad—but legitimate—comparisons between players relative to their era (and credit Joe Posnanski for first running this type of comparison between Mike Trout and Miguel Cabrera—two players having *great* seasons—in 2012).[14]

Let's take a closer look at the "player value" stats for Stargell and Peckinpaugh.

Player	Year	G	PA	Rbat	Rbaser	Rdp	Rfield	Rpos	RAA	RAR	WAR
Peckinpaugh	1926	126	494	-4	2	0	2	8	8	27	2.6
Stargell	1979	126	480	21	-2	-1	-4	-6	9	24	2.5

They played the same number of games, generating essentially the same number of plate appearances. So far, so good. Now let's see what they did with their playing time.

Stargell, a power-hitting first baseman, generated 21 more runs with his bat (Rbat) than the average major league hitter. Peckinpaugh was four runs *worse* than the average hitter. Here is our baseline for value: Runs better (or worse) than average. Stargell comes roaring out of the gate with a 25-run advantage over Peckinpaugh. A significant divide for any player to cross.

As a baserunner (Rbaser), Stargell is two runs *worse* than the average NL player in 1979; Peckinpaugh is two runs *better* than the average AL player in 1925, for a net difference of four runs. Peckinpaugh gains four runs on Stargell with his superior speed and instincts.

The running tally: 19 runs for Stargell, -2 runs for Peck.

The Rdp value determines how many runs a player costs his team by grounding into double plays. Peckinpaugh was a little better than Stargell here, and gains another run.

The score: Willie Stargell, 18 runs; Roger Peckinpaugh, -1 runs. Stargell is still trouncing the Washington shortstop.

Ah, but the operative word here is "shortstop." Peckinpaugh has navigated Stargell's offensive rapids and is about to take the Pittsburgh slugger into deep defensive waters.

Peckinpaugh, in his prime regarded as perhaps the best defensive player in the American league, was no longer a great shortstop in 1925; he was, however, slightly better than league average (at least based on the available data). Stargell, on the other hand, was below average with the glove, costing his team about four runs as compared with a league-average first baseman. Credit Peckinpaugh with another two runs for his defense while deducting four runs from Stargell's account.

Stargell's lead in this race is dwindling: 14 runs for Stargell, three runs for Peckinpaugh.

And now we enter those deep waters: Shortstop is the most demanding position on the field after catcher. First base is the *least* demanding position on the field. WAR is based in large part on the notion of how much better or worse a player is, relative to his league, than a theoretical replacement. It is much harder for a team to replace a league-average shortstop than a league-average first baseman.

In fact, it's harder for a team to replace a *bad* shortstop than it is to replace a *good* first baseman. Because it's really, *really* difficult to play shortstop at the major league level. No position on the field save catcher places greater physical and intellectual demands on a player; no position on the field requires the same level of athleticism. An elite second baseman may have exceptional range and a glove skinned in Velcro, but he won't have exceptional arm strength (if he did, he'd be a shortstop); an elite third baseman may have a firehose for an arm and supernatural reflexes, but he won't have exceptional range (if he did, he'd be a shortstop). This is why teams will tolerate a below-average bat at the position: With apologies to Flannery O'Connor, a good shortstop is hard to find.

WAR takes this into account, and adjusts for positional scarcity (Rpos). Peckinpaugh makes up a ton of ground here, gaining eight runs of extra credit for playing shortstop; Stargell is docked six runs due to having many fewer defensive responsibilities as a first baseman.

That's a 14-run swing in Peckinpaugh's favor. Peck is now rated at nine runs better than the average player (RAA); Stargell rates eight runs better.

WAR then converts runs above average (RAA) into runs above replacement (RAR—remember, a replacement player is the theoretical player called up from the minors), applies a number of formulas and calculations and pixie dust (not really; it's all math) and converts those *runs* above replacement into *wins* above replacement (WAR).

And WAR estimates that Peckinpaugh and Stargell were equally productive as players (which is to say, they were both pretty good, but certainly not great).

Now for the "but." And it's a big one.

Defensive numbers are, on the whole, suspect. And the further back in time we reach, the more suspect the numbers become. Even basic stats like putouts and assists can't be fully trusted. We know that Peckinpaugh was a brilliant defensive player in his prime—his teammates, coaches, and opponents conceded the point. But we can't really quantify it with any certainty, because defensive statistics from the time are close to worthless. We also know that Peckinpaugh was nowhere near his prime in 1925, and he could have been much worse than his defensive stats suggest (he also could have been better, but it's not likely).

That said, we have to go with the available data, no matter how flawed. And the data tells us that Peckinpaugh and Stargell generated less WAR than any other player during their MVP season. Two very different peas in the same pod.

Lowest WAR in an MVP Season

Player	Year	WAR
Willie Stargell	1979	2.5
Roger Peckinpaugh	1925	2.6
Dennis Eckersley	1992	2.9
Bob O'Farrell	1926	3.5
Jeff Burroughs	1974	3.6
Frankie Frisch	1931	3.7
Juan Gonzalez	1998	3.8
Jake Daubert	1913	4.0
Mo Vaughn	1995	4.3
Steve Garvey	1974	4.4

4

Out by a Mile

If you're reading this book, you already know a few things about Babe Ruth. You know he was the greatest hitter who ever lived. You know that before he became the greatest hitter, he was one of the best pitchers in his league. You also know, or have read, or have heard that Ruth was a man of unchecked excess: He drank more booze, ate more food, and bedded more women than any other two players in the league.[1]

Ruth's lifestyle caught up to him in 1925, when he missed more than 50 games due to illness and a team-leveled suspension. It's unfair to pin the fortunes of a team on one player, but the feeling among fans, management, and the press of the day was that Babe Ruth torpedoed the season with his appetites and his attitude.

"The Bellyache Heard Round the World," an unidentified condition variously reported as influenza, exhaustion, indigestion, or an intestinal abscess, waylaid Ruth for more than two months. The exact nature of Ruth's condition was never confirmed, but a surgical scar on his abdomen betrayed something more serious than the flu.[2] He didn't start his first game until June 1, and was clearly weakened as he struggled with a terrible Yankees team that finished seventh in an eight-team league (a shell of his hale and hearty self, Ruth was still a productive hitter in his limited playing time).

Ruth	G	AB	R	H	2B	3B	HR	RBI	BB	K	BA	OBP	SLG	OPS	OPS+
1920–24 avg.	142	491	*145*	182	38	11	*47*	*131*	*138*	83	.370	*.511*	*.777*	*1.288*	*229*
1925	98	359	61	104	12	2	25	67	59	68	.290	.393	.543	.936	137

The only thing worse than the Yankees' on-field performance was Ruth's attitude: Upon his return to the team, the drunken carousing resumed in short order, as did his frequent and petulant confrontations with manager Miller Huggins. Ruth returned from his bellyache only to become a toothache in the clubhouse. After one too many challenges to Huggins' authority, Ruth was suspended "indefinitely" for misconduct on August 29. With little to write about in terms of on-field achievement, the press delighted in reporting the clubhouse melodrama. Ruth looked the big buffoon, the diminutive Huggins the little dictator.[3] After it became clear that team ownership supported Huggins, Ruth apologized and was reinstated after a week—but the damage had been done. The 1925 season couldn't end soon enough for all parties involved.

Much to the delight of management, Ruth—now on the north side of 30—seemed to have something to prove heading into the 1926 season: The Yankees, two years removed from their last pennant, were pleasantly surprised to see their star report for Spring Training in good shape and good spirits. After his health scare, Ruth had apparently exercised a modicum of restraint in the off-season, watching his diet, hitting the gym, and strengthening his legs by playing plenty of golf.

A motivated Ruth was the best player in baseball. The best player who ever lived.

1926 League Leaders, Adjusted Production (OPS+)

1926	WAR	G	AB	R	H	2B	3B	HR	RBI	BB	K	BA	OBP	SLG	OPS	OPS+
Babe Ruth	11.5	152	495	139	184	30	5	47	153	144	76	.372	.516	.737	1.253	225
Heinie Manush	5.1	136	498	95	188	35	8	14	86	31	28	.378	.421	.564	.985	154
Goose Goslin	6.8	147	568	105	201	26	15	17	109	63	38	.354	.425	.542	.967	153
Harry Heilmann	5.2	141	502	90	184	41	8	9	101	67	19	.367	.445	.534	.979	153
Lou Gehrig	6.8	155	572	135	179	47	20	16	109	105	73	.313	.420	.549	.969	152

Nineteen twenty-six isn't usually recognized among Ruth's signature seasons, but that's because he had another nine or ten just like it. That said, 1926 is an amazing display of his specific genius. He simply *dwarfed* the best of his "peers" when it came to hitting.

- Ruth led the league with 47 home runs; Al Simmons of the Philadelphia Athletics was second with 19. Ruth clubbed a home run every 10.5 at-bats—or about twice the rate of his nearest competitor (Ken Williams of the St. Louis Browns, who in 108 games averaged one home run per 20.4 at-bats).
- Ruth led the league with 153 RBI; rookie teammate Tony Lazzeri was second with 117.
- Ruth generated a 1.253 OPS—no other player reached 1.000. His OPS was 268 points higher than runner-up Heinie Manush (whose league-leading .378 BA denied Ruth the Triple Crown).
- Measured by adjusted production (225 OPS+), he was about 50 percent better than the *second* best hitter in the league.[4] He was more than *twice* as good as the *average* AL hitter.

- His 11.5 WAR outpaced teammate Lou Gehrig (6.8) for the league lead by almost five wins. Put another way: To match Babe Ruth's production in 1926, you'd need to combine the second-best player in the league with a major league all-star.

Ruth led the universe in almost every important offensive category, and he led the Yankees back to their familiar perch atop the American League. Baseball's best player and biggest star was back. To call Ruth the most valuable player in the league was an understatement; few players in history have been as valuable to his team as Ruth was to the 1926 Yankees.[5]

Naturally, the AL MVP was awarded to … Cleveland's George Burns, who finished fourth in the league in batting average (.358) while slashing a then-record 64 doubles. Burns' 4.9 WAR was good for 12th in the junior circuit.

Player	WAR	G	AB	R	H	2B	3B	HR	RBI	BB	K	BA	OBP	SLG	OPS	OPS+
Babe Ruth	**11.5**	152	495	**139**	184	30	5	**47**	**153**	**144**	76	.372	**.516**	.737	**1.253**	**225**
George Burns	4.9	151	603	97	**216**	**64**	3	4	115	28	33	.358	.394	.494	.889	130

MVP voters have made some dubious choices, but this one strains credulity. Setting a record for doubles in a season is nice and all, but there was no way the voters could possibly grant that Burns was more valuable to the second-place Indians than Ruth was to the AL champion Yankees.[6]

They didn't. At least not willingly. Under MVP voting rules at the time, a player could only capture the award once during his career; Ruth, the unanimous pick in 1923, wasn't eligible for the award in 1926. It was an absurd rule, one that the players and voters hated (and one of the reasons the AL MVP award, created in 1922, was discontinued after the 1928 season; the NL award lasted until 1929).

With Ruth removed from contention, the voters had what would seem to be a considerably more difficult task: selecting the league's most valuable among Manush, Heilmann, and Goslin.

Instead, Burns was a near-unanimous pick, receiving 63 out of 64 possible votes. Why Burns? Newspaper accounts of the day invoke his doubles record (again, an esoteric peg on which to hang an MVP hat), and Cleveland's second-place finish (they were broadly expected to settle near the bottom of the league). Even under the rules of the day, he was a poor choice for the honor.

◆ ◆ ◆

Before we get to the NL MVP, keep in mind that unlike today, when awards ballots are distributed and collected before the start of the post-season, the MVP award in 1926 was voted on *after* the World Series was concluded.

Now, about that World Series. The 1926 battle between the Yankees and the Cardinals was a spectacular affair, featuring two evenly matched teams and, with Ruth and Cardinals manager/second baseman Rogers Hornsby, two of the game's greatest hitters. Hornsby would prove a non-factor in the series; Ruth, for better and for worse, would have a series for the ages.

The Yankees took the first game behind Herb Pennock's three-hitter; the Cardinals drew even behind the grit and guile of Grover Cleveland ("Pete") Alexander in game two, and took a 2–1 series lead with a 4–0 whitewash in game three.

Game four was won by the Yankees behind one of the greatest performances from the game's greatest performer: Babe Ruth launched three home runs, drove in four, and scored four. His sixth-inning blast (third of the game) to the deepest recesses of the centerfield bleachers was reckoned by many to be the longest ever hit in Sportsman's Park. No one had ever hit three home runs in a World Series game; of *course* Ruth would be the first to achieve this unlikely feat.[7]

The Yankees took game five behind Pennock, and returned to the Bronx confident that victory was in hand. But the redoubtable Alexander had other things in mind, pitching the Cardinals to victory in game six.

The series knotted at three wins apiece, the two teams took the field on a gray, gripping Sunday to determine the world championship. For drama, suspense, and intrigue, few games have matched it.[8]

Ruth staked the Yankees to a 1–0 lead in the third with his fourth home run of the series. It was the last time the Cardinals would pitch to him, walking the Babe his next three trips to the plate.[9] Ruth would contribute in other ways, robbing Cardinals catcher Bob O'Farrell of a potential inside-the-park home run with a racing, tumbling catch that was the defensive highlight of the series.

The Cardinals scored three unearned runs to take the lead in the fourth. Shoddy defense and bad luck conspired against the Yankees, who "cracked and went to pieces in the mist and darkness of a cold October day." Shortstop Mark Koenig booted what should have been a double play off the bat of the Cardinals' Lester Bell; two batters later, with the bases loaded, Bob O'Farrell lifted an easy fly ball to leftfield—the Yankees, who still had a chance to escape the inning unscathed, instead watched the Cardinals tie the game when Bob Meusel dropped the ball. The next batter, shortstop Tommy Thevenow, placed a soft flare just over the head of the Yankees' fine rookie second baseman Tony Lazzeri, scoring two runs.

The Yankees drew within one run in the sixth, setting up a moment of high drama in seventh. With the bases loaded and two outs, Lazzeri stepped to the plate. The rookie had endured a brutal series, but all would be forgotten and forgiven with a well-timed base hit. You know what happened next.

Cardinals starter Jesse Haines had owned the Yankees to this point in the Series, surrendering just two runs over 16 innings. But torn blisters on his pitching hand made it impossible to continue. To the surprise of all who bore witness, Hornsby summoned "Old Pete" Alexander from the bullpen.

The 40-year-old veteran had pitched a complete-game victory the day before (how hard, and for how long, he celebrated that effort is a matter of debate).[10] How much could he possibly have left in what was once the game's greatest arm? The haggard old gunfighter ambled to the mound, the bases soaked with Yankees, the World Series on the line.

Lazzeri dug in against the ancient and exhausted master. First pitch: Low curve, swinging strike. Second pitch: High fastball. Vicious line drive to left … could it be? It could be! Could it be …?! The ball screamed foul. Third pitch: A slop curve nearly in the dirt, swinging strike. Threat averted, inning over.

In the retelling of the 1926 World Series, the Alexander-Lazzeri duel often takes center stage—but the game wasn't over yet: Alexander had to navigate another two innings.

The Yankees went meekly in the top of the eighth; the Cardinals couldn't score in bottom half of the inning. The score held at 3–2 in the ninth when a cautious Alexander walked Babe Ruth with two outs and nobody on base. This brought the dangerous Meusel to the plate; Meusel, who was looking to atone for his costly error in the fourth.

He wouldn't get the chance. As Pete Alexander told Lawrence Ritter in *The Glory of Their Times*: "I'll never know why the guy did it, but on my first pitch to Meusel, the Babe broke for second … I caught the blur of Ruth starting for second as I pitched, and then came the whistle of the ball as O'Farrell rifled it to second. I wheeled around, and there was one of the grandest sights of my life: Hornsby, his foot anchored on the bag and his gloved hand outstretched, was waiting for Ruth to come in." Bob O'Farrell, also in *The Glory of Their Times*, stated, "I wondered why Ruth tried to steal second then. A year or two later … I asked him. Ruth said he thought Alex had forgotten he was there. Also that the way Alex was pitching they'd never get two hits in row off him, so he better get in position to score if they got one. Well maybe that was good thinking and maybe not. In any case, I had him out by a mile at second."

Game over. Series over. The Cardinals stormed the field in jubilation, while the Babe composed, in the words of reporter Frank Getty, "a muddy heap at second base."

◆ ◆ ◆

We can't know for sure that the MVP voters in 1926 let the outcome of the World Series influence their vote. We do know for sure that the newspapers of the day had this to say about Bob O'Farrell's Series performance: "Bob O'Farrell, the St. Louis catcher, was a power on the defense and at bat, and caught one of the best games ever seen in these deciding classics of baseball."[11]

We can't know for sure that O'Farrell's bullet throw to nail Babe Ruth by several feet swung the MVP in his favor. We do know for sure that MVP ballots were sent back to the league for counting *after* the World Series ended on October 10, 1926. O'Farrell, the first catcher honored as most valuable, ran away with the honor, capturing seven of eight first-place votes.

We can't know for sure that O'Farrell's World Series won him the regular season MVP, but we do know for sure that the Associated Press wrote after *game five* (two games *prior* to his harpooning of Ruth at second) that O'Farrell's "brilliant performance" had "emphasized the likelihood" of his being "officially recognized as the most valuable player" of his league.

We can't know for sure that his post-season heroics won him the MVP. We *do* know for sure that it's difficult to find something in his regular-season performance to merit the honor.

1926	WAR	G	AB	R	H	2B	3B	HR	RBI	SB	BB	K	BA	OBP	SLG	OPS	OPS+
O'Farrell	3.5	147	492	63	144	30	9	7	68	1	61	44	.293	.371	.433	.804	112

O'Farrell's 3.5 WAR is among the lowest for any MVP. Defensive statistics of the day are somewhat suspect, but it is clear that O'Farrell possessed a strong throwing arm and had a reputation as a fine handler of pitchers. He was also durable, leading all backstops with 146 games caught. Still ... MVP?

In fairness to the voters, there was almost no right—or wrong—selection. While the NL as a whole scored at about the same rate as the season prior, no player truly distinguished himself through his hitting.

1926 WAR Leaders

1926	WAR	G	AB	R	H	2B	3B	HR	RBI	BB	K	SB	BA	OBP	SLG	OPS	OPS+
Paul Waner	**5.3**	144	536	101	180	35	**22**	8	79	66	19	11	.336	**.413**	.528	.941	148
Hack Wilson	5.2	142	529	97	170	36	8	**21**	109	**69**	61	10	.321	.406	.539	.944	**151**
Kiki Cuyler	4.6	**157**	614	**113**	197	31	15	8	92	50	66	**35**	.321	.380	.459	.840	121
Frankie Frisch	4.6	135	545	75	171	29	4	5	44	33	16	23	.314	.353	.409	.762	106
Travis Jackson	4.5	111	385	64	126	24	8	8	51	20	26	2	.327	.362	.494	.856	130

Pittsburgh's Paul "Big Poison" Waner and Chicago's Hack Wilson sat atop the league in WAR and adjusted production, but their marks were hardly inspiring (combine Wilson and Waner and you still wouldn't match Babe Ruth's production for the year). Waner's 5.3 WAR is the lowest ever to lead position players, while Wilson's 151 OPS+ is the second-lowest mark to ever lead the National League.[12] Despite this modest achievement at the top of the leaderboards, O'Farrell failed to land in the top-ten in any offensive category.

Given the somewhat dreary hitting of the league's best, one might think the NL was dominated by pitching in 1926. It wasn't. Hal Carlson led the league in pitcher WAR, but his excellence was camouflaged by a so-so 17–12 record and a good-not-great 3.23 ERA. Ray Kremer had a fine season for the Pirates, tying (with three others) for most wins and leading the league in ERA and adjusted ERA—but he only started 26 games and finished 11th in innings.

1926	pWAR	W	L	W%	ERA	GS	CG	IP	R	ER	BB	K	ERA+	WHIP	K/BB
Ray Kremer	6.3	**20**	6	**.769**	**2.61**	26	18	231.1	79	67	51	74	**150**	1.176	1.45
Charlie Root	4.8	18	17	.514	2.82	32	21	271.1	104	85	62	127	137	1.213	2.05
Guy Bush	3.1	13	9	.591	2.86	15	7	157.1	58	50	42	32	135	1.214	0.76
Jesse Petty	5.0	17	**17**	.500	2.84	33	23	275.2	118	87	79	101	133	1.179	1.28
Hal Carlson	**8.3**	17	12	.586	3.23	34	20	267.1	116	96	47	55	132	1.272	1.17

The NL in 1926 had achieved an equilibrium of mediocrity, with no player truly separating himself from the rest of the pack. In this environment, the player named most valuable would take the award by default.

Even by the pedestrian standards of the season, Bob O'Farrell wasn't a great pick for MVP—but there *were* no great picks. If the voters were set on recognizing a Cardinal, third baseman Les Bell was probably the best choice (.325/.383/.525; 4.4 WAR)—but he was hardly an obvious pick for the award.

In the absence of a great hitter or a great pitcher, the 1926 MVP race was likely decided by a strong throw to end the World Series. Babe Ruth was so good he won MVPs for other players.

Master of Them All?

Grover Cleveland Alexander's Hall of Fame plaque recounts his 1926 World Series strikeout of Tony Lazzeri. It's a disservice to Alexander, who faced more than 20,000 batters over the course of his superb career (said Alexander of the game years later, "I'm stuck with it like George Washington with the hatchet"). Had the MVP award existed in his prime, Alexander claims at least three trophies.

Christy Mathewson's Hall of Fame plaque ends with the epitaph "Matty Was Master of Them All." It's a somewhat curious inscription. At the time of Mathewson's induction (1936), there was a strong case to be made that Alexander was at least his equal.[13] Like Alexander, Mathewson would have claimed several MVP trophies had the award existed when he was at his best (and he was arguably snubbed for the Chalmers Award in 1911—see Chapter 5 for more).

Mathewson or Alexander. For 70 years, the answer to the question "Who

"Old Pete" Alexander spun the first of four pitching Triple Crowns in 1915 (Bain Collection, Library of Congress, Prints and Photographs Division).

is the most valuable pitcher in National League history?" came down to two choices. Whether you preferred the urbane Mathewson or the frontier-tough Alexander, there was no wrong answer: These two colossi towered above the history of the league.

A sparse list of serious challengers came and went: Warren Spahn approached some of their unassailable career marks; Sandy Koufax, for a time, was favored to knock them off their shared thrones before chronic arm miseries truncated his career; Bob Gibson, Juan Marichal, Steve Carlton—all orbited the twin suns of Mathewson and Alexander.

It wasn't until Tom Seaver was late-career that a serious challenger emerged for the title. Twenty years later, Greg Maddux joined the conversation as the final tallies were being added to his career ledger.[14]

Mathewson, Alexander, Seaver, Maddux: Who then is the NL standard-bearer, the most valuable pitcher ever to grace the league?

◆ ◆ ◆

In chronological order, our candidates are:

- **Christy Mathewson** (1900–16): "Matty" was baseball's first superstar. College educated, blessed with matinee-idol looks and raised with a gentleman's disposition, Matty stood in stark contrast to the uneducated, rough-hewn men who played the game in the first decades of the 20th century. He was the game's most beloved player, and one of its best: He holds National League career records for wins (tied with Alexander), winning percentage, and career ERA.[15]
- **Grover Cleveland Alexander** (1911–30): From the moment he stepped onto a major league ball field at the age of 24, two things were immediately apparent about Pete Alexander: (1) He looked like a middle-aged longshoreman; (2) He was the best pitcher in baseball. These two facts held true over the next two decades. Leathered. Craggy. Briny. Alexander looked old at 24, looked old at 43. In between, he was the best in the game. Alexander accumulated more WAR than any other NL pitcher.
- **Tom Seaver** (1967–86): A well-spoken, college-educated California kid, Seaver immediately and irrevocably captured the affections of New York City's gritty, hardscrabble outer-boroughs with his power and panache. He was the face of one of New York's most beloved teams, the 1969 "Miracle Mets." Named on a then-record 98.8 percent of possible ballots, he's a "hall-of-famer's" Hall of Famer.[16]
- **Greg Maddux** (1986–2008): Pitching against an endless parade of mesomorphic sluggers, Maddux dominated with precision and guile. Maddux wasn't big; he didn't throw hard; he didn't sneer and scowl. Yet in his way he was among the game's great intimidators—he simply *embarrassed* hitters with startling efficiency.

Statistical Record

Player	WAR	W	L	ERA	GS	CG	IP	H	ER	BB	K	ERA+	FIP	WHIP	K/BB
Alexander	*117*	*373*	208	2.56	600	*436*	5190.0	4868	1476	951	2198	135	2.88	1.121	2.31
Maddux	105	355	227	3.16	*740*	109	5008.1	4726	1756	999	3371	132	3.26	1.143	*3.37*
Mathewson	96	*373*	188	*2.13*	552	434	4788.2	4219	1135	848	2507	*137*	*2.26*	*1.058*	2.96
Seaver	95	273	170	2.73	553	213	4131.1	3352	1254	1204	3272	130	2.91	1.103	2.72

Statistically, the four are clustered tightly, with adjusted ERAs 30–37 percent better than the league average (we only use Seaver's 17-season tenure in the National League; this costs him in some of the counting stats like WAR, wins, innings, and strikeouts).[17]

These are the four most accomplished pitchers in league history. The following is only a partial summary of greatness.

- Mathewson: Led his league in wins four times, ERA five times, shutouts five times, fewest walks per nine innings (BB/9) seven times; strikeouts-to-walk ratio nine times. The all-time NL leader in wins, winning percentage, ERA, adjusted ERA (ERA+), WHIP, and fielding-independent pitching (FIP), which assigns an ERA-equivalent value to a composite of a pitcher's home runs and walks allowed, and strikeouts recorded.[18]
- Alexander: Tied with Mathewson for the NL career lead in wins and ERA+. Earned pitching's Triple Crown (wins, era, strikeouts) a record four times, including three consecutive (1915–17). Led his league in innings pitched seven times, wins and strikeouts six times; ERA five times; FIP four times; NL career leader in shutouts with 90.
- Tom Seaver: Holds the lowest career ERA (2.73 NL; 2.86 overall) of the post-war era (min. 3000 IP). Led his league in ERA, wins, adjusted ERA, FIP, and WHIP three times; strikeouts five times; strikeouts per nine innings six times. Established NL record with ten 200-strikeout seasons. Recognized with three Cy Young Awards as the league's best pitcher. Seaver was listed on the MVP ballot in nine different seasons, finishing a close second in 1969.
- Greg Maddux: Led league in wins three times, ERA and FIP four times, ERA+ five times, innings pitched five times, fewest walks per nine innings nine times. Recognized as the league's best pitcher four times. Maddux received MVP support in six different seasons; he should have won the award in 1995. The unassuming Maddux was also the meanest of this quartet, plunking 137 batters; none of the others hit more than 70.

Using the "Black Ink" test as our gauge, Alexander has the most "impressive" statistical resume, followed by Mathewson, Maddux, and Seaver, in that order.

But as a wise man once said, there are three kinds of untruths: "Lies, damned lies, and statistics."

Level of Competition

The old warhorses don't fare well here. The overall quality of play is much higher today than it was when Alexander spun 16 shutouts in a single season. Athleticism, strategy, technique, and statistical analysis are so advanced in the modern game that it's much more difficult to produce extremes in individual performance as compared with 90–100 years ago.[19] As the evolutionary biologist and ardent baseball fan Stephen Jay Gould wrote, "Wee Willie Keeler could hit 'em where they ain't, because fielders didn't yet know where they should be."

And then there's the composition of the talent pool: Mathewson and Alexander pitched in an eight-team league. Seaver pitched in a 12-team league. The NL went from 12 to 16 teams over the course of Maddux' career (not including interleague interstitials).

Obviously, the larger number of players, the harder it is to lead the league in any single statistical category. In Mathewson's Triple Crown season of 1908, there were only 83 pitchers in the entire league; Maddux in 1994 was competing against 235 other pitchers (and that number would exceed 350 in later years).[20]

The fact is, Mathewson and Alexander were able to avoid a significant percentage of the world's best players. Both pitched decades prior to the racial integration of the game. Relative to their era, they were the equal of Seaver and Maddux—but they competed with a much smaller, exclusively Caucasian, exclusively *American* talent pool. The eras don't compare in terms of overall quality of play. Seaver and Maddux plied their trade in a much tougher competitive environment.

Offensive Environment

The chart below provides a measure of context for the environment in which these men pitched. Using a representative season from each man's career (in this case, we used a season in which each pitcher was at or near his very best), we list the league averages in a number of telling categories: Runs scored per game (R/G), ERA, complete game percentage (CG), hits, home runs, walks, strikeouts, and errors per game.

No contest here: Maddux had far and away the worst of it (and 1994 was just *the beginning* of the worst of it; the offensive carnage wouldn't peak until 2000); Mathewson had it the best, followed closely by Alexander.

Player	Year	Tms	#P	R/G	ERA	CG	H9	HR9	BB9	K9	E
Mathewson	1908	8	83	3.33	2.35	0.67	7.7	0.1	2.6	3.4	1.63
Alexander	1915	8	87	3.62	2.75	0.54	8.2	0.2	2.6	3.8	1.49
Seaver	1971	12	175	3.91	3.47	0.28	8.5	0.7	3.1	5.4	0.83
Maddux	1994	14	236	4.62	4.22	0.06	9.2	1.0	3.3	6.4	0.75

Teams averaged 3.33 runs per game in 1908; in 1994 they scored an average of 4.62 runs per game—an increase of about 40 percent. The *league ERA* in Mathewson's signature 1908 season was 2.35—that's a Cy Young Award season for a pitcher in Maddux' time, when the league ERA was nearly two runs higher.

Mathewson spent the entirety of his career in the Deadball era; Alexander a little less than half (albeit his entire prime). These were the days when pitchers defaced and defiled baseballs with abandon, staining them with tobacco spit, scuffing them with emery boards, camouflaging them in clouds of rosin. This abuse was barely warranted; fresh out of the box, the baseballs of the day were practically dead.

Contrast that with Maddux, who spent almost the entirety of his prime pitching in smaller ballparks, to smaller strike zones, against bigger players. No one gave up home runs in Mathewson's day, while Maddux played in the most homer-happy environment in history.

It's also important to note the quality of defense playing behind them: Playing on inconsistently groomed fields with crude, tiny gloves, defenders made twice as many errors behind Mathewson and Alexander as compared with Seaver and Maddux.

This is a double-edged sword: More errors = more base runners = more runs scored. But it also means more *unearned* runs, which could mean artificially low ERAs. Defenders *never* got the benefit of the doubt in the days of Mathewson and Alexander; they almost *always* get the benefit of the doubt in the modern game. With highly calibrated, athletically superior defensive units playing behind them, Seaver and Maddux gave up very few unearned runs. This ultimately helped their won-loss records, but hurt their career ERAs.

Using total runs allowed per nine innings (RA/9), the apparent gap in raw career ERA is closed considerably. Mathewson and Seaver, for example, gave up about the same amount of total runs per nine innings; Mathewson's ERA was penalized at a much lower rate.

Here is another way to look at it: Earned Run Rate (ERR) shows how often a pitcher was on the hook for runs allowed: Mathewson was dinged with an earned run 70 percent of the time a run scored; Seaver, by comparison, saw his account charged 87 percent of the time.[21]

Pitcher	RA/9	ERA	Diff	ERR
Mathewson	3.05	2.13	-.92	70%
Alexander	3.21	2.56	-.65	80%
Seaver	3.15	2.73	-.42	87%
Maddux	3.56	3.21	-.35	90%

The net result? Using this methodology, if Seaver was charged with earned runs at the same rate as Mathewson, his career ERA would be 2.20; if Mathewson was charged with earned runs at the same rate as Seaver, his career ERA climbs to 2.65.

Durability

Pitchers in the first quarter of the 20th century compiled enormous innings totals; it wasn't unusual for the league leaders to approach (and at times, surpass) 400 innings in a season.

- Maddux, despite pitching in a five-man rotation the entirety of his career, made more starts than any other pitcher in NL history.
- Seaver never led his league in innings, but he was far from lazy, completing 47 percent of his starts and leading all NL pitchers in innings over the first decade of his career.
- Mathewson collected his 4714 innings in 15 full seasons (averaging 321 IP from 1901 to 1915). He only led the league once (with 390 IP in 1908), but his cumulative body of work leads all pitchers over the time period (and *dwarfs* his closest NL competitor: Vic Willis compiled 3342 innings before retiring at age 34).
- Alexander was a horse, leading his league in innings seven times, and complete games six times. From 1911 to 1917, Alexander *averaged* 356 innings per season. He was indefatigable, even by the standards of his day.

But the key phrase here is "standards of his day." Hitters in 1908 launched a home run about once every nine or ten days; in 1915, they left the park once every five games. In 1994, hitters averaged one home run per *game*. Pitching in vast ballparks to a larger strike zone, using dark, wet baseballs with dead cores, pitchers (and managers) in Matty's day didn't have to worry that the slightest mistake meant surrendering a lead—they pitched to contact, often against hitters who were trying to bunt their way on (or bunt a base runner over). While we don't have official records, it's somewhat obvious that pitchers threw far fewer pitches per inning in the early 1900s as compared with modern hurlers.

As a result, it was *much* easier to go the distance: NL pitchers completed *two-thirds* of their starts in 1908; by 1994, complete games were virtually extinct. Running a nightly gauntlet of hulking mashers, starters went the distance only once in 16 tries. They weren't *less* durable than star hurlers of the past—if anything, pitchers in Maddux's time were *more* durable, on a pitch-by-pitch basis, than their turn-of-the-century counterparts. They just had to throw many more pitches—at maximum effort—to get through fewer innings. With his 5000 innings spread across 23 seasons, Greg Maddux is the standard-bearer for durability.

Reputation

We'll call this one a four-way tie. All four were considered the best pitcher in baseball for an extended period during their respective careers; each has been considered the best pitcher in the history of their league. Seaver, as previously mentioned, long held the record for Hall of Fame induction percentage (98.8), but all four are inner-circle immortals.

Peak Performance

Here is where Maddux distances himself from the rest of this quartet. His four-, five-, six-, and seven-year consecutive peaks are arguably the best in league history. If we restrict "peak" to the five best seasons, period (i.e., non-consecutive), it looks like this.

5-YR Peak	Mathewson	Alexander	Seaver	Maddux
pWAR	48.1	51.3	42.5	42.3
ERA + (avg.)	190	178	166	215

WAR and adjusted ERA are, admittedly, blunt instruments. Mathewson and Alexander, with their extraordinary innings totals, are probably overvalued. WAR correctly values innings pitched within a given era, but doesn't yet make fine distinctions for degree of difficulty *across* eras. In other words, an inning of work in 1915 is very different than an inning of work in 1999.[22] Maddux and that 215 adjusted ERA—meaning his ERA was more than twice as good as league average in his five best seasons—is probably the most impressive statistic you'll see in this chapter.[23]

Odds and Ends

Best Nickname: Tom Seaver—"The Franchise," "Tom Terrific." Can't do much better than that. "Big Six," "Old Pete," and "Mad Dog"?'Let's call it a three-way tie for "not nearly as good as Seaver."

Post-Season: Mathewson has a claim as the best post-season pitcher ever: 101 IP, 0.97 ERA, 0.836 WHIP; he was about twice as good in the World Series as he was in the regular season. Maddux pitched nearly 200 post-season innings at about the same rate of effectiveness as the regular season; he neither burnishes nor hurts his cause. Fair or not, Seaver and Alexander simply didn't get the same opportunities to distinguish themselves in the post-season. Both pitched great, but in *many* fewer innings.

Signature Moment: Seaver struck out 19 men, including the last ten he faced, on April 22, 1970. Alexander, of course, has his legendary dispatch of Tony Lazzeri in Game Seven of the 1926 World Series. Maddux has an honorary statistic named for him: A player achieves a "Maddux" by pitching a complete game shut-out with fewer than 100 pitches. But the winner in this category is Mathewson, who in 1905 produced this World Series line: Three starts, three shutouts, three wins.

Master of Them All?

The four greatest pitchers in National League history. Who then, is the unquestioned best? The numbers have been crunched and re-crunched, and the conclusion is inescapable: Greg Maddux is the most durable, precise, and efficient pitcher to spend the entirety of his career in the senior circuit. Based on his dominance relative to his era, Greg Maddux is the most valuable (and best) pitcher in the history of the National League, with Seaver, Alexander, and Mathewson, worthy travel companions (in that order).

5
Revisionist History 101

Having been named American League MVP in 1923, Babe Ruth was rendered ineligible for another award until 1931, when the Baseball Writers Association of America created the modern MVP award. Because of timing (there was no AL award from 1915 to 1921, and again in 1929–30) and eligibility restrictions, the most valuable player in the history of the game was named MVP only once.

For all its perceived faults, the system put into place in 1931 (and still in use today) at the very least defines consistent voting parameters: *All* players are eligible; ballots must be returned before the post-season begins; players can win more than once. Prior to 1931, in those years when an MVP award existed, the rules differed by year and by league (explaining, in some measure, why the award didn't catch on until *after* reforms were made in 1931).

But what if things were different? What would MVP history look like if the award created by the BBWAA in 1931 had been in place since 1901 (the year the major leagues as we know them were established)? No product placement disguised as an individual honor; no decade-long award droughts; no "league awards" with their onerous eligibility requirements.

What would MVP history look like if we had the power to fill in the blanks and right past wrongs?[1]

National League

1901–1910: No Award Given

There was no formal recognition of outstanding player performance during MLB's first official decade.

1901: Honus Wagner, OF-SS-1B, Pittsburgh Pirates

St. Louis leftfielder Jesse Burkett leads the league in runs, hits, average, on-base, and adjusted production, but the Browns are a lousy team, finishing fourth. Wagner doesn't compile the "black ink" like Burkett, but essentially matches him as an offensive force while establishing himself as the league's most versatile defender and fastest baserunner. Wagner is the best player on the best team in the league, and he's the MVP.

1902: Wagner

WAR rates the Cubs' Jack Tayler (1.29 ERA in 333.2 IP) as the best player in the league, but the Cubs finish 34 games back. Pittsburgh *destroys* the league in 1902, pacing second-place Brooklyn by 27.5 games. Wagner himself later called this team the greatest in league history, and he had a case: At 103–36, Pittsburgh's lead over Brooklyn is greater than Brooklyn's lead over the last-place Giants. The MVP is coming from the NL champion Pittsburgh Pirates, and if the MVP is coming from the Pirates, that means the MVP is Honus Wagner. Playing outfield, first base, and shortstop, the Pirates' superman leads the league in runs, doubles, RBI, slugging, and adjusted production (although his 7.3 WAR is pedestrian by his standards).[2]

1903: Iron Man Joe McGinnity, P, NY Giants

1903	pWAR	W	L	W%	ERA	GS	CG	SHO	IP	H	ER	BB	K	ERA+	WHIP	K/BB
McGinnity	*11.3*	*31*	20	.608	2.43	*48*	*44*	3	*434*	391	117	109	171	139	1.152	1.57
Mathewson	10.2	30	13	.698	2.26	42	37	3	366.1	*321*	92	100	*267*	149	1.149	2.67

The Giants had a pretty good one-two punch in Joe McGinnity and Christy Mathewson. Matty was nominally better in 1903, but there's no denying those 434 innings—an exceptional feat even by the standards of the day.

1904: Joe McGinnity

McGinnity and Mathewson combine for a 68–20 record as the Giants loosen Pittsburgh's stranglehold on the pennant. Fatigue is clearly setting in for the Iron Man: He can muster but 408 innings pitched in 1904. He's still able to squeeze out a league-leading 35 wins (and a league-leading five saves).

1905: Christy Mathewson, P, NY Giants

1905	pWAR	W	L	W%	ERA	G	GS	CG	SHO	IP	H	ER	BB	K	ERA+	WHIP	K/BB
Mathewson	9.1	*31*	9	.775	*1.28*	43	37	32	8	338.2	252	48	64	*206*	*230*	*0.933*	3.22

Mathewson capped his superb season with three complete-game shutouts in the World Series. In 27 WS innings, he allowed no runs, 13 hits, and one walk while striking out 18. Is it the best pitching performance in World Series history? The contenders:

- Sandy Koufax, 1965: "The Left Arm of God" yields two runs (one earned) against the Twins in the sixth inning of game two. It's the last time he's touched in the series. His final line: One earned run (0.38 ERA) over 24 innings. He fans 29 and walks five.
- Bob Gibson, 1967: Three starts, three complete games, three earned runs, three wins. The indomitable right-hander strikes out 26 and walks five. Gibson would make nine career WS starts, completing eight of them (and going eight innings in the other). His career WS line: 7–2, 1.89 ERA, 92K in 81 IP.
- Madison Bumgarner, 2014: Allows one run in 21 World Series innings, for a nifty 0.43 ERA. Pitching on two days' rest, he follows a Game Five shutout with five scoreless innings in Game Seven to secure the save and the world's championship. More remarkable: Bumgarner threw 52 post-season innings in 2014, or about twice as many as the other pitchers on this list.

1906: Frank Chance, 1B-Mgr., Chicago Cubs

1906	pWAR	W	L	W%	ERA	GS	CG	SHO	IP	H	ER	BB	K	ERA+	WHIP	FIP	K/BB
Brown	7.1	26	6	.813	**1.04**	32	27	**9**	277.1	198	32	61	144	**253**	**0.934**	**2.08**	2.36

We'll get to Chance in a moment. That's Mordecai Brown's pitching line, and that's not a misprint: "Three Finger" Brown pitched to a 1.04 ERA in 1906. Even at the height of the Deadball era, that shiny penny is going to catch your eye. Slam dunk for the MVP, right? Not so fast.

The 1906 Cubs stand among the greatest of all teams; their .763 winning percentage (116–36) is a record that has never been challenged.[3] Manager-first baseman Frank Chance (known as the "Peerless Leader") was probably the most respected personality in the league, anchoring the famed Tinker-Evers-Chance infield that some consider the best defensive unit of all time.[4] Chance had a fine season, leading the league in runs and stolen bases and ranking third in WAR (behind Wagner and the NY Giants' Art Devlin).

1906	WAR	G	AB	R	H	2B	3B	HR	RBI	SB	CS	BB	K	BA	OBP	SLG	OPS	OPS+
Chance	7.3	136	474	**103**	151	24	10	3	71	**57**	—	70	31	.319	.419	.430	.849	158

The Peerless Leader Frank Chance, at the height of his powers in 1910. His fortunes within the game would change dramatically over the next few years (Bain Collection, Library of Congress, Prints and Photographs Division).

"OK," you're thinking. "Chance was good. But 1.04 is 1.04. Why are we having this discussion?"

Remember, this is just about the toughest environment *ever* for hitters. If you normalize their statistics to historical offensive averages (as of 2014 defined as approximately 715 team runs scored per 162 games), Chance starts to look better and Brown starts to look ... well, something more than mortal but something less than supernatural.

	W	L	W%	ERA	IP	H	ER	BB	K	WHIP	K/BB			
Normalized Brown	23	9	.719	2.03	292.0	242	66	75	151	1.086	2.01			

	G	AB	R	H	2B	3B	HR	RBI	SB	BB	K	BA	OBP	SLG	OPS
Normalized Chance	143	515	127	175	28	12	3	87	66	81	33	.340	.443	.458	.901

Frank Chance is now Wade Boggs with Kenny Lofton speed—and normalized statistics undersell Chance's power: Home runs were non-existent in his day (Tim Jordan of the Brooklyn Superbas led the league with 12). Chance would likely be good for low double-digits in a normal hitting environment.

And then there's Brown's 1.04 ERA. It's spectacular. But a deeper dive into his performance reveals an element of luck is at play (as there is with any statistical outlier). As noted earlier, Fielding Independent Pitching (FIP) assigns an ERA-equivalent value to a composite total of a pitcher's home runs and walks allowed (including HBP), and strikeouts. FIP essentially attempts to strip team defense out of the equation to give us an idea of how well a pitcher handles the things directly under his control. If a pitcher's FIP is significantly *lower* than his actual ERA, it's reasonable to conclude that his defense cost him

Tinker, Evers, and Chance got the publicity, but Mordecai Brown was the heart of the 1906-10 Cubs dynasty (Bain Collection, Library of Congress, Prints and Photographs Division).

some runs (or he was just unlucky); if a pitcher's FIP is notably *higher* than his actual ERA, it's reasonable to conclude that his defense bailed him out of a few jams along the way.

Brown's 1906 FIP is 2.08—exactly *twice* as high as his actual ERA. A FIP that registers twice as high as an actual ERA is unusual; it means there was a lot of luck involved in a pitcher's performance (it should be noted that Brown led the league in FIP, nipping Pittsburgh's Deacon Phillippe 2.08 to 2.11; Phillippe finished with a 15–11 record, and a then-pedestrian 2.47 ERA).

There's also the matter of Brown's "earned run rate" (ERR). Brown allowed 56 runners to cross home plate in 1906, but only 32 (57 percent) of those runs were charged to the great right-hander—an unusually low percentage, even by Deadball standards.

And then there's his volume of work: Today, Brown's 277 IP would lead baseball by a comfortable margin. But in 1906, it registered *15th* in the league. Brown was the best pitcher in the league on an inning-by-inning basis, but Pittsburgh's Vic Willis, by virtue of his 1.73 ERA in 322 innings, led all pitchers in WAR (8.3).

We're not picking on Ol' Miner Brown. He was magnificent in 1906. But he threw in front of one of the best defensive units of all time, never had to fear the home run, and wasn't especially durable relative to his day. Chance, with his strong hitting performance, excellent defense and base running, and reputation as a leader among men, would have gotten the nod as MVP.

1907: WAGNER

1907	WAR	G	AB	R	H	2B	3B	HR	RBI	SB	CS	BB	K	BA	OBP	SLG	OPS	OPS+
Wagner	8.9	142	515	98	180	38	14	6	82	61	—	46	40	.350	.408	.513	.921	187

According to the August 1913 *Baseball Magazine*, "Hans Wagner is the greatest player in the National League. Whether he may fairly be compared with Ty Cobb is a matter of opinion. So far as length of record is concerned it is all Wagner. In some respects the Pittsburgher has the superior record irrespective of length. He has never batted for .400, but he has played the difficult position of shortstop and is one of the greatest fielders who ever lived. There is small comparison between shortstop and outfield.... He is one of the few greatest players of all time."

The Cubs make a mockery of the league, winning 107 games and pacing the circuit by 17 games. But like the 1998 Yankees, they're victims of their own extraordinary skill (at least when it comes to the MVP vote). Johnny Evers leads Cubs position players with a modest (compared with Wagner) 5.3 WAR—most of it tied to his defense. The Cubs pitching staff features *five* starters with a sub-1.70 ERA; choosing the most valuable among this rotation is a fool's errand, and opens the door for a dominant Wagner to pick up his third MVP of the decade.

1908: MATHEWSON

1908	pWAR	W	L	W%	ERA	GS	CG	SHO	IP	H	R	ER	BB	K	ERA+	WHIP	K/BB
Mathewson	11.1	37	11	.771	1.43	44	34	11	390.2	281	85	62	42	259	168	0.827	6.17

In October 1916, *Baseball Magazine* had this to say about Mathewson: "The real secret of Mathewson's success, the thing above all others which accounted for his brilliant career, was that simple but all important faculty of control. For to Mathewson more than to any other pitcher of his time, or of any other time, was given the gift of placing a baseball exactly where he wanted it."

In perhaps the most thrilling and compelling pennant race in history, the Cubs claim the flag by a single game over the Giants and Pirates. Mathewson is at his Olympian peak in 1908.

It's worth noting that Honus Wagner is at his absolute best in 1908 (11.5 WAR; a total never exceeded by another shortstop), and there's no real argument *against* him. As you'll note, the same rationale applies in 1909.

1909: WAGNER

1909	WAR	G	AB	R	H	2B	3B	HR	RBI	SB	CS	BB	K	BA	OBP	SLG	OPS	OPS+
Wagner	9.2	137	495	92	168	39	10	5	100	35	—	66	24	.339	.420	.489	.909	177

Fair or not, this one is decided by team records: Pittsburgh was astonishing, going 110–42 to claim the pennant and interrupt the Cubs' dynasty. Wagner, the best player in baseball, gets the conditional nod—but you'll get no argument in these quarters if you prefer one of the pitchers.

1909	pWAR	W	L	W%	ERA	G	GS	CG	SHO	IP	H	ER	BB	K	ERA+	WHIP	K/BB
Mathewson	9.2	25	6	.806	1.14	37	33	26	8	275.1	192	35	36	149	222	0.828	4.14
Brown	8.7	27	9	.750	1.31	50	34	32	8	342.2	246	50	53	172	193	0.873	3.25

1910: Mathewson

The Cubs dominate the league, but they field no dominant players, with Solly Hofman (5.3 WAR) and King Cole (5.6 pWAR) their top player and pitcher, respectively. Mathewson leads the league in WAR and wins (and places among the top-three in every important pitching category) for the second-place Giants.

1911–1914: Chalmers Award

The Chalmers Award for the player deemed "most useful to his club" was given out in the NL from 1911 to 1914 (the 1910 version of the award was given to the batting titlist). While the Chalmers committee was handing out MVPs (and cars) to the likes of Ty Cobb, Tris Speaker, and Walter Johnson in the American League, the NL list of winners was … less inspired. That said, none of the honorees were aided or hurt by eligibility restrictions. The actual award winners stand in our retroactive accounting:

- **1911: Frank Schulte, OF, Chicago Cubs**

    Schulte had a nice season, leading the league in home runs, RBI, and adjusted production. Mathewson was probably a better choice for MVP.

- **1912: Larry Doyle, 2B, NY Giants**

    "Laughing Larry" Doyle led the league in exactly zero offensive categories. He wasn't much on defense. The Giants won the pennant and Doyle somehow won MVP over his more deserving teammates Christy Mathewson and Rube Maquard. A terrible selection.[5]

    Doyle was presented a beautiful new "Model 36" by Hugh Chalmers prior to game one of the 1912 World Series. In introducing Chalmers, Ren Mulford said, "What Lipton is to yachting and Vanderbilt is to automobile racing, Hugh Chalmers is to baseball. The Chalmers Trophy is now a recognized baseball classic."

Chalmers would discontinue the award two seasons hence.

- **1913: Jake Daubert, 1B, Brooklyn Superbas**

   He was thought of primarily as a glove man his first few years in the league—called the "Hal Chase of the National League." Unlike the vile and crooked Chase, Daubert was a hard-working man of integrity.

   As a boy, Daubert was pulled out of school and put to work in the Pennsylvania mines shortly after the death of his mother. He toiled in the grit and the black for more than a decade, first as a "breaker boy" picking shards of slate from jagged mounds of coal, and later as a miner, descending into the pitch with pick and bucket. The mines took his brother's life, and rendered his father a near-cripple. Daubert never forgot this filthy, harrowing work.

   He didn't make his major league debut until the age of 26, but was immediately recognized as a deft touch around the bag. By his own admission, he wasn't a natural hitter. "I used to dream about hitting .300 in the Majors, but I never expected to get there," said the earnest Daubert in 1912. "Two seasons I hit for .307, but I couldn't believe I deserved that average."

   Daubert exceeded his dreams by hitting .350 to lead the league in 1913. He defended his batting title in 1914 (hitting .329), and finished his 15-year career with a .303 lifetime average. His driving ambition was to succeed in the major leagues so his own son could avoid the mines. He didn't deserve the MVP in 1913 (Philadelphia's "Cactus Gavvy" Cravath was clearly the league's best hitter, and he played for a much better team),[6] but there was never a player who was easier to root for than Daubert.

   Sadly, Daubert took ill and died at the age of 40. He was an active major leaguer at the time of his passing.

- **1914: Johnny Evers, 2B-Mgr., Boston Braves**

   The January 1914 *Baseball Magazine* said of Evers, "One would imagine that these officials would get used to Evers and pay no attention to him, but they say this is impossible, for he always springs something that sinks in deep, and when he gets something on an umpire he will wait for weeks for an opportune time to land it."

1915–1924: No Award Given

Hugh Chalmers cancelled his annual trophy (and the awarding of the car that went with it) after the 1914 season. It would be nearly a decade before the

The modest and unassuming Jake Daubert was awarded the Chalmers Trophy in 1913 (Bain Collection, Library of Congress, Prints and Photographs Division).

National League reinstated some form of recognition for the player deemed most valuable.

1915–1917: Grover Cleveland Alexander, P, Philadelphia Phillies

Alexander	pWAR	W	L	W%	ERA	G	GS	CG	SHO	IP	H	ER	BB	K	ERA+	WHIP	K/BB
1915	10.9	31	10	.756	1.22	49	42	36	12	376.1	253	51	64	241	225	0.842	3.77
1916	9.6	33	12	.733	1.55	48	45	38	16	389.0	323	67	50	167	172	0.959	3.34
1917	9.3	30	13	.698	1.83	45	44	34	8	388.0	336	79	56	200	154	1.010	3.57

Pete Alexander has a case as the greatest pitcher in National League history.

1918: Jim "Hippo" Vaughn, P, Chicago Cubs

1918	pWAR	W	L	W%	ERA	G	GS	CG	SHO	IP	H	ER	BB	K	ERA+	WHIP	K/BB
Vaughn	7.8	22	10	.688	1.74	35	33	27	8	290.1	216	56	76	148	159	1.006	1.95

Despite a heroic effort (27 IP, 1.00 ERA), Vaughn was unable to pitch the Cubs past the Red Sox in the World Series. He dropped game one to Babe

Ruth by a score of 1–0; Carl Mays beat him 2–1 in game three; Vaughn returned on two days rest to craft a five-hit shutout in game five, but he was forestalling the inevitable: The Sox closed out the series the next day.[7]

1919: HEINIE GROH, 3B, CINCINNATI REDS

1919	WAR	G	AB	R	H	2B	3B	HR	RBI	SB	CS	BB	K	BA	OBP	SLG	OPS	OPS+
Heinie Groh	5.4	122	448	79	139	17	11	5	63	21	—	56	26	.310	.392	.431	**.823**	149
Edd Roush	5.1	133	504	73	162	19	12	4	71	20	–	42	19	**.321**	.380	.431	.811	146

Little known fact: Dante originally described *ten* circles of hell, the last and worst being National League Baseball in the late 1910s. *The Inferno* tells us of sinners being torn to pieces by dogs, incinerated by burning rain, drowning in the river Styx ... but the thought of watching NL hitters push and peck for an eternity was deemed too horrible for readers to contemplate, so the poet cut it from his manuscript.[8]

Welcome to the game when spitballs were legal, baseballs were brown, and players carried cement pylons to the plate.

1919 League Leaders

WAR: Hornsby, 6.7	HR: Cravath, 12	OBP: Burns, .396
R: Burns, 86	RBI: Myers, 73	SLG: Myers, .436
H: Olson, 164	SB: Burns, 40	OPS: Groh, .823
2B: Youngs, 31	BB: Burns, 82	OPS+: Hornsby, 150
3B: Southworth, Myers, 14	BA: Roush, .321	XBH: Kauff, 44

We're still in the Deadball dark ages, so we expect to see a dozen home runs lead the league. But these other numbers are historically bad. Hi Myers' 73 RBI is the lowest total ever by a league leader; the same holds true for his .436 SLG. Groh's .823 OPS is the lowest to ever lead the league (Edd Roush matched that tepid .823 in 1918). George Burns' 86 runs scored; Benny Kauff's 44 extra base hits; Youngs' 31 doubles; Olson's 164 hits—all the second-lowest totals to ever lead the league (most of the all-time marks for futility were set the season prior).

Unlike 1918 (another anemic year for individual hitting performances), there is no dominant pitcher to give us an obvious choice for MVP. So we sift through the charts, tables, lists, and press clippings and arrive at Heinie Groh and Edd Roush, teammates on the world champion Cincinnati Reds.[9] Groh's a third baseman; Roush a centerfielder. Statistically, they're basically twins. Groh wins the coin flip in a landslide.

1920: Burleigh Grimes, P, Brooklyn Robins

1920	pWAR	W	L	W%	ERA	G	GS	CG	SV	IP	R	ER	HR	BB	K	ERA+	WHIP	K/BB
Grimes	6.8	23	11	.676	2.22	40	33	25	2	303.2	101	75	5	67	131	144	1.113	1.96

Pete Alexander, now bearing the scars of his time at the front during World War I (half deaf, fully in the clutches of PTSD, given to epileptic seizures, he treated his afflictions with whiskey) claims his fourth pitching Triple Crown. But the Phillies finish dead last in the standings. Is Alexander the best player in the league? Of course he is—his 12.1 WAR stands among the best of the 20th century. But he has no chance at the award, which is claimed by Burleigh Grimes, the ace of the NL champion Brooklyn Robins.

1921–1922: Rogers Hornsby, 2B, St. Louis Cardinals

Hornsby	WAR	G	AB	R	H	2B	3B	HR	RBI	SB	CS	BB	K	BA	OBP	SLG	OPS	OPS+
1921	10.8	154	592	131	235	44	18	21	126	13	13	60	48	.397	.458	.639	1.097	191
1922	10	154	623	141	250	46	14	42	152	17	12	65	50	.401	.459	.722	1.181	207

Hornsby is just about the last person you'd want sitting next to you at a dinner party. He famously eschewed any activity that would "strain" his eyes. This meant no reading and no movies. He wasn't much of a conversationalist, and when he did talk, he was often an abrasive sort. But *by god*, the man could hit.

1923: Dolf Luque, P, NY Giants

1923	pWAR	W	L	W%	ERA	G	GS	CG	SHO	IP	H	ER	BB	K	ERA+	WHIP	K/BB
Luque	10.6	27	8	.771	1.93	41	37	28	6	322.0	279	69	88	151	201	1.140	1.72

Adolfo Domingo de Guzman Luque wasn't quite a one-hit wonder—he also led the league in ERA in 1925. But aside from his wonderful 1923 season, he was a sub-.500 pitcher (despite an adjusted career ERA 18 percent better than the league average). He was the first Cuban-born player to gain a measure of stardom in the majors.

1924–1929: League Awards

The National League introduced its version of the MVP award in 1924, without the strict eligibility restrictions enforced by the AL. The actual winners of the 1924–29 period remain unchanged in our revised list.

- **1924: Dazzy Vance, P, Brooklyn Robins**
  A controversial selection at the time (Hornsby hit .424), but Vance was a deserving MVP. By some measures, his 1924 masterpiece is one of the

three or four most dominant seasons *ever* by a pitcher. Vance *towered* over the league in 1924. His 28 victories were six more than the next highest total; his 2.16 ERA was more than half a run lower than the next best; his 262 strikeouts were nearly twice as many as runner-up Burleigh Grimes (the only other pitcher in the league to record more than 100 strikeouts).

- **1925: Hornsby**

  Another year, another Triple Crown. Ho hum. From 1921 to 1925, Hornsby *averaged* .402/.471/.690.

- **1926: Bob O'Farrell, C, St. Louis Cardinals**

  What *was* Ruth thinking?

- **1927: Paul Waner, 1B, Pittsburgh Pirates**

  "Big Poison" paced the league with a .380 BA., but it's tough to make a case for him as MVP. The voters probably felt they couldn't give it to Hornsby every year.

- **1928: Jim Bottomley, 1B, St. Louis Cardinals**

  Bottomley led the league in triples, home runs, and RBI, but he was a terrible choice for MVP (5.3 WAR). Vance (10.1 pWAR) should have claimed his second trophy.

- **1929: Hornsby, Chicago Cubs**

  Hornsby's last great season: .380/.459/.679, 10.4 WAR.

1930: No Award Given

So we'll give it to ... Hack Wilson, OF, Chicago Cubs.

1930	WAR	G	AB	R	H	2B	3B	HR	RBI	SB	CS	BB	K	BA	OBP	SLG	OPS	OPS+
Wilson	7.4	155	585	146	208	35	6	**56**	**191**	3	—	**105**	**84**	.356	.454	**.723**	**1.177**	**177**

Wilson sets the single-season RBI record with 191 (and the NL home run record, which would stand for 68 years). It nets him the theoretical MVP, but it must be said that Wilson's season isn't nearly as good as it seems. Here's his stat line adjusted for 2014, assuming the same league, same home park:

"2014"	AB	R	H	2B	3B	HR	RBI	SB	BB	K	BA	OBP	SLG	OPS
Wilson	569	109	175	29	5	48	142	3	88	88	.308	.401	.629	1.030

A fine effort, but no one would remember this season 85 years later. National League teams scored 5.7 runs per game in 1930—the highest scoring season on record. The league averaged only 3.95 R/G in 2014—or 44 percent less than in Wilson's time.

How crazy was 1930? The league *as a whole* hit .303; 12 men hit .340 or better (led by Bill Terry at .401). In a league where 63 men qualified for the batting title, *17 of them drove in 100 or more runs.*

Wilson was a good hitter for a few years, but his RBI record is one of baseball's biggest flukes.

American League

1901–1910: No Award Given

The American League was founded in 1901. It was grudgingly recognized as on par with the National League when Cy Young's Boston Americans bested Honus Wagner's Pittsburgh Pirates in the first World Series (1903).

1901: Napoleon Lajoie, 2B, Philadelphia Athletics

1901	WAR	G	AB	R	H	2B	3B	HR	RBI	SB	CS	BB	K	BA	OBP	SLG	OPS	OPS+
Lajoie	8.4	131	544	145	232	48	14	*14*	125	27	—	24	9	.426	.463	.643	1.106	198

In the American League's inaugural season, Lajoie is a man among boys.

1902: Cy Young, P, Boston Red Sox

1902	pWAR	W	L	W%	ERA	G	GS	CG	SHO	IP	H	ER	BB	K	ERA+	WHIP	K/BB
Young	*10*	32	11	.744	2.15	45	43	41	3	384.2	350	92	53	160	164	1.048	3.02

Cy Young was 35 years old in 1902. Check that: With more than 500 games and 4400 innings behind him, Cy Young was an *ancient* 35 in 1902. Old and fat, Cy showed the upstart American League how the grown-ups played ball. The only plausible explanation is that Young kept a portrait of his right arm locked away in a closet somewhere.

1903: Young

Cy Young was 36 years old in 1903. Check that: With more than 550 games and 4800 innings behind him, Cy Young was an *ancient* 36 in 1903. Old and fat, Cy showed the American League how the grown-ups played ball. The Cyclone led the league in wins, innings, complete games, shutouts, and strikeout-to-walk ratio. With a 125 OPS+ in 146 PA, Young was also one of the better hitters on the pennant-winning Red Sox.

1904: Jack Chesbro, P, NY Highlanders

1904	pWAR	W	L	W%	ERA	G	GS	CG	SHO	IP	H	ER	BB	K	ERA+	WHIP	K/BB
Chesbro	10.2	**41**	12	.774	1.82	**55**	**51**	**48**	6	**454.2**	338	92	88	239	150	0.937	2.72
Waddell	**10.5**	25	19	.568	1.62	46	46	39	8	383.0	307	69	91	**349**	**165**	1.039	3.84

Edward "Rube" Waddell was the best pitcher in the league in 1904 (and probably the best pitcher in the league from 1902 to 1906), but Jack Chesbro was the most valuable, relative to his team. Forty-one wins is 41 wins; 450 innings is 450 innings.

A special Veteran's Committee inducted Chesbro into the Hall of Fame in 1946—almost entirely on the strength of this one great year. Joining him in the class of '46 was Waddell. Unlike Chesbro, he was deserving of the honor.

Waddell was one of the game's greatest characters and eccentrics. With a crackling fastball and sharp curve, the lefthander led the decade (1900–09) in strikeouts (including six consecutive seasons, 1902–07), shutouts, and FIP; he placed among the top three in WAR, ERA, and ERA+.

He was dominant to an extent that few pitchers have ever been. His strikeout totals in a high-contact era were *ungodly*. Take 1904: With 349 strikeouts (110 more than runner-up Chesbro), Waddell set a major league record that would endure 51 years.[10] To put this in perspective: American League hitters in 1904 struck out 4.1 times per nine innings; Waddell fanned 8.2 batters per nine innings. On a rate basis, Waddell's 8.2 K/9 in 1904 is equivalent to *15.4 K/9 in 2014*. Randy Johnson, an apt comparison to Waddell in terms of dominance and ability, holds the K/9 mark for a starting pitcher with 13.4 K/9 (Johnson in 2001 fanned 372 batters in only 249.2 innings).

1905: Rube Waddell, P, Philadelphia Athletics

1905	pWAR	W	L	W%	ERA	G	GS	CG	SHO	IP	H	ER	BB	K	ERA+	WHIP	K/BB
Waddell	**9.2**	27	10	.730	**1.48**	46	34	27	7	328.2	231	54	90	**287**	**179**	0.977	3.19

Connie Mack, in *Baseball Magazine* in 1912, said, "We used to put Rube in centerfield when we weren't pitching him. He never wanted to sit on the bench, and we had to humor him or he wouldn't have stayed on the lot. One day we were being hard pressed. With only one out, the other team filled the bases in the fifth inning. We had two strikes on the next man up, and then something happened: A black cloud of smoke appeared in the sky back of centerfield fence. Then came the clanking of fire bells, and the clatter of horses' hoofs. I happened to look in the direction of the blaze. High up on the centerfield fence I saw Rube perched, looking at the blaze.... I let out a blast that nearly woke the dead. Rube heard me and looked around. He seemed undecided as to his next move, but he wasn't long in making up his mind. With a graceful salute of his hand, as if to say, 'So long, fellows!' he dropped from sight on the other side of the fence, and was on his way to the fire."

Waddell was by turns the most infuriating and endearing player of his day. Fans flocked to see him pitch. He had the disposition, attention span, and emotional maturity of a child. He also had the best arm in the league (and a serious drinking problem). As is the case with many great characters, his legend was burnished by teammates and the press of the day. It has only grown in the century since Waddell last threw a pitch.

There are scores of anecdotes, many of which strain credulity, about his baffling behavior. One thing is clear: He was unpredictable and unreliable; more than once he abandoned his team in favor of a drinking binge. He would also disappear to go fishing, chase fires, or pitch for semi-pro teams (stories of the day also had him missing starts to shoot marbles with children and—wait for it—wrestle alligators).[11]

He was at the height of his powers in 1905, but as was so often the case with Waddell, he was undermined by his own poor judgment. He missed most of the last month of the 1905 season for nebulous reasons (Waddle claimed he was injured wrestling with teammate Andy Coakley over a hat; rumors of the day had it that he was bribed by gamblers to *fake* an injury). Wherever the truth lies, we know one thing for certain: The world was denied Waddell vs. Mathewson in the 1905 World Series.

1906: Lajoie, 2B, Cleveland Naps[12]

Lajoie was the AL version of Honus Wagner: He was better at everything than everybody else. Unlike Wagner, who may have been the most awkward great player in history, Lajoie was known for his smooth, graceful style in the field. They may have gone about it in different ways, but both were among the premier defensive players of their generation.

1907: Ty Cobb, OF, Detroit Tigers

1907	WAR	G	AB	R	H	2B	3B	HR	RBI	SB	CS	BB	K	BA	OBP	SLG	OPS	OPS+
Cobb	6.8	150	605	97	*212*	28	14	5	*119*	53	—	24	55	*.350*	.380	*.468*	*.848*	*167*

Taking the first of his 11 batting titles with a .350 average, Cobb begins his run of American League dominance in 1907. All of 20 years old, he's still learning how to hit.

1908: Ed Walsh, P, Chicago White Sox

1908	pWAR	W	L	W%	ERA	G	GS	CG	SHO	IP	H	ER	BB	K	ERA+	WHIP	K/BB
Walsh	10.1	40	15	.727	1.42	66	49	42	11	464	343	73	56	269	162	0.860	4.80

"Big Ed" Walsh was an ornery sort. He wasn't the type of guy who went in for small talk. He intimidated opponents and teammates alike. He was also tougher than glove leather, starting a *third* of Chicago's games in 1908. The spitballer *almost* willed the White Sox to the pennant (they fell 1.5 games short of the Tigers).

1909: Cobb

1909	WAR	G	AB	R	H	2B	3B	HR	RBI	SB	CS	BB	K	BA	OBP	SLG	OPS	OPS+
Cobb	9.8	156	573	116	216	33	10	9	107	76	—	48	45	.377	.431	.517	.947	193

Ty Cobb captures the "Quadruple Crown" in 1909, leading in average, home runs, RBI, and stolen bases (the only man to ever accomplish this feat). As improbable as this sounds, 1909 might not place among Cobb's three best seasons.

1910: Cobb. Maybe.

1910	WAR	G	AB	R	H	2B	3B	HR	RBI	SB	CS	BB	K	BA	OBP	SLG	OPS	OPS+
Lajoie	9.8	159	591	94	227	51	7	4	76	26	—	60	18	.384	.445	.514	.960	199
Cobb	10.5	140	506	106	194	35	13	8	91	65	—	64	46	.383	.456	.551	1.008	206
Collins	10.5	153	581	81	188	16	15	3	81	81	—	49	41	.324	.382	.418	.800	152

Lajoie and Cobb are clearly the two dominant offensive forces in the league. If we dismiss Lajoie's tainted 8-for-8 final day, we widen the gap between them as hitters. It's tempting to redress the shenanigans in St. Louis and just give the retroactive MVP to Cobb. Except it's not quite that simple.

Enter Eddie Collins, second baseman for the AL champion Philadelphia Athletics. Collins, while not in the same class as Lajoie and Cobb as a hitter, places among the top-five in virtually every major hitting category while leading the league in stolen bases. He's an elite defender at a premium position, and a superb baserunner. WAR recognizes his all-around contributions as equal to the batting duelists.

Collins also gets a boost from team performance: His Athletics capture the pennant with ease, while Cobb's Tigers finish a distant third, 18 games back. Lajoie's Naps are 32 games adrift in fifth place. Collins doesn't have the fame (or notoriety) of his two competitors for the award, but he's recognized by insiders as the best second baseman in the game. One can easily make the argument that Cobb and Lajoie, those two great rivals, "cancel one another out" in this mythical MVP race, allowing Collins to scamper home with the 1910 award.

Further muddling the 1910 MVP picture is Collins' teammate "Colby Jack" Coombs.

1910	pWAR	W	L	W%	ERA	G	GS	CG	SHO	IP	H	ER	BB	K	ERA+	WHIP	K/BB
Coombs	9.7	31	9	.775	1.30	45	38	35	13	353	248	51	115	224	182	1.028	1.95

Coombs is one of the best three or four pitchers in the game, but the Athletics *as a team* post a 1.79 ERA. Coombs is clearly the ace of this rotation for the ages, but it can't be ignored that staff-mates Chief Bender (1.55 ERA), Cy Morgan (1.58 ERA), and Eddie Plank (2.01 ERA) were nearly as good (albeit in far fewer innings).[13]

The uneasy pick here is Cobb, and it boils down to how much weight one places on defense. Collins was universally hailed as a superb gloveman, but it's impossible to quantify with statistical certainty. The theory here is not that Cobb and Lajoie split the MVP vote—it's that stellar teammates Collins and Coombs divide the affections of the voters, allowing Cobb to capture a plurality of the vote.

1911–1914 Chalmers Awards

1911: COBB

The Reach Official American League Base Ball Guide for 1912: "In individual work Cobb, in the 1911 season, overtopped all other players in all departments of the game, as in addition to his wonderful batting average [.420] he established a new American League base-stealing record with 83 stolen bases, and also led his league in run-scoring and made a new American League record with 248 safe hits in the season, and another league record by batting safely in 40 consecutive games. This is an individual record which for all-round excellence in one season has never been exceeded by any player."

1912: TRIS SPEAKER, OF, BOSTON RED SOX

Tris Speaker was the Willie Mays of his time—he wasn't just acknowledged as the best centerfielder in the game, he was unanimously hailed as the best defensive outfielder *ever*. And that's before we get to his hitting (superb) and base running (excellent). He was at the height of his powers in 1912, batting .383, leading position players in WAR (10.1), and pacing the league in runs, doubles, home runs, and on-base percentage.

Despite his excellence, Speaker wasn't a mortal lock for the Chalmers. A magnificent trio of pitchers staked a claim.

1912	pWAR	W	L	W%	ERA	G	GS	SV	IP	H	R	ER	BB	K	ERA+	WHIP	K/BB
Johnson	**13.5**	33	12	.733	**1.39**	50	37	2	369.0	259	89	57	76	**303**	**240**	**0.908**	3.99
Walsh	11.4	27	17	.614	2.15	62	41	**10**	**393.0**	332	125	94	94	254	149	1.084	2.70
Wood	10.4	**34**	5	**.872**	1.91	43	38	1	344.0	267	104	73	82	258	179	1.015	3.15

Walter Johnson had one of his best years in 1912, but Speaker's Red Sox were a juggernaut (105–47), taking the pennant by 14 games over Johnson's suddenly-not-terrible Senators. Boston's dominance makes Smoky Joe Wood's showing in the vote somewhat perplexing; the young superstar was only able to muster a fifth-place finish in the vote despite those 34 wins (against only five losses).

In one of the most thrilling World Series ever played, the Red Sox triumphed over Mathewson's Giants in eight games (game two a called tie on account of darkness). Down 2–1 to Mathewson in the bottom of the 10th inning of game eight, Speaker tied the game with a line drive to right; an intentional walk and a sacrifice fly later, the Red Sox were world champs.

1913: Walter Johnson, P, Washington Senators

1913	pWAR	W	L	W%	ERA	G	GS	CG	SHO	IP	H	R	ER	BB	K	ERA+	WHIP	K/BB
Johnson	14.6	36	7	.837	1.14	48	36	29	11	346.0	232	56	44	38	**243**	**259**	**0.780**	6.39

Probably the single greatest season ever for a pitcher.

1914: Eddie Collins, 2B, Philadelphia Athletics

Hugh Chalmers cancelled his annual award after the 1914 season. He claimed it was always his intent for the award to last five years, establishing an honorary "baseball hall of fame." The Chalmers HOF was a bit underwhelming; it comprised the nine players who received a car from his company. This is not to denigrate the fine work of Eddie Collins, who had a case as the best position player in the game from 1913 to 1915.

1915: Cobb

1915	WAR	G	AB	R	H	2B	3B	HR	RBI	SB	CS	BB	K	BA	OBP	SLG	OPS	OPS+
Cobb	**9.5**	156	563	**144**	**208**	31	13	3	99	**96**	38	118	43	**.369**	**.486**	.487	**.973**	**185**

At this point, the voters are looking for excuses not to give it to Cobb[14]; they can't find any in 1915. Walter Johnson was still the most valuable commodity in the game, but his Senators finish a distant fourth in the league. Eddie Collins is Cobb's equal as a player, but his White Sox finish a tepid third (13.5 games behind the pennant-winning Red Sox). The Tigers finish just 2.5 games back of the Red Sox, and Cobb sets a record for base thefts while leading the league in all the usual categories. The stolen base mark was considered a very big deal at the time—but Cobb's success rate (72 percent) was nothing special.[15] Since he was caught a league-high 38 times, he netted but 58 bases for his team. Fritz Maisel, with 51 thefts in 63 tries, generated about the same value on the bases for the Yankees.

1916: BABE RUTH, P, RED SOX

1916	WAR	W	L	W%	ERA	G	GS	CG	SHO	IP	H	ER	BB	K	ERA+	WHIP	K/BB
Ruth	10.4	23	12	.657	**1.75**	44	**40**	23	**9**	323.2	230	63	118	170	**158**	1.075	1.44

In a shocking move, the world champion Red Sox sold their best player, centerfielder nonpareil Tris Speaker, to the Cleveland Indians at the outset of the 1916 season. Baseball's standard-bearer on defense, the 28-year-old Speaker had an "off-year" in 1915, hitting .322/.416/.411 for an OPS+ of 151 (leading the team by a mile in all categories). Boston owner J.J. Lannin, believing (or, at least, publicly grousing while in contract negotiations with his centerfielder) that Speaker was in decline, offloaded his star for a record sum of more than $50,000.

The deal sparked a fair amount of outrage in the press. Even in an off year, the beloved Speaker was still one of the two or three best players in the game. His departure from Boston, it was assumed, all but guaranteed the Red Sox would relinquish their title without a fight. It was seen as a betrayal of the city and its fans.

Lannin shrugged off the criticism, gloating about the heist he perpetrated on Cleveland: "I never dreamed that I could get so much money for his release," he said. "But when [Cleveland] told me the price that owner James C. Dunn was willing to pay I quickly changed my mind. I do not believe that any ball player is worth the money I have received for Speaker." In a parting shot, Lannin added: "I also wish to say that Speaker isn't worth the salary he demanded."[16]

Cleveland was a *terrible* team (finishing 57–95 in 1915), but such was Speaker's stature that they were now considered a contender for the 1916 pennant. Wrote *The Sporting Life* on April 15, 1916, "With the coming of Speaker, who is without doubt the best defensive outfielder baseball has ever known, and who ranks next to Ty Cobb and right alongside of Eddie Collins as the world's best offensive-player, the 'Critics' will have to revise their dope a second time and give the Indians a look-in at a first division berth."

Well ... let's not get ahead of ourselves. Speaker did his part, exceeding any reasonable expectations with one of his best seasons. But Cleveland was Cleveland. They finished the 1916 season in sixth place (they did, however, improve by 18 games over the year prior).

1916	WAR	G	AB	R	H	2B	3B	HR	RBI	SB	CS	BB	K	BA	OBP	SLG	OPS	OPS+
Speaker	*8.6*	151	546	102	*211*	*41*	8	2	79	35	27	82	20	.386	.470	.502	.972	*186*

And what of Speaker's former team, the Red Sox? As predicted, the Sox offense suffered from his loss, falling from third in runs scored (4.3 R/G) in 1915 to sixth in 1916 (3.5). Their win-loss record took a corresponding hit.

Red Sox	Record	W-L%	R/Game	RA/Game
1915	101–50	.669	4.3	3.2
1916	91–63	.591	3.5	3.1

But timing is sometimes everything: The Red Sox were indisputably worse without Speaker—but the Detroit Tigers, their chief rivals for the pennant in 1915, were also worse, winning just 87 in games in 1916 as compared with 100 the season prior.

The end result was a wash: The Red Sox again took the pennant, and they took it with pitching. Their star was a raw-boned, barrel chested, hard-throwing lefty named Ruth. His control wasn't much, but when he was on, the 21-year-old was near unhittable (and he contributed a 121 OPS+ with the bat). As would often be the case in his later years, Ruth was at his best in the World Series, spinning a 14-inning, six-hit, one-run victory in game two (Boston would dispatch Brooklyn in five games to repeat as champions).

1917: EDDIE CICOTTE, P, CHICAGO WHITE SOX

1917	pWAR	W	L	W%	ERA	G	GS	CG	SHO	IP	H	ER	BB	K	ERA+	WHIP	K/BB
Cicotte	*11.4*	28	12	.700	*1.53*	49	35	29	7	346.2	246	59	70	150	*174*	*0.912*	2.14

Eddie Cicotte was the best pitcher in the world in 1917. He was just about as good in 1919. He is rightfully remembered, however, for his role in the 1919 Black Sox scandal.

1918: JOHNSON

The Big Train notches his third "Pitching Triple Crown." You can, without much effort, make the case that Walter Johnson was the most valuable player in the league *every* year from 1910 to 1918.

1919–1921: BABE RUTH, OF-P, BOSTON RED SOX, NY YANKEES

1919	WAR	G	AB	R	H	2B	3B	HR	RBI	SB	CS	BB	K	BA	OBP	SLG	OPS	OPS+
Ruth	*10.2*	130	432	*103*	139	34	12	*29*	*113*	7	—	101	58	.322	*.456*	*.657*	*1.114*	*217*

Red Sox outfielder Harry Hooper said in *Glory of Their Times*, "I still remember when the Babe was switched from pitching to become an outfielder. I finally convinced Ed Barrow to play him out there to get his bat in the lineup every day.... Well, Ruth might have been a natural as a pitcher and as a hitter, but he sure wasn't a born outfielder."

In addition to setting a new single-season home run record, Ruth went 9–5 as a pitcher for the 1919 Red Sox.

Ruth	WAR	G	AB	R	H	2B	3B	HR	RBI	SB	CS	BB	K	BA	OBP	SLG	OPS	OPS+
1920	*11.9*	142	458	*158*	172	36	9	*54*	*135*	14	14	*150*	80	.376	*.532*	*.847*	*1.379*	*255*
1921	*12.9*	152	540	*177*	204	44	16	*59*	*168*	17	13	*145*	81	.378	*.512*	*.846*	*1.359*	*238*

The Spalding Guide, 1921, said, "In connection with this, one must not forget that it was very seldom that Ruth got a really good ball at which he could swing. His skill is best understood when we consider that he made his home runs when the ball was at his knee equally as well as when the ball was at his shoulder. The extraordinary power which he puts into that wicked golf swing from behind his shoulder seems able to drive a ball out of any ordinary fenced ground."

1922–1928: LEAGUE AWARDS

The American League introduced its league Most Valuable Player award in 1922. It was a flop. Blame the voting rules and eligibility requirements: A player could only win the award once; player-managers were not eligible; and the writers could only vote for one player per team. From an available talent pool of more than 200 players, only a handful were seriously considered for the award. Below are the MVP choices had the award existed under today's rules.

1922: GEORGE SISLER, 1B, ST. LOUIS BROWNS

Often forgotten in the wake of Gehrig and Foxx, Sisler at his peak was the best first baseman of the game's first quarter-century. His finest season was probably 1920, but he was pretty good in 1922 as well, when he hit .420, also leading the league in WAR (8.7) runs, hits, triples, and stolen bases. Sisler was recognized as the MVP by the writers, and this recognition stands in our revised list.

1923–1924: RUTH, OF

Detroit's Harry Heilmann denied Ruth the 1923 Triple Crown when he outhit him .403 to .393. As of August 30, Ruth stood at .405/32 HR/104 RBI, leading the league in all three categories. Heilmann, second in average at .396, hit .423 for September, while Ruth "slumped" to .357. They engaged in a thrilling chase for the batting title, separated by a single point of average as late as September 20. Heilmann got serious over the last two weeks of the season, scalding the ball at a .553 clip. Not even the Babe could keep pace. No Triple Crown for the Ruth, but he was compensated with his only MVP award.

Ruth captured his only batting title in 1924, but was again denied the Triple Crown when he fell six RBI shy of league leader Goose Goslin. Walter Johnson was named MVP, but Ruth was clearly the most deserving of the honor.

1925: GOOSE GOSLIN, OF, WASHINGTON SENATORS

1925	WAR	G	AB	R	H	2B	3B	HR	RBI	SB	CS	BB	K	BA	OBP	SLG	OPS	OPS+
Goslin	6.5	150	601	116	201	34	20	18	113	27	8	53	50	.334	.394	.547	.941	139

As noted earlier, actual MVP Roger Peckinpaugh was a *terrible* choice for the award. Goose Goslin was the best player on the AL champion Senators, one of the best players in the league, and should have been recognized for his efforts.

1926: RUTH

With 47 HR, Ruth comfortably exceeded the *combined* total of his two closest competitors in that category. Al Simmons (19) and Tony Lazzeri (18).

1927: Gehrig, 1B, NY Yankees (Actual MVP)

1927	WAR	G	AB	R	H	2B	3B	HR	RBI	BB	K	BA	OBP	SLG	OPS	OPS+
Gehrig	11.8	155	584	149	218	52	18	47	*173*	109	84	.373	.474	.765	1.240	220

A tough call—this is the year Ruth clouts 60. But Gehrig was nearly his equal at the plate, and the voters would likely be suffering from Babe fatigue. And it's not like they'd need excuses to vote for the Yankees' first baseman: His 47 HR and .765 SLG were the highest totals ever recorded by anyone other than the Babe; his 173 RBI established a new single-season record; and he led the league in doubles and total bases. His actual MVP stands.

1928: Ruth

Ruth's 54 HR in 1928 were exactly twice as many as runner-up Gehrig.

1929–1930: No Award Given

The American League abruptly cancelled its MVP award prior to the 1929 season, claiming that it bred "jealousy" among the players. The real reason was that MVP winners (and players named on the ballot) cited their MVP recognition during salary negotiations. The National League followed suit after the 1929 season, but the hiatus was short-lived: The BBWAA instituted the modern version of the award in 1931.

1929: Al Simmons, OF, Philadelphia Athletics

1930	G	WAR	AB	R	H	2B	3B	HR	RBI	SB	CS	BB	K	BA	OBP	SLG	OPS	OPS+
Simmons	143	7.9	581	114	212	41	9	34	*157*	4	3	31	38	.365	.398	.642	1.040	159
Foxx	149	7.9	517	123	183	23	9	33	118	9	7	103	70	.354	*.463*	.625	1.088	173
Ruth	135	*8.0*	499	121	172	26	6	*46*	154	5	3	72	60	.345	.430	*.697*	*1.128*	*193*

A potentially fascinating MVP ballot: Ruth is nominally the best player in the league, but 21-year-old Jimmy Foxx is in the conversation, as is his veteran teammate Al Simmons. Given the Athletics' dominance (they took the pennant by 18 games over Ruth's Yankees), the MVP likely falls to one of the two Philadelphia sluggers. It's Simmons by the slimmest of margins.

1930: GEHRIG

1930	WAR	G	AB	R	H	2B	3B	HR	RBI	BB	K	BA	OBP	SLG	OPS	OPS+
Gehrig	9.6	154	581	143	220	42	17	41	173	101	63	.379	.473	.721	1.194	203

Philadelphia once again takes the pennant with ease, but two Yankees are the most dominant players in the league. WAR rates Ruth slightly higher, but Gehrig gets the nod as the MVP. Clearly there is a sense a torch is passing.

Superficially, Al Simmons generated statistics (.381/.423/.708, with 36 HR and 165 RBI) nearly the equal of Ruth and Gehrig—but his numbers were significantly inflated by his home park. Simmons raked at a .395/.435/.807 clip at Shibe Park; .364/.408/.593 on the road.

Gehrig, on the other hand, saw his numbers *suppressed* by Yankees Stadium. "The Iron Horse" hit .348/.450/.637 at home, but his *road* numbers in 1930 show his true worth as a hitter: .405/.495/.794 with 27 HR and 115 RBI in 76 games. Adjusted Production (OPS+) and WAR recognize the true gap between Gehrig (205 OPS+, 9.6 WAR) and Simmons (175 OPS+, 7.8 WAR).[17]

Final Tally

Ruth leads our revisionist MVP list with eight awards (one as a pitcher). Ty Cobb follows with five. Rogers Hornsby and Honus Wagner trail with four. Walter Johnson, Pete Alexander, and Christy Mathewson are three-time honorees.

6
Black Mike and the Triple Crown

When Detroit slugger Miguel Cabrera became the first player in 45 years to capture the Triple Crown (Carl Yastrzemski had been the last player to turn the trick, in 1967), he was recognized with the 2012 American League MVP award. It wasn't a close vote, as Cabrera outpaced runner up Mike Trout by a comfortable margin. But it was the most breathlessly analyzed, contentiously debated MVP race ... well, perhaps ever (see Chapter 20 for more).[1]

2012	WAR	AB	R	H	2B	3B	HR	RBI	SB	BB	BA	OBP	SLG	OPS	OPS+
Trout	**10.8**	559	**129**	182	27	8	30	83	**49**	67	.326	**.399**	.564	.963	**168**
Cabrera	7.2	622	109	205	40	0	**44**	**139**	4	66	**.330**	.393	**.606**	**.999**	164

The Cabrera selection as most valuable was controversial in many quarters. Trout had produced not just the greatest rookie season in the history of baseball, but the best all-around season by an AL player in 20 years. That said, there's really no way to begrudge the Cabrera pick: The guy hit for the *Triple Crown*, after all, and Triple Crowns earn MVPs. Except when they don't.

♦ ♦ ♦

In the 45 years since Yaz staked his claim, the Triple Crown had, by the time Cabrera assaulted the record books, been elevated (and relegated) to myth. It's one of those rare achievements that is at once extraordinary and not quite as amazing as one would think.

Extraordinary, because it almost never happens: Fewer men have hit for a Triple Crown than have pitched a perfect game.

Extraordinary, because the level of difficulty in today's game is much higher than it was 70 years ago. Today's player pool is much larger—and the talent level much deeper—than it was back in the days of Ted Williams, Rogers Hornsby, and Jimmy Foxx. Pitching and defense are highly specialized and

Two-time AL MVP Miguel Cabrera is the best hitter of his generation (courtesy Keith Allison, https://creativecommons.org/licenses/by-sa/2.0/legalcode).

finely calibrated, which in turn helps to mitigate extreme outliers in performance.

Extraordinary, because hitting for average and hitting for power are two different skillsets (think Minnesota teammates Harmon Killebrew and Rod Carew). There are only a handful of players who have led the league in all three Triple Crown categories at various points over a *career*, let alone a single season.[2]

Extraordinary, because at the end of the day, it is impossible to achieve the Triple Crown and *not* produce an extraordinary season: Triple Crowns always lead the league in slugging, usually lead the league in runs, on-base percentage, and adjusted OPS, and almost always lead all position players in WAR (Cabrera and 1912 titlist Heinie Zimmerman the two exceptions).

The feat is also not *quite* as amazing as we've been led to believe. Not quite as amazing, because the Triple Crown categories are somewhat arbitrary. Home runs make perfect sense, but why RBI and not runs scored? Why batting average and not on-base or slugging percentage? The Triple Crown ignores base-running entirely.

Not quite as amazing, because today we have a much better understanding of how an offense works. The so-called "slash-line Triple Crown" (BA/OBP/

SLG) is a much better barometer of hitting prowess. Adjusted production (OPS+), which measures a player's offensive production relative to the league average while adjusting for park effects, is better still. We've known for decades now that the single most important skill for a hitter is the ability to avoid *creating outs* (hence, on-base percentage is the single most important offensive stat). We know RBIs are probably the *least* accurate way to measure player production, because they are so heavily reliant on external factors (i.e., RBI *opportunities*).

Not quite as amazing, because leading the league in those three arbitrary stats doesn't give a *complete* picture of greatness. While 2012 will undoubtedly remain his signature season, Cabrera followed it up with an even better 2013. In fact, Cabrera's Triple Crown year was arguably his *weakest* in a brilliant four-season stretch that saw him garner three batting titles while leading the league in on-base percentage three times, RBI and slugging twice, home runs, doubles, and MVP arguments.[3]

Extraordinary, and not quite as amazing as one would think. In fact, the press played scant attention to baseball's "Triple Crown" until the late 1940s; it doesn't become the familiar mid-summer storyline we know today ("*Can Player X Capture the Triple Crown?*") until Cleveland's Al Rosen made a spirited but thwarted run at the achievement in 1953 (missing the honor by one point of batting average on the season's final day).[4]

That said, you earn the Triple Crown and odds are you were the most valuable player in your league. Except, of course, when you're not.

Triple Crown Seasons 1900–Present

Player	Year	WAR	AB	R	H	2B	3B	HR	RBI	SB	BB	BA	OBP	SLG	OPS	OPS+
Cabrera	2012	7.2	622	109	205	40	0	44	139	4	66	.330	.393	.606	.999	164
Yazstremski	1967	12.4	579	112	189	31	4	44	121	10	91	.326	.418	.622	1.040	193
Robinson	1966	7.7	576	122	182	34	2	49	122	8	87	.316	.410	.637	1.047	198
Mantle	1956	11.2	533	132	188	22	5	52	130	10	112	.353	.464	.705	1.169	210
Williams	1947	9.9	528	125	181	40	9	32	114	0	162	.343	.499	.634	1.133	205
Williams	1942	10.6	522	141	186	34	5	36	137	3	145	.356	.499	.648	1.147	216
Medwick	1937	8.5	633	111	237	56	10	31	154	4	41	.374	.414	.641	1.056	182
Gehrig	1934	10.4	579	128	210	40	6	49	166	9	109	.363	.465	.706	1.172	206
Foxx	1933	9.2	573	125	204	37	9	48	163	2	96	.356	.449	.703	1.153	201
Klein	1933	7.5	606	101	223	44	7	28	120	15	56	.368	.422	.602	1.025	176
Hornsby	1925	10.3	504	133	203	41	10	39	143	5	83	.403	.489	.756	1.245	210
Hornsby	1922	11.2	623	141	250	46	14	42	152	17	65	.401	.459	.722	1.181	207
Zimmerman	1912	7.0	557	95	207	41	14	14	104	23	38	.372	.418	.571	.989	169
Cobb[5]	1909	9.8	573	116	216	33	10	9	107	76	48	.377	.431	.517	.947	193
Lajoie	1901	8.4	544	145	232	48	14	14	125	27	24	.426	.463	.643	1.106	198

There have been 15 Triple Crowns since 1900, with an MVP award in existence for 12 of them (there was no MVP award when Nap Lajoie [1901], Ty Cobb

[1909], and Rogers Hornsby [1922] paced their leagues in AVG/HR/RBI; Cobb produced a "quadruple crown" of sorts, also leading the league in stolen bases). Those 12 seasons produced seven MVPs, meaning Triple Crown titlists have been named most valuable 58 percent of the time. Let's look at who didn't make the cut.

- **1912: Heinie Zimmerman.** WAR rates Zimmerman the second-best player in the league, behind Wagner. As a hitter, he had no peers—his 169 OPS+ led the league by a significant margin. But Zimmerman's Cubs placed third, 11.5 games behind the pennant-winning Giants, and Zimmerman was a non-factor in the MVP race. Zimmerman's sixth-place showing on the MVP ballot is the worst of any Triple Crown hitter. He really deserved much better: His weak-hitting teammate Joe Tinker (.282/.331/.358) somehow placed fourth in the vote. Never underestimate the power of a good reputation.
- **1942, 1947: Ted Williams.** Williams failed to capture MVP in both his Triple Crown seasons. He was robbed both times. The Joe Gordon victory in 1942 was simple theft; Joe DiMaggio's 1947 award (by a single vote) was grand larceny. DiMaggio, battling injuries all season, accrued 4.8 WAR and a .315/.391/.515 line, with 20 HR and 97 RBI. Compare that to Williams' line above. The 1947 vote was clearly among the worst of all time (see Chapter 8 for more).[6]
- **1933: Chuck Klein.** Klein finished a distant second to MVP winner Carl Hubbell, and that's about right. WAR rates Hubbell as the most valuable player in the league. In a sense, it's an "apples-to-oranges" comparison—but there's no denying that Hubbell was a monster in 1933, leading the league in ERA and adjusted ERA, innings, WHIP and shutouts, while finishing second in strikeouts. He made a fine MVP choice. Hubbell's line:

1933	pWAR	W	L	ERA	G	GS	CG	SV	SHO	IP	H	BB	K	ERA+	WHIP	K/BB
Hubbell	**8.8**	23	12	**1.66**	45	33	22	5	**10**	308.2	256	47	156	**193**	**0.982**	3.32

Now about that Triple Crown for Klein...

Klein '33	G	AB	R	H	2B	3B	HR	RBI	SB	CS	BB	K	BA	OBP	SLG	OPS
Home	72	285	62	133	28	2	20	81	8	0	29	12	.467	.516	.789	1.305
Away	80	321	39	90	16	5	8	39	7	0	27	24	.280	.338	.436	.774

Notice anything strange about his numbers?

Through the end of the 1933 season, Klein's career batting average stood at .359, good for second all-time behind Ty Cobb. After five full seasons in the league, Klein had amassed four home run titles, led the league in runs three times, RBI twice, and even threw in a stolen-base crown. Those 28 HR were his *lowest* full-season total to that point in his career. He was named league MVP in 1932, and claimed runner-up status in 1931 and 1933.

Klein is the only reigning Triple Crown titlist to be traded. Faced with potentially crippling debt, Phillies owner Gerald Nugent sent Klein to the Cubs (who had long coveted the Philadelphia star) in exchange for three players and $65,000 in cash. Klein spent two injury-compromised seasons with the Cubs (where he was derided as a flop despite being a productive hitter when able to take the field) before returning to the Phillies.

For his career, which also included a half-season stint with the Pirates, Klein hit .354/.410/.618 at home, .286/.346/.466 on the road. If we *only* include games in Philadelphia's Baker Bowl (only 280 feet down the right-field line) things go from absurd to Dali-esque: Klein was a career .395 hitter over 581 games in the league's tightest bandbox.

Klein was a fine player, but his batting record is more artifice than art. His career batting average after being traded away from the swaddling comfort of Philadelphia was .278.

- **1934: Lou Gehrig**. In addition to the Triple Crown categories, Gehrig also paced the circuit in WAR, OBP, SLG, OPS+, and total bases. He finished second in runs, hits, and walks. His most amazing (if not necessarily most important) stat: He smashed 49 home runs while striking out *31* times. Put another way, Gehrig was 50 percent more likely to hit a home run than to strike out.[7] In one of the worst MVP votes of all time, he finished fifth on the ballot.

◆ ◆ ◆

About that ballot: The 1934 AL vote was one of the closest in history, with Detroit catcher-manager Mickey Cochrane claiming the prize by a mere two points over teammate Charlie Gehringer. Any of the top five finishers could have been named MVP if a handful of votes had gone a different way.

The tight clustering at the top of the ballot was unnecessary, as Lou Gehrig was clearly the most valuable player in the league. WAR rates him at least two wins better than his MVP competition—and more than *six* wins better than MVP Mickey Cochrane.

6. Black Mike and the Triple Crown 79

1934	Vote	WAR	G	AB	R	H	2B	3B	HR	RBI	SB	BB	BA	OBP	SLG	OPS	OPS+
Cochrane	84%	4.0	129	437	74	140	32	1	2	76	8	78	.320	.428	.412	.840	117
Gehringer	81%	8.4	*154*	601	*134*	*214*	50	7	11	127	11	99	.356	.450	.517	.967	149
Gehrig	68%	*10.4*	*154*	579	128	210	40	6	*49*	*166*	9	109	*.363*	*.465*	*.706*	*1.172*	*206*

1934	Vote	pWAR	W	L	ERA	WHIP	G	GS	IP	H	BB	K	FIP	WHIP	ERA+
Gomez	75%	7.7	*26*	5	*2.33*	*1.133*	38	33	*281.2*	223	96	*158*	3.57	*1.133*	*176*
Rowe	74%	7.1	24	8	3.45	1.278	45	30	266	259	81	149	3.51	1.278	127

Tigers second baseman Charlie Gehringer produced a wonderful season, and deserved his runner-up designation. Yankees ace Lefty Gomez captured the pitching version of the Triple Crown (and led the league in just about every other meaningful pitching category) so he's a solid top-three choice. Schoolboy Rowe was a poor man's Gomez.

And what of MVP Cochrane?

By 1934, Gordon Stanley Cochrane had been a star for the better part of a decade. He claimed his first MVP award (and became the first catcher to do so) for Connie Mack's Athletics in 1928, and was considered the heart of a Philadelphia dynasty that made three consecutive World Series appearances (1929–31). A two-time champion, "Black Mike" (so nicknamed for his swarthy complexion and thick head of black hair) was the undisputed leader of the squad, an acknowledged on-field general recognized as one of the best catchers of all-time.

Beset by financial trouble, Athletics owner Connie Mack reluctantly sold his superb catcher to Detroit after the 1933 season (Cochrane at the time owned a .321/.412/.490 career batting line). The Tigers installed Cochrane as player-manager, and he inherited a squad that finished in fifth place the prior season, 25 games behind the flag-bearer Washington Senators.[8] This was an *improvement* compared with the previous six seasons, which saw Detroit finish an average of 33 *games* out of first place. Perennial disappointments, the Tigers hadn't been a team of consequence in more than two decades.

Enter Cochrane. His arrival coincided with an immediate and dramatic improvement in the fortunes of the team. The 1934 squad shocked baseball by winning 101 games, capturing the AL pennant with room to spare (Gehrig's Yankees took second place, trailing by seven lengths).[9] Cochrane, who in 1934 produced the weakest season of his career in terms of on-field performance, got the lion's share of the credit. He didn't deserve it.

In recalling the 1934 season, Hall of Fame first baseman Hank Greenberg would describe Cochrane as "the spark that ignited us. We needed someone to take charge and show us how to win, and that's what Mickey did." Greenberg, obviously, offers an educated perspective. But it's impossible to know how much Cochrane's leadership contributed to the Tigers' won-loss record. We do know Cochrane made above-average, but certainly not spectacular, contributions on the field.[10]

We also know 1934 was the year Greenberg became *Greenberg* (.339/.404/.600 with 26 HR and 63 2B); future HOFer Goose Goslin joined the club and provided an immediate upgrade in the outfield; third baseman Marv Owen contributed a career-best .317/.385/.451 line; Gehringer was brilliant[11]; even banjo-hitting SS Billy Rogell got in on the act, driving in 100 runs with just three home runs. The Tigers were an offensive juggernaut in 1934, leading the league in runs scored with 958—*236 more* than they scored the prior season. In a nutshell, the offense coalesced in a dramatic way, the pitching remained very good (second in the league in runs allowed), and the Tigers made an abrupt and immediate ascension to elite status (losing the World Series to the Gashouse Gang Cardinals in seven games).

Gehrig, of course, had long terrorized the league with his rifle-report line drives. He was extraordinary in 1934; he was basically as good (or better) in a half-dozen other seasons. Had Gehrig finished second or third in the voting, we could easily chalk it up to voter preference for a pennant winner; his fifth-place finish defies logic.

In photos taken during his playing days, Cochrane sometimes had the visage of a coal miner—and he was renowned for his tough, uncompromising style of play. Off the field, the warm and approachable Cochrane was universally admired, a hard-scrabble symbol of pluck and determination for a Depression-era country attempting to crawl out of an economic abyss. When his Tigers captured their first World Series title in 1935, he was embraced by his city as few athletes have ever been. His career ended just two seasons later, the victim of a near-fatal beanball. Cochrane eventually recovered, but he never took the field again. He was a superb player, comfortably leading all backstops in career BA (.320) and OBP (.419—top 15 all time).

Gehrig, of course, was one of the most stoic and agreeable men to ever play the game. He was the most devastating hitter, save Ruth, that the game had yet seen, and remains to this day one of the best batsmen of all time.[12]

Both were monuments of dignity on and off the field. Given our knowledge of the character of both men, its doubtful Gehrig cared much about the award, just as its doubtful the modest and unassuming Cochrane felt he earned it.

If It's Such a Big Deal, Why Didn't the Babe Do It?

The concept of the "Triple Crown" in baseball didn't exist prior to the 1940s. No mention of the feat was made when Nap Lajoie accomplished the trick in 1901; the newspapers of the day paid much more attention to Cobb's batting title and base-running exploits than they did his league-leading home runs and RBI in 1909[13]; Hornsby's two Triple Crowns were but background noise to his .400 averages.

In 1933, *two* players hit their way to the mythical title, with Jimmy Foxx and Chuck Klein dominating their respective leagues. Again, no mention of a "Triple Crown." The Associated Press (October 12, 1933) acknowledges that AL MVP Foxx did some collateral damage with his 48 home runs: "Decisive factors in favor of Foxx [as MVP] were that, in addition to retaining the home run crown, he led all American League hitters with an unofficial mark of .356 and topped the clouters of both big leagues in runs batted in, with 159."

With Gehrig's 1934 masterpiece, the as-yet-unnamed Triple Crown had now been accomplished eight times in 33 years—about as rare as a U.S. presidential election or the Olympics.[14] Still nary a mention of the term.

Joe Medwick made it nine times in 36 years with his 1937 campaign. In

Left to right: **Lou Gehrig, Joe Cronin, Bill Dickey, Joe DiMaggio, Charley Gehringer, Jimmie Foxx, and Hank Greenberg. Seven Hall of Famers with 11 MVPs between them** (Harris and Ewing Collection, Library of Congress, Prints and Photographs Division).

reporting his superb season (for which he was awarded the NL MVP), the press listed his accomplishments in order of importance. As always, the batting title came first, as the United Press noted on November 10, 1937: "Medwick, in addition to winning the batting title, also led the league in other departments. He had the most runs, 111; most hits, 237; most two-baggers, 57; most runs batted in, 154; and tied Mel Ott of the Giants for home run honors, each getting 31."

All of this is to say that the notion of a player leading the league in average, home runs, and RBI just wasn't thought of as a singular accomplishment. It wasn't until 1941, July 3, to be precise, that the phrase "Triple Crown" (as it applied in baseball; the term had been in use for years in horse racing) seems to have first surfaced in the major media of the day (the Associated Press): "Poker-faced Joe DiMaggio, the greatest player, excluding pitchers, in the present era of baseball, has reached his goal of a new all-time major league record for hitting in 45 consecutive games, and now can try shooting for another prize—the 'Triple Crown of batting.' This bauble is the three-way championship in percentage hitting, home runs and runs batted in and is one of the most elusive batting honors in the game."

DiMaggio, of course, didn't capture the "Triple Crown of batting"—but Ted Williams accomplished the feat in 1942 and 1947. Coverage of Williams' seasons focused more on his league-leading batting averages, all-around hitting dominance, and lack of support in the MVP vote. The term "Triple Crown" was rarely employed.

As noted earlier, Al Rosen's 1953 bid seems to be the tipping point for the term's use. With the Indians' pennant hopes dashed by mid–August, the lead storyline out of Cleveland was Rosen's pursuit of the mythical title. The Associated Press, on August 25, 1953, reported, "Cleveland's vanishing Indians rate as the biggest flop in the American League but Al Rosen, their chief hatchet man, is heading for the Triple Crown as well as the circuit's Most Valuable Player Award."

It appears the annual tradition of premature Triple Crown speculation began in earnest in 1956, with Mickey Mantle's then-nascent "pursuit" of the achievement. Again, the Associated Press, on May 7, 1952, said, "It may be a little too early to predict that Mickey Mantle will win the Triple Crown in the American League. But at the rate he's going, who is going to beat him?"

Since then, of course, a version of the Mantle story has been written *ad nauseum*, appearing every time a player gets off to an early season hot streak, or hovers near the top of the leaderboards in all three categories.[15] The reliable and routine coverage of the chase (and, from 1967 until Cabrera's 2012 season, the reliable and inevitable failure of the player attempting to lead the league in all three categories) served only to build the Triple Crown into the stuff of legend.

Contemporary statistical analysis has dulled some of the luster of the achievement, but it still rates as one of the most unique and exclusive hitting accomplishments available a player.

7

The Octopus

How, then, to value defense?

First, a little thought experiment. Picture in your mind's eye the following hypothetical situation: It's 2015. The Atlanta Braves are hosting the Pittsburgh Pirates. Top of the sixth, Braves clinging to a one-run lead, Pirates threatening: Two out, men dancing off second and third. Right-handed pull hitter at the plate.

Pitch delivered, crack of the bat, sharp groundball—*major league* groundball—to the left side of the infield, buzzing toward the daylight between third base and shortstop. Third baseman is guarding the line—he's in no position to make the play. A sure base hit.

Except. Braves shortstop Andrelton Simmons ranges into the next zip code, backhands the bobbing, weaving groundball, plants his feet while transferring the ball from his glove to his throwing hand (in a motion so deft, so quick, so undetectable, card sharps swoon), and unleashes—there's no other word for it—*unleashes* a throw from short leftfield that carries the diamond on a fixed plane, a throw arriving with such force it feels like the first baseman should be wearing a chest protector. Runner out by a stride. Rally over. Inning over. Another day at the office for Andrelton.[1]

To anybody watching the play unfold, it's clear Simmons prevented a base hit, stranding two runners that would otherwise have scored. To anybody following the National League, it's clear that very few (if any) other shortstops make that play.

Let's get back to the game. Top of the ninth inning. Braves still clinging to their one-run lead. Runner leading off second, but he's on a short tether. The Bucs' best hitter, Andrew McCutchen, is working the count.

Pitch delivered, crack of the bat. Screaming, rising line drive. McCutchen knows immediately. The pitcher knows immediately. The stunned, silent crowd knows immediately. Home run, left centerfield. Pirates take the lead.

7. The Octopus

Braves fail to answer in the home half of the ninth. Game over. Pirates victory. The "Mc-CLUTCH-en" headlines hit the blogs before the grounds crew hits the field for its post-game tending of the diamond.

How then do we place a value on the Simmons play three innings prior? How do we quantify Simmons' contribution? It will be counted, of course: As a chance accepted, an assist delivered. His defensive WAR total will receive an incremental boost. His "Zone Rating" (UZR) will benefit, as will his "Defensive Runs Saved" (DRS) and "range factor per nine innings" (RF/9) numbers. But no one really knows what those things mean—if they in fact *have* meaning.

So how then is the MVP voter to value defense? If Simmons had hit a two-run home run early in the game, the credit is indelibly and irrevocably reflected in his BA/OBP/SLG line; the home run goes into his account, regardless of whether or not the Braves win the game. His heart-stopping illusion of a catch-and-throw? It's recorded less by the Elias Sports Bureau[2] and more by our collective (but fleeting) appreciation. The Simmons play *prevented* two runs; the McCutchen play *produced* two runs. But we know the two don't cancel each other out: McCutchen's home run will be counted as far more valuable in the box scores. In baseball, the math isn't always neat; two runs saved isn't necessarily two runs earned.

How to assign value to the ineffable? It's a question that has vexed not just MVP voters, but talent evaluators, coaches, and the executives charged with building major league rosters. Everybody agrees defense is important, but nobody seems to know just *how important*, relative to other aspects of the game, defense is to winning. Is defense 25 percent of the game? 50 percent? 10 percent? The game's best minds have yet to arrive on a definitive answer. Defense has remained the one area of the game stubbornly resistant to quantitative analysis.[3]

It's therefore understandable that MVP voters have never quite known what to do with defense. They either overvalue it when handing out awards to the likes of Roger Peckinpaugh and Frankie Frisch (1931), or undervalue it when denying the award to, say, Alan Trammell in 1984 or 1987.

◆ ◆ ◆

The MVP is a *hitting* award; only eight players have ranked as the best defender in the league (as measured by dWAR) the year they claimed their trophy.

MVP	Year	dWAR	G	AB	R	H	2B	3B	HR	RBI	BB	K	BA	OBP	SLG	OPS	OPS+
Marion	1944	**3.6**	144	506	50	135	26	2	6	63	43	50	.267	.324	.362	.686	90
Boudreau	1948	**3.0**	152	560	116	199	34	6	18	106	98	9	.355	.453	.534	.987	165
Mays	1954	**2.0**	151	565	119	195	33	**13**	41	110	66	57	**.345**	.411	**.667**	**1.078**	175

MVP	Year	dWAR	G	AB	R	H	2B	3B	HR	RBI	BB	K	BA	OBP	SLG	OPS	OPS+
Banks	1959	**3.5**	155	589	97	179	25	6	45	**143**	64	72	.304	.374	.596	.970	156
Fox	1959	**2.6**	156	**624**	84	191	34	6	2	70	71	13	.306	.380	.389	.770	113
Groat	1960	**2.6**	138	573	85	186	26	4	2	50	39	35	**.325**	.371	.394	.766	110
Versalles	1965	**3.0**	160	**666**	182	**126**	**45**	**12**	19	77	41	**122**	.273	.319	.462	.781	115
Ripken	1991	**3.4**	162	650	210	99	46	5	34	114	53	46	.323	.374	.566	.940	162

Superb defense had little to do with the awards for Lou Boudreau, Willie Mays, Ernie Banks, and Cal Ripken; their contributions with the glove were just the exclamation point on magnificent all-around seasons. Zoilo Versalles was one of the American League's most dynamic offensive players in 1965; if he hews to his career 86 OPS+, Zoilo watches teammate Tony Oliva capture the award. Dick Groat led the National League in batting average during his 1960 campaign—without that batting title, it's doubtful he receives strong MVP support. Nellie Fox, among the most respected players in the league, was above-average at the plate in 1959; if the scrappy Fox hits .286 instead of .306, it's doubtful he claims the award.[4]

That leaves Marty Marion.

Lean, lanky, and long, the 6'2" Marion used an endless wingspan and quick feet to grab anything hit to the left side of the infield.[5] He had a powerful arm and an extrasensory ability to anticipate where the ball was going to be hit. His teammates nicknamed him "Slats" for his wiry frame; sportswriters called him "The Octopus." Eventually, he came to be known as "Mr. Shortstop," in deference to the wonders he accomplished with his glove. In 1944, Marion became the only player to claim the MVP based solely and indisputably on defensive performance.[6]

The St. Louis Cardinals' shortstop took the award by one point over Bill Nicholson of the Cubs. It was, at the time, the closest vote in award history (matched three years later when Joe DiMaggio edged Ted Williams by a single misguided tally).

1944	WAR	G	AB	R	H	2B	3B	HR	RBI	SB	CS	BB	K	BA	OBP	SLG	OPS	OPS+
Marion	4.7	144	506	50	135	26	2	6	63	1	—	43	50	.267	.324	.362	.686	90
Nicholson	6.0	156	582	**116**	167	35	8	**33**	**122**	3	—	93	71	.287	.391	.545	.935	162

Marion's selection didn't stir much controversy at the time, but he was a terrible choice as the league's most valuable. Or was he?

"For some reason I never had the chance to see Wagner play. I know he must have been a wonder," said Connie Mack shortly after the St. Louis Cardinals won the 1944 World Series. "But Marion is the greatest shortstop I've ever seen and I've been around several years. What a ballplayer. My goodness."

The Sporting News also invoked Wagner in naming Marion their player of the year, calling him the greatest shortstop since the Pittsburgh icon.

The Associated Press wrote that it was "the unanimous opinion that Marion is the best and most colorful shortstop in baseball today, and they are starting to compare him with Honus Wagner."[7]

"Maybe I'm prejudiced because I see him every day—but he's the best ever. Some of the things he does have to be seen to be believed," said St. Louis manager Billy Southworth.

The growing chorus of affirmation grew into consensus acclaim, with Marion appointed MVP by late summer in many journalistic quarters. That the final vote was so close was a bigger surprise than Marion's MVP victory.

Is preventing two runs as valuable as plating two runs? There is little doubt that Marion's defensive play lived up to its reputation—modern-day statistical analysis supports the widespread anecdotal support of Marion as the best defensive shortstop of his day. It also seems intuitive that defense was much more important in Marion's day than it is today: Contact rates were *much* higher for hitters in the 1940s (only 3.3 K/9 as compared with 7.7 K/9 in 2014); defensive shifts were rare; bullpens weren't stocked with genetically engineered, fire-breathing robot dragons designed to throw 101 MPH until their connective tissue disconnects. The game was a much looser exercise than the highly calibrated affair we see today; quick wits and good hands were paramount for a middle infielder.

In this context, Marion's artistry was as prominent as the profile this regal crane of a man cut on the field. The question isn't "Was Marion a great defender?" He was. The question is "Did Marion's defense make up for the fact that he was one of the worst hitters in baseball history?"[8]

◆ ◆ ◆

The Cardinals were a wartime dynasty, claiming four pennants (by wide margins) and three World Series titles from 1942 to 1946. The 1944 squad was a balanced dynamo, leading the league in runs scored while allowing the fewest (the third consecutive year they would achieve those vaunted bookends).

Despite their obvious and sustained superiority over the rest of the league, influential *New York Times* columnist Arthur Daley wrote of Marion: "One thing [managers] are unanimous about is that he is the most vital cog in the Cardinal machine.... Without him, the Cards are an ordinary ball club. With him, they are a great one."

The notion that St. Louis was "an ordinary team" without Marion is absurd.[9] The Cardinals had—*by far*—the best pitching in baseball (granting, of course, that pitching and defense are interwoven threads in the same tapestry). They allowed the fewest runs, surrendered the fewest hits, posted the most shut-outs, and sent more opposing batters back to the dugout muttering in frustration than any other team in the league.[10] With an adjusted ERA 34 percent better than the league average (by way of comparison, the legendary Atlanta Braves' staff of 1993 to 2002 peaked at 133 ERA+), the Cardinals staff was deep and balanced.[11] The rotation was anchored by 1942 MVP Mort Cooper, and bolstered by 28-year-old rookie Ted Wilks, who had toiled for six years in the minors before finally getting his shot thanks to war-depleted rosters. Wilks made the most of it, winning 11 consecutive games en route to a 17–4 record.

1944 St. Louis Starting Rotation

1944	pWAR	W	L	W%	ERA	G	GS	IP	H	ER	HR	BB	K	ERA+	WHIP	K/BB
Mort Cooper	5.3	22	7	.759	2.46	34	33	252.1	227	69	6	60	97	145	1.137	1.62
Max Lanier	3.4	17	12	.586	2.65	33	30	224.1	192	66	5	71	141	135	1.172	1.99
Ted Wilks	4.5	17	4	**.810**	2.64	36	21	207.2	173	61	12	49	70	135	**1.069**	1.43
Harry Brecheen	2.9	16	5	.762	2.85	30	22	189.1	174	60	8	46	88	126	1.162	1.91
Red Munger	4.1	11	3	.786	1.34	21	12	121.0	92	18	2	41	55	268	1.099	1.34

Their hitting was also fantastic: The Cards led the league in runs scored, home runs, hits, doubles, total bases, batting, slugging, and on-base percentages. The only element of team offense they failed to dominate was stolen bases (37), but this was largely irrelevant; no one ran in those days. Relative to their time, they were an offensive juggernaut.

Marion, hitting sixth, seventh, or eighth in the lineup, was the weak link in the offensive chain.[12] He was also the most inept hitter to ever claim the league's highest individual honor.

Worst Hitting Performances by an MVP

Player	Year	G	AB	R	H	2B	3B	HR	RBI	SB	CS	BB	K	BA	OBP	SLG	OPS	OPS+
Marion	1944	144	506	50	135	26	2	6	63	1	—	43	50	.267	.324	.362	.686	90
Peckinpaugh	1925	126	422	67	124	16	4	4	64	13	4	49	23	.294	.367	.379	.746	91

The two worst hitting performances by an MVP belong to Marion and 1925 winner Roger Peckinpaugh. As measured by adjusted production (OPS+), they both rate as about 10 percent less productive than a league-average hitter. While their anemic batting lines bear superficial resemblance, Marion's performance was *much* worse.

By 1944, the vast majority of young, able-bodied major leaguers had been enlisted in war efforts, with more than 500 players serving in some capacity. These 500 open slots weren't filled by the best players from the minors—they were filled by middle-aged farmers and truck drivers; by semi-pro washouts; by unqualified rookies who were too young, too old, or physically unable to serve in the military. Major League clubs didn't want to put this product on the field, but they were left with no choice: Minor league clubs had sent more than 4000 young men into service, prompting a shutdown of most leagues during the height of military operations (1943–44).[13] There simply wasn't any available talent to fill major league rosters.

Hitting against bartenders, hat salesmen, and auto mechanics, Marion produced the lowest batting, on-base, and slugging percentages of any MVP. He scored the fewest runs, and generated the worst OPS+ (90) of any player deemed most valuable. And given the level of competition, his hitting performance is significantly *worse* than the numbers would suggest. One shudders to think what Marion would have hit against *professional* pitching.[14]

And therein lies the major difference between Marion and Peckinpaugh as hitters: Marion wasn't hitting against major league pitching; Peckinpaugh was (even if he didn't *quite* hold his own).

To be clear, Marion's 1944 season isn't the worst all-around performance of any MVP. His 4.7 WAR dwarfs that of Peckinpaugh, Stargell, and several others. But it was the worst *hitting* performance of any player voted most valuable.

So we've established that Marion couldn't hit. But his young teammate sure could.

1944	WAR	G	AB	R	H	2B	3B	HR	RBI	SB	CS	BB	K	BA	OBP	SLG	OPS	OPS+
Musial	**8.8**	146	568	112	**197**	**51**	14	12	94	7	—	90	28	.347	**.440**	**.549**	**.990**	**174**

In retrospect, the injustice isn't that Marion edged Bill Nicholson for most valuable; it's that Marion took honors over Stan Musial. Having claimed honors in 1943, Musial was exactly as good in 1944, the undisputed lynchpin of the Cardinals' lineup, the best player in baseball. He placed fourth on the ballot.

Did Marion's defense make up for the fact that he was one of the worst hitters in baseball history? In a sense, yes. He was clearly a valuable and productive player (in 1944, and throughout his 14-year career). Was he the most valuable player in his league? Not by a longshot. He wasn't the most valuable player on his own team.

How, then, to value defense?

In Marion's case, it's clear that the voters *overvalued* his contributions in the field; the 1942–45 Cardinals are one of the great teams (relative to their league) in history, and the 1944 squad would have captured the NL pennant with any competent glove man at shortstop. In fact, one might argue that Marion's talents were superfluous on a team with such overwhelming powers.[15] And then there's the comparison to Musial: No amount of acrobatic catches and laser throws could hope to measure up against that batting line. Had Marion been a league-average hitter, he might have had a legitimate case as the National League's most valuable—but on both counts, he wasn't.

Forcing a Hand, Dealing an Ace

Marion's selection as MVP cost St. Louis its best pitcher—but didn't prove costly.

In the wake of his MVP award, Marion asked for and received a bump in salary for the 1945 season; the best defensive shortstop in baseball would make $13,000 for his services. Marion's play *also* garnered a raise for St. Louis ace Mort Cooper and his battery-mate brother Walker, who had been promised by Cardinals owner Sam Breadon in 1944 that "no player on the club would receive more pay than they" in 1945.

Breadon, as tight with a dollar as any owner in the game, apparently lived up to his word by offering the Cooper brothers $13,500 for the 1945 season. Easy, right? Let's play ball! Not so fast.

According to the Associated Press on May 24, 1945, "Walker Cooper, who has since been inducted into the Navy, said the new offer was rejected, explaining that they had signed for $12,000 [in 1944] with the understanding that it was the ceiling salary for the club.... If Breadon could go beyond that figure to $13,500, he also could "tilt it to $15,000."

While the exact terms of their gentlemen's agreement were open to debate, one thing was clear—neither side was given to compromise: The Cooper brothers felt like they had been bamboozled the season prior; Breadon felt like he was being held-up without a gun.[16]

As noted in the excerpt above, Walker Cooper would spend the 1945 season in service to his country—*his* conversations with Breadon would have to wait until he returned to the team. That left Mort to wrangle with the club, and negotiations between Cooper and Breadon went nowhere. Cooper held out during spring training, joined the club at the start of the season (pitching to sterling 1.52 ERA in 23.2 innings) then abruptly walked out on the team in mid–May, refusing to pitch until the salary dispute was resolved. "I won't put on a uniform until this thing is solved," said Cooper, at the same time making it clear where his loyalties lay: "But I don't want to be traded. I'd rather play baseball for the Cards than anybody else. I'm not mad at anyone."

The same couldn't be said for the Cardinals' owner. An exasperated Breadon sold his star pitcher to the perpetually forlorn Boston Braves on May 21, for an estimated $60,000. The Braves threw in unheralded junk-baller Red Barrett as part of the deal.[17]

Mort Cooper, 1942–44

Cooper	pWAR	W	L	W%	ERA	G	GS	IP	H	ER	HR	BB	K	ERA+	WHIP	K/BB
1942	**8.4**	22	7	.759	**1.78**	37	35	278.2	207	55	9	68	152	**192**	0.987	2.24
1943	5.9	21	8	.724	2.30	37	32	274.0	228	70	5	79	141	147	1.120	1.78
1944	5.3	22	7	.759	2.46	34	33	252.1	227	69	6	60	97	145	1.137	1.62

The sale was seen as coup for the Braves. Over the previous three seasons, Cooper had led the league in pitcher WAR (a full six wins better than his nearest competitor) wins, winning percentage, ERA, adjusted ERA, strikeouts, shutouts (ten more than runner-up Bucky Walters) and WHIP, while placing in the top-three in all other significant pitching categories. He was named 1942 MVP, and placed fifth on the ballot in 1944. By any measure, he was the league's most successful pitcher. Braves General Manager John Quinn spoke for most observers of the game at the time when he said "I think he's the best pitcher in the league, and naturally any club is happy to get the best."

Said Cooper, "I've been sold. Everybody's happy."

The Cardinals had the deepest rotation in the game, but this was the equivalent of the 1995 Braves selling Tom Glavine to the Milwaukee Brewers. No staff could absorb such a loss—or could it?

Red Barrett, Mort Cooper After May 22, 1945

Player	pWAR	W	L	W%	ERA	GS	IP	H	ER	HR	BB	K	BF	ERA+	WHIP	K9	K/BB
Barrett	5.6	21	9	.700	2.74	29	**246.2**	244	75	12	38	63	1001	138	1.143	2.3	1.66
Cooper	.07	7	4	.636	3.35	11	78.0	77	29	4	27	45	329	115	1.333	5.2	1.67

Astonishingly, the heretofore middling Barrett—a bit player in the transaction—stepped into Cooper's role and pitched, well, *exactly* like Mort Cooper, leading the major leagues in total wins (23 between St. Louis and Boston), innings, and complete games. Unfortunately, the rest of the staff didn't fare so well: The Cardinals' runs allowed per game went from a league-leading 3.1 in 1944 to 3.8 in 1945. It was enough to derail their three-year death grip on the NL pennant, as they finished three games behind the Cubs. The Cardinals' slip from the top of the league certainly wasn't due to the efforts of Barrett, who was recognized with a third-place finish in the 1945 MVP vote.

Cooper for his part developed a sore arm with the Braves, and was only able to muster 78 innings with his new club. He would never be healthy again, and retired after a disastrous 1947 season (3–10, 5.40 ERA). He attempted a comeback in 1949 (after losing 25 lbs. by giving up beer and meat, and subsisting, in his words, "on gruel"), but lasted just one inning before calling it quits for good.

Despite his production in 1945, Barrett was considered a war-time flash-in-the-pan by the Cards, and relegated to spot-starting and mop-up duty in 1946.[18] The Cards traded him to the cross-town Browns prior to the 1947 season, where he hung on for three years before being released in 1949. He wouldn't find work with another major league club, but pitched for years with minor-league and semi-pro teams.

The Cooper deal also underscores just how much the Cardinals valued Marty Marion. Herb Pennock, general manager of the Phillies, told the Associated Press in June of 1945 that he offered the then-staggering sum of $250,000 to Sam Breadon for the combined services of MVP Marion and Cardinals third baseman Whitey Kurowski. The breakdown of the offer wasn't made public, but Marion would certainly have been the centerpiece. According to Pennock, Breadon waved off the offer without a thought. "Herb," said Breadon, "I might as well sell the franchise as let Marion and Kurowski go."

Lightning Strikes Once: The Worst Hitters to Claim MVP...

Lowest Career Adjusted Production (OPS+) by an MVP

Player	G	AB	R	H	2B	3B	HR	RBI	BB	BA	OBP	SLG	OPS	OPS+	MVP+
Rizzuto	1661	5816	877	1588	239	62	38	563	651	.273	.351	.355	.706	93	122
Pendleton	1893	7032	851	1897	356	39	140	946	486	.270	.316	.391	.707	92	139
Groat	1929	7484	829	2138	352	67	39	707	490	.286	.330	.366	.696	89	110
Wills	1942	7588	1067	2134	177	71	20	458	552	.281	.330	.331	.661	88	99
Peckinpaugh	2012	7233	1006	1876	256	75	48	740	814	.259	.336	.335	.672	86	91
Versalles	1400	5141	650	1246	230	63	95	471	318	.242	.290	.367	.657	82	115
Marion	1572	5506	602	1448	272	37	36	624	470	.263	.323	.345	.668	81	90

That "MVP+" column shows us how they hit during their MVP campaign, listing adjusted production for that season. Terry Pendleton is downright good: After adjusting for park effects, Pendleton is 39 percent more productive than the league average in his 1991 campaign. Wills' 99 OPS+ undersells his offensive contributions, as he obviously brought significant value with his base running (104 SB, only 13 CS). He was still among the worst MVP selections ever (See Chapter 8 for more).

... Or Doesn't Strike at All: Best Hitters to Never Claim an MVP

Ranked by Adjusted Production (OPS+)

Player	G	AB	R	H	2B	3B	HR	RBI	BB	K	BA	OBP	SLG	OPS	OPS+
Mark McGwire	1874	6187	1167	1626	252	6	583	1414	1317	1596	.263	.394	.588	.982	163
Johnny Mize	1884	6443	1118	2011	367	83	359	1337	856	524	.312	.397	.562	.959	158

7. The Octopus

Player	G	AB	R	H	2B	3B	HR	RBI	BB	K	BA	OBP	SLG	OPS	OPS+
Mel Ott	2730	9456	1859	2876	488	72	511	1860	1708	896	.304	.414	.533	.947	155
Manny Ramirez	2302	8244	1544	2574	547	20	555	1831	1329	1813	.312	.411	.585	.996	154
Ralph Kiner	1472	5205	971	1451	216	39	369	1015	1011	749	.279	.398	.548	.946	149
Edgar Martinez	2055	7213	1219	2247	514	15	309	1261	1283	1202	.312	.418	.515	.933	147
Jim Thome	2543	8422	1583	2328	451	26	612	1699	1747	2548	.276	.402	.554	.956	147
Eddie Mathews	2391	8537	1509	2315	354	72	512	1453	1444	1487	.271	.376	.509	.885	143

Ott and Mathews, of course, head anybody's list of "Greatest Players to Never Win MVP." Ralph Kiner put up MVP-worthy statistics several times for terrible teams. Manny Ramirez was an extraordinary hitter, but he played the outfield like a man trying to remember where he left his keys.

It might be surprising to see Mark McGwire at the top of this chart; it might be more surprising to see Johnny "Big Cat" Mize a close second. Despite his Hall-of-Fame credentials, Mize is often overlooked when discussing the great sluggers. He was a superb hitter whose career totals are suppressed by missing three seasons to military service in his prime. Mize breeched the top-five in MVP voting four times, and probably should have claimed the award in 1940. Instead, it went to an undeserving Frank McCormick, first baseman for the Cincinnati Reds (McCormick's Reds ran away with the NL pennant, while Mize's Cardinals finished in third place, 16 games back).

1940	WAR	G	AB	R	H	2B	3B	HR	RBI	SB	CS	BB	K	BA	OBP	SLG	OPS	OPS+
McCormick	5.7	155	**618**	93	**191**	**44**	3	19	127	2	—	52	26	.309	.367	.482	.850	132
Mize	7.4	155	579	111	182	31	13	**43**	**137**	7	—	82	49	.314	.404	**.636**	**1.039**	**177**

As for McGwire: He should have been named NL MVP in 1998, but placed a distant second to his partner (or accomplice, depending on one's point of view) in home run heroics, Sammy Sosa. McGwire's critics characterize him as a one-dimensional slugger. Even if that were true, *what* a dimension: McGwire hit home runs with greater frequency than any other player in MLB history. His career OPS+ of 163 lands him among the top-10 of all time (tied with Jimmy Foxx).[19] His batting average is low, but with that sparkling on-base percentage, it's also irrelevant. McGwire excelled at the two most important aspects of hitting: power and patience. The year he hit 70 home runs, he also set an NL record for walks (subsequently shattered by Barry Bonds).

McGwire was an enormous man with bad legs, so he couldn't run at all. He struck out too much. Despite these flaws, he was still one of the most devastating hitters in history.

8

Sticking It to the Splinter: Most Career MVP Snubs

Barry Bonds was named National League MVP seven times. He didn't just win the award, he won it in bruising fashion, never capturing less than 90 percent of the vote in any of his MVP seasons. No other player can claim more than three trophies.[1]

Of course, most baseball fans can probably tell you Bonds holds the career record for MVP awards. It's staggering to think Bonds could have won even more. He had a legitimate case several other seasons, but was never really the victim of outright theft, unlike three great players who were routinely victimized by the voting: Ted Williams, Mickey Mantle, and Willie Mays.[2]

It's a dubious honor, holding claim to most career MVP disappointments. On the one hand, getting robbed multiple times speaks to the sustained greatness of a player; on the other, it must really stick in one's craw to know *your* trophy is being polished with another man's rag.

Williams, Mantle, Mays. The best of the best. But only one can lay claim to the title of "Most Snubbed Player of All Time."[3]

Ted Williams: Won Two, Should Have Won Five

- **1941:** MVP winner Joe DiMaggio had a superb season, but Ted Williams painted his masterpiece.[4]

1941	WAR	G	AB	R	H	2B	3B	HR	RBI	BB	K	BA	OBP	SLG	OPS	OPS+
DiMaggio	9.1	139	541	122	193	43	11	30	**125**	76	13	.357	.440	.643	1.083	184
Williams	**10.6**	143	456	**135**	185	33	3	**37**	120	**147**	27	**.406**	**.553**	**.735**	**1.287**	**235**

Williams overwhelms with the numbers, but the numbers don't quite tell the whole story. While not in Williams' class as a hitter, DiMaggio was no slouch at the plate—that's an MVP-worthy slash line almost any other season. On defense, it wasn't close: DiMaggio was a very good centerfielder who gracefully patrolled the vast green expanse of Yankees Stadium's "Death Valley"; Williams was an indifferent leftfielder who, between pitches to opposing hitters, pantomimed his batting stroke at the foot of the Green Monster.

All things considered, did DiMaggio's superior defense compensate for Williams' astonishing feats at the plate? Probably not. Williams in 1941 came close to his childhood goal of being the best hitter who ever lived. But the MVP vote wasn't a travesty: DiMaggio was the best player on the best team in baseball (at 101–53, the Yankees took AL honors by 17.5 games over the second-place Red Sox). DiMaggio wasn't as great as Williams, but he *was* great (and you may also recall that DiMaggio had himself a nice little hot streak over the summer).

- **1942**: In reporting the selection of Yankees second baseman Joe Gordon as MVP, the *New York Times* wrote: "The surprise selection will leave Boston fans in general, and Ted Williams in particular, startled."

   The notoriously prickly Williams had a right to be annoyed with this one.[5] MVP Joe Gordon had a wonderful season: The Yankees' second baseman was the best player on the best team, exceptional with that bat and brilliant with the glove. But Williams was playing a *different game* than everyone else in 1942. He didn't just capture the Triple Crown—he lapped the field.

1942	WAR	G	AB	R	H	2B	3B	HR	RBI	BB	K	BA	OBP	SLG	OPS	OPS+
Gordon	8.2	147	538	88	173	29	4	18	103	79	**95**	.322	.409	.491	.900	154
Williams	10.6	*150*	*522*	*141*	*186*	*34*	*5*	**36**	**137**	**145**	51	**.356**	**.499**	**.648**	**1.147**	**216**

His league-leading 1.147 OPS dwarfed runner-up Charlie Keller by more than 200 points. He won the batting title by 25 points; led the league in home runs by nine (no other player hit as many as 30); and paced the league in RBI by 23. There was no one within a country mile of his slugging or on-base marks (Williams' *on-base* percentage was higher than Gordon's *slugging* percentage).

In a show of equanimity, the New York chapter of the Baseball Writers Association of America honored Williams with its Player of the Year award. As bad as this MVP vote was, Williams' second-place showing in 1942 wasn't the worst snub of his career.

- **1947**: George McQuinn was a decent player with the St. Louis Browns in the late-1930s/mid–40s. You've probably never heard of him. He was good for 15ish HR and 80ish RBI a year. He had a reputation as a good glove man at first base, and he was a tough so-and-so, taking the field every day despite an ailing back that plagued him for years.

  In 1947, at the age of 37, McQuinn landed with the Yankees, where he improbably had his best season. The veteran contributed a nice .304/.395/.437 line to the ledger of the World Champions. For his efforts, he received three first-place votes on the MVP ballot.

  Williams, who captured his second Triple Crown in 1947, also received three first-place votes.

  "Fireman" Joe Page pitched in parts of seven seasons with the Yankees, peaking in 1947 when he led the league in appearances (56) and saves (17). He pitched to a sharp 2.48 ERA over 141 innings. He fared extraordinarily well in the MVP voting relative to his performance: Page received *seven* first-place votes.

  Seven. That's four more than Williams, who in addition to claiming the Triple Crown also paced the circuit in WAR, runs, walks, on-base, slugging, total bases, and adjusted production.

  Philadelphia Athletics shortstop Eddie Joost was hopeless with the bat.[6] A career .225 hitter entering the 1947 season, Joost was only able to muster a feeble .206 BA for the campaign. On the bright side, his 13 HRs were a career high; on the not-so-bright side, his 110 Ks were also a career high (and led the league). Joost was known for his quick feet and exceptional range at short. In 1947 he led all shortstops in putouts; unfortunately, he also committed 38 errors, second in the league. He got to everything, but didn't always know what to do once he arrived.

  You've probably never heard of Eddie Joost, but in 1947 he received two first-place votes for MVP.

  Only one less than *Ted Williams*.

  You have certainly heard of Joe DiMaggio. Joe D. was a great player. He was named MVP of the league three times, including 1947. DiMaggio took the honors over Williams by a single voting point (203–202). It was a terrible ballot that occupies a deserved spot at or near the top of any "worst MVPs of all time" list.[7]

1947	WAR	G	AB	R	H	2B	3B	HR	RBI	BB	K	BA	OBP	SLG	OPS	OPS+
DiMaggio	4.8	141	534	97	168	31	10	20	97	64	32	.315	.391	.522	.913	154
Williams	*9.9*	156	528	*125*	181	40	9	*32*	*114*	*162*	47	*.343*	*.499*	*.634*	*1.133*	*205*

8. Sticking It to the Splinter: Most Career MVP Snubs 97

As usual, DiMaggio was one of the better players in the game—but his selection as the league's most valuable can't be justified by reasonable means. That's not to say the media of the day didn't try. The Associated Press on November 28, 1947, wrote, "It was DiMaggio's great team play, and courageous work under extreme adverse conditions that caused the writers to lean toward him [as MVP]. The star ... underwent a heel operation during the winter, and entered the line-up when things weren't going so well for the Yankees despite the fact his injured heel had not fully recovered ..."

Reading the *AP* account, one might infer the great DiMaggio rushed his way back from serious injury to help his struggling teammates salvage a vanishing season. Here's what actually happened: DiMaggio missed the first *three games* of the season. When he made his debut April 18, the Yankees record stood at 2–1 (thank goodness the Clipper was able to right the ship with only 152 games left to play).[8] They went on to take the AL flag by 12 games.

The 1947 MVP vote was the worst slight of Williams' career, a bitter pill that stuck in his throat for decades, with Williams recalling in his 1969 autobiography that Boston writer Mel Webb cost him the award by leaving him off the ballot. Williams was mistaken: Webb didn't have a vote that year, and the identity of the writer who felt Williams wasn't one of the ten best players in the league has been lost to history.

It's also irrelevant. The fact is, that spiteful little omission didn't cost Williams the MVP. Had any of the voters who gave first-place nods to the likes of Joost, McQuinn, or Page (12 wasted votes; 12 chances to do the right thing) instead recognized Williams, he would have received the honor befitting his magnificent season.

Statistical Records of Players Receiving First-Place Votes, 1947

1947	1st	WAR	G	AB	R	H	HR	RBI	BB	BA	OBP	SLG	OPS	OPS+
DiMaggio	8.0	4.8	141	534	97	168	20	97	64	.315	.391	.522	.913	154
McQuinn	3.0	4.4	144	517	84	157	13	80	78	.304	.395	.437	.832	132
Joost	2.0	2.2	151	540	76	111	13	64	114	.206	.348	.330	.678	88
Boudreau	1.0	7.5	150	538	79	165	4	67	67	.307	.388	.424	.811	128
Williams	3.0	9.9	156	528	125	181	32	114	162	.343	.499	.634	1.133	205

1947	1st	pWAR	W	L	ERA	WHIP	G	SV	IP	H	HR	BB	K
Page	7.0	3.8	14	8	2.48	1.252	56	17	141.1	105	5	72	116

Mickey Mantle: Won Three, Should Have Won Six

Calvin Griffith, owner of the Washington Senators, wasn't all that impressed with that kid in New York. Holding court at the beginning of the 1954 season, Griffith opined, "Mickey Mantle is probably the most overrated player in baseball. Sure, he's a good outfielder, but he isn't as good as [Senators outfielder Jim] Busby."[9]

While acknowledging the New York centerfielder's power, Griffith went on to say that if Mantle were playing for anybody but the Yankees, "you'd hardly ever hear of him."[10]

As you know, Mantle went on to do some things in the game: Seven World Series wins in 12 appearances, 536 HRs (the most ever for a switch hitter) a Triple Crown, and three MVPs.

He probably should have won six, including four in a row from 1955 to 1958 (he took honors in 1956–57).

- **1955**: From the day he reached the majors in 1951 at the age of 19, Mantle was breathlessly hyped as The Next Big Thing. The New York press corps (with an able and vocal assist from Yankees Manager Casey Stengel) anointed Mantle the successor to Ruth, Gehrig, and DiMaggio, and despite three all-star appearances by the age of 22, Mantle was derided in some corners as a disappointment. While no one was as foolishly dismissive as Calvin Griffith, the chorus went something like this: "We were told we were getting a better version of DiMaggio, and all we got was an all-star centerfielder. I want my refund."

  That changed in 1955, when Mantle became the dominant player in the American League—a designation he would hold for a decade. Leading the league in triples, home runs, walks, on-base percentage, slugging, adjusted production, and WAR, Mantle was clearly the best player on the best team in baseball.

  While no one was calling Mantle a bust anymore, the MVP voters got it very, very wrong in 1955: Mantle didn't receive a single first-place vote, finishing a distant fifth on the ballot behind MVP teammate Yogi Berra, who copped his third award. Berra had a fine season, and is one of the two or three best catchers ever—but he had no business taking home the plaque in 1955.[11]

1955	WAR	G	AB	R	H	2B	3B	HR	RBI	SB	BB	BA	OBP	SLG	OPS	OPS+
Berra	4.5	147	541	84	147	20	3	27	108	1	60	.272	.349	.470	.819	136
Mantle	**9.5**	147	517	121	158	25	**11**	**37**	99	8	**113**	**.306**	**.431**	**.611**	**1.042**	**180**

- **1958**: Despite being the most productive hitter in the league (and despite another Yankees championship), Mantle placed fifth in the MVP voting. The award went to Red Sox outfielder Jackie Jensen (and his league-leading 122 RBI). In fairness, 1958 Mantle wasn't the overwhelming force of the previous three seasons, but he was clearly the best player in the league.[12] Blame voter fatigue for Mantle's poor showing on the ballot. After back-to-back awards in 1956–57, it seems an "anyone-but-Mantle" mindset was at work. And if that was the case, Cleveland's Rocky Colavito and Kansas City's Bob Cerv were more deserving of the award than Jensen.

1958	WAR	G	AB	R	H	2B	3B	HR	RBI	SB	BB	BA	OBP	SLG	OPS	OPS+
Jensen	4.9	154	548	83	157	31	0	35	**122**	9	99	.286	.396	.535	.931	148
Colavito	6.0	143	489	80	148	26	3	41	113	0	84	.303	.405	**.620**	1.024	180
Cerv	6.3	141	515	93	157	20	7	38	104	3	50	.305	.371	.592	.963	159
Mantle	*8.7*	*150*	*519*	***127***	*158*	*21*	*1*	***42***	*97*	*18*	***129***	*.304*	*.443*	*.592*	*1.035*	***188***

- **1961**: You may have read a thing or two about this season.[13] Maris got the glory, but Mantle should have received the MVP trophy (the ballot was extraordinarily close, with Maris outpointing Mantle 202 to 198, seven first-place votes to six).

  The single-season HR record was at the time the most glamorous mark in professional sports, and the writers were going to recognize this singular accomplishment.[14] It was a terrible vote. Maris was great in 1961, but Mantle was much, much better.

1961	WAR	G	AB	R	H	2B	3B	HR	RBI	SB	BB	BA	OBP	SLG	OPS	OPS+
Maris	6.9	161	590	**132**	159	16	4	**61**	**141**	0	94	.269	.372	.620	.993	167
Mantle	**10.5**	*153*	*514*	*131*	*163*	*16*	*6*	*54*	*128*	*12*	***126***	*.317*	*.448*	***.687***	*1.135*	***205***

Willie Mays: Won Two, Should Have Won ... Infinity?

Willie Mays was pretty good at baseball. In fact, he was better at baseball than almost anybody else who ever lived. How good was he? Among position players, his career WAR (156) ranks third, behind Babe Ruth and Barry Bonds.[15] If you prefer "peak value" over "career value," Mays averaged 9.9 WAR over 13 seasons (1954–66), an extended run second only to Ruth in baseball history.[16]

Competing against what was perhaps the 20th century's greatest assemblage of talent, Mays excelled for more than a decade. He was the best hitter. The best fielder. The best baserunner. The most fun to watch. From 1954 to

1966, he led NL position players in WAR *ten times*. He led the league in slugging five times, adjusted production five times, home runs four times, stolen bases four times, triples thrice, runs twice, average once. He led baseball in *joie de vivre*, style, and flair every year. He won 12 Gold Gloves and would have won three more if the award existed prior to 1957. He brought more joy to more people than perhaps any player before or since.

As others have contended, if the MVP was just given to the best player, Willie Mays would have won every year. It's certainly true that Mays *could* have won every year, and none of those MVPs would have generated the least bit of controversy. Instead, he picked up two awards (1954 and 1965) over his incomparable career. It seems like an incongruous and irreconcilable delta between performance on the field and recognition from the electorate. Mays' play was worthy of eight or nine awards (at least), and his relatively pedestrian showing in the MVP vote represents one of the great extended injustices in the award's history.

Or does it?

The fact is, just because Mays *could* have won the award every year doesn't mean he *should* have won the award every year. Between 1955 and 1966, he was competing with the likes of Hank Aaron (1957 MVP), Ernie Banks (1958–59), Frank Robinson (1961), Sandy Koufax (1963), and Roberto Clemente (1966). Well-earned MVPs, all. Mays in 1955–56 was outpaced on the ballot by Brooklyn battery-mates Roy Campanella and Don Newcombe, respectively. Both were questionable choices for the award, but Mays wasn't necessarily the logical alternative (Brooklyn centerfielder Duke Snider would have been the best choice both years).[17]

That leaves three specific instances where Mays would seem to have been the obvious and sensible choice for MVP.

- **1960**: Despite a poor second half (.280/.336/.461, as compared with a first-half line of .361/426/.653), Mays rates as the best player in the league. Pirates shortstop Dick Groat took the batting title by six points over Mays, and it won him the MVP. Bucs' third baseman Don Hoak placed second in the voting, with Mays trailing at a considerable distance.

RK	1960	WAR	G	AB	R	H	2B	3B	HR	RBI	SB	BB	BA	OBP	SLG	OPS	OPS+
1	Groat	6.2	138	573	85	186	26	4	2	50	0	39	.325	.371	.394	.766	110
2	Hoak	5.4	155	553	97	156	24	9	16	79	3	74	.282	.366	.445	.810	120
3	Mays	9.5	153	595	107	**190**	29	12	29	103	25	61	.319	.381	.555	.936	160

This ballot often sits near the top of "worst-ever MVP" lists, and it's true that Groat wasn't a great choice for MVP. But the writers were going to give it to a member of the Pirates, who in 1960 captured their first pennant in 35 years. A brilliant shortstop, Groat was their best player and acknowledged on-field leader—and while he fares poorly in comparison to Mays, there is a kernel of logic to his selection (not so much for Hoak's runner-up status). Groat hit well for his position and anchored a spectacular defense (with Hoak, second baseman Bill Mazeroski and catcher Smokey Burgess among the best at their respective positions). If not for first baseman Dick Stuart, this could have been the best defensive unit to ever man an infield.[18]

- **1962**: MVP voters are a fickle bunch. Maury Wills narrowly edged Willie Mays for the award when he swiped a then-record 104 bases. Twelve years later, Lou Brock finishes a strong second in the voting when he establishes a new record of 118 SB. Rickey Henderson smashes the record in 1982 with 130 SB, yet finishes a distant 10th on the ballot.

  Back to 1962: Wills could have stolen 200 bases and not been as valuable as Mays. This vote more than earns its status as one of the worst ever cast.

1962	WAR	G	AB	R	H	2B	3B	HR	RBI	SB	CS	BB	K	BA	OBP	SLG	OPS	OPS+
Wills	6.0	165	695	130	208	13	**10**	6	48	**104**	13	51	57	.299	.347	.373	.720	99
Mays	**10.5**	162	621	130	189	36	5	**49**	141	18	2	78	85	.304	.384	.615	.999	165

- **1964**: Terrible. Mays is the best player in the league by a league, generates 11 WAR, and finishes *sixth* in the voting. How good is 11 WAR? There have only been 20 seasons of 11+ WAR in modern baseball history (Bonds was the last to do it in his 2002 MVP campaign). St. Louis third baseman Ken Boyer leads the league in RBI (and the Cardinals lead the league in wins) and gets the glory.

1964	WAR	G	AB	R	H	HR	RBI	SB	BB	BA	OBP	SLG	OPS	OPS+
Boyer	6.1	162	628	100	185	24	**119**	3	70	.295	.365	.489	.854	130
Mays	**11.1**	157	578	121	171	**47**	111	19	82	.296	.383	**.607**	**.990**	**172**

The 1964 pennant race, won by St. Louis on the final day of the season, is among the most thrilling of all-time, with the Reds and Phillies finishing a single game out of the running.[19] The Giants finished fourth, only three games out. The Cards stormed to the pennant on the strength of a 22–10 record over the final month of the season (and a stunning Phillies collapse). Boyer did his part, hitting .270/.371/.533 during this frenetic stretch drive—solid, but hardly the engine that drove the Cards to the finish. That engine was Bob Gibson, who started *eight* games (and added a four-inning relief appearance) the final month of the season. If the writers insisted on giving the MVP to a Cardinal, Gibson (19–12/3.01/245K, 6 pWAR) was the best pick (but not the *right* pick; that would be Mays).

Bob Gibson, September 2–October 4, 1964

1964	G	GS	CG	W–L	IP	H	R	ER	BB	K	ERA	Scowls	Glares
Gibson	9	8	6	7–2	73.2	55	18	16	21	65	1.95	67*	156*

*estimate

Should Mays have challenged Bonds' record of seven MVPs? The data tells us that Mays was a strong MVP candidate 11 times, but was "cheated" out of the honor only three times (he was *probably* the best choice in 1960; the *clear* MVP in 1962, 1964). There's no conspiracy afoot when you're finishing behind the likes of Hank Aaron, Frank Robinson, Ernie Banks, and Sandy Koufax.

◆ ◆ ◆

In the end, we have a three-way tie for the dubious distinction of "Most Career MVP Snubs." Who got the worst of it? If pure hitting genius is your criteria, than Williams is your man. If you prefer a more balanced excellence, you'll give the nod to Mays. If you prefer your stars to burn brief, but brighter than any other in the sky, you'll likely go with Mantle.

The 1947 vote might be the worst ever, so we'll give the nod to Teddy Ballgame. If we're ranking the votes in descending order of incompetence, it would look something like this.

1. Williams, 1947
2. Mays, 1964
3. Williams, 1942
4. Mantle, 1961
5. Mantle, 1955
6. Mays, 1962
7. Williams, 1941
8. Mantle, 1958
9. Mays, 1960

9

The Gym Teacher Who Came in from the Cold

In photos taken at the time, Jim Konstanty looks exactly like how you'd *expect* a gym teacher in the 1950s to look: The close-cropped hair of an enlisted man; thick-framed, thick-lensed glasses; a fleshy countenance. His chin isn't particularly strong; his eyes are a touch narrow. At 6'1", 200 pounds, he's big-but-not-too-big, carrying the remnants of a once athletic build that has steadily been accruing suburban comfort over the years.

Mr. Konstanty. He even had the name for a gym teacher. "*Mr. Konstanty*, can we take a break from dodgeball? My head hurts." "*Mr. Konstanty*, how do I throw a spiral?" "*Mr. Konstanty*, Billy got sick on the wrestling mat."

It would seem Konstanty, by name and appearance, was predestined to become a physical education teacher—and for a short time, he did indeed fulfill that destiny. But jumping jacks weren't the only plans destiny had for Konstanty: He was also a major league pitcher who was named MVP of the National League. And while he didn't really deserve the honor (the 1950 ballot as a whole is a head scratcher), his MVP season *is* among the more interesting selections.

◆ ◆ ◆

Casimir James Konstanty was the very definition of a late-bloomer. He began his professional career at the age of 24 (after his stint as a P.E. instructor) and languished in the minors for the better part of a decade. His lot in life looked to be that of a career farmhand (he in fact threw more career innings in the minors than the majors). He wasn't called up to the major leagues for the first time until he was 27; he didn't *stick* until he was 32. At 33, his second full season, he won league MVP while pitching for the 1950 Phillies—the pennant-winning "Whiz Kids."

So, the story so far: Start your career way too late; compile a mediocre minor-league resume; catch on with the big club at 32; win MVP for the league champion at 33. Makes perfect sense.

Konstanty's career path wasn't the norm—and his 1950 MVP might be as much about acknowledging a singularity as it was about recognizing performance. Relying on a bat-deadening "palm ball" (essentially a sinking change-up) and an array of breaking slop, the bespectacled Konstanty appeared in a then-record 74 games, throwing 152 innings and leading the league in saves with 22. Along the way, he picked up 16 wins while pitching to a 2.66 ERA. On an inning-by-inning basis, he was about as good as any pitcher in the league.[1]

How he compiled those innings probably had as much to do with his MVP as what he *did* in those 152 IP. To wit: Konstanty didn't start a single regular-season game in 1950, but twice went nine innings or more. He threw three or more innings in a game 17 times, two innings or more 41 times (often on back-to-back days). He appeared in both ends of a doubleheader *six* times. His resilience didn't go unnoticed. The Associated Press reported on August 10, 1950, "Jim Konstanty, the Phils rubber-armed reliefer [*sic*], looks like the most important single factor in the National League race. As long as Jim holds up, the Phils should ride high. Konstanty won't miss many of the last 46 down the pennant stretch."

The AP story proved prescient as the Phils wrung every last fluttering, off-speed pitch they could out of Konstanty's arm. He had an interesting week in late August: Against Pittsburgh on the 25th, he entered the game in the sixth inning and picked up the win with a *nine-inning* relief appearance. The Phillies rewarded him for this monumental effort by giving him the next day off. He was back August 27, throwing 3.2 innings against the Cubs. The next day, he did it again: another 3.2 innings against Chicago. August 29 was a day off of sorts: he was brought in for an out against the Cardinals. Revived by his mini-vacation, Konstanty was brought in the next day to throw two innings against those same Cards.

If you're keeping score: Five appearances and 18 innings in six days. He pitched beautifully, yielding only three earned runs over that span (the nine-inning appearance wasn't even a personal best; he outdid himself with a *10-inning* appearance on September 15).

Konstanty's unique usage pattern carried into the post season. The Phillies, having secured their first pennant in 35 years, were facing DiMaggio's Yankees in the World Series. Konstanty, who had led the league in appearances, games finished, and saves, who hadn't started a game in the big leagues in *five years*, was naturally tabbed as the game one *starter*. He gave a valiant effort, yielding one run over eight innings. Unfortunately for Konstanty and the

Phillies, the Yankees' Vic Raschi was brilliant, hurling a two-hit shutout. *That*, as they say, was *that* for the Phils, who were swept in four games.

Konstanty never came close to replicating his 1950 success, but he would hang on for a few more years, pitching well for those same Yankees in 1955 before retiring the next season.

◆ ◆ ◆

So, who was more deserving of the award than Konstanty? Runner-up Stan Musial had a persuasive statistical argument (.346/.437/.596), leading the league in batting and slugging. But Musial had already pocketed three MVPs and finished second in 1949. One gets the feeling that with Musial, the writers had become inured to greatness (call it the "Mays Effect"). Run off season-after-season-after-season of extraordinary performances, and the extraordinary becomes routine. Musial's *average* year through the 1950 season:

Musial	WAR	G	AB	R	H	2B	3B	HR	RBI	BB	K	BA	OBP	SLG	OPS	OPS+
1942–50	8.0	151	580	114	200	42	14	22	101	81	29	.346	.429	.580	1.009	171

So his 1950 campaign—a career year for 99 percent of those who have ever played the game—was in most respects an average year for The Man.

New York Giants second baseman Eddie Stanky finished third in the voting, leading the league in walks and on-base percentage. His inter-borough counterpart Jackie Robinson, who had been recognized as MVP the year prior, had a compelling argument as the best overall player in the league (.328/.423/.500 with his typically superb defense and base running). He finished 15th in the voting.

The oddest aspect of the voting in 1950 isn't that Musial finished second; it isn't that Stanky finished third, or that Robinson finished deep in the ballot.[2]

The baffling aspect of the voting isn't even that Konstanty won the award. One can understand (while not necessarily agreeing with the premise) how the voters might view him as the most valuable component on a team that wasn't supposed to go anywhere. Philadelphia had finished 16 games behind powerhouse Brooklyn the prior season, and the club wasn't expected to do much of anything in 1950. But the perennial also-rans, fielding one of the youngest teams in the league, ran away with the pennant. Writers love a story, and the Whiz Kids were a story. *Konstanty* was a story: The ancient gym teacher with the rubber arm pitches the Whiz Kids to the pennant! He wasn't the best player in the league that year (this vote would go to Robinson), but he was perhaps its best narrative.

No, the baffling aspect of the voting is how the writers viewed Konstanty's teammate, Robin Roberts. Roberts was clearly one of the best two pitchers in the league, pacing the circuit in pitcher WAR, starts and shutouts; second in wins, innings, and WHIP; and top five in ERA, strikeouts, and complete games.[3] He placed *seventh* in the voting, despite pitching *twice* as many innings as his MVP teammate.

1950	pWAR	W	L	ERA	G	GS	CG	SHO	SV	IP	H	HR	BB	K	FIP	WHIP	ERA+
Konstanty	4.4	16	7	2.66	74	0	—	—	22	152.0	108	11	50	56	3.77	1.039	151
Roberts	**6.8**	20	11	3.02	40	**39**	21	**5**	1	304.1	282	29	77	146	3.64	1.180	133

Roberts and Konstanty played the same position. Roberts played it twice as much, at about the same rate of effectiveness. Konstanty was deemed more valuable. And that wasn't the worst of it for Roberts as far as the MVP vote was concerned. For his efforts, Roberts was recognized as the fourth most valuable player on his *own team* by the writers. Outfielder Del Ennis, who had a fine year, and shortstop Granny Hamner—he of a .270/.314/.380 slash line good for 83 OPS+—finished ahead of Roberts in the voting.

The Konstanty MVP represented a departure for the BBWAA in that he was the first reliever honored with the award. He wouldn't be the last. The voters would misunderstand the nature (and overstate the value) of relief pitching for decades.

10

Curiouser and Curiouser

There are some votes that defy easy explanation.

These aren't your run-of-the-mill terrible MVP selections, your 1995 Mo Vaughns or your 1979 Willie Stargells or your dozens of others. We *understand* terrible selections. They exasperate, they disappoint, but they don't strike us as inscrutable. We *get* them. With a little effort, one can rationalize (while not condoning) a bad vote. Maury Wills over Willie Mays in 1962? Dreadful, but understandable (stolen base record, premiere defensive position on a team that won 102 games). Mickey Cochrane over Triple Crown slugger Lou Gehrig in 1934? Absurd, but according to the unwritten tenets of the "most valuable vs. best player" argument, Cochrane had a case (premiere position, decent production, unquestioned leader of a surprise pennant-winner).

The truly inscrutable votes—the ones that brazenly ignore the precedents and preferences of the MVP electorate—are few and far between.

◆ ◆ ◆

From day one, MVP voters have been a consistent lot when it comes to the impact of team performance on individual player honors. MVPs, almost without exception, come from winning teams (fully 97 percent since 1931); more often than not, the league's most valuable player comes from a division or league champion, or a strong contender.

So it was something of a story when Hank Sauer, popular first baseman for the lowly Chicago Cubs, took National League honors in 1952. With his award, Sauer became the first player from a second-division club to claim the prize.[1] He is among the most curious (and dubious) MVP selections of all time.

NL WAR Leaders (Position Players), 1952

1952	WAR	G	AB	R	H	2B	3B	HR	RBI	BB	K	SB	CS	BA	OBP	SLG	OPS	OPS+
Robinson	8.5	149	510	104	157	17	3	19	75	106	40	24	7	.308	**.440**	.465	.904	149
Musial	8.0	**154**	578	**105**	**194**	**42**	6	21	91	96	29	7	7	**.336**	.432	**.538**	**.970**	**167**
Hemus	6.7	151	570	**105**	153	28	8	15	52	96	55	1	5	.268	.392	.425	.817	126
Dark	5.8	151	589	92	177	29	3	14	73	47	39	6	6	.301	.357	.431	.788	117
Sauer	5.7	151	567	89	153	31	3	**37**	**121**	77	92	1	2	.270	.361	.531	.892	143

The 1952 vote was a very tight three-man race with Sauer (eight first-place votes; 226 points) edging two pitchers—Philadelphia's Robin Roberts (seven first-place votes, 210 points) and Brooklyn's rookie relief sensation Joe Black (eight first-place votes, 208 points)—for honors. It's a confounding vote for several reasons: 1) at 77–77, the fifth-place Cubs were the platonic ideal of mediocrity[2]; 2) despite his leading home run and RBI totals, Sauer's body of work falls short when compared with the league's elite players; 3) Sauer was a construct of his home park, and faded badly down the stretch; 4) the league's best teams fielded legitimate MVP candidates.

The genial and unassuming Sauer was the sole power threat in a tepid Cubs lineup, tying Pittsburgh's Ralph Kiner for the home run title while pacing the circuit in RBI. Known as the "Mayor of Wrigley Field," Sauer was one of the more popular players in the history of the franchise. The feeling was mutual. "I loved playing at Wrigley Field," an appreciative Sauer once said. "Fans would throw tobacco to me."[3]

It wasn't just the free chaw: Wrigley was very good to Sauer, and he can thank his home park (and the misguided writers) for his Most Valuable trophy.

Hank Sauer, 1952 Home-Road Split

1952	G	AB	R	H	2B	3B	HR	RBI	SB	CS	BB	K	BA	OBP	SLG	OPS
Home	74	283	43	89	19	3	23	76	1	2	32	42	.314	.386	.647	1.033
Away	77	284	46	64	12	0	14	45	0	0	45	50	.225	.337	.415	.753

The large, lumbering Sauer couldn't run a lick; in the outfield, he got an "A" for effort, but a "D-minus" for execution (once, after misplaying a routine fly ball during a night game, he famously told then-manager manager Frankie Frisch that he "lost the ball in the moon"). His game was based solely on his power, and the only argument for his award, of course, are those 37 HR and 121 RBI (achieved despite a slump that saw him hit .205 with 3 HR and 13 RBI over the last 33 games of the season).[4]

It's not a case you'd want to present to a jury. The list of men who had accomplished the HR/RBI "double-double" prior to Sauer and *not* been accorded the MVP is a long one. It includes names like Lou Gehrig, Babe Ruth,

Ted Williams, Joe DiMaggio, and Johnny Mize. And as Gehrig and Williams could attest, several men had notched a *Triple Crown* and seen their MVP fortunes dashed on the jagged rocks of team performance. The precedent, ignored by the writers in 1952, had clearly been set: League-leading power numbers *always* deferred to team won-loss records.[5]

What makes the Sauer vote so inexplicable is the fact that three of the four teams finishing ahead of the Cubs offered a vastly superior candidate for the award.

- Brooklyn's Jackie Robinson had a case as the best all-around player in the league, pacing the circuit in WAR and on-base percentage while playing with his customary flair and fire. The Dodgers assumed first place on June 1, and never looked back. Arguably the best hitter, defender, and baserunner in the game, Robinson was clearly the engine that powered this train. Somehow, rookie relief ace Joe Black (more on him in a moment) cornered the Brooklyn MVP vote. Robinson was barely considered by the voters, finishing seventh on the ballot.
- Assuming his customary perch at the top of the hitting mountain, Stan Musial led the league in runs, hits, doubles, slugging, batting average, and adjusted production for a strong St. Louis team. His utter lack of support (a fifth-place finish, but not a single first-place vote) is defies explanation.
- And then there's Robin Roberts, of the fourth-place Philadelphia Phillies. Relying on a crackling fastball, a complementary curve ball (thrown mainly as a change-of-pace), and unerring control, Roberts was the best pitcher in baseball. Roberts pitched *40 more innings* (or about five starts worth), won ten more games, and completed nine more starts *than any other pitcher* in the league. He easily led all pitchers in WAR (8.3), but that number doesn't do him justice: The indefatigable Roberts went 17–1 over the second half of the season, completing 12 of his last 13 starts—including a *17-inning* complete game against the forlorn Braves on September 6th.[6] In an act of omission comparable to the Williams snub of 1947, one writer failed to list the great right-hander on his ballot. According to this anonymous voter, Robin Roberts wasn't one of the ten most valuable players in the league.
- Nipping at Roberts' heels on the ballot was Brooklyn reliever Joe Black. As was the case with Jim Konstanty's 1950 award, the writers greatly overvalued a reliever's contributions at the expense of Roberts. Black was excellent, but to suggest he was as valuable as Roberts is a stretch. Black accumulated 142 innings over 52 appearances out of the Brook-

lyn bullpen, and the 28-year-old rookie was excellent—but Roberts pitched nearly *200 additional innings*, at a comparable rate of effectiveness.

1952	pWAR	W	L	W%	ERA	GS	CG	SHO	IP	H	R	ER	BB	K	ERA+	FIP	WHIP	K/BB
Roberts	**8.3**	28	7	.800	2.59	**37**	**30**	3	**330**	292	104	95	45	148	141	2.82	1.021	3.29
Black	4.4	15	4	.789	2.15		2	—	—	142.1	102	40	34	41	85	171	2.90	1.005	2.02

That said, Black had a very good season and clearly merited deserved *some* consideration (Dodgers manager Charlie Dressen stumped loudly for his reliever, citing the rookie as the primary reason his club took the pennant). Despite Black's strong third-place finish in the voting, it raised several eyebrows when it was revealed that three writers had failed to list him on the ballot, thereby costing him the award.

"Any system that can produce a judge who fails to give one vote to Joe Black or Robin Roberts, ignoring both completely, has the kiss of death attached," wrote famed sportswriter Grantland Rice. "Here we have a case of rank prejudice and stupidity lumped together in one sad mess."[7]

It's impossible to know if personal animus or bigotry played a role in the vote (Black was African American), but Rice was correct when he called out the one writer who dismissed Roberts as unworthy of even a tenth-place vote. It's not a defensible position. Writing for the *New York Times*, Arthur Daley concurred: "It has become increasingly obvious—and this year's Sauer selection proves it—that there are fundamental flaws in the writers' system. They are destroying the value of the most valuable award. How could anyone in conscience disregard Black and Roberts?"[8]

Of course, both Daley and Rice were wrong in predicting the impending collapse of the award. It wasn't the first time—and it certainly wouldn't be the last—that the MVP voting system would come under fire. As it had in the past (and would again many times in the future), the award weathered a terrible vote and retained its relevancy.

◆ ◆ ◆

Sauer's MVP was curious, but in the end it reflected a plurality of sentiment from the 1952 voting bloc. Not so for the solo acts, the *singularities,* those seemingly random first-place votes for a player who otherwise has no business being placed on a ballot. These are the lone tallies that occasionally pop up to mar an otherwise slam-dunk, no-brainer, foregone conclusion of a ballot. These are the most curious votes of them all. Sometimes, the writer who cast the offending vote will offer an explanation for the otherwise unexplainable (but as often as not, we'll wish he hadn't).[9]

Michael Young, Texas Rangers, 2011
(MVP: Justin Verlander)

2011	WAR	G	AB	R	H	2B	3B	HR	RBI	SB	CS	BB	K	BA	OBP	SLG	OPS	OPS+
Young	2.4	159	631	88	**213**	41	6	11	106	6	2	47	78	.338	.380	.474	.854	125

Taken out of context, a nice all-around season for Young—but MVP-worthy? Despite ample evidence to the contrary, one voter thought so, gifting Young with a vote that rightfully belonged to MVP claimant Justin Verlander (who led the league in just about every meaningful pitching category, including WAR) Jose Bautista, Miguel Cabrera, or Jacoby Ellsbury.

2011	WAR	G	AB	R	H	2B	3B	HR	RBI	SB	CS	BB	K	BA	OBP	SLG	OPS	OPS+
Ellsbury	**8.1**	158	660	119	212	46	5	32	105	39	15	52	98	.321	.376	.552	.928	146
Bautista	**8.1**	149	513	105	155	24	2	**43**	103	9	5	**132**	111	.302	.447	**.608**	**1.056**	**182**
Cabrera	7.5	161	572	111	197	**48**	0	30	105	2	1	108	89	**.344**	**.448**	.586	1.033	179

Young's .338 batting average catches the eye, but his offensive production isn't notable for a man paid to hit. Young's home park (then known as the Stadium at Arlington) played like Coors Field on the plains, and Young was the beneficiary of Texas largesse, hitting ten of his 11 home runs at home.[10] Taking park factors into account, Young was about 25 percent more productive than a league-average hitter. A nice season with the bat, but Young contributed little with his glove or on the base paths (as compared with, say, Ellsbury, who earned his Gold Glove in centerfield while out-hitting Young).

In explaining his vote for Young, *Dallas Morning News* reporter Evan Grant cited his contributions "in clutch situations" (for what it's worth, Young did hit .377 with runners in scoring position), and his consistent, steadying presence in the Texas lineup while key teammates fell to injuries.[11] And it's true: Young was a selfless player who went where he was needed, playing every infield position when he wasn't DHing. Maybe not the best rationale for according a player the league's highest honor, but maybe not the worst.

But Grant didn't stop there: "When somebody can quickly explain the complexities of the concept and standardize the WAR formula, I'll spend more time with it. In the meantime, I'll go with what my eyes told me. My eyes told me Michael Young meant more to the Texas Rangers and their success than any player in the American League."

We won't knock Grant for casting a withering and circumspect glare on WAR—especially not in 2011, when the statistic was still on the fringes on mainstream acceptance. But the "eye test" argument falls short of the standards of evidence. With some mental gymnastics, one can justify some down-ballot support for the respected Michael Young. That first-place vote is undeserved.

As you'll read, this isn't the last we'll hear from Grant.

MIGUEL CABRERA, DETROIT TIGERS, 2009 (MVP: JOE MAUER)

2009	WAR	G	AB	R	H	2B	3B	HR	RBI	SB	CS	BB	K	BA	OBP	SLG	OPS	OPS+
Mauer	7.8	138	523	94	191	30	1	28	96	4	1	76	63	**.365**	**.444**	**.587**	**1.031**	**171**
Cabrera	5.1	160	611	96	198	34	0	34	103	6	2	68	107	.324	.396	.547	.942	144

A single vote for Miguel Cabrera cost Minnesota's Joe Mauer the elite distinction of being named unanimous MVP. Months after the fact, reporter Keizo Konishi explained his pick to the *New York Times*. "If I took Cabrera out of the Tigers' lineup, I thought it would be a very different team. If I did the same thing for the Twins, if I picked Mauer out of the lineup, they would still have a better lineup compared to the Tigers."

Konishi's defense of his vote started well enough. Unfortunately, he then proceeded to go off the rails, citing Cabrera's performance in the 2009 World Baseball Classic, an international off-season tournament that concluded *prior* to the start of 2009 season. "The World Baseball Classic is a huge deal for the Japanese people—enormous. And Cabrera played to the semi-finals. Mauer didn't."

In some respects, this is akin to awarding the heavyweight championship of the world to the winner of an amateur boxing tournament. Featuring a mix of established major league stars, amateur standouts, and professional players from 16 countries,[12] the overall level of play of the WBC is akin to that of the high minor leagues (granting that the national teams of Cuba, Japan, the Dominican Republic, and others clearly field world-class talent). Many major leaguers skip the tournament for fear of injury, unwillingness to travel, or simply because they have other off-season commitments. Statistics compiled over the course of the tournament are not recognized by MLB. But give Konishi credit— he was willing to publically defend his vote, which is more than could be said for the writer who stiffed Robin Roberts in 1952.

RICK CERONE, NEW YORK YANKEES, 1980 (MVP: GEORGE BRETT)

1980	WAR	G	AB	R	H	2B	3B	HR	RBI	SB	CS	BB	K	BA	OBP	SLG	OPS	OPS+
Brett	9.4	117	449	87	175	33	9	24	118	15	6	58	22	**.390**	**.454**	**.664**	**1.118**	**203**
Cerone	4.2	147	519	70	144	30	4	14	85	1	3	32	56	.277	.321	.432	.753	107

A sole writer felt Yankees catcher Rick Cerone was more valuable than MVP George Brett. Being contrarian for contrarian's sake doesn't make one a rebel or an iconoclast; it makes one a boor.

Cesar Tovar, Minnesota Twins, 1967
(MVP: Carl Yastrzemski)

1977	WAR	G	AB	R	H	2B	3B	HR	RBI	SB	CS	BB	K	BA	OBP	SLG	OPS	OPS+
Yaz	*12.4*	161	579	*112*	*189*	31	4	*44*	*121*	10	8	91	69	*.326*	*.418*	*.622*	*1.040*	*193*
Tovar	2.4	*164*	*649*	98	173	32	7	6	47	19	11	46	51	.267	.325	.365	.691	97

Yastrzemski's Triple Crown *undersells* his amazing performance. His 12.4 WAR is the highest single-season total for non-pitchers since 1927 (Ruth's 60-HR monument). That's 88 years, if you're counting. He was a near-unanimous pick for MVP, receiving 19 out of 20 first-place votes.

Minneapolis Star writer Max Nichols was the lone dissenter, giving his vote to Minnesota's Cesar Tovar. Cesar Tovar. A utility player who manned six positions. None particularly well.

The vote was met with scorn, but Nichols remained defiant in the face of criticism. Of Tovar, he said: "We didn't have the best of player relations on our club, but Tovar never got mixed up in any of the clubhouse politics.[13] He kept plugging away, no matter where they put him, and to me he did a tremendous job … Tovar was my choice and, if I had to do it all over again, I'd vote for him again."

It's difficult to pinpoint the worst single vote in the history of the award (especially in this company), but it can be said with confidence that there are no *worse* votes than this.[14] Twins manager Billy Martin resorted to hypotheticals in trying to defend the pick.[15] "I'd have voted for him too," said Martin. "What if we had won the pennant? Look, Yaz had a great year. But if we won, Tovar would have been the one who did it for us, the same way Yaz did it for Boston. The way I saw it, I'd have to vote for Tovar as the MVP."

The point, of course, is that the Twins *didn't* win the pennant, finishing one game behind Yastrzemski's Red Sox—and even if they had, the Tovar vote remains indefensible.

Alvin Dark, Boston Braves, 1948 (MVP: Stan Musial)

1948	WAR	G	AB	R	H	2B	3B	HR	RBI	SB	CS	BB	K	BA	OBP	SLG	OPS	OPS+
Musial	*11.1*	155	611	*135*	*230*	*46*	*18*	39	*131*	7	—	79	34	*.376*	*.450*	*.702*	*1.152*	*200*
Dark	4.3	137	543	85	175	39	6	3	48	4	—	24	36	.322	.353	.433	.786	112

Producing the best season of his remarkable career, Stan Musial deservedly ran away with the 1948 NL award, capturing 18 first-place votes.

But one can understand how five writers decided Johnny Sain was more valuable to the Boston Braves than Stan Musial was to the St. Louis Cardinals.

Sain (24–15, 2.60 ERA, 137 K; 8.4 pWAR) was magnificent, leading the National League in starts, wins, complete games, innings, and pitcher WAR. The lowly Braves claimed their first pennant since the miracle run of 1914, and it's a certainty they don't do it without Sain.

So we *get* it, we get how five writers thought him more valuable than Stan the Man. Not so much for the one writer who thought Braves rookie Alvin Dark was the league's most valuable.[16] No, not so much.

Tony Lazzeri, New York Yankees, 1927
(MVP: Lou Gehrig)

1927	WAR	G	AB	R	H	2B	3B	HR	RBI	SB	CS	BB	K	BA	OBP	SLG	OPS	OPS+
Gehrig	11.8	**155**	584	149	218	**52**	18	47	**173**	10	8	109	84	.373	.474	.765	1.240	220
Lazzeri	6.3	153	570	92	176	29	8	18	102	22	14	69	82	.309	.383	.482	.866	125

Under the rules at the time, Babe Ruth was ineligible for the 1927 award, robbing fans of a potentially fascinating MVP vote (Ruth with his record 60 HR, Gehrig his record 173 RBI). As it stands, Gehrig made for an excellent choice, capturing seven of eight first-place votes. The dissenting vote went to teammate Tony Lazzeri. An on-the-record explanation for the Lazzeri vote remains to be found. Perhaps it's better this way, else we might stumble on something like this from Richards Vidmer in the *New York Times* on August 3, 1927: "It seems to this writer, there has been no more valuable player on the Yanks this season than Mr. Wilcy Moore. Without him the Yanks would not have made a joke of the American League race…. Old Doc Moore has come to the rescue of many a game that was just about to die on the Yanks hands."

When Vidmer published his column, the Yankees' record stood at 74–29. Versatile reliever Wilcy Moore's record stood at 11–5, with ten saves.[17] Lou Gehrig was leading the league in batting (.388), runs scored, home runs, RBI, slugging, and total bases, hitting at a pace unmatched by any hitter in history save the Babe himself.

We don't know if Richards Vidmer had an MVP vote in 1927, so we can't blame him for the Lazzeri fiasco (though he did put forth Lazzeri as a viable candidate in the same August 3rd column). We *can* wonder if Vidmer was still feeling the effects of a night out on the town with the Babe when he wrote his endorsement of Moore for MVP.

While we're on the subject of singularities, a few notes about sports writer Richards Vidmer, who in many ways was more interesting than the subjects he covered. The son of a brigadier general, Vidmer served as a pilot in World War I (nearly losing his leg in a stateside aerial collision), and on General Eisenhower's staff in World War II, where one of his duties as an intelligence officer was to chaperone (and report on) Eleanor Roosevelt for a full month. "I thought it was going to be one hell of an assignment," said Vidmer. "But to put it briefly, Mrs. Roosevelt charmed me. I thought she was delightful."[18]

Between wars, he was a prolific beat writer covering the Yankees for the *New York Times*, and later a columnist and reporter for the *New York Herald Tribune*. An accomplished athlete himself—he played football at George Washington University, and played minor-league baseball—Vidmer was friendlier with the athletes he covered than with his colleagues in the press box. The Yankees, among others, appreciated his discretion. "Hell, I could have written a story every day on the Babe," he recalled 50 years after the fact. "But I never wrote about his personal life, not if it would hurt him. Babe couldn't say no to certain things. Hot dogs was the least of 'em. There were other things that were worse. Hell, sometimes I thought it was one long line."

The roguish Vidmer was no slouch in that department himself, and served as the inspiration for *Young Man of Manhattan*, a best-selling romantic novel about a playboy sportswriter.[19]

After the war, Vidmer found it impossible to return to sports writing ("Sports was no longer glamorous to me, not in comparison to what had gone on over there"). He became a European correspondent for the *Herald Tribune*, married the daughter of a rajah of Borneo (the second of three marriages for Vidmer), and for a time pursued the easy life as an ersatz golf pro in Barbados.

Vidmer passed away in 1978, at the age of 79, but not before he offered a delightful, extended reminiscence in Jerome Holtzman's oral history of the golden age of sports writing, *No Cheering from the Press Box*.

"The thing that saved my life in the newspaper business was that I never had any desire to have a drink until five o'clock, until after my work was done," said Vidmer. "Then, I could catch up with anybody."

BOBBY BONILLA, PITTSBURGH PIRATES, 1990
(MVP: BARRY BONDS)

1990	WAR	G	AB	R	H	2B	3B	HR	RBI	SB	CS	BB	K	BA	OBP	SLG	OPS	OPS+
Bonds	9.7	151	519	104	156	32	3	33	114	52	13	93	83	.301	.406	**.565**	**.970**	**170**
Bonilla	3.9	160	625	112	175	39	7	32	120	4	3	45	103	.280	.322	.518	.841	132

It was in 1990 that Barry Bonds, lean gazelle of an outfielder for the Pittsburgh Pirates, first established himself as the game's best. Bonds was almost demure when learning of his selection as Most Valuable: "This was just an unreal year. I don't know if I can ever do this again, but I can tell my kids and grandkids that, for six months, I was up there with the best of them."

His tenure among the best of them lasted a little longer than six months. While his physique (and his public persona) would change over the next 15 years, his status as the game's greatest player remained intact. Bonds' numbers in 1990 seem almost quaint when compared with his late-career supernova peak, but coupled with his superb defense and superior base running, there was no questioning his credentials as the National League's Most Valuable Player. Well, there was *some* question—at least in the mind of one writer, who gave his first-place vote to Bonds' teammate Bobby Bonilla.

RBI. Always with the RBI.

ALVIN DARK, NY GIANTS, 1954 (MVP: WILLIE MAYS)

1954	WAR	G	AB	R	H	2B	3B	HR	RBI	SB	CS	BB	K	BA	OBP	SLG	OPS	OPS+
Mays	10.6	151	565	119	195	33	13	41	110	8	5	66	57	.345	.411	.667	1.078	175
Dark	3.6	154	644	98	189	26	6	20	70	5	3	27	40	.293	.325	.446	.770	98

Dark makes the list *twice*. This time, one voter thought him more valuable than his teammate Mays. Look, no harm done: Mays took the award in a landslide (though he was far from a unanimous choice, with Cincinnati's Ted Kluszewski receiving significant support). But there is no reconciling this vote. No one in good conscience could honestly believe Alvin Dark in 1954 was more valuable to the Giants than Willie Mays.

HARRY DANNING, NY GIANTS, 1937 (MVP: JOE MEDWICK)

1937	WAR	G	AB	R	H	2B	3B	HR	RBI	SB	CS	BB	K	BA	OBP	SLG	OPS	OPS+
Medwick	8.5	156	633	111	237	56	10	31	154	4	-	41	50	.374	.414	.641	1.056	182
Danning	1.7	93	292	30	84	12	4	8	51	0	-	18	20	.288	.331	.438	.770	106

Joe Medwick in 1937 nearly joined Lou Gehrig, Ted Williams, and Chuck Klein in the dubious distinction of players who hit for the Triple Crown but were passed over for their league's Most Valuable Player award. Doing his superb work for the third-place Cardinals, Medwick *barely* took MVP honors (70 points to 68) over runner-up Gabby Hartnett (a brilliant catcher who played but 110 games for the second-place Chicago Cubs).

The 1937 MVP vote was an interesting affair. Despite Medwick's utter dominance of the league, five different players were awarded first-place votes, with three of those going to members of the pennant-winning New York Giants: Ace pitcher Carl Hubbell, by then a two-time MVP, was an annual fixture on the ballot; shortstop Dick Bartell was a tougher sell, but his .306/.367/.469 line, coupled with strong defense, was good for 6.6 WAR, second in the league to Medwick. The outlier in this company, the singularity that can't be supported by empirical or anecdotal evidence, is the vote cast for Giants catcher Harry "The Horse" Danning.

A good player for several years, Danning in 1937 shared catching duties with Gus Mancuso. *Combined*, the two backstops generated 2.6 wins above replacement. Voters of the time afforded catchers a great deal of respect (respect, it could be argued, that contemporary voters sorely lack), but Danning and his grand total of 30 runs scored doesn't deserve to be anywhere *near* this ballot. His first-place vote was the *only* vote he received—and it was a dishonest mistake.

Joey Jay, Cincinnati Reds, 1961 (MVP: Frank Robinson)

1961	WAR	G	AB	R	H	2B	3B	HR	RBI	SB	CS	BB	K	BA	OBP	SLG	OPS	OPS+
Robinson	7.7	153	545	117	176	32	7	37	124	22	3	71	64	.323	.404	*.611*	*1.015*	*164*

This, of course, is the year of Mantle and Maris—but Frank Robinson's fine work in the senior circuit shouldn't be lost to history. Robinson wasn't chasing Ruth, but he did power the Reds to their first pennant in 20 years. He was recognized for his efforts with the NL MVP award, claiming 15 of 16 first-place votes. Costing "The Judge" unanimous affirmation was teammate Joey Jay, who pitched a fine season but wasn't one of the dozen or so best players in the league.

1961	pWAR	W	L	W%	ERA	G	GS	IP	H	R	ER	BB	K	ERA+	FIP	WHIP	K/BB
Jay	4.4	*21*	10	.677	3.53	34	34	247.1	217	102	97	92	157	114	3.80	1.249	1.71

Jay's lone vote is a function of his 21 wins (tied with Warren Spahn for the league lead), but he clearly wasn't as good as teammate Jim O'Toole (19–9, 3.10, 178K). It's telling that despite finishing fifth in the MVP vote, Jay didn't receive a single first-place vote for the MLB Cy Young Award (his performance down the stretch didn't help his cause: 3–3, 5.44 ERA over his last eight starts of the season).

Robinson would capture a unanimous MVP five years later with his 1966 Triple Crown effort for the Baltimore Orioles.

A Man Stands Alone

Johan Santana, Minnesota Twins, 2006 (MVP: Justin Morneau)

2006	WAR	G	AB	R	H	2B	3B	HR	RBI	SB	CS	BB	K	BA	OBP	SLG	OPS	OPS+
Morneau	4.3	157	592	97	190	37	1	34	130	3	3	53	93	.321	.375	.559	.934	140
Jeter	5.5	154	623	118	214	39	3	14	97	34	5	69	102	.343	.417	.483	.900	132

And then there's the singular vote that makes this chapter for a different reason.

The 2006 MVP ballot saw the Twins' Justin Morneau edge the Yankees' Derek Jeter in a highly anticipated (and extensively debated) vote. Between the two of them, Morneau and Jeter collected 27 of 28 first-place votes (15 for Morneau to Jeter's 12).

The lone holdout was again *Dallas Morning News* reporter Evan Grant, who cast his ballot for Twins left-hander Johan Santana. "Maybe because of the team I cover [the heavy-hitting, weak-pitching Texas Rangers] I over-value the starting pitcher," said Grant in explaining his vote. "But the Twins were 27–7 when Santana pitched, 14–0 at home."

2006	pWAR	W	L	W%	ERA	GS	IP	H	R	ER	BB	K	ERA+	FIP	WHIP	K/BB
Santana	7.5	19	6	.760	2.77	34	233.2	186	79	72	47	245	162	3.04	.997	5.21

Jeter and Morneau were both excellent hitters who made significant contributions to first-place teams—but Santana was *superb*, leading the league in just about every meaningful pitching category. The question wasn't "Is Johan Santana the best pitcher in the league?" The question was "Is there anybody who deserves to be mentioned in the same breath as Santana as the best pitcher in the league?"

The answer, at least in 2006, was an emphatic "No." He was clearly the league's most important player. Simply put, the Twins—who captured their division by a single game over the second-place Tigers—would not have made the post-season without their ace. He was recognized for his pitching excellence with a unanimous Cy Young award, but that doesn't accurately capture his importance to the Twins.

In casting his support for Santana in 2006, Grant again makes this list of voting singularities. But this time it's for the *right* reason: In bucking the majority (and refusing to perpetuate the silly bias against starting pitchers), Grant cast the single *best* vote on the 2006 MVP ballot.

11

"What are we going to do? Break it in half?"

The voters named three MVPs in in 1979. They got it right once.

The 1979 NL ballot is unique in MVP lore: For the only time in the award's history, the vote ended in a tie, with Keith Hernandez of the Cardinals and Willie Stargell of the Pirates sharing honors (asked Stargell, "What are we going to do? Break it in half?"). According to BaseballAnalysts.com, Stargell garnered ten first-place votes, three seconds, four thirds, a fourth, and two sixths; he was left off four ballots. Hernandez was named on all ballots, receiving four first-place votes, eight seconds, seven thirds, two fourths, and three fifths. When the ballots were totaled, each stood at 216 points in the BBWAA voting system.[1]

1979	WAR	G	AB	R	H	2B	3B	HR	RBI	SB	CS	BB	K	BA	OBP	SLG	OPS	OPS+
Stargell	2.5	126	424	60	119	19	0	32	82	0	1	47	105	.281	.352	.552	.904	139
Hernandez	7.6	161	610	116	210	48	11	11	105	11	6	80	78	**.344**	.417	.513	.930	151

Hernandez should have won it outright. The St. Louis first baseman was one of the two or three best players in the league, taking the batting title, leading the league in runs and doubles (with a robust .417 OBP), and playing his position like a virtuoso.[2] In terms of personal achievement, 1979 was the pinnacle of his distinguished career.

Stargell, the long-time Pittsburgh icon, produced a solid, injury-truncated season for the "We Are Fam-i-ly" Pirates, who eventually went on to win the World Series. Essentially a part-time player, Stargell appeared in a mere 126 games (starting but 108). Stargell was still capable of inflicting violence on a baseball, as evidenced by his 32 HR in only 424 AB, but he was a poor defender and a plodding baserunner (his knees were strictly ornamental at this point in his career). Based on his overall contributions on the field, "Pops" wasn't one of the 30 best players in the league, let alone the most valuable.

He was, of course, the heart and soul of a plucky Pittsburgh team that overcame the odds to win the NL East. Stargell, with a September for the ages (he launched eight HR as the Pirates went 20–10 for the month to turn back the hard-charging Montreal Expos) refused to lose—chiding, inspiring, motivating, and leading his team to victory. Or so the story went at the time.

That the Pirates were a powerhouse in the 1970s, claiming six division titles (as many as the Big Red Machine) didn't quite fit this narrative; that Stargell hit .222/.328/.485 for September (significantly *below* his season averages heading into the month) didn't quite fit this narrative; that teammate and defending MVP Dave Parker was the Pirates' best player didn't quite fit this narrative. But the voters never let the facts get in the way of a good MVP story. The Stargell vote was really just a thinly disguised "lifetime achievement award."

"Pops," then in his 18th season, was clearly winding down a storied career. The civic-minded, charitable Stargell was one of the most respected and beloved players of his generation, and at one time had been the most intimidating power hitter in the league.[3] Hall of Fame pitcher Don Sutton once quipped, "He doesn't just hit pitchers. He takes their dignity."

For nearly two decades, Stargell hit monstrous home runs and drove in plenty. He had a reputation as "clutch." He was affable and quotable, two qualities that never hurt with the voters. He was genuinely liked and admired throughout the league. Despite being the most productive and popular player on an excellent team, a player that seemed to fill every box on the hypothetical MVP checklist, Stargell failed to capture an MVP.

Why? Injuries and timing. Stargell, who never played in as many as 150 games in any of his 21 seasons (he only reached 140 games six times), generated relative production on par with Hank Aaron; the key difference between them was that Aaron was indestructible, while Stargell was injury prone.

In addition to his injury history, Stargell had the misfortune of playing the bulk of his prime (the late 1960s) in the most difficult hitter's environment since the Deadball era. Compounding the issue was Stargell's home field for the first half of his career: Forbes Field was an enormous park that punished power hitters (at its apex, the right centerfield wall was 408 feet from home plate; the centerfield wall was 430 feet away). Here are Stargell's averages for his first seven full seasons (1963–69; we don't include 1970 because the Pirates moved out of Forbes Field at the All-Star break):

Stargell	G	AB	R	H	2B	3B	HR	RBI	BB	K	BA	OBP	SLG	OPS	OPS+
1963–69	131	452	63	125	21	5	24	81	43	106	.277	.343	.502	.845	137

Stargell was a productive hitter; a 137 OPS+ is excellent. But he went from productive to *profound* once the Pirates left the oppressive expanse of Forbes

11. "What are we going to do? Break it in half?"

Field for the more reasonable, symmetrical dimensions of Three Rivers Stadium.[4]

Stargell's first three seasons in his new home park:

Stargell	G	AB	R	H	2B	3B	HR	RBI	BB	K	BA	OBP	SLG	OPS	OPS+	MVP
1971	141	511	104	151	26	0	48	125	83	154	.295	.398	.628	1.026	185	2
1972	138	495	74	145	28	2	33	112	65	129	.293	.373	.558	.930	164	3
1973	148	522	106	156	43	3	44	119	80	129	.299	.392	**.646**	**1.038**	**186**	2

Three consecutive MVP finishes in the top three, but no wins. Again, he was a victim of timing.

Stargell's peak coincided with the rise of Johnny Bench, Pete Rose, and the rest of the "Big Red Machine." His best chance at the award was probably 1971: With 30 HRs at the all-star break, he seemed destined to challenge Ruth and Maris. Alas, the injury bug bit him again—this time a knee problem that compromised his power over the second half of the season. In a unanimous and questionable decision by the voters, the MVP ultimately went to Joe Torre, who led the league in batting and RBI. Stargell, the engine that powered a division-leading Pittsburgh club, finished a distant second.

Stargell was exactly as good in 1973, again amassing 30 HRs at the break. He failed to maintain his torrid pace over the second half of the season, but still finished as the most productive hitter in the league. In a very close vote, the MVP went to Pete Rose, who hit .338 while playing the game with a maniacal flourish that voters found irresistible. That the Pirates finished third in their division (with a losing record, after three consecutive NL East titles) undoubtedly played a factor in the vote.

The Pittsburgh slugger followed with strong years in 1974–75, but mounting injuries took their toll and he was simply unable to stay on the field long enough to accumulate the counting stats needed for award consideration.

By the time the Pirates captured another division title in 1979, Stargell had arguably been passed over twice in the MVP voting (1971 and 1973). All the while, his fame and legend continued to grow. Now a beloved elder statesman of the game, his unexpected renaissance at 39 gave the voters an opportunity to honor him with a farewell MVP.[5]

Both men were magnanimous when learning of the MVP tie. "I'm glad we could share it," said Hernandez. "The fact that it's a tie makes it all the better because Willie's a great man and it's an honor just for me to have my name next to his."[6]

The typically retiring Stargell said, "I thought it would go to the guys who played every day. But I am happy for myself and for Hernandez.... I know what kind of player he is."

Stargell, who despite being elected to the Hall of Fame is probably underrated as a hitter due to his era and his original home park, *should* be recognized for his achievements as a player and a person—but it was more appropriate to honor him with a statue at the ball park (which the Pirates erected in 2001), not a watered-down MVP he didn't earn.

◆ ◆ ◆

The AL vote wasn't nearly as bad, but it sure wasn't good. MVP Don Baylor led the league in runs (120) and RBI (139) for the AL West division-leading California Angels. In hindsight, Baylor's MVP just seems like a *lazy* pick: Give it to the slugger who drove in a lot of runs, and we'll call it a day.[7]

Baylor's pick is egregious when viewed in context. The AL had a surfeit of strong candidates in 1979, led by Boston centerfielder Fred Lynn, who placed fourth on the ballot. A superficial glance at the table below suggests that the stat lines of the top-five finishers were nearly interchangeable; in reality, Lynn was the most productive hitter in the league, and probably its best player.[8] MVP runner-up Ken Singleton was the offensive linchpin of a powerhouse Baltimore team, while third-place finisher Brett would have to wait until next season to claim his only MVP.

RK	Name	WAR	AB	R	H	2B	3B	HR	RBI	SB	BB	BA	OBP	SLG	OPS	OPS+
1	Baylor	3.7	628	**120**	186	33	3	36	**139**	22	71	.296	.371	.530	.901	145
2	Singleton	5.2	570	93	168	29	1	35	111	3	109	.295	.405	.533	.938	155
3	Brett	8.6	645	119	**212**	42	**20**	23	107	17	51	.329	.376	.563	.939	148
4	Lynn	**8.8**	531	116	177	42	1	39	122	2	82	**.333**	**.423**	**.637**	**1.059**	**176**
5	Jim Rice	6.3	619	117	201	39	6	39	130	9	57	.325	.381	.596	.977	154

Baylor, of course, had a nice season at the plate. You lead the league in runs scored and RBI, you've had a nice season. He was a hard-nosed player and a respected presence in the clubhouse. But MVP? That honor should have gone to Lynn, who led the league in batting, slugging, on-base percentage, adjusted production, and WAR. The list of centerfielders to sweep those categories in a single season is a short one: Tris Speaker (1916), Ty Cobb (1917), and Lynn.

And then there's the small matter of defense: Whereas Baylor was among the worst leftfielders in the league, Lynn was an above-average *centerfielder*. Defensive metrics rate Baylor as costing his team 15 runs as compared with an average outfielder (which is worse than it sounds: Baylor played only 97 games in the field),[9] while Lynn *saved* his team nine runs as compared with the average fielder. On defense alone, Lynn—the best hitter in the league—contributed 24 more runs than Baylor.

None of this made for a compelling argument in the minds of the voters, who all but ignored Lynn's wonderful season (he didn't receive a single first-place vote). Baylor was the productive clean-up hitter on a division-leading squad, while Lynn's Red Sox placed a distant third in the AL East. Along with those league-leading RBI, Baylor locked up the "MVPs should come from play-off teams" vote (it should be noted, the Red Sox finished with a better record than the Angels). With 20 first-place votes, he took the award in a landslide.

According to the law of baseball averages, 1-for-3 (.333) is a fine day at the plate; not so for the bestowing of the sport's highest single-season honor.

12

MVP Mosts (and Leasts)

That Guy.... What's His Name?

The most anonymous MVP? Bob O'Farrell is probably your guy. Catching for the 1926 St. Louis Cardinals, O'Farrell produced an uninspiring .293/.371/.433 line (with seven HR and 68 RBI). He was somehow a near-unanimous pick.

O'Farrell had a few decent years, but 1926 marked the only time in a 21-year career he would receive a *single* MVP vote.

Most Unlikely to Succeed

Probably Zoilo Versalles, 1965. The slick-fielding shortstop had made one All-Star appearance prior to his 1965 MVP season, but his has to stand as the most unlikely MVP season ever. To that point in his career, his OPS+ was 86, meaning he was 15 percent worse than the average hitter. His career .255/.299/.393 slash line prior to 1965 was poor even by the standards of the day.

And then, something clicked. Playing all-world defense at short, Versalles led the league in runs, doubles, triples, total bases, and extra-base hits. He stole 27 bases and was caught just 5 times. He hit 19 HR when this total was rare for a shortstop. Versalles in 1965 had a strong case as the best player in the league, and he was deserving of his MVP.

And that, unfortunately, was it for Zoilo Versalles. He played six injury-compromised seasons after 1965, producing a dreadful .217/.270/.304 line. He accumulated 12.3 total WAR over the course of his 13-year career, with more than half (7.2) coming in his 1965 season.

Worst Timing for the Best Season of Your Career

Joe Jackson had himself a *year* in 1911: The White Sox' rookie from Pickens County, SC hit .408, led the league in on-base percentage, and dazzled the baseball world with his all-around game.[1]

Chalmers Award winner Ty Cobb had himself a better year. Sorry about that, Joe. But keep your nose clean, run with the right crowd, and you'll have a future in this game.

Name	WAR	G	AB	R	H	HR	RBI	SB	BB	BA	OBP	SLG	OPS	OPS+
Ty Cobb	**10.7**	146	591	**147**	**248**	8	**127**	**83**	44	**.420**	.467	**.621**	**1.088**	**196**
Joe Jackson	9.2	147	571	126	233	7		83	41	56	.408	**.468**	.590	1.058	193

Now You're Just Piling On

1913	WAR	W	L	%	ERA	IP	H	R	ER	BB	K	ERA+	FIP	WHIP	K/BB
Johnson	**16**	**36**	7	**.837**	**1.14**	**346**	232	56	44	38	**243**	**259**	**1.90**	**0.780**	**6.39**

Walter Johnson's 16 WAR (14.6 as a pitcher, 1.4 as a hitter; Johnson's .261/.293/.433 batting line was good for a 110 OPS+) is *seven* full wins ahead of the next highest total in the league. To steal a line from Bill James, you could split 1913 Walter Johnson in half, and you'd have two MVPs.

WAR, What Is It Good For?

Cal Ripken tied for dead last on the 1984 ballot despite leading the league with 10 WAR (see Chapter 13 for more).

Good Things Come in Small Packages

At 5'6", Bobby Shantz is the shortest man ever named MVP. Two-time honoree Joe Morgan was listed at an optimistic 5'7", 160 pounds. Johnny Evers, of "Tinker to Evers to Chance" fame, was listed at 5'9", 125 pounds. Evers had the metabolism of a humming bird; he would eat candy bars before going to bed in an attempt to gain weight.

Good Things Come in Large Packages

Baseball Almanac lists two-time honoree Frank Thomas at 6'5", 275 pounds. That's more than two of Johnny Evers.

Yeah, but Intangibles Add Another 40 Points of Batting Average

With an OPS+ of 90, Marty Marion wasn't even a league-average hitter in his 1944 campaign (see Chapter 7 for a list of the worst hitters to ever claim the prize).

A Virtuoso on the Banjo

That would be Johnny Evers, who clubbed one home run in his 1914 Chalmers Award season.

I'm More of a Table-Setter, Really

Evers also holds the record for fewest RBI in an MVP season. He drove in a scant 40 runs in 1914.

Quality Over Quantity

Cubs catcher Gabby Hartnett took 1935 MVP honors despite playing a mere 116 games.

Quality Over Quantity, Pitcher Edition

Dennis Eckersley threw but 80 innings in his 1992 AL MVP campaign.

The View Is Much Better When You're the Lead Dog

Three-time MVPs Stan Musial and Albert Pujols were also four-time runner-ups.

Dr. Strangeglove Award

Worst fielding MVP? We hate to be unkind, but it's between Frank Thomas, 1993; Jason Giambi, 2000; and Juan Gonzalez, 1996/1998. When you hope they hit it to Gonzalez, you know something's very, very wrong.

On the other hand, this trio of sluggers has more than 1300 career home runs among them. That makes up for a lot of misplayed pop-ups.

Three-time MVP Albert Pujols was also runner-up four times (courtesy Keith Allison, https://creativecommons.org/licenses/by-sa/2.0/legalcode).

A Streaking Comet

Rickey was the greatest base stealer. Cobb the most ferocious baserunner. But Mickey Mantle was the fastest.

I Run Just as Hard as I Used To—I Just Don't Go as Fast

Ernie Lombardi, MVP catcher for the 1938 Cincinnati Reds, wasn't just slow: He was a glacier in spikes. He was also known for hitting the most consistently ferocious line drives in the league. Lombardi hit .342 in his MVP season, and may have challenged .400 if he was ambulatory. Infielders, knowing they could throw him out from anywhere on the diamond, played him so deep he once quipped, "Pee Wee Reese was in the league three years before I realized he wasn't an outfielder." How sluggish was Lombardi? His Hall of Fame plaque reads: "Hit .306 … despite slowness afoot."

Why Run If You Don't Have To?

Barry Bonds holds the record for most walks in an MVP—or any other—season, with 232 free passes (120 *intentional*) in 2004.

Making the Most of My Opportunities

MVP George Brett was able to suit up for just 117 games in 1980. He still led the league in WAR (9.4).

Worst Role Model

Plenty to choose from, of course. We'll go with Denny McLain. As early as his 1968 AL MVP campaign, rumors were circulating around the league regarding McLain's connections to criminal elements. He was suspended in 1970 for his part in an illegal book-making operation. In 1985, long after he retired, McLain was found guilty of federal charges involving racketeering, extortion, and narcotics. He avoided jail time, but not for long: A decade later he was convicted for conspiracy, theft, money laundering, and mail fraud in connection with a failed pension fund. He served six years in a federal penitentiary.

Most Virtuous MVP

Roberto Clemente. Clemente, as you know, met his premature end delivering humanitarian aid to earthquake-ravaged Nicaragua.

Most Courageous MVP (and MVP Vote)

Jackie Robinson, 1949. What Jackie Robinson accomplished in his time seems almost impossible.[2]

• • •

The Haves and the Have-Nots

The New York Yankees can claim the most total awards, with 22 plaques earned by 13 players (the Cardinals are second, with 19 awards claimed by 15 players). As of this writing, four teams have never had an MVP on their roster.

A Change in Perspective

Don Mattingly, MVP runner-up, 1986: "A guy like Clemens does a great job every fifth day, but the other four days you're counting on somebody else. It's hard for me to conceive that a guy who is in 33 or 34 games can be as valuable … as an everyday guy who is out there 162 games."

Don Mattingly, Dodgers manager, 2014, on his MVP pitcher Clayton Kershaw: "As a manager, you see how valuable a guy like Clayton is—or Clemens, or whoever that dominant guy is."

Most Valuable Out Machine

Jimmy Rollins made 527 outs the year he was named MVP (2007). To put that into context, there have only been 20 seasons in the history of the game where a player made *more* than 527 outs (Omar Moreno holds the record with 560 outs made in 1980). That's a *lot* of outs. Rollins was still a very productive hitter, due chiefly to his extra-base power. He generated 380 total bases in-between all of those outs.

Once in a Blue Moon

Vida Blue is the youngest MVP in the award's history (age 22). He is also the last "switch-hitter" to take AL MVP honors (the American League introduced the designated hitter in 1974; prior to that, pitchers grabbed a bat).

13
A Certain Kind of Logic

"You're kidding."

Bob Gibson, the Cardinals' ace of aces, had just been informed he was named 1968 National League MVP. Given his numbers, one might think Gibson was playing coy in expressing his disbelief—but it wasn't false modesty on the great pitcher's part: As he pointed out at the time, "Pitchers don't usually win MVP awards."

Bob Gibson: Master on the mound, master of understatement.

What is it with pitchers and the MVP award? When Justin Verlander claimed the AL prize in 2011, he was the first starting pitcher so recognized in 25 seasons. Before Clayton Kershaw in 2014, *46 years* had passed since the voters last named a pitcher MVP of the National League (the incredulous Gibson). It has become nearly impossible for a starter to win the plaque.

It wasn't always so: Looking back across the entire history of the award—beginning with the Chalmers trophy in 1911—pitchers aren't underrepresented in MVP voting. In all, 22 pitchers have won 25 out of a total of 190 MVPs, or about 13 percent of the available hardware. Breaking it down by league, ten pitchers have won 11 out of 94 total MVPs (about 12 percent) in the NL; 12 pitchers have won 14 of 96 awards (about 15 percent) in the AL. But if we narrow our focus to the past 60 years or so, trends clearly emerge along league lines.

MVP voting changed, of course, with the introduction of the Cy Young Award in 1956. Pitchers now had "their own award," and pitcher MVPs, at least in the National League, have essentially dried up. To wit, Don Newcombe (1956), Sandy Koufax (1963), Gibson (1968), and Kershaw (2014) are the only NL pitchers to win the award since 1956.

That's it. No Tom Seaver, no Fergie Jenkins, no Randy Johnson; no Tom Glavine, no Steve Carlton, no Juan Marichal. No 1985 Dwight Gooden. No 1995 Greg Maddux.

This bears repeating: No 1985 Gooden. No 1995 Maddux.

Player	Year	WAR	W	L	WL%	ERA	GS	IP	H	HR	BB	K	ERA+	FIP	WHIP	K/BB
Gooden	1985	13.3	24	4	.857	1.53	35	276.2	198	13	69	268	229	2.13	0.965	3.88
Maddux	1995	9.7	19	2	.905	1.63	28	209.2	147	8	23	181	260	2.26	0.811	7.87

Refusing to recognize a pitcher as the league's most valuable player because they have their "own award" clearly holds a certain kind of logic for a certain kind of voter—especially if they equate MVP with "best position player."[1] Of course, if one were so inclined, one could point out that pitcher *is* a position. The *most important* position. One could also note that the Baseball Writers Association of America is quite clear on the matter of pitcher eligibility for the MVP. From the official BBWAA MVP ballot: *"Keep in mind that all players are eligible for MVP, including pitchers and designated hitters."*[2]

Prior to Kershaw's win (largely a function of no dominant hitting performance in the NL), the MVP pitcher looked to be extinct in the National League. The American League, on the other hand, has been lousy with MVP pitchers. McLain and his 31 wins in 1968, Vida Blue (1971), Rollie Fingers (1981), Willie Hernandez (1984), Roger Clemens (1986), Dennis Eckersley (1992) and the aforementioned Verlander. Seven MVPs, with three of them going to relief pitchers.

Digest that for a second. While the writers are denying Doc Gooden an MVP (see Chapter 15), they're handing out awards to Rollie Fingers, Willie Hernandez, and Dennis Eckersley. A certain kind of logic.

◆ ◆ ◆

Let's start with Fingers in 1981. And let's start with the assertion that relievers should probably never win the MVP (or, realistically, the Cy Young Award). Because relievers are never the most valuable or best player in the league. They are rarely, if ever, the most valuable player on their *own team*.

A pitching truism is that volume equals value; quantity is a measure of quality. In other words, innings matter. And while it's true that not all innings are created equal—high-leverage situations do have a multiplier effect—a league-average starter who throws more than 200 innings will almost always provide significantly more value to a team than all but the very best relievers. And league-average starters never win MVPs. In the National League, *the best pitching seasons in the past 100 years* didn't win MVPs.

Back to Rollie Fingers in 1981. He pitched to a dazzling 1.04 ERA in 78 innings, while leading the league in saves. He was brilliant down the stretch, allowing a total of three runs in his last 37.2 innings, striking out 25 and walking only four. His 4.2 WAR doesn't crack the league's top-10, but he was fourth in pitcher WAR, trailing three starters: Cleveland's Bert Blyleven, Oakland's Steve McCatty and Toronto's Dave Stieb.

1981	pWAR	G	W	L	ERA	SV	IP	H	ER	BB	K	BF	ERA+	FIP	WHIP	K/BB
Fingers	4.2	47	6	3	1.04	**28**	78.0	55	9	13	61	297	333	2.07	0.872	4.69

Fingers was the league's best reliever. Check that: On an inning-by-inning basis, he might have been the league's best *pitcher*.[3] But he wasn't a defensible choice as MVP. It comes down to those innings.

How did Fingers claim the prize? There's that nifty ERA, of course. And then there's the season itself: The bifurcated 1981 season was a farce. On June 12, the player's union called a work stoppage to protest owner attempts to curtail free agency and player arbitration. By the time the two sides reached an accord on August 9, a third of the season was lost.

Rather than allow the division races to resume where they left off, Commissioner Bowie Kuhn, in a misguided attempt to reignite fan interest in a lost season, pushed the "reset" button: The season would be split into two halves. Division leaders at the time of the June 12 work stoppage were guaranteed playoff berths.[4] A second season began August 10, with everybody's slate wiped clean. Teams were now battling for the right to face the "First Season" winners in a best-of-five playoff series to determine who would move on to the League Championship Series.

If it sounds absurd, it sounds about right. The Yankees, for example, finished *fourth* in their division but made the playoffs (eventually losing to the Dodgers in the World Series) due to their division lead as of June 12. Cincinnati, owners of baseball's best overall record at 66–42, failed to make the playoffs—they finished second in their division in *both* halves of the season.

At the end of the year, Milwaukee stood tall amid the wreckage, owning the best record in the AL East division. And the voters gave a lot of the credit to Fingers. They should have given it to Milwaukee's hitters: The Brewers finished 12th out of 14 teams in ERA, but second in runs scored. They won because of their bats.

As for Most Valuable Player, Rickey Henderson (who finished a close second to Fingers on the ballot), Buddy Bell, Dwight Evans, and Bobby Grich were all fine candidates. Prefer a pitcher? McCatty was excellent for division-winner Oakland, pacing the league in ERA and tying for the lead in wins. But in a watered-down, joyless, fractured season, no American League player had a stand-out performance. So Fingers got the nod because … they needed to give it to somebody.[5]

◆ ◆ ◆

Anchoring the bullpen for the 1984 Tigers—a remorseless juggernaut of a team—Guillermo Hernandez had the season of his life, logging 140 innings while pitching to a 1.92 ERA. He led the league with 80 appearances, notching 32 saves (in 33 opportunities). He pitched very well, he pitched every other day, and he was an uninspired choice as league MVP.

1984	pWAR	G	W	L	SV	IP	H	ER	BB	K	ERA	BF	ERA+	FIP	WHIP	K/BB
Hernandez	4.8	80	9	3	32	140.1	96	30	36	112	1.92	548	204	2.58	0.941	3.11

The 1984 Tigers are best known for their record 35–5 start, which essentially rendered the rest of the season moot (with Hernandez making 19 appearances and pitching to a 3.03 ERA during this period). While it's true that they rode one of history's greatest hot streaks to a division title (when seeding "History's Best Teams" bracket, critics point out they "only" went 69–53 over the remaining three quarters of the season), it should be noted that these Tigers were much more than a brilliant two months. Sparky Anderson's club was an exceptionally well-balanced team, leading the league in runs scored while allowing the fewest. They could bludgeon opponents into submission, or beat them with pitching and finesse.

Hernandez, of course, was excellent out of the Tigers' bullpen. Hit hard in April (his ERA stood at 4.86 after 12 appearances), Hernandez found his groove in early May and never lost it, pitching to a superb 1.53 ERA over the final five months of the season (the same ERA, you'll note, that Dwight Gooden spun over 276 innings in 1985).

It would be reasonable to conclude that his workload earned him recognition as his league's most valuable. With 140 innings spread over 80 appearances, one might think Hernandez was a stalwart link to a bygone era, a *tougher* era; a rubber-armed, mustachioed anachronism who mocked the coddled, one-inning-at-a-time relievers of his time with every short-armed screwball he twisted into the dirt.

It's true that Hernandez racked up a ton of innings for a reliever; it's not true that what he did was unique by the standards of the day. Hernandez wasn't even unique on his own team: Tigers set-up man Aurelio Lopez logged 137.2 innings in 71 appearances. Kansas City's Dan Quisenberry (who placed third on the MVP ballot), Cleveland's Ernie Camacho, Oakland's Keith Atherton, New York's Jay Howell, Boston's Bob Stanley—all pitched 100 innings or more out of the bullpen. The league was still a few years away from the specialist revolution wrought by Tony La Russa and his late-80s Oakland bullpen, and firemen were expected to work for their supper.

Again, Hernandez was great. But MVP? Instead of, say, teammate Alan Trammell?

1984	WAR	G	AB	R	H	2B	3B	HR	RBI	SB	CS	BB	K	BA	OBP	SLG	OPS	OPS+
Trammell	6.7	139	555	85	174	34	5	14	69	19	13	60	63	.314	.382	.468	.851	136

Valuing a relief pitcher over an elite shortstop seems like a tough sell. Of course, it depends on who's doing the selling: Sparky Anderson, as tenacious a PR man as ever helmed a major league bench, waged a one-man campaign on his reliever's behalf that just may have earned Hernandez MVP honors (Sparky on the 1984 season: "First I thanked God, then I thanked Hernandez").[6] Anderson's crowing was curious; it's not like he didn't know the value of a player like Trammell. But his marketing and promotion efforts were behind his closer, and Trammell was relegated to a desultory ninth on the ballot.

As weak as the Hernandez pick was, it's not why the 1984 AL ballot makes the "worst-of-all-time" list. Hernandez wasn't a great choice, but he did have a fine season. To find out what makes the 1984 vote so terrible, you have to take the elevator all the way down to the bottom of the ballot. On your way down, you'll pass Juan Beniquez and George Bell. You'll pass Willie Upshaw, Lance Parrish, and Dave Kingman. You'll pass Steve Balboni. And when you finally land in the damp, moldy sub-basement of the ballot, when you finally hit rock bottom, there sits Cal Ripken, Jr. And his 10 WAR.

1984 AL Leaders, WAR

Player	WAR	G	AB	R	H	2B	3B	HR	RBI	BB	K	SB	CS	BA	OBP	SLG
Ripken	**10**	162	641	103	195	37	7	27	86	71	89	2	1	.304	.374	.510
Moseby	7.2	158	592	97	166	28	**15**	18	92	78	122	39	9	.280	.368	.470
Murray	7.1	**162**	588	97	180	26	3	29	110	**107**	87	10	2	.306	**.410**	.509
Trammell	6.7	139	555	85	174	34	5	14	69	60	63	19	13	.314	.382	.468
Mattingly	6.3	153	603	91	**207**	**44**	2	23	110	41	33	1	1	**.343**	.381	.537

How good is 10 WAR? In the American League, the mark has only been exceeded six times since 1984 (three times by position players).

Voters in 1984, of course, had no notion of WAR.[7] So one can't blame them for not leveraging advanced analysis in their consideration for their awards picks.

But how much analysis did one need to see that Ripken was the best player in the league? After two decades of the likes of Derek Jeter, Troy Tulowitzki, and Alex Rodriguez, it's difficult to remember a time when an All-Star shortstop was a wiry acrobat who caught the ball, stole some bases, and hit .260 with five accidental home runs (Ernie Banks the exception, of course). Cal Ripken came along and changed *everything*. He wasn't just great, he was unique. Supposedly far too large a man to field the position, he fielded it beautifully—and he hit like a corner outfielder.

And it wasn't as if Ripken snuck up on people in 1984. Rookie of the Year in 1982, MVP in 1983, he was established as one the game's brightest lights.

His performance in 1984 was every bit as good—maybe better, when factoring defense—as his 1983 MVP campaign.

Ripken	WAR	G	AB	R	H	2B	3B	HR	RBI	BB	K	BA	OBP	SLG	OPS	OPS+
1983	8.2	162	663	121	211	47	2	27	102	58	97	.318	.371	.517	.888	144
1984	10	162	641	103	195	37	7	27	86	71	89	.304	.374	.510	.884	146

In addition to matching his offensive production of the year before, he led all shortstops in putouts, assists and double plays. His defensive range was the best in the league (owner of the best infield arm of his generation, Ripken could play the deepest shortstop in baseball). Ripken was the preeminent defensive player in the league and, by some metrics, the best offensive player in the league (his stat line might seem modest by today's standards; in 1984, it was unheard of for a shortstop other than Ripken to hit like this). What else do you need?

Ripken's only crime was that the Orioles went from first to fifth in the standings—and Ripken went from MVP to invisible man. He was, by a significant margin, the best player in the league; yet 25 men were deemed more valuable than the best shortstop since Honus Wagner.[8]

◆ ◆ ◆

Which stands as the worst MVP vote of all time? The answer really depends on frame of measurement. If total WAR is the criteria, Roger Peckinpaugh in 1925 is the worst of the worst; if the performance delta between the league's best player and the player who was voted MVP is the criteria, then Mickey Cochrane's 1934 selection might serve as a touchstone (Cochrane compiled a mere 4.0 WAR, compared with Lou Gehrig's 10.4). If (alleged) voter spite is the measuring stick, the Joe DiMaggio vote in 1947 rises to the top of the list. If critical thinking is the criteria ... actually, before we get to that, let's play a little "Pitcher A/Pitcher B."

1992	pWAR	W	L	W%	ERA	G	IP	H	R	ER	HR	BB	K	BF	ERA+	FIP	WHIP	K/BB
Pitcher A	2.9	7	1	.875	1.91	69	80	62	17	17	5	11	93	309	195	1.72	0.913	8.45
Pitcher B	3.1	7	4	.636	1.95	79	101.1	76	27	22	5	39	103	414	209	2.58	1.135	2.64

Who was better? It's about as close as it gets: WAR rates them essentially equal, as does adjusted ERA. Pitcher A was more dominant, Pitcher B more durable. Both pitched for division-winning teams. On an inning-by-inning basis, Pitcher A might be a fraction better on the strength of his superb command, but based on overall body of work, this is a toss-up.

Pitcher A, as you know, is Dennis Eckersley. He was named the 1992 MVP and Cy Young winner. Pitcher B is Toronto's Duane Ward. He failed to receive a *single* vote for either award. Ward deserved some recognition for his efforts, but his non-showing on the ballots hews a lot closer to reality than Eckersley's sweep of the hardware. Why the overwhelming affection for Eckersley and the outright rejection of Ward? One stat we failed to include in the table above: Eckersley, in his closer role for Oakland, compiled 51 saves. Ward, a set-up man for Toronto, collected only 12.

Things have (thankfully) changed since 1992; while bullpens have become more specialized, more important, and more dominant than ever, the "save" statistic seems to have been placed in proper context and perspective. Saves, like RBI, are largely a matter of opportunity and circumstance, having more to do with pitcher assignments than pitcher skill (securing three outs to preserve a three-run lead isn't exactly an assignment worthy of Walter Johnson). It seems unlikely that the single-inning closer will ever garner an MVP again. Unfortunately, the damage has been done: The 1992 vote stands among the worst of all time.[9]

1992 MVP Finish, Pitchers

MVP	Player	pWAR	W	L	ERA	G	GS	SV	IP	BB	K	BF	ERA+	FIP	WHIP	K/BB
1	Eckersley	2.9	7	1	1.91	69	0	51	80.0	11	93	309	195	1.72	0.913	8.45
13	Morris	2.9	21	6	4.04	34	34	0	240.2	80	132	1005	101	3.78	1.255	1.65
14	Clemens	**8.8**	18	11	**2.41**	32	32	0	246.2	62	208	989	**174**	**2.54**	**1.074**	**3.35**
19	McDowell	5.3	20	10	3.18	34	34	0	260.2	75	178	1079	122	3.41	1.235	2.37
21	Mussina	8.2	18	5	2.54	32	32	0	241.0	48	130	957	157	3.19	1.079	2.71

The table above lists the five pitchers who received 1992 MVP consideration in order of finish on the ballot. The table speaks volumes, so we'll just point out a few things.

- Eckersley's 2.9 pWAR is the third-lowest of any MVP winner, trailing only Roger Peckinpaugh and Willie Stargell. His innings total is the second-lowest, behind Rollie Fingers (who worked the strike-shortened 1981 season).
- As measured by pWAR, Boston's Roger Clemens was *three times* as valuable as Dennis Eckersley. How is this possible? Simple, really: Clemens pitched three times as many innings as Eckersley, and faced three times as many batters as Eckersley—at about the same rate of effectiveness. Not shown on the table above: Rocket's Red Sox finished with a 73–89 record; Eck's Athletics paced the league at 96–66.
- Mike Mussina, who also pitched three times as many innings for a winning Baltimore squad, was more than twice as valuable as Eckersley. He somehow ended up in the deepest recesses of the ballot, behind ...

- ... Jack Morris, who *also* pitched three times as many innings as Eckersley. Morris' 21–6 record is one of the better statistical "gotchas!" you'll ever come across: He was a league-average pitcher on a very good team.[10] Give Morris extra credit for being a horse, and his 13th place finish on the ballot seems about right.

This isn't to argue that Roger Clemens should have been named AL MVP (although he had the most impressive statistical resume); it's tough to argue a pitcher as MVP when his team finishes last in the standings.[11] This *does* argue that Dennis Eckersley should have finished much, *much* lower on the ballot.[12]

How low? Before we answer, let's mention Cal Eldred. Cal Eldred was a big right-hander who broke in with the Milwaukee Brewers in the early 1990s. In 1992, Eldred had a fine rookie campaign.

Eldred	pWAR	W	L	W%	ERA	G	GS	IP	H	R	ER	HR	BB	K	ERA+	FIP	WHIP	K/BB
1992	4.2	11	2	.846	1.79	14	14	100.1	76	21	20	4	23	62	217	2.81	0.987	2.70

Extrapolated over a full year, that's Cy Young-caliber pitching. *MVP*-caliber pitching. But Eldred didn't make his season debut until mid–July, and accumulated but 100 innings (he faced 394 batters; a major league starter might face upwards of 1000 hitters over a full season). No one in their right mind would consider Eldred one of the more valuable commodities in baseball on less than half a season (and no one did). But it was an excellent start to his major league career (he pitched more innings, faced more batters, and compiled a lower ERA than Eckersley), and he was recognized with a fourth-place finish in the rookie of the year vote. He didn't receive any Cy Young or MVP support.

We should also mention fire-balling rookie reliever Roberto Hernandez, who had an impressive debut for the White Sox.

1992	pWAR	W	L	W%	ERA	G	IP	H	R	ER	HR	BB	K	BF	ERA+	FIP	WHIP	K/BB
Hernandez	2.7	7	3	.700	1.65	43	71	45	15	13	4	20	68	277	236	2.61	0.915	3.40
Eckersley	2.9	7	1	.875	1.91	69	80	62	17	17	5	11	93	309	195	1.72	0.913	8.45

Hernandez got to the majors late (he was a 27-year-old rookie), but made the most of it once he arrived with his excellent work out of the Chicago bullpen. He didn't receive any support for any individual honors, but you can't blame the voters for that: He pitched a scant 71 innings.

All of which is to say, Eckersley wasn't really better, on an inning-by-inning basis, than Duane Ward, Cal Eldred, or Roberto Hernandez. Combined, those three men received *zero* MVP votes. If we feel like beating a dead horse, we can use the tired arms of Terry Leach, Jeff Montgomery, and several others who pitched almost exactly as well (and as often) as Eckersley. Again, combined, these pitchers received not a single tally on the ballot.

The 1992 AL vote doesn't look any better when we turn our attention to the hitters. In order of MVP finish:

MVP	Player	WAR	G	PA	AB	R	H	2B	3B	HR	RBI	BB	BA	OBP	SLG	OPS	OPS+
2	Puckett	**7.1**	160	696	639	104	**210**	38	4	19	110	44	.329	.374	.490	.864	139
3	Carter	2.5	158	683	622	97	164	30	7	34	119	36	.264	.309	.498	.808	120
4	McGwire	6.4	139	571	467	87	125	22	0	42	104	90	.268	.385	**.585**	.970	**176**
5	Winfield	4.1	156	670	583	92	169	33	3	26	108	82	.290	.377	.491	.867	138
6	Alomar	6.6	152	671	571	105	177	27	8	8	76	87	.310	.405	.427	.832	130

If the writers were looking to pin the award on a great player from a winning team, they had several from which to choose: Kirby Puckett, the game's most popular and charismatic player at the time, led all position players in WAR for the second-place Minnesota Twins[13]; Eckersley teammate Mark McGwire was the league's most dominant power hitter (in a sense, the voters were saying Eck's 51 saves were more important to Oakland than Big Mac's 42 home runs); Toronto's dazzling second baseman Roberto Alomar was among the league's most complete players, while teammate Dave Winfield inspired with an improbable renaissance at the age of 40. Not shown above is the superb batting line produced by Chicago's Frank Thomas (.323/.439/.536, leading the league in doubles and walks). All would have made a far, *far* better choice than the Oakland closer as the league's most valuable.[14]

Given the abundance of qualified candidates the Eckersley award is inexplicable.[15] Is it the worst vote in the history of the award? We'll let the reader decide. It's clearly *among* the worst (and it's the worst of the three MVPs handed out to AL relief pitchers).

It's undeniable that Eckersley brought presence to the mound—as the game's best closer playing for the game's best team he brought a sense of ... *finality* to the game whenever he entered the game. This was worth *something*. A top-20 MVP finish seems about right.

MVP Seasons by a Pitcher Since 1956

Since the Cy Young Award was introduced in 1956, 11 pitchers have claimed league MVP. While the AL has been overly generous with the hardware—highlighted by that dubious, decade-long fascination with relief pitchers—NL voters went nearly half a century between pitcher MVPs.

Pitcher MVPs, American League

Name	Year	WAR	W	L	W%	ERA	G	GS	SV	IP	H	ER	BB	K	ERA+	WHIP	K/BB
Verlander	2011	8.4	24	5	.828	2.40	34	34	0	251.0	174	67	57	250	172	0.920	4.39
Clemens	1986	8.9	24	4	.857	2.48	33	33	0	254.0	179	70	67	238	169	0.969	3.55
Eckersley	1992	2.9	7	1	.875	1.91	69	0	51	80.0	62	17	11	93	195	0.913	8.45
Hernandez	1984	4.8	9	3	.750	1.92	80	0	32	140.1	96	30	36	112	204	0.941	3.11
Fingers	1981	4.2	6	3	.667	1.04	47	0	28	78.0	55	9	13	61	333	0.872	4.69
Blue	1971	9.0	24	8	.750	1.82	39	39	0	312.0	209	63	88	301	183	0.952	3.42
McLain	1968	7.4	31	6	.838	1.96	41	41	0	336.0	241	73	63	280	154	0.905	4.44

Denny McLain's 1968 selection was probably the only foregone MVP conclusion: His 31 wins was the most in the major leagues since 1931, and only Bob Welch in 1990 has come within five of that total. Unless pitcher usage patterns change dramatically in the future, McLain is the game's last 30-game winner.

He had a wonderful season, but it's difficult to make a case for it as one of the best in the Cy Young Award era (1956—present). This was "The Year of the Pitcher," with league scoring levels (3.41 runs per game) at their lowest levels *ever*. The league as a whole in 1968 hit .230, also a record for futility. Pitchers ruled the game, and in this context, McLain's season loses a touch of luster. He was workhorse, but his 154 ERA+ and 7.4 WAR are the lowest of any AL starting pitcher to claim MVP honors.

Clemens is the only pitcher on the list whose MVP season *didn't* count as his career year. He was just as good in 1987 and 1992, and better in 1990, 1997, and 1998.

In this company, the presence of Eckersley, Hernandez, and Fingers is jarring.

Pitcher MVPs, National League

Name	Year	WAR	W	L	W%	ERA	G	GS	SV	IP	H	ER	BB	K	ERA+	WHIP	K/BB
Kershaw	2014	8.0	21	3	.875	1.77	27	27	0	198.1	139	39	31	239	197	0.857	7.71
Gibson	1968	11.2	22	9	.710	1.12	34	34	0	304.2	198	38	62	268	258	0.853	4.30
Koufax	1963	10.7	25	5	.833	1.88	40	40	0	311.0	214	65	58	306	159	0.875	5.28
Newcombe	1956	4.5	27	7	.794	3.06	38	36	0	268.0	219	91	46	139	131	0.989	3.02

If the AL has been profligate, the NL has been parsimonious. Bob Gibson joins a trio of Dodgers as the only starting pitchers to claim the award.

You already know about Gibson and his immortal 1968. Koufax was the best pitcher in the world from 1962 to 1966. WAR rates 1963 as his best season, but he was just about as good in 1965–66.

Kershaw was brilliant in 2014, but hardly historic: His 198 innings pitched is the lowest total for any starting pitcher who took MVP (or Cy Young) honors. The Koufax comparisons began in earnest after Kershaw took his second Cy Young award in 2013, and intensified in 2014. He hasn't yet matched the 1962–

66 Koufax peak, but after a superb 2015 (16–7, 2.13 ERA, 301K), he's not far off. If Kershaw can stay healthy, he will go down as the greatest pitcher in Dodgers history.

The outlier in this company is the pioneering Don Newcombe, the first black pitcher to be named rookie of the year (1949), start a World Series game (1949), and win 20 games in the major leagues (1951). Newcombe was the inaugural Cy Young winner in 1956 (prior to 1967, only one award was given for the entirety of major league baseball), and the first pitcher to claim Cy Young and MVP honors in the same season.

He didn't deserve it. "Newk" pitched well in 1956, but his 27 wins are illusory, a function of team performance. The pennant-winning Dodgers scored six or more runs for Newcombe *18* times (exactly half of his starts). Newcombe pitched poorly in these starts—his 4.64 ERA in 118 innings was more than 20 percent worse than the league ERA of 3.77—but his team's largesse rewarded him with a 13–1 record.[16]

Newcombe	W	L	W%	ERA	G	GS	GF	IP	H	R	ER	HR	BB	K	WHIP	K9	K/BB
6+ Runs	13	1	.929	4.64	18	18	0	118.1	118	63	61	20	18	59	1.149	4.5	3.28

In addition, Newcombe *feasted* on the cellar-dwelling teams, going a combined 12–1 with a 1.77 ERA against also-rans Pittsburgh and Chicago. Against the rest of the league, he was a healthy 15–6, but with a pedestrian 3.73 ERA.

Again, Newcombe pitched well in 1956. He was among the league's five best starters—but he was a poor choice for the MVP. Teammate Duke Snider, who led the league in WAR, home runs, on-base percentage, and slugging, would have been the better choice (the Duke finished a curious 10th in the voting).

14

Out of Character: MVP Flukes

As noted earlier, Zoilo Versalles is probably the least likely MVP ever. His 1965 campaign also stands as one of the great fluke seasons of all time.

"Unlikely" vs. "fluke." It may seem like we're splitting semantic hairs, but there is a difference between a fluke season and an unlikely season—and that difference is timing. We judge how *likely* a player's performance is in a given season based on what we've observed about the player to that point in his career; we can't know if the season was a *fluke* until after his career is over, and we can assess his entire body of work.

Take Sammy Sosa. Based on his career performance through 1997, it was highly unlikely—*extraordinarily* unlikely—that Sosa would launch 66 home runs on his way to claiming the 1998 NL MVP.[1] But it obviously wasn't a fluke, as he went on to erase the 60-HR line three times in four seasons.

So think of a fluke season as a one-off, something never to be repeated. There are tons of examples sprinkled throughout the history of the game: Earl Webb, for instance, hit a record 67 doubles in 1931; he didn't exceed 30 in any other season. Brady Anderson and his 50 home runs in 1996; he never collected even half as many in any other of his 15 seasons.

An accounting of the "flukiest" and/or most unlikely MVP seasons includes the following (statistics through 2015 season):

Joe Medwick, 1937

Medwick	WAR	G	AB	R	H	2B	3B	HR	RBI	SB	CS	BB	K	BA	OBP	SLG	OPS	OPS+
1937	8.5	*156*	*633*	*111*	*237*	*56*	10	*31*	*154*	4	—	41	50	*.374*	.414	*.641*	*1.056*	*182*
Career	55.5	1984	7635	1198	2471	540	113	205	1383	42	—	437	551	.324	.362	.505	.867	134

We'll call this one a minor fluke. Medwick was a very good hitter who had produced several strong seasons leading up to his monstrous 1937 campaign. He led the league in RBI three times, doubles three times (including 64 in 1936), and hits twice. But no one would have predicted a Triple Crown for the St. Louis leftfielder. Those 31 HR (tying Mel Ott for the league lead) represent the only time in Medwick's 17-year career he hit more than 23. Medwick in 1937 also posted career highs in hits, RBI, on-base percentage, and slugging.

Lou Boudreau, 1948

Boudreau	WAR	G	PA	AB	R	H	2B	3B	HR	RBI	BB	K	BA	OBP	SLG	OPS	OPS+
1948	**10.4**	152	676	560	116	199	34	6	18	106	98	9	.355	.453	.534	.987	165
Career	63	1646	7024	6029	861	1779	385	66	68	789	796	309	.295	.380	.415	.795	120

Despite being one of the slower players in baseball, Boudreau was an outstanding defensive shortstop. Considered the smartest player in the game, he compensated for his lack of quickness with a strong arm and unerring defensive positioning.

Boudreau was a great player, but no one saw this coming; he was Wagneresque in 1948. As player-manager for the Cleveland Indians, Boudreau had compiled a career .292 batting average heading into the 1948 season. He had never hit more than ten home runs in a season, never scored even 100 runs. Leading his team to the 1948 championship, Boudreau set career highs in runs, hits, home runs, RBI, walks, average, on-base and slugging percentages, and adjusted production. For every one of his nine (total) strikeouts on the season, Boudreau walked 11 times. His numbers plummeted in 1949—in fact, Boudreau hit .275 with a *combined* ten HR from 1949 to 1952. As measured by WAR, Boudreau's 1948 ranks among the five best seasons ever for a shortstop.

◆ ◆ ◆

Phil Rizzuto, 1950

Rizzuto	WAR	G	AB	R	H	2B	3B	HR	RBI	BB	K	BA	OBP	SLG	OPS	OPS+
1950	6.7	155	617	125	200	36	7	7	66	92	39	.324	.418	.439	.857	122
Career	40.6	1661	5816	877	1588	239	62	38	58	651	398	.273	.351	.355	.706	93

Boudreau's only rival for the honorary title of best defensive shortstop in baseball. A fluke year, yes—Rizzuto was a *much* better hitter in 1950 than at any other point in his career—but you can't say Rizzuto's MVP was "unlikely." He finished a solid second in the voting to Ted Williams the season prior, so there's a sense the voters were looking for a reason to give the Scooter an MVP. He obliged them with a career year in 1950. "This club can get along without me

14. *Out of Character: MVP Flukes* 143

or anyone else—except one," said teammate Tommy Henrich. "We just keep praying that nothing happens to that little scamp at shortstop."

About that second-place finish in 1949:

RK	Name	1st	Share	WAR	G	AB	R	H	HR	RBI	SB	BB	BA	OBP	SLG	OPS	OPS+
1	Williams	13.0	81%	*9.1*	155	566	150	194	43	159	1	162	.343	*.490*	*.650*	*1.141*	*191*
2	Rizzuto	5.0	52%	2.9	153	614	110	169	5	65	18	72	.275	.352	.358	.711	88

Detroit's George Kell hit .34291 to Williams' .34275, costing the Splinter his third Triple Crown.[2] Williams received his well-deserved MVP, but *five* first-place votes for Rizzuto? *Three* first-place votes for Yankees reliever Joe Page? Absurd. Yet long-time *New York Times* columnist Arthur Daley called the Williams selection "incomprehensible," a "cruel blow" to Rizzuto and Page, the "two most deserving candidates." "Incomprehensible" is one word to describe Daley's thinking.[3]

JIM KONSTANTY, 1950

Over the course of his unique 13-year career, Konstanty struck out 268 batters and walked 269 in 945 innings.

Four pitchers with a minimum of 900 IP have compiled *exactly* the same number of career strikeouts and walks. As you might expect, none of them were all that great. A K/BB ratio of 1:1 means you're walking lots of batters while striking out very few.

Player	IP	BB	K	ERA	ERA+
Ned Garver	2477.1	881	881	3.73	112
Sheldon Jones	920	413	413	3.96	101
Atley Donald	932	369	369	3.52	107
Al Smith	1662.1	587	587	3.72	99

Ned Garver was the best of the bunch. Pitching for some terrible teams, Garver finished with a career record of 129–157, despite an adjusted ERA that was 12 percent better than the league average. Garver pulled off quite the magic trick in 1951, compiling a 20–12 record for a pathetic St. Louis Browns club that went 52–102. Garver became the first pitcher to win 20 games for a team that lost more than 100. He struck out 84 while walking 96.

BOBBY SHANTZ, 1952

Shantz	pWAR	W	L	W%	ERA	G	GS	IP	H	ER	HR	BB	K	ERA+	FIP	WHIP	K/BB
1952	*9.1*	24	7	.774	2.48	33	33	279.2	230	77	21	63	152	159	3.00	*1.048*	*2.41*

"The Tiny Titan." "The Little Lefty." "The Magnificent Midget." "The Wee Wizard." Nicknames were a little less enlightened in Shantz's day.[4] But you get it: Shantz was a small guy (listed at 5'6", 140 pounds). In addition to leading the league in wins, walks plus hits per nine innings, and strikeout-to-walk ratio, Shantz placed in the top-five in just about every other meaningful pitching category. He won 24 games for a fourth-place Philadelphia Athletics team that went a dreary 79–75 (and they weren't as good as their record suggests; the Athletics went 54–67 in games Shantz *didn't* start). He was something of a surprise pick—not because he wasn't deserving, but because he toiled for a second-division team. Shantz would pay a heavy price for his excellence.

Bobby Shantz Through August 5, 1952

W	L	W%	G	GS	CG	IP	H	R	ER	BB	K	HR	ERA	oppBA	oppOBP	oppSLG
20	3	.870	23	23	21	203	143	44	35	41	114	13	1.55	.198	.244	.284

Bobby Shantz After August 5, 1952

W	L	W%	G	GS	CG	IP	H	R	ER	BB	K	HR	ERA	oppBA	oppOBP	oppSLG
4	4	.500	10	10	6	76.2	87	43	42	22	38	8	4.93	.289	.340	.389

After Shantz won his 20th game on August 5, Manager Jimmy Dykes told reporters: "He's the greatest I ever saw in all the time I've been here, and that's been 35 years. He's a marvel."

There is no evidence to suggest he then added, out of earshot, "Now I must destroy that which I love."

There *is* ample evidence that Dykes overworked his diminutive star: Through August 5th, Shantz completed an astonishing 21 of 23 starts (91 percent), including a 14-inning affair on May 30.[5] By late August, the workload was clearly taking its toll: Shantz surrendered 29 runs in 30 innings over a four-start stretch beginning August 31. He rebounded with one last great start, a September 19 shutout against Casey Stengel's Yankees—but with hindsight, it was clear the damage had been done.[6]

The following season, Dykes and the Athletics continued the pattern: Shantz completed four of his first five starts, pitching reasonably well. But the wheels started to fall off May 8, when he was lit up by the lowly Senators for eight runs in seven innings. He was just as bad over his next two starts before he felt something pop in his shoulder on May 21. Shantz couldn't know it at the time, but he had just begun a four-year injury nightmare: He would miss more than half the 1953 season with arm woes, all but two games in 1954, and about half the season in 1955. In 1956, the Athletics tried to convert him to a reliever, with mixed results. He was able to take the mound for 45 appearances, but pitched to a league-average 4.35 ERA.

In the four seasons since his MVP campaign, Shantz had won 13, lost 26 and compiled a 4.42 ERA. No one doubted his courage, but no one was laying odds that he would ever pitch well again. The Athletics finally cut ties with him in 1957, packaging the damaged lefty as part of a 13-player deal with the Yankees.[7]

And then, something remarkable happened: Casey Stengel, that shrewd old wizard, was somehow able to coax 21 starts and 173 innings out of Shantz, who rewarded him with a league-leading 2.45 ERA (originally slated for bullpen duty, Shantz was pressed into starting service when Yankees ace Whitey Ford went down with an injury). It bordered on the unbelievable, and the BBWAA named the well-liked Shantz the American League's Comeback Player of the Year.

A rejuvenated Shantz would pitch well for the Yankees for three seasons (primarily out of the bullpen after 1957). He was claimed by Washington in the 1960 expansion draft and immediately traded to Pittsburgh, where he began an itinerant run that saw him pitch for five clubs in four years, providing 70–80 innings of effective left-handed relief every season.

Shantz retired after the 1964 season. He never again approached the dizzying heights of his 1952 MVP season, but it is something of a miracle of perseverance that he was able to build a nice 16-year career on that slight frame and damaged arm.

Roger Maris, 1961

Maris was known for his strong arm.

Brooks Robinson, 1964

Robinson	WAR	G	AB	R	H	2B	3B	HR	RBI	BB	K	BA	OBP	SLG	OPS	OPS+
1964	8.1	*163*	612	82	194	35	3	28	*118*	51	64	.317	.368	.521	.889	145
Career	78.3	2896	10654	1232	2848	482	68	268	1357	860	990	.267	.322	.401	.723	104

Robinson is a deserving member of the Hall of Fame, but you probably think he's a better hitter than he really was. He was every inch as good with the glove as you've heard.

Zoilo Versalles, 1965

The *Pittsburgh Press* said of Versalles on October 7, 1965, "In 1964, Versalles made the All-Star team for the first time, replacing Luis Aparicio of the Orioles as the acknowledged No. 1 shortstop. Long before that, Zoilo would say, 'I think I'm the best. My arm, she is a rifle. Aparicio? Zoilo can make all the plays he can. Why is he the big hero and Zoilo is nothing?'" The same article continued, "'If we're playing the Yankees,' a teammate once noted, 'he's sensational. If we're playing the Athletics, he just stands around.'"

Recognized by many as the greatest MVP fluke of all time.

VIDA BLUE, 1971

Blue	pWAR	W	L	W%	ERA	G	GS	IP	H	ER	HR	BB	K	ERA+	FIP	WHIP	K/BB
1971	9.0	24	8	.750	**1.82**	39	39	312	209	63	19	88	301	183	**2.20**	**0.952**	3.42
Career	45	209	161	.565	3.27	502	473	3343.1	2939	1213	263	1185	2175	108	3.43	1.233	1.84

Vida Blue struck out 301 batters in his 1971 MVP campaign. It was the only time in his productive career he'd exceed even *200* strikeouts in a season. A mild fluke, as Blue was excellent in 1976 (7.7 WAR) and very good in 1978 (5.8 WAR).

GUILLERMO HERNANDEZ, 1984

Hernandez	pWAR	W	L	W%	ERA	G	SV	IP	H	R	ER	HR	BB	K	ERA+	WHIP	K/BB
1984	4.8	9	3	.750	1.92	**80**	**32**	140.1	96	30	30	6	36	112	204	0.941	3.11
Career	16.6	70	63	.526	3.38	744	147	1044.2	952	431	392	97	349	788	119	1.245	2.26

Sparky Anderson said of the Tigers' 1984 season, "First I thanked God. Then I thanked Hernandez."

Hernandez would pay a price for Anderson's well-intentioned hype: As the lefthander's effectiveness waned in 1986–87, the fans turned on their former favorite. Frustrated by the constant heckling (they needled Hernandez—who repeatedly asked the media to call him by his given name, *Guillermo*—with signs that read "Send Willie Home"), Hernandez publically asked for a trade. The Tigers never obliged, and he endured several unpleasant years before an arm injury finished his career with Detroit in 1989.

KEVIN MITCHELL, 1989

Mitchell	WAR	G	AB	R	H	2B	3B	HR	RBI	CS	BB	K	BA	OBP	SLG	OPS	OPS+
1989	7.8	154	543	100	158	34	6	**47**	**125**	4	87	115	.291	.388	**.635**	**1.023**	**189**
Career	33.1	1223	4134	630	1173	224	25	234	760	31	491	719	.284	.360	.520	.880	142

For those who saw the overweight, immobile Mitchell at the tail end of his career, it might be hard to process that he once played shortstop. In fact, Mitchell played *every* position—save catcher and pitcher—for the 1986 World

Champion Mets, earning him the nickname "World" (as in, "he can play anywhere in the...").

Mitchell's 1989 MVP season with the San Francisco Giants might fall on the "unlikely" side of the unlikely/fluke fence.[8] His power totals were certainly unexpected: Entering the season, Mitchell's previous career high in home runs was 22. But if we consider 1989 a fluke, it's not because it was an outlier in terms of performance. He was the league's most devastating hitter in 1989; he was every bit as good in 1993–94, when injuries and a work stoppage limited him to fewer than 100 games per season (Mitchell in fact never played as many as 100 games a year after his age-29 season).

Two things conspired to keep Mitchell from being remembered as one of the great hitters of his generation: Health and attitude.

Mitchell thrived on the field during his time with the Giants, leading all of baseball in home runs, slugging, and adjusted production from 1989 to 1991. But allegations of disturbing off-the field behavior plagued Mitchell over the course of his San Francisco tenure, and he had several highly publicized scrapes with the law.[9]

Mitchell was never tried for a crime, but by 1991 the Giants had reached their limit, trading him in the off-season to the Seattle Mariners for what amounted to pennies on the dollar. In addition to Mitchell's off-field transgressions, the Giants accused him of heavy drinking, clashing with teammates and organizational personnel, and, in what was later revealed as the proverbial last straw, begging out of games. "Headaches, stomach aches, it's always something with this guy," said an exasperated Al Rosen, then general manager of the club. "We're paying him more than $3 million, telling everybody what a tough guy he is, and then this is what happens?"[10]

Hangovers aside, Mitchell was also a victim of circumstances beyond his control, making annual and extended trips to the disabled list with knee, shoulder, wrist, and groin injuries (his ballooning weight certainly didn't help).

He would last but one injury-truncated season with the Mariners before being traded to the Reds, where he was once again one of the league's best hitters. Mitchell was enjoying his best year in 1994 (.326/.429/.681 with 30 HR in 95 games) when the player's strike guillotined the season August 12.

When the work stoppage extended into the winter of 1995, Mitchell signed a record $4.5 million free-agent contract with the Daiei Hawks of Japan's Pacific League. It was a short-lived disaster: Mitchell abandoned the Hawks in late May over an injury dispute. Mitchell claimed he couldn't play due to a sore knee; the team disagreed. When the Hawks ordered him to rehab his knee with a minor-league affiliate, Mitchell packed his bags and flew back to the United States. He sat out the rest of the 1995 season.

He returned to MLB the following year, but was never again in playing shape. Brief stops followed with the Red Sox, Reds (where he was suspended for the final three weeks of the 1996 season for failing to join the team on a road trip), Indians, and finally, the Athletics.[11] Mitchell revealed in a 2009 interview that he had been diagnosed with type-2 diabetes shortly after being released by the Athletics in 1998. The untreated disease doubtlessly compromised his play, but by then too many bridges had been burned, too many excuses rendered, too many mistakes made.

Mitchell played for eight teams in 13 seasons, which tells you everything you need to know about his comportment and his talent. Had he stayed healthy and out of trouble, he might have put together an Albert Belle–type career. He was a wonderful hitter.

Terry Pendleton, 1991

Pendleton	WAR	G	AB	R	H	2B	3B	HR	RBI	BB	K	BA	OBP	SLG	OPS	OPS+
1991	6.1	153	586	94	187	34	8	22	86	43	70	*.319*	.363	.517	.880	139
Career	28.2	1893	7637	851	1897	356	39	140	946	486	979	.270	.316	.391	.707	92

There's really no other way to say it: Pendleton was a lousy hitter through 1990, averaging .259/.308/.356 over his first seven seasons. But he was so good with the glove he provided a net positive value to his teams. No one—*no one*—would consider Pendleton a potential MVP candidate at the age of 30, but the third baseman, like the fabled "Worst to First" 1991 Braves, surprised everyone with a strong season at the plate.

"I never dreamed about winning the National League MVP award," said a grateful Pendleton. Referring to the slim voting margin between himself and MVP runner-up Barry Bonds, Pendleton was refreshingly forthright: "If we had finished second, I don`t think I'd be standing here now."

He was almost as good in 1992, but he regressed with the bat after that and never approached anything resembling a strong offensive performance again. He finished his 16-year career with an adjusted OPS of 92, meaning he was 8 percent worse than a league-average hitter.

Ken Caminiti, 1996

Caminiti	WAR	G	AB	R	H	2B	3B	HR	RBI	BB	K	BA	OBP	SLG	OPS	OPS+
1996	7.6	146	546	109	178	37	2	40	130	78	99	.326	.408	.621	1.028	174
Career	33.3	1760	6288	894	1710	348	17	239	983	727	1163	.272	.347	.447	.794	116

Caminiti set career highs—by significant margins—in just about every meaningful offensive category.

Joe Mauer, 2009

Mauer	WAR	G	AB	R	H	2B	3B	HR	RBI	BB	K	BA	OBP	SLG	OPS	OPS+
2009	7.8	138	523	94	191	30	1	28	96	76	63	**.365**	**.444**	**.587**	**1.031**	171
Career	47.8	1456	5425	817	1697	343	24	119	755	743	772	.313	.394	.451	.845	129

Joe Mauer was an excellent hitter the minute he stepped onto a major league field at the age of 21. He was a *legendary* hitter in 2009, posting one of the great seasons ever by a catcher. Even in the context of his fantastic career, Mauer's 2009 season stands as an outlier: His 28 home runs are more than double his next highest total (13); his .587 slugging dwarfs his next best mark of .507 and is 136 points higher than his career percentage.

Top-10 Seasons by a Catcher as Ranked by WAR

RK	Player	Year	WAR	G	AB	R	H	2B	3B	HR	RBI	BB	K	BA	OBP	SLG	OPS
1	Mike Piazza	1997	8.7	152	556	104	201	32	1	40	124	69	77	.362	.431	.638	1.070
2	Gary Carter	1982	**8.6**	154	557	91	163	32	1	29	97	78	64	.293	.381	.510	.890
3	Johnny Bench	1972	8.6	147	538	87	145	22	2	**40**	**125**	100	84	.270	.379	.541	.920
4	Joe Mauer	2009	**7.8***	138	523	94	191	30	1	28	96	76	63	**.365**	**.444**	**.587**	**1.031**
5	Johnny Bench	1974	7.8	160	621	108	174	38	2	33	**129**	80	90	.280	.363	.507	.870
6	Darrell Porter	1979	7.6	157	533	101	155	23	10	20	112	**121**	65	.291	.421	.484	.905
7	Gary Carter	1984	7.4	159	596	75	175	32	1	27	**106**	64	57	.294	.366	.487	.853
8	Johnny Bench	1970	**7.4**	158	605	97	177	35	4	**45**	148	54	102	.293	.345	.587	.932
9	Buster Posey	2012	**7.3**	148	530	78	178	39	1	24	103	69	96	**.336**	.408	.549	.957
10	Carlton Fisk	1972	7.3	131	457	74	134	28	**9**	22	61	52	83	.293	.370	.538	.909

*Led *position* players; Kansas City right-hander Zack Greinke led all players with 10.4 pWAR.

15

Meet the Mets, Greet the ... Team That Has Never Had an MVP

In the long, absurd, glorious, convoluted history of the MVP award, four teams have failed to capture honors even once: The New York Mets, the Miami Marlins, the Tampa Bay Rays, and the Arizona Diamondbacks.

As of this writing (just prior to the 2016 season), these teams have played a combined 113 seasons without an MVP; 113 seasons in which thousands of players have taken the field, a composite roster comprising dozens of All-Stars and several Hall of Famers. As improbable as it may seem, more than a century of assembled talent has failed to produce a player deemed "most valuable."

Is it sheer coincidence? Unfortunate timing? Voter ineptitude? A combination of all three?

NEW YORK METS: 54 SEASONS

At 54 seasons and counting, the Mets have cultivated the longest MVP drought in history. Mets fans are no strangers to this type of multi-generational futility (half a century passed before Johan Santana threw the team's first and only no-hitter). Long consigned to second-class citizenry in a city besotted with the cross-town Yankees, the Mets—with two glorious exceptions in 1969 and 1986—have stood as stalwarts of sorrow. This is especially true when it comes to MVP voting: The Mets have seriously challenged for the award only once in their colorful history; meanwhile, 13 Yankees players have captured the award a combined 22 times, with five of those trophies coming since the 1962 debut of the Metropolitans.[1]

This MVP futility is undeserved. Dwight Gooden's 1985 season has a case

15. Meet the Mets, Greet the ... Team That Has Never Had an MVP

for best pitching season of the past 100 years.[2] It is probably the most *famous* pitching season of the past 100 years.[3] It is, by one measure (13.3 total WAR), the single best season by *any player at any position* since Babe Ruth's 1923 campaign.[4] Better than anything put up by Mantle, Bonds, Williams, or Mays. Better than every Triple Crown titlist. Better than every .400 hitter. Better than every 60-homer slugger. He was clearly baseball's most valuable commodity in 1985.

He achieved his success with essentially two pitches: A four-seam comet of a fastball, and that *curveball*. Great curveballs buckle a hitter's knees; Gooden's bucked the laws of physics.[5]

These two weapons produced this line.

1985	WAR	W	L	W%	ERA	G	GS	CG	SHO	IP	H	HR	BB	K	ERA+	WHIP	FIP	K/BB
Gooden	13.3*	24	4	.857	1.53	35	35	16	8	276.2	198	13	69	268	229	0.965	2.13	3.88

*Of his 13.3 total WAR, 12.2 came from his excellence as a pitcher; he padded his total a bit with his contributions at the plate and in the field.

Gooden's performance was all the more impressive considering the pressure bearing down on his shoulders. The Mets were locked in a thrilling divisional race with arch-rival St. Louis, with the two teams trading first place several times over the course of the summer. Entering September, the Cardinals clung to a two-game lead, which they would relinquish, then recapture, several times over the final few weeks of the season. With every game a "must-win," Gooden took the mound six times during the season's final month. His body of work during the stretch drive:

Gooden	GS	W	L	IP	H	ER	BB	K	HR	ERA	OppBA	OppOBP	OppSLG
9/6–10/2/1985	6	4	0	53	33	2	13	49	0	0.34	.175	.228	.212

For those counting, Gooden surrendered two earned runs in 53 innings. His 0.34 ERA might *undersell* his dominance, as he didn't allow an earned run until his final start of the season (a complete-game victory against the Cardinals).

On a start-by-start basis, it reads as fiction.

- September 6: Dominates the Dodgers with nine scoreless innings (10K, no walks), but Fernando Valenzuela matches him inning-for-inning (Fernando went *11 innings* this storied night). Gooden exits with a no-decision.
- September 11: Gooden blanks the Cardinals for nine innings; again, his teammates can't score and he leaves with a no-decision. The Cardinals' John Tudor throws ten scoreless innings, and the Mets lose 1–0.[6]
- September 16: In his third consecutive 9-inning, no-run game, Gooden hurls a two-hit, 11K masterpiece against the Phillies.

- September 21: Gooden goes eight, allowing an unearned run to the Pirates.
- September 26: Another shutout, this time against the Cubs.
- October 2: In the biggest game of the year, Gooden spins a two-run, 10K complete game against the Cardinals. The victory leaves the Mets one game behind with four to play. The Mets lose three of their last four to concede to division.
- November 16: Gooden turns 21. Yep. The kid was *three years out of high school* in 1985.

Gooden was the unanimous Cy Young winner that year. He fared much worse in the MVP vote, placing a distant (and disrespectful) fourth.

Fourth. Behind MVP winner Willie McGee (who led the league with a .353 average while playing a sturdy centerfield for the Cardinals), Cincinnati's Dave Parker, and Los Angeles' Pedro Guerrero (both of whom had very nice, very forgettable seasons). In one of the worst ballots in MVP history, "Dr. K" received a single first-place vote (utterly confounding, given the fact that each city receives two MVP ballots—one of two New York writers decided Dwight Gooden *wasn't* the most valuable player in the league).

Gooden didn't just lap the field with his performance on the mound—he was a national media phenomenon in 1985, and baseball's best story: A lanky, soft-spoken 20-year-old with an electrifying mound presence; the shy kid from Tampa whose magic arm made the Mets *relevant* again (and relegated the Yankees to second-in-the-city status). Gooden was also the unquestioned *box-office* MVP: The Mets averaged 40,072 paying fans in Gooden's 18 home starts; 34,005 in all others.

Despite ticking every box on the imaginary MVP checklist—dominant performance, winning team, great narrative, clutch down the stretch—the young pitcher was an MVP afterthought.

While Gooden produced the single best season in Mets history, several teammates have fared better in the MVP voting.

- 1969: Tom Seaver, the greatest Met of them all, placed a very close second to San Francisco's slugging first baseman Willie McCovey (a fine choice for the award). Seaver and McCovey each received 11 first-place votes, with McCovey receiving stronger all-around support at the top of the ballot. Seaver was even better in 1971 (ninth in the voting) and 1973 (eighth), receiving tepid support both years.
- 1988: Darryl Strawberry (a fairly close second) and Kevin McReynolds (an undeserving third) crowded the top of the ballot in 1988, finishing

15. Meet the Mets, Greet the ... Team That Has Never Had an MVP

behind the Dodgers' Kirk Gibson (whose intense style of play and brooding inapproachability had reporters waxing nostalgic for the days of Cobb and John McGraw). Gibson is a perfectly defensible choice for MVP, even if his raw offensive totals seem quaint by today's standards. His all-around game in a tough hitter's environment placed him among the league's best players.

- 2000: When it comes to MVP balloting, Mike Piazza has been a victim of capricious timing. Here are Piazza's stats in the four seasons he finished in the top-four of MVP voting (the first three with the Dodgers). Keep in mind, he was a playing his home games in two of the most unforgiving hitter's parks in baseball (LA's Dodgers Stadium, New York's Shea Stadium):

Piazza	WAR	G	AB	R	H	2B	3B	HR	RBI	BB	K	BA	OBP	SLG	OPS	OPS+	MVP
1995	6.2	112	434	82	150	17	0	32	93	39	80	.346	.400	.606	1.006	*172*	4
1996	5.4	148	547	87	184	16	0	36	105	81	93	.336	.422	.563	.985	166	2
1997	8.7	152	556	104	201	32	1	40	124	69	77	.362	.431	.638	1.070	*185*	2
2000	5.1	136	482	90	156	26	0	38	113	58	69	.324	.398	.614	1.012	155	3

It's hard to say Piazza was robbed in any of these seasons. He probably should have finished second in 1995 (Barry Larkin, a great player but a terrible choice for MVP, took honors; Greg Maddux should have won).

Piazza had a case in 1996, but so did MVP-select Ken Caminiti, Barry Bonds, and several others.

The following year was probably Piazza's strongest case for the award. But Colorado's Larry Walker also put up extraordinary numbers in 1997, with strong defense and superb base running. It's tough to argue against Larry Walker as NL MVP in 1997.

1997	WAR	G	AB	R	H	2B	3B	HR	RBI	SB	CS	BB	BA	OBP	SLG	OPS	OPS+
Walker	9.8	153	568	143	208	46	4	*49*	130	33	8	78	.366	*.452*	*.720*	*1.172*	178

Walker wasn't an altitude-induced mirage, either. He was just as good away from Coors Field.

1997	G	AB	R	H	2B	3B	HR	RBI	SB	CS	BB	BA	OBP	SLG	OPS
Home	78	302	82	116	30	4	20	68	17	3	36	.384	.460	.709	1.169
Away	75	266	61	92	16	0	29	62	16	5	42	.346	.443	.733	1.176

Piazza, now with the Mets, was a better choice for the award in 2000 than winner Jeff Kent—but Bonds was the best player in the league that year.

Despite producing some of the best seasons ever by a catcher, Piazza never claimed an MVP. Inducted into the Hall of Fame in 2016, he'll be able to console himself with the knowledge that he is the best hitter to ever play his position.

Miami Marlins: 23 Seasons

The Marlins have never really come close to claiming the award, but with outfielder Giancarlo Stanton under contract through 2027, an MVP seems inevitable.

- 2014: On his way to becoming the best player in franchise history, Stanton places a respectable second behind Clayton Kershaw. Leading the league in home runs, RBIs, walks, and slugging in early September, Stanton was probably the MVP favorite heading into the stretch drive; a season-ending fastball to the face torpedoed his chances, and Kershaw took honors with room to spare.
- 2009: Hanley Ramirez captured a pyrrhic second-place finish (the vote gap between unanimous winner Albert Pujols and runner-up Ramirez was greater than the gap between Ramirez and 20th place on the ballot). This isn't a knock on Ramirez, who was one of the best players in the league. Pujols was otherworldly.

Arizona Diamondbacks: 18 Seasons

Randy Johnson is the best—and most valuable—player in the 18-year history of the Arizona franchise. Each of his four consecutive Cy Young seasons deserved MVP consideration. His best finish was a seventh-place showing in 2002.

Johnson	pWAR	W	L	W-L%	ERA	GS	CG	IP	H	R	ER	BB	K	ERA+	WHIP	K/BB
1999	9.2	17	9	.654	2.48	35	12	271.2	207	86	75	70	364	184	1.020	5.20
2000	8.1	19	7	.731	2.64	35	8	248.2	202	89	73	76	347	181	1.118	4.57
2001	10	21	6	.778	2.49	34	3	249.2	181	74	69	71	372	188	1.009	5.24
2002	10.9	24	5	.828	2.32	35	8	260.0	197	78	67	71	334	195	1.031	4.70

The table above represents one of the great peaks any pitcher has ever produced. Compare any of these four seasons to Clayton Kershaw's 2014 MVP campaign, and Johnson rates as superior by almost any measure. Kershaw posted lower ERAs (pitching far fewer innings in a *much* friendlier environment), but Johnson's overall value was significantly greater.

"The Big Unit" deserved better in the voting, but it's hard to make an argument for Johnson as MVP in any of those years, with the possible exception of 1999 (when he led the league in WAR, but placed 15th on the ballot).[7] As noted above, Bonds and Piazza each had a strong claim to the award in 2000 (though Johnson was a better choice than winner Jeff Kent), and Bonds was the clear-cut MVP in 2001–02. Chalk the D-Backs' lack of MVP hardware

15. Meet the Mets, Greet the ... Team That Has Never Had an MVP

up to timing (and the voter aversion to recognizing that pitchers provide value).

Only two Diamondbacks have cracked the top-three in MVP voting.

- 2001: Luis Gonzalez, who produced one of those dubious, monster, Selig-era seasons in 2001, finishing a distant third in the voting. His 57 HRs were good for third in the league, 16 behind Bonds.[8]
- 2013: First baseman Paul Goldschmidt has a wonderful season, pacing the league in home runs, RBI, slugging, and adjusted production. He places a distant second in the vote to the Pirates' Andrew McCutchen.
- Goldschmidt is even better in 2015, but his 8.8 WAR (to go with a .321/.435/.570 batting line) again nets him a distant second place to unanimous MVP pick Bryce Harper.

Tampa Rays: 19 Seasons

The Tampa Rays have never come close to producing an MVP over their 18-year history. Ben Zobrist, a solid hitter and renaissance-man defender (he was very good at just about every position on the field) owns the two best seasons by WAR in team history (2009, 2011). Zobrist was a fine player, but it was a stretch to consider him an MVP-caliber force (and the voters didn't—his best finish was eighth on the 2009 ballot).

Evan Longoria is the best player in the team's brief history. Long considered an MVP-in-waiting, inconsistency and injuries have "relegated" Longoria to merely excellent. His two sixth-place finishes (in 2010 and 2013) represent the Rays' best showing in the MVP vote.

And a Child Shall Lead Them

Days shy of his 23rd birthday at season's end, Bryce Harper in 2015 became the youngest *unanimous* MVP in the award's history. With a performance for the ages, the brash and boisterous outfielder ended nearly half a century of MVP frustration for a Washington, D.C., franchise that traces its lineage back almost 50 years to the vibrant city of Montreal, Quebec, Canada.

2015	WAR	G	AB	R	H	2B	3B	HR	RBI	SB	CS	BB	BA	OBP	SLG	OPS	OPS+
Harper	*9.9*	153	521	*118*	172	38	1	*42*	99	6	4	131	.330	*.460*	*.649*	*1.109*	*195*

Montreal in 1969 became the first city outside of U.S. borders to field a major league franchise. *Les Expos de Montréal* debuted to great fanfare, if some-

2015 NL MVP Bryce Harper is the youngest unanimous MVP (courtesy Keith Allison, https://creativecommons.org/licenses/by-sa/2.0/legalcode).

what limited initial success: The hapless Expos would lose 110 games in their first year of existence, and average 91 losses per year for a decade before breaking through with a 95-win, second-place finish in 1979. They'd also finish in second place in 1980–81, slip back into the pool of low expectations for the next decade, and make a doomed run at glory during the stricken season of 1994.[9]

A snake-bitten franchise, the Expos played in one of the worst stadiums ever built: The soulless, practically shapeless concrete abomination known as the *Stade Olympique*.[10] With the worst home park in the majors, the fans' growing resentment and distrust of ownership (who simply refused to support the team—the Expos finished near the bottom of the payroll scale every year), and a consistently mediocre product on the field, the Expos finished last in attendance for seven consecutive seasons before relocating to Washington, D.C., in 2005, where they re-branded as the Nationals.[11]

While team success proved elusive, Montreal developed its fair share of great players—three of whom (Andre Dawson, Larry Walker and Vladimir Guerrero) were named MVP. Representative of Montreal's baseball fortunes, all three were playing for *other* teams when they won the award.

Montreal's best showing in the annual vote came from Gary Carter (1980) and Andre Dawson (1983), who each finished a distant second while playing for the Expos (behind landslide winners Mike Schmidt and Dale Murphy, respectively).

Carter would have made a fine choice for the award in 1982, as he was arguably the best player in the league. Instead, he finished a misguided 12th in the balloting—ahead of teammate Dawson, who also had a reasonable claim as the best player in the NL (this claim secured him 21st place on the ballot). The award went to Murphy, whose league-leading home run and RBI totals secured a comfortable margin of victory in the voting.

The best player in Montreal/Washington history, Carter never did secure an MVP. He had to leave Montreal to finally secure a world championship, but he's wearing an Expos cap on his Hall of Fame plaque.

16

The Greatest Season That Never Was

It's the spring of 1987 and a man is enjoying a walk along the shore. He happens upon an ancient, tarnished oil lamp. He figures it might fetch two bucks at a yard sale and picks it up. Within moments of cleaning the sand and seaweed from the artifact, a genie appears (well of course it does).

The genie, in a booming voice that belies his diminutive stature, says, "As you have liberated me from my eternal prison, I shall grant you wishes three."

The man has already started to pick out colors for his private jet when the genie continues: "There is but one condition: The wishes must be used to create the perfect baseball player."

As one might expect, the man's amazement and delight is somewhat tempered by this clause in the agreement. But he's a baseball fan, so he takes the genie up on his offer.

"Obviously, he has to have enormous power," the man says. "*Light-tower power*, as they say in Detroit. Fifty home runs won't be a problem for this guy."

"Done!" says the genie.

"He has to have amazing speed," the man says. "But not just raw speed. He has to have the guts to use it. He has to have larceny in his heart. This guy should steal 80 bags, easy."

"Done!" says the genie.

"And he has to play defense like the laws of gravity don't apply," says the man. "He should be a centerfielder, where his athletic gifts are on full display."

"Done!" says the genie.

With that, the genie transforms into a cloud of smoke. As he's carried away on the ocean breeze, he tells the man one last thing: "Start checking the box scores tomorrow. I think you'll like that kid in Cincinnati."

16. The Greatest Season That Never Was

So our man checks the scores every day. He notices Reds centerfielder Eric Davis having himself a nice April. Seven home runs, nine stolen bases through the first month. Really good, but not *three wishes* good. Our man gets distracted by life, goes a few weeks without following the box scores. He checks again on May 31, and his eyes grow wide.

At the end of May, despite having missed seven games, Eric Davis has amassed 19 HR, 20 SB, and lots of other serious stats.

Eric Davis Through May 31, 1987

G	AB	R	H	2B	3B	HR	RBI	BB	SB	CS	BA	OBP	SLG	OPS
42	159	43	55	11	1	19	52	21	20	2	.346	.420	.786	1.206

"Well, I'll be!" thinks our man down the shore. "It's really happening. I've created the perfect baseball player!"

This being 1987, our man didn't have Baseball-Reference.com to project those numbers over a 162-game season, but if he had, he would have seen that Davis was prorated for 74 HR, 78 SB, 201 RBI and 166 R.[1]

"MVP?" thinks our man. "Please. They'll need to re-name the award 'The Eric Davis.'"

But over the next few weeks, our man notices something: Davis begins to slow down. Clearly playing hurt, he's missed 14 games at the halfway point of the season. His breathtaking, daredevil play in centerfield doesn't help his cause: When he isn't scaling the centerfield wall, he's doing his best to crash through it. He tumbles like a gymnast to prevent any ball from touching the turf; unfortunately, there isn't anything he can do to prevent his *body* from hitting the carpeted concrete that passes for an outfield at Riverfront Stadium.[2]

Still, after 81 team games (with Davis suiting up for 67 of them), his line reads like this.

G	AB	R	H	2B	3B	HR	RBI	BB	SB	CS	BA	OBP	SLG	OPS
81	247	70	77	14	2	24	64	40	33	3	.312	.406	.676	1.082

"Ok, so maybe he's not destined for a 75 home runs and 75 stolen bases," our man thinks. "But simple math tells me he's on pace for 48 and 66. And if he can manage to stay healthy, he'll get to 50–70. No one has ever approached those numbers in the same season."

Alas, it is not to be. The sprains, strains, contusions and collisions continue to mount, and the home runs and stolen bases come with less frequency. Davis would ultimately play in 129 games, starting 127 of them (and only Davis and the Genie can say how many of those games were played in full health).

Eric Davis' final line for the year:

1987	WAR	G	AB	R	H	2B	3B	HR	RBI	SB	CS	BB	K	BA	OBP	SLG	OPS	OPS+
Davis	7.9	129	474	120	139	23	4	37	100	50	6	84	134	.293	.399	.593	.991	155

There is no shame in such a season, of course. It's a magnificent season. No player has ever hit as many home runs in a season in which they also stole 50 bases. Despite missing more than a month, Davis placed in the top-five in WAR, runs, home runs, slugging, adjusted OPS, and stolen bases; he finished in the top-10 in walks, on-base percentage, RBI, and runs created. He was awarded—and deserved—a Gold Glove for his play in centerfield. On a game-by-game basis, he was the best player in the league; unfortunately, he didn't play enough games, and placed seventh in the MVP voting.

Of course, there was no genie. But for the first half of the 1987 season, "magic" Eric Davis was a real and true thing; a whippet-thin construction of sinew and speed that seemed poised to redefine what was possible on a baseball diamond.[3]

Real Eric Davis, when he was able to take the field, was the most gifted player *on* the field. Real Eric Davis, after the best start to a season any player has ever had, finished with 37 home runs, 50 stolen bases, and 120 runs scored in 129 games.[4]

But the *real* Eric Davis got hurt in 1987, like he did every year (Davis missed hundreds of games over the course of his career due to serious injuries).[5]

In creating the perfect baseball player, our man down the shore had wished for power, speed and grace.

If only he had wished for invincibility.

◆ ◆ ◆

The 1987 NL MVP vote doesn't make our chronicle of the worst ballots because Eric Davis placed seventh (though he deserved better). It makes the list because Andre Dawson was named MVP over more deserving candidates Tony Gwynn, Dale Murphy, and St. Louis stars Jack Clark and Ozzie Smith.

Dawson's selection was not without controversy at the time. Plying his trade for the lowly Cubs, Dawson became the first player from a last-place team to ever win the award.[6] "How valuable can he be?" the traditionalists asked. "The Cubs would have finished last without him."[7]

In fairness, the Cubs would have been even worse without 'The Hawk.' He had a nice season, leading the league in HR (49) and RBI (137). Impressive totals to be sure, but because Dawson never took a walk (posting an anemic .328 OBP—the second lowest in the history of MVP award), and contributed little by way of defense and base running, his season falls into the "good, but nothing to write home about" category.[8] His OPS+ of 130 doesn't crack the top-10, and is dwarfed by league leader Jack Clark (176). Dawson's 4.0 WAR ranked 19th in the league, tied with Philadelphia's Milt Thompson (who is nowhere to be found on the ballot).

Here is the top of the 1987 NL MVP ballot.

RK	Name	WAR	G	AB	R	H	HR	RBI	SB	BB	BA	OBP	SLG	OPS
1	Andre Dawson	4.0	153	621	90	178	**49**	**137**	11	32	.287	.328	.568	.896
2	Ozzie Smith	6.4	158	600	104	182	0	75	43	89	.303	.392	.383	.775
3	Jack Clark	5.4	131	419	93	120	35	106	1	**136**	.286	**.459**	**.597**	**1.055**
4	Tim Wallach	4.3	153	593	89	177	26	123	9	37	.298	.343	.514	.858
5	Will Clark	4.2	150	529	89	163	35	91	5	49	.308	.371	.580	.951

Here is the top-five as sorted by WAR. Dawson isn't within hailing distance of this crew.

RK	Name	WAR	G	AB	R	H	HR	RBI	SB	BB	BA	OBP	SLG	OPS
1	Tony Gwynn	**8.5**	157	589	119	**218**	7	54	56	82	**.370**	.447	.511	.958
2	Eric Davis	7.9	129	474	120	139	37	100	50	84	.293	.399	.593	.991
3	Dale Murphy	7.7	159	566	115	167	44	105	16	115	.295	.417	.580	.997
4	Tim Raines	6.7	139	530	**123**	175	18	68	50	90	.330	.429	.526	.955
5	Ozzie Smith	6.4	158	600	104	182	0	75	43	89	.303	.392	.383	.775
(19)	*Dawson*	4.0	153	621	90	178	**49**	137	11	32	.287	.328	.568	.896

WAR, of course, is not the final word on MVP voting (nor should it be, since it didn't exist in 1987). Tony Gwynn doesn't deserve the 1987 NL MVP because he scores fractionally better than Eric Davis in a retroactively applied, somewhat esoteric stat. But did voters need quantitative analysis to see that Jack Clark was a far superior hitter to Dawson?[9] It wasn't obvious that Tony Gwynn, with a .370 avg., 56 SB and excellent defense was the much better player?

The voters almost—*almost*—made a bold (and far more appropriate) choice in Ozzie Smith, who placed second on the ballot. The Wizard[10] and the Hawk offered voters a fascinating contrast in styles: The slugger vs. the defensive genius; ivy-clearing blasts vs. infield singles; runs batted in vs. runs saved with the glove.

At the time, it didn't seem like a fair fight: Dawson out-homered Smith 49 to *zero*. But a closer inspection of the numbers levels the playing field: Smith's enormous advantages in OBP (.392 to Dawson .328), walks (89 for Smith, 32 for Dawson) and base running (Ozzie led in steals 43 to 11, hit into 6 fewer double plays, and was recognized as one of the smartest base runners in the game) resulted in Smith scoring more runs (and making fewer outs) than Dawson. WAR actually rates Smith as the superior *offensive* player in 1987—and while that seems a stretch, the delta between the two isn't nearly as wide as those 49 HRs would suggest. Factor in Ozzie's nonpareil defense, and you have a strong case as the most valuable player in the league. Teammate

Jack Clark, an overwhelming offensive force, was probably the next-best choice for the award (though, in fairness, Clark did miss the last few weeks of the regular season due to an ankle injury).

◆ ◆ ◆

Andre Dawson was a poor choice for MVP, but he one could argue he wasn't the worst Most Valuable Player of 1987. In a close and controversial vote, Toronto Blue Jays outfielder George Bell outpolled Detroit Tigers shortstop Alan Trammell for the American League award. With parallels to the NL ballot, voters went with the traditional glamour stats of home runs and RBI over superior all-around production. It was one of the worst selections in the history of the award.

Name	WAR	G	AB	R	H	2B	3B	HR	RBI	SB	BB	BA	OBP	SLG	OPS+
Alan Trammell	8.2	151	597	109	205	34	3	28	105	21	60	.343	.402	.551	155
George Bell	5.0	156	610	111	188	32	4	47	**134**	5	39	.308	.352	.605	146

When informed of his runner-up status, the gracious Trammell was generous with his praise. "George Bell had an outstanding year. He certainly deserved to win. I think [he] did a better job of carrying the Blue Jays. I didn't carry the Tigers. I just contributed."

With all due respect to Trammell, he was dead wrong in his assessment of his own MVP qualifications. He *did* carry the Tigers, and he *did* deserve the MVP.

Bell, a defensive liability in the leftfield, led the league in RBI (134) while placing second in home runs (47) and slugging (.605). He ranked sixth in OPS+ (a healthy 146). Without much to offer by way of plate discipline (only 39 walks—nine of which were intentional) or defense, Bell barely cracked the top-10 in WAR (5.0). He obviously hit a ton, but *everybody* hit a ton in 1987. Players launched a then-record 4458 HR (averaging more than one per game for the first time in the game's history), while teams averaged 4.72 runs per game—a scoring level not seen since the 1930s (and not seen again until the "Selig Era" of 1994–2006).[11]

1987 AL OPS+ Leaders

RK	Name	G	R	H	2B	3B	HR	RBI	SB	BB	BA	OBP	SLG	OPS	OPS+
1	Wade Boggs	147	108	200	40	6	24	89	1	105	**.363**	**.461**	.588	**1.049**	**174**
2	Mark McGwire	151	97	161	28	4	**49**	118	1	71	.289	.370	**.618**	.987	164
3	Paul Molitor	118	**114**	164	41	5	16	75	45	69	.353	.438	.566	1.003	161
4	Dwight Evans	154	109	165	37	2	34	123	4	106	.305	.417	.569	.986	157
5	Alan Trammell	151	109	205	34	3	28	105	21	60	.343	.402	.551	.953	155
6t	Don Mattingly	141	93	186	38	2	30	115	1	51	.327	.378	.559	.937	146
6t	*George Bell*	*156*	*111*	*188*	*32*	*4*	*47*	*134*	*5*	*39*	*.308*	*.352*	*.605*	*.957*	*146*

Bell's MVP is almost certainly a function of his league-leading RBI total. If the writers wanted offense, they had plenty to choose from—and Trammell acquits himself just fine in this company. He was a better hitter than Bell, and much, much more valuable as a defender.

There is also the small matter of *the collapse*.

Leading Detroit by 3.5 games with seven left to play, the Blue Jays, remarkably, lost their final seven games to hand the division to Trammel's Tigers. And while no one should bow to the tyranny of small sample sizes, it's worth noting that Bell hit .111/.250/.111 (three singles in 27 at-bats) with one RBI over that span. Trammell, on the other hand, hit .333/.419/.519 as the Tigers won five of their last seven to claim the AL East.

Clearly, Bell doesn't deserve the blame for the Jays' collapse—but he certainly didn't come through when the stakes were highest. With the season on the line, Detroit swept the Jays by scores of 4–3, 3–2 and 1–0 in the final series of the year. Bell could only muster a single in 11 at-bats.

In short, Trammell was the best all-around player in the league, and he exceeded *any* reasonable criteria for MVP honors: An elite defensive shortstop who hits .340 with power, drives in a bushel of runs, and leads his team to a first-place finish. Trammell didn't carry the Tigers? He hit .417/.490/.677 over the final month of the season as the Tigers scratched and clawed their way to a division title. It's the *very definition* of "carrying" a team. What more could anybody *possibly* want from an MVP candidate?

Apparently, 29 additional RBI.

17

Never Mind, Juan Gone— It's the 90s

By the slimmest of margins, Texas outfielder Juan Gonzalez (11 first-place votes, 290 points) edged Seattle shortstop Alex Rodriguez (10 first-place votes, 287 points) for the 1996 American League MVP.

It was among the most contentious and controversial MVP ballots—had Rodriguez (who had the *far* superior season by any objective reckoning) garnered one more third-place vote, he would have become the youngest MVP in history. As it turned out, A-Rod would have to wait seven years before capturing his first trophy. The writers, it seemed, had to get the 90s out of their system.

◆ ◆ ◆

Juan Gonzalez was a hulking outfielder who hit lots of home runs and compiled lots of RBI for the Texas Rangers. He was a powerful slugger who played in an extreme hitter's park, during an extreme era for offense.[1] He posted excellent totals in the aforementioned glamor stats while contributing little by way of defense and base running.[2]

Gonzalez was named AL MVP in 1996 and 1998. Both are considered among the worst selections of all time. His 1996 MVP is probably the more egregious of the two.

Without context, his batting line from 1996 is fantastic. Excellent power numbers, respectable on-base percentage, more than an RBI per game.

1996	WAR	G	AB	R	H	2B	3B	HR	RBI	BB	BA	OBP	SLG	OPS	OPS+
Gonzalez	3.8	134	541	89	170	33	2	47	144	45	.314	.368	.643	1.011	145

But context matters. By the mid-90s, offensive production had reached levels not seen since 1930. American League teams averaged 5.387 runs per game in 1996—the third highest per-game average in league history, and a full

20 percent higher than historic norms. AL hitters clubbed 2742 home runs—to that point, the most ever in a single season. In 1996, everybody hit like Hank Aaron.

In fact, Aaron's 1971 season might help place Gonzalez' 1996 MVP campaign in proper context.

Season	WAR	G	AB	R	H	2B	3B	HR	RBI	BB	BA	OBP	SLG	OPS
Aaron 1971	7.2	139	495	95	162	22	3	47	118	71	.327	.410	.669	1.079
Gonzalez 1996	3.8	134	541	89	170	33	2	47	144	45	.314	.368	.643	1.011

At first glance, the two seasons appear quite similar. Overall, you'd give the nod to Aaron, but the difference isn't too dramatic. Gonzalez certainly acquits himself well.

Except, the difference *is* dramatic. Aaron plied his trade in a *much* tougher environment for hitters.

- The National League as a whole in hit .252/.316/.366 (.672 OPS) in 1971, while the American League in 1996 clouted .277/.350/.445 (.795 OPS).
- NL teams in 1971 averaged 3.9 runs per game—scoring 28 percent fewer runs than AL teams did in 1996 (5.4 R/G).
- NL hitters in 1971 hit *half* as many HRs as AL hitters did in 1996.

As measured by OPS+, Gonzalez in 1996 was 45 percent more productive than the average AL hitter—very good. Aaron in 1971 was *94 percent* more productive than the average NL hitter—that's *Ted Williams* good. While their raw numbers were essentially the same, Aaron was twice as productive, relative to his time and place, as Gonzalez was to his era. WAR supports this argument, with Aaron (7.2 WAR) nearly doubling "Juan Gone" (3.8 WAR).

Still not convinced?

Ok. A little thought experiment with the help of Baseball-Reference.com's "Neutralized Batting" tool[3]: Let's pretend we can transport 1971 Aaron to the American league in 1996, while Gonzalez is sent back in time to the National league circa 1971. We'll have them swap teams, as well. Aaron is now hitting in Arlington Stadium, while Gonzalez plays his home games in Atlanta. We then adjust their levels of production to their new surroundings.

Space-Time Rift	G	AB	R	H	2B	3B	HR	RBI	BB	BA	OBP	SLG	OPS
Aaron "1996"	139	530	130	197	27	4	57	162	87	.372	.458	.760	1.218
Gonzalez "1971"	134	517	69	146	29	2	40	112	38	.282	.333	.578	.911

These two seasons bear no resemblance to each other. Aaron's is better by an order of magnitude. Numbers can *lie*.[4] Context *matters*.

Which brings us back to the 1996 MVP ballot. Gonzalez took the honors on the strength of his .314/47/144 season for the division-leading Texas Rangers. Just how impressive *were* his impressive power totals?

In 1996:

- A record 22 players hit 30 or more HR; eight players cleared 40 HR.
- A record 30 players amassed 100 or more RBI; six players collected more than *135 RBI*.[5]

Gonzalez didn't lead the league in any offensive category. His OPS ranked ninth in the league (and lagged leader Mark McGwire by nearly *200 points*); his adjusted production of 145 doesn't crack his league's top-10. As measured by WAR (3.8), he ranks as the *30th* best player in the league. He was simply the wrong choice for the award.

In fairness to Gonzalez, he accepted the award with humility: "All year, people talked about Alex [Rodriguez] as the number one contender for the award," he said. "Right now, I'm surprised myself."

Even when stripping away some of the artifice around to his numbers, Gonzalez remains a very good hitter—in any era. But in 1996, there were at least a dozen players more valuable to their teams (led by Ken Griffey, Jr., who was delivering a season that would make Willie Mays proud, and the aforementioned Alex Rodriguez).[6]

1996 AL WAR Leaders

Player	WAR	G	AB	R	H	HR	RBI	SB	BB	AVG	OBP	SLG	OPS	MVP RK
Ken Griffey	9.7	140	545	125	165	49	140	16	78	.303	.392	.628	1.020	4
Alex Rodriguez	9.4	146	601	**141**	**215**	36	123	15	59	**.358**	.414	.631	1.045	2
Chuck Knoblauch	8.6	153	578	140	197	13	72	45	98	.341	.448	.517	.965	16
Jim Thome	7.5	151	505	122	157	38	116	2	**123**	.311	.450	.612	1.062	15
Brady Anderson	6.9	149	579	117	172	50	110	21	76	.297	.396	.637	1.034	9
Mark McGwire	6.4	130	423	104	132	**52**	113	0	116	.312	**.467**	**.730**	**1.198**	7
Ivan Rodriguez	6.1	153	639	116	192	19	86	5	38	.300	.342	.473	.814	10
Albert Belle	5.7	158	602	124	187	48	**148**	11	99	.311	.410	.623	1.033	3
Mo Vaughn	5.6	161	635	118	207	44	143	2	95	.326	.420	.583	1.003	5
Frank Thomas	5.5	141	527	110	184	40	134	1	109	.349	.459	.626	1.085	8

♦ ♦ ♦

The same arguments apply to 1998, with A-Rod, Junior, Derek Jeter, Roger Clemens, Nomar Garciaparra, Albert Belle, Manny Ramirez … well, there's no point in listing the 15 or so players with more robust MVP qualifications than Gonzalez, who again took the honor because he drove in a lot of runs for a division-leading team.

Suffice it to say, his two selections are bewildering. But it was a bewildering time for the game, marked by Olympian highs (Cal Ripken's Iron Man record, the 1998 home run chase, the Yankees dynastic excellence, a decade of dominance in Atlanta), Stygian lows (an extended strike that cancelled the 1994 World Series), and an all-out assault on pitching fed by juiced players, juiced balls, shrinking ballparks, and a shrinking strike zone.[7]

There was a lot of weirdness in baseball in the 90s. And the MVP ballots of the time reflected this weirdness. The voters got it wrong far more than they got it right.

A year-by-year accounting:

1990: Rickey Henderson, AL; Barry Bonds, NL
The voters got it right up and down both ballots.

1991: Cal Ripken, AL; Terry Pendleton, NL
One for two. Ripken was historic—his 11.5 WAR is tied for the highest ever posted by a shortstop (Wagner), and remains the highest by any AL player since Yastrzemski's 1967 Triple Crown season.

Pendleton wasn't the best choice for MVP (the conventional wisdom has Bonds as the more appropriate pick), but he was one of the best players in the league as measured by WAR (and was, at least according to the narrative of the time, the leader of a previously forlorn Braves team that went from "Worst to First"). The best player in the league that year? It wasn't Bonds. Tom Glavine posted 9.3 WAR in pitching the Braves to respectability, beginning their 14-year run of excellence. Glavine finished 11th in the voting (reflecting the NL attitude toward starting pitchers).

1992: Dennis Eckersley, AL; Bonds, NL
Eck? Ecch.

1993: Frank Thomas, AL; Bonds, NL
Not good. Thomas had a fine season and was voted the unanimous MVP. But why Thomas and not one of the five or six players who, at least superficially, put up nearly identical seasons?[8]

1993	WAR	G	AB	R	HR	RBI	SB	BB	BA	OBP	SLG	OPS	OPS+
Player 1	**8.7**	156	582	113	45	109	17	96	.309	.408	.617	1.025	171
Player 2	7.7	158	551	109	24	107	0	**114**	**.363**	**.473**	.599	**1.072**	**186**
Player 3	6.8	126	419	80	29	82	1	69	.310	.416	.585	1.001	162
Player 4	6.5	140	536	105	**46**	118	4	37	.310	.368	**.632**	1.000	169
Thomas	6.2	153	549	106	*41*	128	4	112	.317	.426	.607	1.033	177

Thomas doesn't fare poorly in this group. He was obviously a superb hitter. But not obviously superior to the four guys ahead of him on this list. It's notable that he failed to lead the league in any meaningful offensive category. Sorted by WAR, Thomas barely rates as one of the ten best players in the league.

Player 4, as you probably know, is Juan Gonzalez; 1993 was his strongest case for MVP, and it wasn't that strong. Player 3 is Chris Hoiles, catcher for the Baltimore Orioles. Player 2 is Toronto first baseman John Olerud, doing his best Edgar Martinez impression. For the record, Ken Griffey Jr.—Player 1 in the chart above—should have been the clear choice for MVP. He was Thomas' equal as a hitter, and played a breathtaking centerfield.[9]

1994: Thomas, AL; Jeff Bagwell, NL

The voters essentially got it right, up and down both ballots. But 1994 poses an interesting philosophical question on the notion of "most valuable." A players' strike ended the season August 12. With literally nothing to play for—no division races, no playoffs, no World Series—what value, exactly, did Bagwell and Thomas bring to their teams? This is not to denigrate two superb seasons, but to point out that the Most Valuable Player Award in 1994 was clearly the "Best Player Award" (or in Thomas' case, the "Best Hitter Award").

1995: Mo Vaughn, AL; Barry Larkin, NL

This was a doozy of a ballot in both leagues. In one of the closest (and worst) AL votes of all time, Boston's Mo Vaughn squeaked by Cleveland's Albert Belle (12 first-place votes to 11). Belle was superior in every facet of the game, except public relations.[10] Notorious for being unfriendly (the Associated Press called him "downright rude") when engaging with the media, Belle was doubtlessly the victim of his disposition. "I guess it really does say something," said Vaughn when learning of his MVP honor. "People are looking at the whole thing and that it's just not the numbers. If it's just numbers, he [Belle] probably would win."

1995	WAR	G	AB	R	H	2B	3B	HR	RBI	BB	AVG	OBP	SLG	OPS	OPS+
Vaughn	4.3	140	550	98	165	28	3	39	**126**	68	.300	.388	.575	.963	144
Belle	6.9	143	546	**121**	173	**52**	1	**50**	**126**	73	.317	.401	**.690**	1.091	177

And then there's sixth-place finisher Randy Johnson, far and away the most productive player in the American league. In a strike-shortened season, The Big Unit did *this*[11]:

1995	pWAR	W	L	ERA	GS	CG	SHO	IP	BB	K	ERA+	FIP	WHIP	K/9	BB/9	K/BB
Johnson	8.6	18	2	2.48	30	6	3	214.1	65	294	193	2.08	1.045	12.3	2.7	**4.52**

Amazing. But not quite as amazing as *this*:

1995	pWAR	W	L	ERA	GS	CG	SHO	IP	BB	K	ERA+	FIP	WHIP	K/9	BB/9	K/BB
Maddux	9.7	19	2	1.63	28	10	3	209.2	23	181	260	2.26	0.811	7.8	1.0	7.87

That, of course, is Greg Maddux' legendary 1995 season. Somehow, the NL voters considered Barry Larkin and Dante Bichette (he of 1.1 WAR) more valuable than Maddux. Bichette's runner-up showing nestles comfortably among the worst votes in the history of MVP balloting; his hitting was a distorted construct of Coors Field, and his play in left field ... well, perhaps the less said the better.[12]

At 9.7 WAR, Maddux was markedly better than Larkin (5.9) and Bichette *combined*.

1996: Gonzalez, AL; Ken Caminiti NL

Caminiti is a defensible choice for MVP—he had a fine season. But a *unanimous* pick? Barry Bonds and his 40/40, 9+ WAR season barely cracks the top-five? Mike Piazza (.336/.422/.563 ... as catcher... in Dodgers Stadium) doesn't get a single first-place vote? Couldn't find a vote for Kevin Brown, John Smoltz, or Gary Sheffield—each of whom put up MVP-worthy seasons?

1997: Griffey, AL; Larry Walker, NL

The voters got it right up and down the ballot. Walker and Griffey were both overwhelming, "five-tool" forces in 1997. This was Griffey's only MVP; a case can be made that he should have three trophies on his mantle.

1998: Gonzalez, AL; Sammy Sosa, NL

The second of Gonzalez' ill-gotten MVP gains.[13] Over in the NL ... well, it's tough to say a player was robbed when he places runner-up to a man who hit 66 HR and drove in 158—but Mark McGwire was robbed. Sosa may have kept pace in their thrilling race, but McGwire lapped him in overall production. Enhanced or not, McGwire delivered one of the ten best seasons by a hitter in NL history.

Name	WAR	G	AB	R	H	2B	3B	HR	RBI	SB	CS	BB	K	BA	OBP	SLG	OPS	OPS+
McGwire	7.5	155	509	130	152	21	0	70	147	1	0	162	155	.299	.470	.752	1.222	216
Sosa	6.4	159	643	134	198	20	0	66	158	18	9	73	171	.308	.377	.647	1.024	160

1999: Ivan Rodriguez, AL; Chipper Jones, NL

Was Pudge Rodriguez the most valuable player in the AL? No. But if as a catcher you hit .332/.356/.558 (with 25 SB) while playing indisputably great defense for a playoff team, you're going to get your share of votes. What makes this ballot terrible is the treatment afforded Boston's Pedro Martinez.[14]

1999	WAR	W	L	W%	ERA	GS	CG	IP	BB	K	ERA+	FIP	WHIP	BB9	K9	K/BB
Martinez	9.7	23	4	.852	2.07	29	5	213.1	37	313	243	1.39	0.923	1.6	13.2	8.46

Two writers—George King of the *New York Post* and La Velle E. Neal III of the *Minneapolis Star Tribune*—failed to list the amazing Martinez on their ballot.[15] Said Ted Williams of this ghastly omission: "What game were those guys watching?"

Of the two snubs, the King non-vote was the more galling. La Velle Neal had been consistent in his position that the award should go to an everyday player. He was pilloried in the media for his vote, but met the criticism with good humor and a reasoned defense of his ballot. "I just feel that in order to be an MVP you have to be in the battle every day," said Neal. "If I believe a pitcher should not be in the running, why would I put him on the ballot at all?"[16]

King, on the other hand, had some explaining to do. Despite listing pitchers David Wells and Rick Helling on his ballot the year prior, King defended his snub of Martinez by saying the "MVP is for everyday players. Pitchers have their own award." David Wells in 1998 was very good; Pedro Martinez in 1999 tested the limits of human performance. King, a beat writer covering the Yankees, was guilty of abject homerism. His vote was so bad that *his own newspaper* called it "bunch of hogwash."[17]

If you're keeping score, the voters got it 100 percent right *twice* in the decade (1990, 1997). Arguably, four out of ten ballots are among the worst ever (1993, 95–96 and 98).

The '90s also underscore that when judging how good or bad the MVP vote is in a particular season, one must view the voting in its entirety. A questionable choice for MVP (Caminiti in 1996, for example) doesn't necessarily mean the entire vote was terrible; how we *arrive* at that choice can determine whether or not a ballot makes the "all-time worst" list.

In 1996, one writer somehow left Alex Rodriquez off his ballot; had Rodriguez placed even *third* on this ballot, he wins the MVP over the undeserving Gonzalez. In 1999, Pedro Martinez garnered more first-place votes than MVP winner Pudge Rodriguez; had Pedro placed higher on another few ballots (or not been *left off* two ballots), he would have added the trophy to his mantle. There are no "throw-away" votes when it comes to determining the most valuable player.

Sometimes the Voters Get the Tough Calls Right

With hindsight, it seems obvious.

1990	WAR	G	AB	R	H	2B	3B	HR	RBI	SB	CS	BB	BA	OBP	SLG	OPS	OPS+
Henderson	**9.9**	136	489	**119**	159	33	3	28	61	**65**	10	97	.325	**.439**	.577	**1.016**	**189**
Fielder	6.5	159	573	104	159	25	1	**51**	**132**	0	1	90	.277	.377	**.592**	.969	167

Oakland's Rickey Henderson was the best hitter, the best baserunner, the best *player* in baseball. But Henderson's anointment as the 1990 American League MVP was anything but certain. In fact, if you were a betting man (or woman), the smart money in the 1990 AL MVP race might have been on Cecil Fielder of the Detroit Tigers. And why not? Fielder didn't just check off the boxes that MVP voters love—he checked them with broad, heavy strokes.

Fielder's 51 HRs seem almost quaint now, but in 1990 his season had an air of the historic. His home run total was the most in the majors since George Foster clubbed 52 in 1977. Fielder, in fact, was the first American League player in 30 years to clear the 50-HR barrier. It was considered a monumental number, the provenance of Mays, Mantle, and Ruth. Fifty was the stuff of myth and legend.[18]

Fielder's 133 RBI were also exceptional—and the one stat voters at the time valued above all else was RBI. For good measure, he played every day, scored more than 100 runs, and led the league in total bases (339) and slugging, approaching .600 when .600 was something to write home about.

Throw in his narrative: He was a likeable slugger who seemed to materialize overnight. A part-time player who showed flashes of power for the Toronto Blue Jays over four seasons, Fielder was released after the 1988 season. Failing to catch on with a major league team, he was forced to ply his trade in Japan (where he hit 38 HR in 106 games). "Big Daddy" (a cool nickname can't be discounted in MVP narratives) found his way back to the majors in 1990 and took the American League by storm.

By most measures, and certainly by the standards of the day, he was an easy choice for MVP.

Despite the stats and the story, Fielder finished second in the voting—and the voters got it right. Henderson, a two-time victim of MVP robbery (arguably the best player in baseball in 1981; certainly the best position player in 1985), took the prize in a vote that was closer than it should have been (although, again, not by the standards of the time).

Henderson was at his best in 1990. Despite missing 26 games, he led the league in runs, on-base percentage, adjusted production (OPS+), and WAR (9.9).[19] He slugged .577 (playing in a home park that suppressed offense) while leading the league with 65 stolen bases. This just isn't done.[20]

In addition to correctly naming Henderson the league's most valuable, the 1990 MVP voters did a better job than the 1990 Cy Young voters in identifying the best starting pitchers of the year.

1990 Cy Young Ballot, with MVP Rank

CY RK	Name	pWAR	W	L	W%	ERA	GS	IP	R	ER	BB	K	WHIP	ERA+	MVP RK
1	Welch	3.0	**27**	6	**.818**	2.95	35	238	90	78	77	127	1.223	125	9
2	Clemens	**10.6**	21	6	.778	**1.93**	31	228.1	59	49	54	209	1.082	**211**	3
3	Stewart	5.2	22	11	.667	2.56	36	**267**	84	76	83	166	1.157	144	8

Follow the thread here.

- Oakland's Bob Welch, who took Cy Young honors with a 27-win season, placed ninth on the MVP ballot. This was about right. Welch had a fine year and deserved the MVP recognition. He was a terrible choice for Cy Young honors.
- Welch's rotation mate Dave Stewart placed eighth in the MVP vote. Stewart, who received a fraction of Welch's Cy Young support, finished ahead of his teammate in MVP voting (appropriate, since he was the better pitcher).
- Roger Clemens, runner-up to Welch in the Cy Young vote, finished third in the MVP vote—*six places ahead* of Welch. The writers *overwhelmingly* chose Clemens as the most "valuable" pitcher in the league in 1990, but somehow chose Welch as the "best" pitcher in the league. This is one of the worst Cy Young snubs in the history of the award.

Did Rickey's election as MVP (and the consideration given Clemens) usher in a new era of MVP voting based on thoughtful statistical analysis? Well, no. Things regressed to their unfortunate norm in 1992 when Oakland reliever Dennis Eckersley took MVP honors. But for one season, the voters made the tough—and correct—call.

18

Are MVP Voters Racist?

In 1960, an enraged Roberto Clemente called out what he saw as a racially motivated "injustice" perpetrated by NL MVP voters—not because he didn't claim the award, but because he placed eighth on the ballot, behind several of his teammates (the award went to Pirates shortstop Dick Groat). It was a slight the sensitive and proud Clemente couldn't forgive, and he was convinced his Puerto Rican heritage had something to do with his showing on the ballot.

1960	MVP	WAR	G	AB	R	H	2B	3B	HR	RBI	SB	BB	BA	OBP	SLG	OPS	OPS+
Groat	1	6.2	138	573	85	186	26	4	2	50	0	39	.325	.371	.394	.766	110
Hoak	2	5.4	155	553	97	156	24	9	16	79	3	74	.282	.366	.445	.810	120
Clemente	8	3.9	144	570	89	179	22	6	16	94	4	39	.314	.357	.458	.815	121

One can't blame the Pittsburgh rightfielder for venting his frustration. The dark-skinned Clemente *was* treated as a caricature by the press of the day, who often ascribed a Speedy Gonzalez-esque accent to the dignified and intelligent star (to paraphrase: "Aye yaye yaye. He very good pitcher. It hard to heet thee ball").

While Clemente had a case against certain writers for the ignorant and offensive portrait they painted of him, it's not clear that Clemente had a case as MVP: Other than his customary fine batting average, 1960 wasn't a banner year for the great rightfielder. As ranked by WAR, he's not among the ten best players in the league. One might argue he deserved better than an eighth-place showing, but the numbers don't necessarily support that argument.[1]

But Clemente raised a much more important question: Do attitudes toward race influence MVP selections?

◆ ◆ ◆

So. Anyone notice that black players aren't named MVP in the American League?

Granted, that's not *entirely* accurate. Black players have captured a total of 12 AL MVP awards in the 68 seasons since Jackie Robinson pioneered integration efforts in 1947 (as compared with 33 MVPs awarded to black players in the National League over the same time period).[2]

More troubling? No black player has been named the American League MVP since 1997; only two black players (Ken Griffey Jr., 1997, and Mo Vaughn, 1995) have claimed the award in the last *20 years* (as compared with seven black players in the NL).

Something seems amiss, no? It seems ... *odd* that since 1947 black players have captured the MVP *half* the time in the NL, as compared with only 18 percent of the hardware in the AL.

But before we condemn the AL voters and congratulate the NL's ... anyone notice that Hispanic players aren't named MVP in the National League?

From 1947 to 2015, NL voters have given the award to an Hispanic player only six times—with three of those awards going to Albert Pujols (2005, 2008–09). Over in the America league, Hispanic players have captured 15 total awards, or 22 percent of the available MVP hardware.

Coincidence? Or something more sinister and sad? Are AL and NL MVP voters biased against specific racial and/or ethnic groups?

No, they aren't—although a casual look at the winners over the past seven decades in both leagues would make one wonder whether American League voters have it in for African Americans, and National League voters eschew Hispanics. But a deeper examination debunks that theory.

◆ ◆ ◆

Looking over voting patterns since 1949 (when Robinson was the first black player named MVP), clear themes emerge: From 1949 to 1969, black players claimed 14 of 21 National League awards—and it easily could have been 16 or 17, had voters properly appreciated Willie Mays. Things were very different in the American League: Elston Howard and Frank Robinson are the only African American players named MVP during this period.

It seems like a damning indictment of voter attitudes, but the facts say otherwise. It's inarguable that the National League had a near-monopoly on black superstars in the 1950s and 60s (of course, this was because the NL was much more progressive when it came to employing black players). This was the heyday of Campanella and Banks, Mays and McCovey, Aaron and Gibson. The AL simply had no comparable black players. We should also grant that the MVP award, like the league championship, was being passed around the Yankees' clubhouse during this period. With 14 pennants in 16 years, it's to be expected that New York was going to be disproportionately represented in the AL MVP voting (and they were, taking nine awards from 1950 to 1962).

Most Valuable Players, 1949–69

	National League	American League
1969	Willie McCovey	Harmon Killebrew
1968	Bob Gibson	Denny McLain
1967	Orlando Cepeda	Carl Yastrzemski
1966	Roberto Clemente	Frank Robinson
1965	Willie Mays	Zoilo Versalles
1964	Ken Boyer	Brooks Robinson
1963	Sandy Koufax	Elston Howard
1962	Maury Wills	Mickey Mantle
1961	Frank Robinson	Roger Maris
1960	Dick Groat	Roger Maris
1959	Ernie Banks	Nellie Fox
1958	Ernie Banks	Jackie Jensen
1957	Hank Aaron	Mickey Mantle
1956	Don Newcombe	Mickey Mantle
1955	Roy Campanella	Yogi Berra
1954	Willie Mays	Yogi Berra
1953	Roy Campanella	Al Rosen
1952	Hank Sauer	Bobby Shantz
1951	Roy Campanella	Yogi Berra
1950	Jim Konstanty	Phil Rizzuto
1949	Jackie Robinson	Ted Williams

Despite only two MVPs awarded to black players, it's tough to find a truly terrible American League vote over the time period. Reggie Jackson was the league's best position player 1969, but there's nothing insidious about the Killebrew award (the "Killer" paced the league in home runs, RBI, walks, and on-base percentage for the division-winning Twins); 1954 MVP runner-up Larry Doby certainly had a case—but voters *loved* catchers around this time, explaining Berra's second nod as Most Valuable.[3]

Things started to even out a bit in the 70s, with five black MVPs in the National League (we count the 1979 tie vote), six in the American League.

	National League	American League
1979	Keith Hernandez (tie) Willie Stargell	Don Baylor
1978	Dave Parker	Jim Rice
1977	George Foster	Rod Carew
1976	Joe Morgan	Thurman Munson
1975	Joe Morgan	Fred Lynn
1974	Steve Garvey	Jeff Burroughs
1973	Pete Rose	Reggie Jackson
1972	Johnny Bench	Dick Allen
1971	Joe Torre	Vida Blue
1970	Johnny Bench	Boog Powell

Sure, there were some questionable choices (Willie Stargell was probably the best choice for the NL award in 1971, but he was a poor choice in 1979; Steve Garvey and Jeff Burroughs were both terrible picks in 1974), but again, nothing to suggest anything other than poor judgment (and an infatuation with RBI) on the part of the voters.

From 1980 on, it's not close: The National League has seen a black player claim the award 13 times, while the AL can only claim five such awards.

The optics seem to get worse when we focus on the last 18 years.

	National League	American League
2015	Bryce Harper	Josh Donaldson
2014	Clayton Kershaw	Mike Trout
2013	Andrew McCutchen	Miguel Cabrera
2012	Buster Posey	Miguel Cabrera
2011	Ryan Braun	Justin Verlander
2010	Joey Votto	Josh Hamilton
2009	Albert Pujols	Joe Mauer
2008	Albert Pujols	Dustin Pedroia
2007	Jimmy Rollins	Alex Rodriguez
2006	Ryan Howard	Justin Morneau
2005	Albert Pujols	Alex Rodriguez
2004	Barry Bonds	Vladimir Guerrero
2003	Barry Bonds	Alex Rodriguez
2002	Barry Bonds	Miguel Tejada
2001	Barry Bonds	Ichiro Suzuki
2000	Jeff Kent	Jason Giambi
1999	Chipper Jones	Ivan Rodriguez
1998	Sammy Sosa	Juan Gonzalez
1997	Larry Walker	Ken Griffey

Since Griffey's AL MVP in 1997, the National League has seen the MVP go to African American players seven times; as mentioned earlier, *no* African American player has claimed the award in the American League over the same time period.

At first glance, the discrepancy seems troubling—*seven to zero?* But the *second* glance reveals why: Of the seven awards handed out to NL players, Barry Bonds owns *four*. Take Bonds out of the equation, and the NL count seems less impressive.

And then there are demographic factors at play. Since peaking at nearly 19 percent of the player population in 1981, the number of African Americans in baseball has been in decline. According to Mark Armour and Daniel R. Levitt, "Baseball Demographics, 1947–2012," on SABR.org, "The percentage of African Americans held steady between 16 percent and 19 percent for a quarter-century (1972–1996) but has since plummeted by more than half. There is seemingly no end to theories as to why this happened, but most of them are speculative…. The prevalent opinion seems to be that the cause of the decline in African Americans is external to major league baseball: that African Americans are focusing on other sports as youths, either by choice or because of fewer opportunities to play baseball."

As of Opening Day 2014, African Americans comprised only 8.3 percent of the player population. At the same time, the number of Hispanic players has steadily risen from barely countable in the early 1950s to more than 27 percent as of 2012. Major League Baseball's racial composition might go a long way in explaining MVP demographics. According to Jens Manuel Krogstad of the respected Pew Research Center: "In 2012, whites comprised about the same share of the population (63 percent) as they did in Major League Baseball, according to the most recent comparable data. By contrast, Hispanics were overrepresented in baseball, comprising 26.9 percent of players and 17 percent of the U.S. population. In 2012, blacks were underrepresented in baseball, making up 7.2 percent of players and 13 percent of the nation's population. Asians made up 1.9 percent of players in 2012 and 5 percent of the U.S. population."[4]

Given baseball's player demographics from 1947 to 2015, it's clear that on an institutional level, race has not played a factor in AL MVP voting: With 18 percent of MVP awards going to African American players, the AL vote has essentially aligned with the historical composition of the player population; the NL vote has *dramatically exceeded* what one would expect given the composition of the player population—and this discrepancy can in large part be explained by the imbalance of great black players between the two leagues in the 1950s-'60s, and the preponderance of multiple winners in the NL. Joe Morgan, Barry Bonds, Roy Campanella, Ernie Banks, and Willie Mays have 16 awards among them; in the AL, only Frank Thomas can claim two awards. This has nothing to do with racial attitudes of MVP voters, and everything to do with player performance (or dumb voting—Griffey should count at least two or possibly three awards in his trophy case).

◆ ◆ ◆

And what of the NL?

Since 1996, when the Latino player population first exceeded 20 percent, Pujols and Sammy Sosa (1998) are the only two Latino players named NL MVP; the AL counts *six* players over the same time period.

What gives? Latino players have, on the whole, totaled about 25 percent of the player population since 1996. It is reasonable to project this player segment to capture about one out of every four MVP awards. Is bias at play?

It would seem not. For the same reasons African American players dominated the National League vote for decades, Latino players have been relatively overrepresented in recent AL votes, capturing 50 percent of available awards since 1996: Alex Rodriguez (2003, 2005, 2007), Juan Gonzalez (1996, 1998), Miguel Cabrera (2012–13) Vladimir Guerrero (2004), Miguel Tejada (2002), and Ivan Rodriguez (1999) have ten awards among them.[5]

While it's true that Latino players have been underrepresented in the NL vote, it's simply been a matter of timing. Here, again, is the MVP roll call since 2001.

	National League	American League
2015	Bryce Harper	Josh Donaldson
2014	Clayton Kershaw	Mike Trout
2013	Andrew McCutchen	Miguel Cabrera
2012	Buster Posey	Miguel Cabrera
2011	Ryan Braun	Justin Verlander
2010	Joey Votto	Josh Hamilton
2009	Albert Pujols	Joe Mauer
2008	Albert Pujols	Dustin Pedroia
2007	Jimmy Rollins	Alex Rodriguez
2006	Ryan Howard	Justin Morneau
2005	Albert Pujols	Alex Rodriguez
2004	Barry Bonds	Vladimir Guerrero
2003	Barry Bonds	Alex Rodriguez
2002	Barry Bonds	Miguel Tejada
2001	Barry Bonds	Ichiro Suzuki

Who in the NL are you going to bump off the MVP list?

- Bonds was easily the most productive player in the league during his 2001–2004 run.
- You can certainly make a strong case for Pujols over Howard in 2006, but Howard did hit .313/.425/.659, with a league-leading 58 HR and 149 RBI.
- Jimmy Rollins wasn't the best choice for the award in 2007; Pujols would have been a better option—as would have David Wright, Chase Utley, or Chipper Jones (with this vote going to Utley).
- Votto is a perfectly fine choice in 2010, even if Pujols was just as good.
- The only legitimate option to Ryan Braun in 2011 is the Dodgers' Matt Kemp, who is African American.
- The Cardinals' Yadier Molina was spectacular in 2012; MVP Buster Posey was better.
- Molina was again a legitimate MVP candidate in 2013, but McCutchen was the best all-around player in the league for a Pirates team that shrugged off two decades of mediocrity to claim a post-season berth.
- Kershaw was clearly the league's most valuable player in 2014; the same is true of Harper in 2015.

We can't know what lies in the hearts and minds of individual voters, and it would be naive to think that *some* form of individual bias—whether it be personal animus toward a player, or attitude toward an entire race—has never influenced an MVP ballot. But as a whole, the MVP electorate has been color-blind. While voters *en masse* have made some terrible choices over the years, race seems to have had nothing to do with it.

19

Fun with Arbitrary Endpoints: MVPs of the Decade

1900–09: Honus Wagner

1900s	WAR	G	AB	R	H	2B	3B	HR	RBI	BB	K	BA	OBP	SLG	OPS	OPS+
Wagner	86	1391	5254	1014	1847	372	148	51	956	518	338	.352	.417	.508	.925	175

Called the "nearest thing to a perfect ballplayer" by the legendary John McGraw, Wagner was one of the game's first superstars—and probably its first superhuman. Wagner looked like he was sutured together by a grave-robbing mad scientist: Enormous hands at the end of long, stove-pipe arms; broad shoulders and barrel chest; a short torso supported by severely bowed legs that suggested he spent the off-season in the saddle.

Wagner's asymmetrical physique belied the best athlete in the game. He was blazingly fast, if not especially graceful, as he rounded the bases with the most distinctive running style in the game (picture a toddler chasing after the family dog). His arm was the stuff of legend—the young Wagner once threw a baseball that carried more than 400 feet in the air.[1]

"Wahoo" Sam Crawford, who played alongside Ty Cobb in Detroit for eight years, was adamant when asked to name history's best player.[2] "Cobb was great, there's no doubt about that," said Crawford, himself a Hall-of-Fame outfielder. "But Honus Wagner could play any position except pitcher and be easily the best in the league at it. The greatest player who ever lived, in my book." Few who saw the Pittsburgh shortstop would argue. He dominated every facet of the game during his time.

Wagner, of course, built his legend at shortstop, but his versatility allowed him to play nearly 1000 games at other positions. "Honus was the best third baseman in the league ... he was also the best first baseman, the best second baseman, the best shortstop and the best outfielder. And since he led the league in batting eight times you know he was the best hitter, too," recalled Wagner's teammate, Pirates third baseman Tommy Leach.³

The best hitter of his era, the best baserunner, the best defender, Wagner did everything better than everybody else. During the decade, he led the league in batting seven times, doubles eight times, slugging six times, on-base percentage six times, doubles seven times, stolen bases five times ... the list goes on and on. Among his contemporaries, only Nap Lajoie approaches Wagner's brilliance over this period.

The obvious MVP of the decade, Wagner is one of the five greatest players in the game's history.

Honus Wagner in 1911. Note that his baseball glove is on his left hand (Bain Collection, Library of Congress, Prints and Photographs Division).

1910–19: The Contenders: Walter Johnson, Ty Cobb

1910s	pWAR	W	L	W%	ERA	G	GS	IP	H	BB	K	ERA+	WHIP	FIP	K/BB
Johnson	108	265	143	.650	1.59	454	361	3427.2	2604	661	2219	183	0.953	1.96	3.36

Nothing against Cy Young, but it really should be called the "Walter Johnson Award."⁴ Johnson is the most valuable performer in the game during the second decade of the 20th century. Those numbers above might *undersell* his dominance: Johnson threw 675 more innings, struck out 680 more batters, and completed 85 more games than his nearest competitor in those categories (Grover Cleveland Alexander). No one comes within a country mile of his actual and adjusted ERA. His 108 WAR for the decade is the greatest total by *any* player over *any* ten consecutive seasons.

1910s	WAR	G	AB	R	H	2B	3B	HR	RBI	BB	K	BA	OBP	SLG	OPS	OPS+
Cobb	84	1334	5034	*1049*	*1948*	313	*161*	47	*823*	602	331	*.387*	*.457*	*.541*	*.998*	*193*

Honorable mention goes to Ty Cobb. Among position players, Cobb towers over the rest of MLB. Those numbers aren't a misprint: He hit .387 for the decade, and led *everybody* in just about *everything*. Ah, capricious whims of arbitrary endpoints: Cobb is the easy pick as most valuable if Walter Johnson begins his career a few years earlier or later.

1920–29: BABE RUTH

1920s	WAR	G	AB	R	H	2B	3B	HR	RBI	BB	K	BA	OBP	SLG	OPS	OPS+
Ruth	*102*	1399	4884	*1365*	1734	314	82	*467*	*1338*	*1240*	795	.355	*.488*	*.740*	*1.228*	*216*

The inscription on Babe Ruth's Hall of Fame plaque starts with "The greatest drawing card in the history of baseball."

In many ways, it's a perfect encapsulation of the man: The greatest drawing card, the greatest character, the greatest player of his or any time. His Roaring Twenties peak is the most dominant 10-year hitting performance the game has seen. And, as his plaque says, he made more money for more people than any other athlete. He was baseball's most valuable commodity in every way.

Let's be sure to mention Rogers Hornsby, who would take the honorary title of "Player of the Decade" in just about any other 10-year stretch. Like Cobb, he's a victim of timing.

1920s	WAR	G	AB	R	H	2B	3B	HR	RBI	BB	K	BA	OBP	SLG	OPS	OPS+
Hornsby	93	1430	5451	1195	*2085*	*405*	115	250	1153	753	431	*.382*	.460	.637	1.096	188

1930–39: THE CONTENDERS: LOU GEHRIG, LEFTY GROVE

1930s	pWAR	W	L	W%	ERA	G	GS	IP	H	BB	K	ERA+	WHIP	FIP	K/BB
Grove	78	*199*	76	*.724*	*2.91*	351	268	2399.0	2344	639	1313	*162*	1.243	3.33	2.05

Joe Sewell, the most accomplished contact hitter in the game's history, said this about Grove's fastball: "It looked like a flash of white sewing thread coming up at you. Inning after inning, he never slowed up. I don't know where he got it all from."[5]

The dour Grove ("I'm a serious man, and baseball is a serious business") threw that fastball into the teeth of the most violent offensive storm of the 20th century. His era, his home parks (Shibe Park, and later Fenway—two of the best hitter's parks in the league), and several wasted years in the minors conspired to mute his raw numbers. Don't be fooled: Grove has the second-best adjusted ERA in history, behind Pedro Martinez. He led the league in traditional ERA a record nine times; strikeouts seven times (consecutively); strikeout-to-walk ratio eight times; complete games and shutouts three times apiece. And he didn't make his big league debut until he was 25.[6] Grove is in the discussion for best pitcher of all time.

1930s	WAR	G	AB	R	H	2B	3B	HR	RBI	BB	K	BA	OBP	SLG	OPS	OPS+
Gehrig	73	1397	5255	*1257*	1802	328	91	347	1360	*1028*	439	.343	*.453*	.638	*1.091*	**181**

Lou Gehrig? Well, you know about Lou Gehrig. At the time, he was the most devastating hitter, save Ruth, the game had seen.

Tough choice for MVP of the decade. Grove and Gehrig both debuted in 1925, so timing isn't kind to either of them. Gehrig doesn't get to count his incredible run in the late-'20s, and plays his last season in 1938.[7] Despite missing a full season to illness (and playing another while battling the effects of the disease that would take his life at 37), Gehrig leads all position players in WAR. Grove also loses some prime years that would have bolstered his cumulative totals (going a combined 44–14 in 1928–29), but leads the decade in WAR (Carl Hubbell is a distant second among pitchers with 55 WAR). Gehrig slugs his way to a Triple Crown in 1934; Grove twice captures the pitching version (W/ERA/K) of the Triple Crown. Both took one MVP trophy in the decade; both played on powerhouse, dynastic teams. Let's call it a draw. Jimmy Foxx, with three MVPs in the decade and a statistical resume nearly equal to Gehrig, deserves honorable mention.

1940–49: The Contenders: Ted Williams, Lou Boudreau, Stan Musial

1940s	WAR	G	AB	R	H	2B	3B	HR	RBI	BB	K	BA	OBP	SLG	OPS	OPS+
Williams	66	1035	3656	*951*	1303	270	45	*234*	893	*994*	312	*.356*	*.496*	*.647*	*1.143*	**200**
Boudreau	60	1425	5268	758	*1578*	*339*	59	62	692	706	268	.300	.385	.422	.807	126
Musial	58	1072	4133	815	1432	302	*108*	146	706	565	199	.346	.428	.578	1.005	172

Musial falls victim to timing here. Despite impeccable credentials (that batting line, three MVP trophies, three World Series victories, an awesome nickname, the adulation of countless fans), Musial falls to third place in our imaginary standings.

Lou Boudreau. Who knew?

While his batting line seems modest in the company of these two immortals, Boudreau belongs in the discussion of most valuable players of the decade. "Handsome Lou" was an excellent hitter and an elite defender at shortstop for the Cleveland Indians (much of his value is tied to his great defense and, it must be noted, his playing time: Only Bob Elliott, toiling for Pittsburgh and Boston, appeared in more games over the decade, and neither Williams nor Musial came within 350 games played of Boudreau's total). He also *managed* the team, leading them to the 1948 World Series title (the franchise's last). It's easy to dismiss tropes like "leadership" and "intangibles," but in Boudreau's case they apply.[8]

Teddy Ballgame. Williams was named MVP twice, but should have taken four trophies. He played just seven seasons in the 1940s, yet led the decade in runs, home runs, and walks (as well as batting average, on-base percentage, slugging, and adjusted production). If you surveyed the press at the time, the nod for "Player of the Decade" would probably go to Joe DiMaggio—but this is no contest: Ted Williams was the most valuable player of the 1940s.[9]

1950–59: The Contenders: Willie, Mickey, the Duke

1950s	WAR	G	AB	R	H	2B	3B	HR	RBI	BB	K	BA	OBP	SLG	OPS	OPS+
Mantle	68	1246	4478	**994**	1392	208	54	280	841	892	**899**	.311	**.425**	.569	**.994**	**173**
Mays	59	1065	4074	777	1291	204	79	250	709	505	435	.317	.391	**.590**	.981	158
Snider	56	1418	5219	970	1605	274	57	**326**	**1031**	711	851	.308	.390	.569	.959	147

Mickey Mantle may have been the most athletically gifted man to ever play the sport—and no one had such gifts taken from them at such a young age.

As a teenager, Mantle was the fastest player in the game *and* the most powerful. In 1951, Casey Stengel, describing his rookie outfielder, said, "He has more speed than any slugger I've ever seen, and more slug than any other speedster—and nobody has ever had more of both of 'em together. This kid ain't logical."[10]

Mantle would play the first of his 65 career World Series games October 4th, 1951. He was 19 years old, and it was the last pain-free game he would enjoy in his career. The next day, in game two of the Series, Mantle caught his spikes on a drain cover in the outfield, ravaging his right knee.[11] He was carried off the field on a stretcher, and he would never again play a major league game at anything close to full capacity. Osteomyelitis eventually finished his other leg. Dodgers outfielder Kirk Gibson is a folk hero for hitting a World Series home run on one leg; Mantle hit 18 of them (as well as 536 in the regular season).[12]

The relative lack of boldfaced statistics for Mantle and Mays might be surprising, given their stature. The timeframe hurts both players: If, say, we used 1954–63 as our start/end points, Mantle leads all players in on-base, slugging, walks, and adjusted production by comfortable margins; Mays paces the universe in WAR, runs, and home runs.

Snider performs admirably in this comparison, leading the 50s in home runs and RBI. He wasn't quite as good as his fellow NY centerfielders, but he was better than everybody else.[13]

Named MVP twice during the decade (1956–57), "The Mick" should have won four in a row (1955–58).[14] He is the most valuable player of the 1950s.

1960–69: The Contenders: Willie Mays, Hank Aaron

1960s	WAR	G	AB	R	H	2B	3B	HR	RBI	SB	CS	BB	K	BA	OBP	SLG	OPS	OPS+
Mays	84	1498	5459	1050	1635	259	53	350	1003	126	42	681	783	.300	.377	.559	.935	159
Aaron	81	1540	5912	*1091*	1819	309	45	375	*1107*	204	60	672	723	.308	.376	**.565**	.941	162

If WAR is our benchmark, this one is a toss-up. They were both great hitters. Defensively, Mays was better—but Hank Aaron certainly didn't embarrass himself. The constraints of the "Decade" parameter once again hurt Mays, as he loses his great 1954–59 run.

Mays, who led the league in charisma and flair, was the more famous of the two, and undoubtedly the bigger drawing card. Aaron, a man of quiet dignity, was every bit his equal on the field. Mays took one MVP trophy but probably should have won at least three; Aaron was shut out in terms of hardware, but had a strong case several times.

Regrettably, each made the post-season only once during the decade, with Mays' Giants bowing to the Yankees in the 1962 World Series, and Aaron's Braves getting swept in the 1969 NL Championship Series by the "Miracle" Mets (Aaron made the most of his brief opportunity: He was the best player on the field during the three-game sweep).

Reminiscing about his on-field rivalry with Mays, Aaron said in a 2008 interview, "It wasn't about who was better than who. God gave both of us all the talent and we wanted to do everything we could to make sure that that was fulfilled."

They succeeded, and then some. By the *slimmest* of margins, Mays gets the vote as of MVP of the Decade.

1970–79: The Contenders: Joe Morgan, Tom Seaver

1970s	WAR	G	AB	R	H	2B	3B	HR	RBI	SB	CS	BB	K	BA	OBP	SLG	OPS	OPS+
Morgan	67	1458	5139	1005	1451	275	47	173	720	488	105	*1071*	517	.282	.404	.455	.860	140

Morgan's raw offensive totals—while outstanding—probably don't do him justice. He was the best player on what some consider baseball's all-time greatest team. A superb hitter, a superb baserunner, a superb mind for the game. A fantastic defender at a premium position. He was voted MVP twice in the decade

(1975–76) and had a top-five showing on two other occasions. His brilliant play in the 1976 World Series helped spark the Reds dismissive sweep of the Yankees.[15]

For all of Morgan's greatness, he was never the biggest star on his own team, let alone all of baseball (playing alongside Johnny Bench and Pete Rose will do that). The garrulous Rose might have been the media's indispensable "quote," but Morgan was the team's indispensable player. He wasn't, however, the MVP of the decade.

1970s	pWAR	W	L	W%	ERA	G	GS	CG	SHO	IP	H	BB	K	ERA+	WHIP	K/BB
Seaver	67	178	101	.638	2.61	348	345	147	40	2652.1	2105	741	2304	**138**	1.073	3.11

June 15, 1977, is recalled by a generation of New York baseball fans as "The Midnight Massacre." It was this evening that the Mets traded Tom Seaver—"The Franchise," the best player in team history, the most popular athlete in the most populous city in the country—to the Cincinnati Reds for four players.[16]

The numbers tell us that from 1970 to the day he was traded, Seaver led the NL in ERA three times, strikeouts five times, WHIP three times. He was honored with the Cy Young trophy twice, and finished second in the voting on another occasion.[17] He led all pitchers in WAR (67) for the decade, with only Jim Palmer and Bert Blyleven within shouting distance.

But the numbers in this case seem insufficient to the task of explaining value. Seaver's departure was seen by many as a betrayal of the New York public trust, and here it might be said that feelings of sadness, loss, and anger do more to define an athlete's value than every number on the back of his baseball card.

It is for these reasons that Tom Seaver gets the nod over Joe Morgan as the decade's MVP.

1980–89: THE CONTENDERS: RICKEY, MIKE SCHMIDT, WADE BOGGS

1980s	WAR	G	AB	R	H	2B	3B	HR	RBI	SB	CS	BB	K	BA	OBP	SLG	OPS	OPS+
Rickey	71	1383	5173	**1122**	1507	248	44	137	535	**838**	**190**	**962**	697	.291	.403	.436	.839	137
Boggs	60	1183	4534	823	1597	314	36	64	523	14	22	754	339	**.352**	**.443**	.480	.922	150
Schmidt	56	1320	4639	832	1287	225	28	**313**	929	57	38	818	925	.277	.385	.540	**.925**	**153**

It's tough to get an invite to this club. Ask Robin Yount, who claimed two MVP awards and led the decade in hits, doubles, and triples. Ask Dale Murphy, who took back-to-back honors in 1982–83, hit more home runs than anybody but Schmidt, drove in more than anybody but Schmidt and Eddie Murray. Ask MVP winners George Brett, Cal Ripken, Jr., and Andre Dawson. They all made the Hall of Fame, but none are in the running for MVP of the 80s.

19. Fun with Arbitrary Endpoints: MVPs of the Decade

With three trophies and a third-place showing, Mike Schmidt was the clear MVP with the voters of the time. For the decade, the greatest third baseman of them all led the league in home runs five times, RBI four times, slugging four times, on-base percentage three times, walks three times, and adjusted production *six* times. Schmidt was the most productive hitter in baseball, and we haven't even touched on his wonderful defense.

Wade Boggs dominated the decade in ways that weren't fully understood or appreciated at the time. The five batting titles and .352 BA are great, but they don't fully capture his brilliance. Dismissed by many as a "slap hitter," Boggs' .480 slugging places him among the top 15 of the decade (ranking higher than noted mashers Jim Rice and Reggie Jackson). His .443 OBP (he led the league six times) is *40 points* higher than runner-up Rickey Henderson. Boggs simply refused to make outs, gathering 200 hits and 100 walks in the same season four times. Despite leading position players in WAR three times, Boggs never received any significant support in the MVP voting.

And then there is Rickey Henderson. Like Boggs, Rickey was largely ignored by the voters at the time (he should have taken the award in 1985, and had a case in 1981 and 1989). Don't let the lack of hardware fool you: He was a dynamo, comfortably leading the world in WAR, runs, walks, and stolen bases. Rickey is known as the greatest lead-off hitter ever, but that's damning him with faint praise—he's unique in the game's history.

Schmidt, Boggs, Rickey. Three very different players who shared one very important skill: The ability to make the pitcher meet them on their own terms, i.e., *patience* at the plate. As noted, Rickey led the decade in walks. Schmidt placed fourth, while Boggs, despite ranking 46th in total games played, ranked eighth. Rickey dominated with patience and speed; Schmidt with patience and power; Boggs with patience and precision.

Who then is the standard bearer for the decade? In the end, Rickey's significant WAR lead can't be ignored: He's the MVP of the 80s.[18]

1990–99: Barry Bonds

1990s	WAR	G	AB	R	H	2B	3B	HR	RBI	SB	CS	BB	K	BA	OBP	SLG	OPS	OPS+
Bonds	80	1434	4894	*1091*	1478	299	42	361	1076	343	94	*1146*	747	.302	.434	.602	*1.036*	179

If the 1990s constituted his career in its entirety, Bonds is a Hall of Famer (and his peak was yet to come). Ken Griffey, Jr., is the only challenger for the title of "Best Player in Baseball"—and it's not really close. Bonds, with MVPs in 1990, 1992, and 1993, was the best and most valuable player of the decade.

2000–09: The Contenders: Alex Rodriguez, Albert Pujols, Barry Bonds

2000s	WAR	G	AB	R	H	2B	3B	HR	RBI	BB	K	BA	OBP	SLG	OPS	OPS+
Rodriguez	78	1524	5732	*1190*	1740	285	16	*435*	*1243*	850	1243	.304	.401	.587	.988	153
Pujols	74	1399	5146	1071	1717	387	14	366	1112	811	570	*.334*	.427	.628	1.055	172
Bonds	59	986	2871	772	925	178	12	317	697	*1128*	427	.322	*.517*	.724	*1.241*	*221*

Yep. Issues. But we work with the facts we have. And the facts tell us this:

- Between them, A-Rod, Pujols and Bonds earn *ten* MVP awards in the decade. That's *half* the available hardware.
- Bonds wins four consecutive awards from 2001 to 2004, and accrues 59 WAR in just six full(ish) seasons.[19] He retires after the 2007 season (or, more accurately, is forced to retire when he isn't able to land a job after posting a .480 OBP and hitting 28 HRs in 126 games).[20]
- Pujols has one of the most dominant decades in the history of the game. He garners three MVP trophies (and finishes second three times), leads all players in batting average, and would have

Dogged though he may be by controversy, three-time MVP A-Rod is the player of the decade 2000–2009 (courtesy Keith Allison, https://creativecommons.org/licenses/by-sa/2.0/legalcode).

19. Fun with Arbitrary Endpoints: MVPs of the Decade

led the decade in on-base, slugging, and adjusted production if not for Bonds.

- Rodriguez leads all players in WAR, runs, home runs, and RBI. He sets single-season home run records for a shortstop (57 in 2002) *and* a third baseman (54 in 2007). He leads his league in home runs five times, runs scored and slugging four times apiece, RBI twice. He's named MVP three times and has a case for two more.

Who is the most valuable player of the most complicated decade in baseball history? On a game-by-game basis, it's no contest: Bonds is the best ever. But he just doesn't play enough, so he falls from contention.

That leaves Pujols and Rodriguez, the two best players of their generation. WAR rates them as about equal. Pujols is the superior hitter, Rodriguez the better all-around player. Both lay claim to three MVP awards and a World Series trophy. How do we break the tie?

What about "bang for the buck"?

Using this criteria, it's no contest: Given the cost of purchasing an "added win" on the free-agent market (on average, more than $4 million per win over the course of the decade), Pujols is a *screaming* bargain.[21] St. Louis paid for a Chalmers, but drove a Ferrari.

2000s	WAR	Salary*	Player Cost/WAR	Market Cost/WAR
Pujols	74	$75 M	$1.01 M	$4M +
Rodriguez	78	$224 M	$2.87 M	$4M +

*Rounded to nearest decimal. Source: Baseball-Reference.com; HardballTimes.com

Of course, Rodriguez was a relative bargain as well (despite being the highest-paid player in baseball history). And let's be real: No one considers player contracts when determining most valuable—it's not called "The Biggest Bargain Award." So this is no way to determine the player of the decade.

The post-season might be illustrative. Throughout the decade they're both annual fixtures on the October stage, so we have a decent sample size. Pujols, of course, has a reputation of rising to the occasion; Rodriguez is notorious for disappearing when the pressure is on.

Post-Season	G	AB	R	H	2B	3B	HR	RBI	BB	K	SB	CS	BA	OBP	SLG	OPS
Rodriguez	48	181	34	55	13	0	12	34	29	45	6	3	.304	.420	.575	.995
Pujols	56	199	39	64	10	1	13	36	36	28	0	1	.322	.431	.578	1.009

Wasn't expecting *that*. Rodriguez and Pujols are still tied. Two great players. Six MVPs between them. How to choose?

In the end, it comes down to positional scarcity. Pujols was a fine first baseman, but Rodriguez was an exceptional shortstop (and starting in 2004, a very good third baseman). Swing a dead cat in the 2000s and you'll find a slugging first baseman (though none as good as Pujols); good luck finding a shortstop (or a third baseman) who could hit like Rodriguez—in any decade.[22] A-Rod is the player of the aughts.

20

The Wonderful Argument

The numbers were there. If one were making a case for Don Mattingly as the American League's Most Valuable Player for 1986, the numbers were there.

1986	WAR	G	AB	R	H	2B	3B	HR	RBI	BB	K	BA	OBP	SLG	OPS	OPS+
Mattingly	7.2	162	677	117	238	53	2	31	113	53	35	.352	.394	**.573**	**.967**	**161**

And then there was the crouch, the slightly busy feet in the box (always tinkering), the compact blur of a swing. The eye black. The moustache. Fathers to sons: *"That's* what a ballplayer looks like." Style points count.

That Mattingly was going to capture his second consecutive MVP award was a foregone conclusion, a way to reclaim the headlines from the cross-town Mets (still reveling in World Series glory), and a small measure of consolation for the Yankees' disappointing second-place finish.

The voters had other ideas. The Associated Press, on November 19, 1918, reported, "Roger Clemens, who won his first 14 decisions this season and wound up with a 24–4 record in leading the Boston Red Sox to their division title, capped his dream year yesterday by being voted the league's Most Valuable Player Award."

1986	pWAR	W	L	W%	ERA	G	GS	CG	SHO	IP	H	ER	BB	K	ERA+	WHIP	K/BB
Clemens	8.9	24	4	.857	2.48	33	33	10	1	254	179	70	67	238	**169**	**0.969**	3.55

The news hit the sensibilities of Yankees fans with the impact of a Clemens four-seamer to the ribs. The Boston ace took the award with room to spare (19 first-place votes to five), and the indignation of New York fandom was enflamed.[1] The Clemens MVP was an outrage splashed in 40-point type across the back pages of every tabloid in the city. Hank Aaron called the pick "a joke," adding fuel to a roiling hot-stove debate; NL MVP Mike Schmidt was more diplomatic, but commiserated with Mattingly: "[Clemens] may be an exception, he was so dominant. But I'm not in favor of a pitcher being considered for the MVP." Ron Darling, starting pitcher for the champion Mets, was flabbergasted: "It's hard for me to think how Mattingly could have lost the award. I'm one who believes everyday players should win."

Sure, Clemens went 24–4; sure, the AL champion Red Sox had finished an average of 19 games out of first place the prior three seasons; sure, entering 1986 they were considered bottom-feeders ready to be filleted by the rest of the AL East; and sure, Clemens hoisted this afterthought of a roster onto his broad shoulders and carried them to the World Series.[2] But the best everyday player in the league *has* to be more valuable than, as Mattingly himself would say, "a guy who is in 33 or 34 games." And as the well-tread logic went, Clemens had already been recognized for his work with the AL Cy Young Award.

Is it worth mentioning that eight seasons prior, Yankees fans were apoplectic over the selection of burly Red Sox outfielder Jim Rice over New York's coiled-whip lefthander Ron Guidry? Guidry, who threw seven shutouts after the All-Star break; Guidry, who humiliated the Red Sox down the stretch (3–0, 0.74 ERA after Sept. 9); Guidry, who stabbed slider-after-slider into the sinking, despondent heart of 1978 Red Sox Nation in a sudden-death, one-game playoff for division.

1978	WAR	G	AB	R	H	2B	3B	HR	RBI	BB	K	BA	OBP	SLG	OPS	OPS+
Rice	7.5	*163*	*677*	121	*213*	25	*15*	*46*	*139*	58	126	.315	.370	*.600*	*.970*	*157*

In the end, the writers went with the slugger over the surgeon, deeming Rice the most valuable player in the American League. New York faithful howled at the injustice. Who could be more valuable than an ace pitcher producing a season for the ages? Guidry was gracious in the face of a stinging vote, calling himself Rice's biggest fan—but he couldn't resist a parting shot at the voters: "If they want to leave out pitchers, they ought to put an asterisk next to it and say 'Pitchers: Generally not included.'"[3]

1978	pWAR	W	L	W%	ERA	G	GS	CG	SHO	IP	H	ER	BB	K	ERA+	WHIP	K/BB
Guidry	*9.6*	*25*	3	*.893*	*1.74*	35	35	16	*9*	273	173	53	72	248	*208*	*0.946*	3.44

To summarize:

- 1978: Of course a pitcher can be most valuable!
- 1986: Pitchers have their own award!

When things really matter, passion doesn't owe consistency a thing. And the MVP *mattered*. Almost as much as Opening Day, almost as much as wins and losses.

And it still does. More than any other award in professional sports. Search for "Baseball MVP" and Google returns more than 20 million results—click enough of them, and themes emerge: Impassioned arguments for or against a player; praise or scorn for a ballot; line-by-line parsing of the BBWAA instructions to voters; list after list of "worst MVPs"; and an endless, elliptical consideration of the meaning of the word "value."

It bears asking: Why? Why do we as fans care so much about a plaque hanging in someone else's trophy room?

◆ ◆ ◆

"The games themselves have never been quite enough for sports fans," says Joe Posnanski, author of *The Soul of Baseball*.[4] "We've always wanted to talk about and argue about other things."

ESPN.com senior writer Jerry Crasnick agrees. "Fans and writers love to argue and debate—particularly in a sport with the rich history of baseball—and the definition of the award is just vague enough to leave plenty of wiggle room."

Crasnick and Posnaski aren't kidding: A catalogue of topics guaranteed to agitate discussion includes the pitcher vs. everyday player debate; the slugger vs. all-around player debate; the "MVPs should come from playoff teams" argument; the 'statheads' vs. 'traditionalists' debate; the "team player vs. individual achievement" argument; and, of course, the "how does one define value?" question. These existential motifs fuel endless hours of pontification and prognosticating (and, at times, vitriol) during drive-time talk radio and prime-time sports television; countless conversations and debates on bar stools and at kitchen tables; uncountable tweets, blogs, and message board postings (talk about vitriol).

"I think there's something more specific about baseball and the MVP award," says Posnanski. "Baseball, in my view, is unique among American team sports because of its relationship between the team and the individual."

Baseball, according to Posnanski, is really an individual sport played in a team environment. "Most of what a player does on the baseball field requires individual skills only. Hitting is an individual skill. Catching a fly ball is an individual skill. Pitching, for the most part, is an individual skill. Nobody else is involved in those things. But within that context, there is a wonderful connection between the players. A base runner might be able to distract a pitcher enough to help a hitter. A first baseman can help a shortstop's fielding by scooping a poor throw out of the dirt. A catcher can help a pitcher by perfectly framing strike three."

Because of this, says Posnanski, there's a wonderful argument to be had every year about who is the most valuable player in baseball. "It's not something that works as well in, say, football.... How can you really tell if a receiver is more valuable than a defensive lineman?" In baseball, says Posnanski, "hitters are generally trying to accomplish the same things. Pitchers are generally trying to accomplish the same things. The MVP argument is much more apples to apples."[5]

◆ ◆ ◆

Maybe it matters to us because it matters to *them*. Take 1974.

"I honestly don't consider myself with the people I'm now ranked with, the players who have won before," said an incredulous Jeff Burroughs on learning of his American League MVP award. "Joe DiMaggio, Mickey Mantle, Reggie Jackson—I see my name with theirs and it just doesn't seem realistic."[6]

National League runner-up Lou Brock had a different perspective: "If I steal a thousand bases next year and they offer me the MVP, I wouldn't accept it," said the seething Cardinals star when he learned Steve Garvey was named the NL's most valuable for 1974.

Brock might have been more gracious in defeat, but his candid venting of frustration provided a glimpse into the meaning of the award: Even wealthy, famous athletes crave external validation and recognition for their efforts. No surprise—they've been training and competing for it their entire lives. A perceived snub can stay with a player like a post-career limp: Ted Williams' jaw tightened for *decades* whenever the 1947 vote was brought up. In 2005, Mike Greenwell (1988 AL runner-up) called for an *ex post facto* stripping of the award from Jose Canseco, who by then had chronicled his steroid use in a best-selling memoir. Fifteen years after the 1999 AL vote, Pedro Martinez continued to question the motives of the writers who denied him his MVP.

As Jim Rice said in accepting his 1978 award, "That's what baseball is all about—getting respect."

It *matters*.

◆ ◆ ◆

Are there other factors at play? Something deeper, more central to our core that compels our annual and protracted MVP debate, our "wonderful argument," as Posnanski put it?

Dr. Sheryll M. Casuga, clinical psychologist and certified sports psychologist, thinks that the awards ultimately represent something more than on-field performance. Baseball fans care about these awards because "they look up to athletes not just for their skills, but for their overall qualities as athletes."

It might be easy to reject Dr. Casuga's opinion out of hand: Does anybody really admire athletes anymore? More than 100 players have claimed a version of the MVP award, a roster filled with drunks, racists, steroid users, and gamblers (as well as many decent, honorable men). The days of a complicit press corps whitewashing the transgressions of the players they cover are long gone; on issues of character, we know more about an athlete's deficits than their assets.

But Dr. Casuga is on to something when she says, "[Fans] look up to athletes that have admirable qualities, such as leadership, hard work, being a team player, perseverance, and honesty. Player awards highlight role-models in sports that people can look up to and aspire to become in sports and in life."

Fans admired Mattingly as much for "playing the game the right way" as for his batting stroke. New York Baby Boomers retain a reverential wonder in their voice when recalling a hobbled Mantle as he circled the bases with a mask of pain on his face. The dignified Koufax is more monument than man to generations of fans and players; the same can be said for Hank Aaron, now a living tribute to dignity and grace. Is there a sports fan in the Midwest who doesn't count the generous and genial Stan Musial as a role model and, in many ways, a dear, departed friend?

"In theory, we should just be able to haul out an all-encompassing stat like WAR and anoint the Most Valuable Player in each league each November," says ESPN's Crasnick. "But it's more romantic—and fun, I think—to dig for intangibles that put a given player over the top. It's one thing for a hitter to lead the league in home runs or OPS or any number of offensive categories. But the Most Valuable Player ascends to a different level by playing through injuries, or 'carrying a team on his back down the stretch,' or 'raising the level of play of the people around him.'"

It's an argument as old as the award itself. "Babe Ruth by a popular vote probably would be chosen as the greatest player in baseball," wrote Henry Farrell for the United Press in February of 1922. Farrell was discussing potential MVP candidates for the coming season. "But American League fans do not agree he is the most valuable to his club. Temperament, reliability, unselfishness—in addition to mechanical ability—go to make up a valuable player."

Ruth, coming off the two best seasons by a hitter in baseball history, had just been suspended for the first six weeks of the 1922 season for brazenly violating Commissioner Kenesaw Mountain Landis' rule against barnstorming by players who had participated in the prior-season's World Series.[7] It was a breathtaking display of arrogance on part of the Babe, the ultimate "me first, team second" move. When the 1922 season ended, Ruth was, on a game-by-game basis, still the most productive hitter in baseball—but he was guaranteed to be an MVP also-ran. Five Yankees received some form of MVP consideration in 1922. Despite being the best player on the team, Ruth wasn't one of them.

"Call it hero worship or whatever you want," says Crasnick. "But we like our MVPs to bring more to the table than just gaudy statistics. If they can provide leadership or intensity or a *presence in the clubhouse,* it makes for a more inspirational narrative."

◆ ◆ ◆

Of course, this notion of the inspirational narrative has been the basis of some of the most contentious (and, as Crasnick points out, *fun*) MVP votes of all time. There are camps that dismiss outright the notion of "intangibles" over numbers. These voters choose data over romance, logic over leadership. It speaks to a driving force behind the impassioned arguments that swirl around the Most Valuable Player selection: The notion that the MVP stands as proxy for how an individual approaches and appreciates the game.

Maybe you prefer your MVPs to *play the game the right way (while being a leader in the clubhouse, and showing his team how to win).* Maybe you don't care one bit about any of that; maybe you think the best numbers equate to the best player, and *the best player, by definition, is the most valuable.* Maybe you think MVPs can only come from playoff teams—after all, how valuable can a guy be if his team finishes out of contention? One's point of view about the award often seems to carry as much weight, and stir as much passion, as political conviction.

◆ ◆ ◆

So why does it matter so much?

Rooting interest, celebration of excellence, mark of character, and approach to the game—all play a role in gestating an endless fascination with the award, but none can fully explain it. It's probably a little of all-of-the-above, and a dash of none-of-the-above. In the end, Jerry Crasnick provides an answer as good as any.

"If you log onto Baseball-Reference.com and scan the list of MVP winners, you'll find names like Babe Ruth and Lou Gehrig, Ted Williams and Joe DiMaggio, Hank Aaron and Willie Mays and so many other players who are synonymous with baseball's history and tradition and carry the torch from one generation to the next. Those names," says Crasnick, "help explain why the MVP award has meaning a lot better than I (or anybody else who follows the game) could ever articulate."

21

The Last Worst MVP: The Future of the Award

The subject was the 2006 AL MVP race. Boston's David Ortiz—in the running for the award—had a few things on his mind.

"I'm right there, but I'm not going to win it," said Ortiz in a revealing September interview with the *Boston Globe*'s Gordon Edes. "They give it to Alex [Rodriguez] one year, even though his team was in last place, so now they can't play that BS anymore. But they always have a reason to vote for whatever, so that's why I don't worry about it."

Ortiz, however, clearly *was* worrying about it (or at least thinking about it). After three consecutive top-five finishes—including a runner-up showing to Rodriguez in 2005—it appeared he had a trophy-sized chip on his shoulder. "They'll vote for a position player, use that as an excuse," said the Boston designated hitter.

The 2006 race was a considered a wide-open affair, expected to come down to Minnesota teammates Joe Mauer and Justin Morneau, the Yankees' Derek Jeter, and Ortiz, a dark-horse candidate for the third-place Boston Red Sox.[1]

2006	WAR	G	AB	R	H	2B	3B	HR	RBI	SB	CS	BB	K	BA	OBP	SLG	OPS	OPS+
Morneau	4.3	157	592	97	190	37	1	34	130	3	3	53	93	.321	.375	.559	.934	140
Jeter	5.5	154	623	118	214	39	3	14	97	34	5	69	102	.343	.417	.483	.900	132
Ortiz	5.7	151	558	115	160	29	2	*54*	*137*	1	0	*119*	117	.287	.413	.636	1.049	161
Mauer	5.8	140	521	86	181	36	4	13	84	8	3	79	54	*.347*	.429	.507	.936	144

"They're talking about Jeter a lot, right? He's done a great job, he's having a great season, but Jeter is not a 40-homer hitter or an RBI guy ... the guy who hits 40 home runs and knocks in 100, that's the guy you know helped your team win games."

Ortiz's argument was at once self-servingly progressive (don't penalize a great player because his teammates couldn't get the job done) and defiantly old-school (real men drive in runs; all that other stuff—defense, base running—is for guys who can't hit home runs).

In a close vote, the voters ultimately chose the Twins' slugging first baseman over the hard-hitting shortstop, with Ortiz finishing a distant third on the ballot (Mauer placed an inexplicable sixth). In the end, the voters agreed with Ortiz' point of view and adhered to the primacy of the RBI. But they weren't ready to discount team performance (the Twins, mired in fourth place as of mid–June, stormed the league over the second half to claim a division title), and they weren't ready to give the award to a player who never took the field.

Best MVP Finishes, Designated Hitter

Player	MVP	Year	WAR	G	AB	R	H	2B	3B	HR	RBI	BB	BA	OBP	SLG	OPS	OPS+
Frank Thomas	2	2000	6.0	159	582	115	191	44	0	43	143	112	.328	.436	.625	1.061	163
David Ortiz	2	2005	5.3	159	601	119	180	40	1	47	**148**	102	.300	.397	.604	1.001	158
Paul Molitor	2	1993	5.7	160	636	121	**211**	37	5	22	111	77	.332	.402	.509	.911	143
Edgar Martinez	3	1995	7.0	**145**	511	**121**	182	**52**	0	29	113	116	**.356**	**.479**	.628	**1.107**	**185**
Frank Thomas	3	1991	6.9	158	559	104	178	31	2	32	109	**138**	.318	**.453**	.553	**1.006**	**180**
David Ortiz	3	2006	5.7	151	558	115	160	29	2	**54**	**137**	**119**	.287	.413	.636	1.049	161

The Morneau vote almost always ranks high on anyone's list of "worst MVPs"—and it's true his 4.3 WAR is among the ten worst for an MVP winner (he ranked 23rd in the league in 2006).[2] But his coronation as the league's most valuable doesn't quite crack the worst-of-the-worst when placed in context: The young first baseman had an extended period of strong production (.362/.412/.611, 23 HR 92 RBI over the last 104 games of the season) that coincided with a 71–33 team run that took the Twins from the murky depths of the division to the bright lights of the playoffs.[3] It should also be noted that his primary competition for the award wasn't without flaws.

- Jeter, a better pick for the honor than Morneau, was an excellent hitter and baserunner—but WAR suggests he gave a significant portion of his overall value back with poor defense. Jeter may also have suffered from playing on too *good* a team—with a lineup stacked with All-Stars, the Yankees were an offensive juggernaut, comfortably leading the league in runs scored and pacing the AL East by ten games. Jeter was their best player, but, as several voters noted, the Yankees claim their division with even average production from their shortstop.
- Ortiz was a devastating hitter, launching a *dozen* more home runs than any other player in the league, and leading in walks and RBI.[4] But he was a designated hitter, and that just wasn't going to fly with the voters. With five top-five MVP finishes (2003–2007), Ortiz is the most recog-

nized and acclaimed DH in history—but the 2006 vote served as a final referendum of sorts on the position: If Ortiz couldn't claim the award in a wide-open field, it appears a full-time DH may never take the honor.
- There's a clear and compelling argument to be made for several other players, including the aforementioned Mauer and the third pillar of the Twin Cities' most-valuable troika, Johan Santana (19–6/2.77/245K/ 7.5 pWAR). Objectively speaking, both were more valuable to the team than Morneau. But with the misguided bias against pitchers, Santana had no chance—and Mauer, while more valuable than Morneau, wasn't *demonstrably* better than, say, Jeter.

Let's be clear: The Morneau pick wasn't great. It's probably the most questionable MVP pick of the past 15 years. But given his competition for the award, it's not a travesty akin to Roger Peckinpaugh's 1925 award.

So why mention it in a book that devotes several hundred pages to exploring the worst MVP votes in history?

Because it just might be the last "worst" MVP.

◆ ◆ ◆

Since the modern incarnation of the Most Valuable Player award was introduced in 1931, we've learned a few things along the way.

- The MVP award goes to the best all-around player in the league in a given season—except when it doesn't. MVPs have led their league in WAR about 40 percent of the time (including pitchers).
- The MVP goes to the best player on the best team—except when it doesn't. Cincinnati's "Big Red Machine" produced six MVPs in eight years; the 1996–2000 Yankees, with four World Series championships in five years, produced … none.
- Players from last-place teams never win the MVP—except when they do (Andre Dawson, 1987; Alex Rodriguez, 2003).
- Designated hitters, as David Ortiz can affirm, have no shot at claiming an award.
- Setting a record of some sort goes a long way in the eyes of MVP voters. A record will often overshadow the all-around accomplishments of a superior candidate. George Burns was named AL MVP in 1926 because he hit lots of doubles; Joe DiMaggio's 56-game hitting streak was the main pillar supporting his 1941 award platform; Maury Wills took 1962 honors because he broke Ty Cobb's long-standing stolen

base record; Denny McLain won 31 games in 1968 and took home an MVP to go along with his Cy Young trophy; you know about Roger Maris in 1961.

- All-around players who do everything well tend to do worse in the voting than "specialists" who excel at one thing. That one thing is usually driving in runs. MVP voters historically love RBI. *Love* them. One-third of all MVP selections since 1931 have led their league in RBI; the majority of all MVP selections have finished in the top-five in RBI.

- That said, it looks like those RBI fires *might* be cooling, at least a bit: Since 1998, only one NL MVP has led his league in runs driven in (Ryan Howard, 2006), while four trophies have gone to the RBI leader in the American League (Alex Rodriguez, 2007; Miguel Cabrera, 2012; Mike Trout, 2014; Josh Donaldson, 2015). Out of a total of 33 awards given to position players since 1998, seven have *failed* to place among the league leaders in RBI: Ivan Rodriguez (1999), Ichiro Suzuki (2001), Jimmy Rollins (2007), Dustin Pedroia (2008), Joe Mauer (2009), Josh Hamilton (2010), and Andrew McCutchen (2013).

- MVPs are players who show up for work every day—except when they're not. Gabby Hartnett played a mere 116 games in his 1935 campaign; George Brett suited up for 117 games in 1980; Josh Hamilton missed a month of the season in 2010; Clayton Kershaw made but 27 starts in his 2014 MVP campaign.[5]

- Latter-day MVP voters are somewhat indifferent to defense. While the writers fall for the rakish, hollow charm of the RBI, dependable, drama-free defense often goes ignored.

- MVP voters are suckers for a narrative. Narratives include things like "leadership," "intangibles," "clutch performance," "playing the right way," and "showing a team how to win."

- National League voters hate pitchers (unless that pitcher is Clayton Kershaw). American League voters had a bizarre fascination with relief pitchers for about a decade (those hazy, crazy '80s).

- MVP voters *used* to love catchers and pitchers. Now they love corner outfielders and first basemen. They hate second basemen like an underemployed son-in-law (only ten MVP selections out of the 171 awarded since 1931). They should really love catchers a lot more than they do.

- MVP voters don't love the Triple Crown as much as one would expect. There have been 15 Triple Crowns since 1900—with the MVP award in existence for 12 of them. Those 12 seasons produced seven MVPs,

meaning Triple Crown titlists have been named MVP only 58 percent of the time.
- We've learned that it's really hard to define "value," which is problematic because the award was created to recognize the most valuable player in each league. Many voters employ Justice Stewart's "I know it when I see it" criteria. Using this criteria has led to some highly dubious MVP choices over the years.
- It should also be said that, on the whole, the voters get it right (or at least "right-ish") more often than not.

As the investing disclaimer reads, "Past performance does not suggest future results." What we've learned may not in fact hold predictive value for the award. Historically, MVP voters have proven an obstinate lot, overvaluing RBI and rewarding borderline candidates based on team record. And yet, none of the awards doled out in recent years—and here we include 2006—have been worthy of a general recall. In fact, there really hasn't been an unmitigated disaster of a vote since 1998.

Is a changing game dragging the MVP award into modernity? And what does this mean for the future of the most prized and contentious individual honor in professional sports?

◆ ◆ ◆

Given the current state of the vote, we can venture with some confidence that the future of the award will be marked by three macro trends: 1) an increasing reliance on sophisticated data analysis, especially with regard to defense; 2) pitcher usage patterns; 3) profound shifts in the electorate.

The Defensive Revolution Will Be Televised (and Streamed)

It's been 70 years since Marty Marion caught-and-threw his way to an MVP, and it seems like the baseball world may finally be on the verge of properly quantifying defensive contributions. In April of 2015, MLB officially launched a new tracking technology called "StatCast" that promises to revolutionize the way teams measure defensive contributions

The system, deployed in every major league park, uses advanced radar technology and ultra-high-definition cameras to record just about every movement on the field, from the "spin rate" of a curveball to the "exit velocity" of the ball coming off the bat.

Statcast data includes information such as "first-step" and acceleration of defensive players (does Juan Lagares get a better jump on line drives than Lorenzo Cain?), and release time and velocity of throws (does Yoenis Cespedes have a better arm than Jason Heyward?). According to Major League Baseball, Stat Cast can even determine if an outfielder took an optimal route to the ball.

This data is represented in graphical form, accompanying high-definition video of the play itself. As teams (and third-parties, such as television networks and websites) accumulate and analyze vast amounts of data, it will be fairly easy to determine, for example, who has the greatest range, who has the best arm, who takes the most direct and efficient path to a batted ball. In other words, who *really* makes the plays?

While still in its infancy as of this writing—as might be expected, home run distances are the most popular data point on nightly sports broadcasts—the system should fundamentally reshape player evaluation. Teams are hiring front-office staff dedicated to crunching the data generated by this new technology, and it's clear the future of roster-building lies within the vast amounts of information being generated by StatCast (and proprietary technology in use by every major league franchise).

The question, for our purposes, is how will big data impact MVP voting? Oakland Athletics General Manager Billy Beane took to the editorial pages of *The Wall Street Journal* to offer his perspective: "Whereas current metrics describe players' performance in isolation, front offices will increasingly rely on statistics that measure a player's value in the context of the rest of the team, picking up externalities such as how a player's defensive abilities may compensate for the deficiencies of those playing around him."

It's the grayest of gray areas in terms of player evaluation, and one of the most contentious aspects of the annual MVP debate: Did a player make his teammates better? Is it even *possible* for a player make his teammates better? And if it's possible, is it quantifiable?

As Joe Posnanski noted earlier, "there is a wonderful connection between the players. A base runner might be able to distract a pitcher enough to help a hitter. A first baseman can help a shortstop's fielding by scooping a poor throw out of the dirt. A catcher can help a pitcher by perfectly framing strike three."

With the technology now in place, Beane suggests that these connections between players can be quantified, and the true value of a player's overall contributions—including the things he does to help make his teammates better—revealed. While we're not predicting an MVP win by a "super" utility player, we may indeed see the jack-of-all trades, defensive-minded type (think a Ben Zobrist) fare much better in tomorrow's vote. As teams become more comfortable with this data, the MVP vote should follow course.[6]

A Slightly More Honest Accounting of Pitching

While we'd never say "never," it's a reasonable bet that we've seen the last of the short-reliever MVP. While relief pitching as a whole is more important than ever, individual roles are now being put in proper context, and a credible case for the 70-inning closer as the most useful and valuable to his team simply can't be made. Even the most nostalgic of voters has come to recognize the immense value of innings pitched: Since Dennis Eckersley took honors in 1992, the best showing by a reliever is Eric Gagne's sixth-place finish in 2003—and to get there, Gagne had to convert 55 saves in 55 opportunities, pitch to a 1.20 ERA, and strike out 137 batters in 82 innings.[7]

If we're ever to see another closer as MVP, three things will have to happen: (1) An historic performance, i.e., a season superior to any relief effort that has come before[8]; (2) An utter lack of standout performances across the entirety of the player population; (3) A change in pitcher usage patterns.

The widespread adoption of the one-inning (and in many cases, one-batter) bullpen specialist began in earnest in the 1980s; this trend has continued unabated for 30 years, with bullpen composition reflecting the realities of the contemporary game (and hastened dramatically by the punishing offensive environment of the late '90s/early aughts). Teams now devote *half* of the active roster to the pitching staff, regularly carrying up to 13 pitchers, with each arm machined to fit a precise slot within the flow of the game: Teams have their seventh-inning man, their eighth-inning, or set-up, man, and of course, the alpha-wolf closer. Teams bolster their staffs with archetypes that include the one-batter, slop-throwing, lefty neutralizer; the sinker-balling double-play machine; and the garbage-time, slightly wild speed demon looking to secure his place in the bullpen hierarchy.

Limited roles mean limited opportunities, and today's specialists don't approach even 100 innings in a season. Unless a bold (or, depending on how one looks at it, benighted) General Manager decides to resurrect the classic long man or every-day reliever (those greedy, gluttonous Vultures of yore), it's unlikely we'll ever again see an MVP award wasted on a part-time pitcher. The body of work simply won't be there.

And what of starters? In making an early-season case for Tampa Bay's Chris Archer as a potential 2015 MVP candidate, ESPN.com's Dave Schoenfield wrote: "None of the top five position players ... are on teams currently in a playoff position. That potentially opens the door for a pitcher, and the recent MVP choices of Justin Verlander and Clayton Kershaw indicate voters no longer snub their noses at pitchers."

It would be nice to share Schoenfield's optimism, but the jury, as they say, is still out. Until proven otherwise, the Verlander/Kershaw awards should be considered more outlier than predictor. The evidence is just too overwhelming: Pitcher MVPs, like pitcher W-L records, have less to do with performance, and more to do with external events beyond the control of the player. Plenty of voters still think it's perfectly acceptable to disqualify fully half of the active player population from MVP consideration.

Thirty years ago, Roger Clemens took AL MVP honors. Let's take a look at the best pitching performances since then:

Best Pitching Seasons, 1987–2014 (as Measured by pWAR)

RK	Year	Player	pWAR	GS	CG	W	L	W%	IP	ER	BB	K	ERA	FIP	ERA+	MVP
1	1997	Roger Clemens	11.9	34	9	21	7	.750	264.0	60	68	292	2.05	2.25	222	10
2	2000	Pedro Martinez	11.7	29	7	18	6	.750	217.0	42	32	284	1.74	2.17	291	5
3	2002	Randy Johnson	10.9	35	8	24	5	.828	260.0	67	71	334	2.32	2.66	195	7
4	1990	Roger Clemens	10.6	31	7	21	6	.778	228.1	49	54	209	1.93	2.18	211	3
5	2009	Zack Greinke	10.4	33	6	16	8	.667	229.1	55	51	242	2.16	2.33	205	17
6	2001	Randy Johnson	10	34	3	21	6	.778	249.2	69	71	372	2.49	2.13	188	11
7	1999	Pedro Martinez	9.7	29	5	23	4	.852	213.1	49	37	313	2.07	1.39	243	2
8	1995	Greg Maddux	9.7	28	10	19	2	.905	209.2	38	23	181	1.63	2.26	260	3
9	1989	Bret Saberhagen	9.7	35	12	23	6	.793	262.1	63	43	193	2.16	2.45	180	8
10	1987	Roger Clemens	9.4	36	18	20	9	.690	281.2	93	83	256	2.97	2.91	154	19
						• • •										
31	2011	Justin Verlander	8.4	34	4	24	5	.828	251.0	67	57	250	2.40	2.99	172	1
58	2014	Clayton Kershaw	7.5	27	6	21	3	.875	198.1	39	31	239	1.77	1.81	197	1

Ranking 1997 Clemens over 2000 Pedro or 2002 Johnson is splitting hairs; each has a case as the best pitching season of the past 30 years. In fact, one can easily make a case for five or six of the top-10 seasons listed above as the best performance by a pitcher since 1987.

Not so for Verlander or Kershaw, neither of whom place among the *top 30* individual pitching seasons since 1987 (Kershaw's bid undone by his low innings total, Verlander because he was just slightly less fantastic than the pitchers ahead of him on the list). Yet Kershaw and Verlander were recognized with MVP hardware, while the voters largely ignored the other seasons on this list. Of the two awards, Verlander's was the more surprising (and edifying): The top of the 2011 ballot included first-rate candidates Jose Bautista and Jacoby Ellsbury; that Verlander claimed the prize over legitimate competition bucked decades of established voter attitudes.

Kershaw, on the other hand, had no real challengers for the award. He was incredible, of course, but not demonstrably better than in any of his prior three seasons. His award was as much a function of his performance as it was a lack of credible candidates; front-runner Giancarlo Stanton's bid was undone by an errant fastball to the jaw. Once the Miami outfielder was removed from the MVP equation in mid–September, Kershaw was the only logical choice for the award.

In other words, voters have traditionally looked for reasons *not* to give a pitcher the award; until voting patterns suggest otherwise, we're going to assume that this holds true in the future.

Demographic Shifts in the Electorate

The writing is on the wall for the "old-school" voter. More accurately, the writing is on the mobile device of millions of fans who have enthusiastically adopted a more nuanced and sophisticated view of the game.

A significant contingent of the MVP voting bloc has always been behind the curve when it comes to quantifying player production, lagging GMs, talent evaluators, statisticians, players, and fans. But as the demographics of the MVP electorate change—that is to say, as younger writers well-versed and at ease with data join the ranks of the BBWAA, we can expect to see advanced statistical analysis play a more prominent role in MVP vote.

Nowhere was this more evident than the great Trout vs. Cabrera debate of 2012 –the most contentious MVP argument of the past quarter century. Both players were superb, with Cabrera producing the first Triple Crown in

Supporters of Mike Trout in the great 2012 MVP debate cited his remarkable defense (courtesy Keith Allison, https://creativecommons.org/licenses/by-sa/2.0/legalcode).

more than 40 years, and the preternaturally talented Trout composing the greatest rookie season in major league history.

2012	WAR	G	AB	R	H	2B	3B	HR	RBI	SB	CS	BB	BA	OBP	SLG	OPS	OPS+
Cabrera	7.2	161	622	109	205	40	0	*44*	*139*	4	1	66	*.330*	.393	*.606*	*.999*	164
Trout	*10.9*	139	559	*129*	182	27	8	30	83	*49*	5	67	.326	.399	.564	.963	*168*

Ten years prior, there's no debate: Cabrera's Triple Crown makes him the unanimous MVP. But acceptance of advanced statistical analysis had grown exponentially thanks to Michael Lewis' *Moneyball*, the increased use of advanced stats on mainstream, mass-market websites like ESPN.com, the proliferation of websites and blogs populated by intellectually curious members of the sabermetric community (FanGraphs.com and baseballthinkfactory.org are two that immediately come to mind) and the seemingly instantaneous adoption of a new stat known as Wins Above Replacement (WAR), which assigned a basic integer to the sum total of a player's contributions.

In 2012, your MVP pick revealed who you were as a fan. Less-enlightened characterizations of the debate went something like this: Cabrera your man? You're a codger with misplaced fealty to antiquated stats like batting average and RBI; you ignore things like base running and defense, and can't recognize all-around excellence (as revealed by Trout's otherworldly WAR rating).[9] Fishing for Trout? You're a stat-geek tweeting from your mom's basement; the only thing you know about baseball is that you couldn't make your middle-school team.[10]

The argument raged for weeks, with social media serving as a potent accelerant to the rhetorical flames. As a fan, you couldn't avoid it: It seemed every baseball writer in America had an opinion, as did most public observers of the game. National television broadcasts, talk radio, local games—the topic was unavoidable. In the end, it wasn't close: Cabrera breezed to his first MVP with 92 percent of the vote—but it was clear that the vote was about something much larger, much more personal than the statistical resumes of the two players jostling at the top of the ballot.

The Cabrera vote, in some ways, felt like a defiant last stand.

National media forums for the game have fully and enthusiastically embraced the sabermetric revolution started by Bill James some 30 years ago: *Sports Illustrated*, ESPN.com, and others list WAR, OPS+, and FIP alongside batting average, home runs, and innings pitched; today's younger voters spend more time thinking about the finer points of pitch framing, the impact of park effects, and variances in BABIP than they do things like "mental toughness" and "showing a team how to win."

In time, these voters will compose the majority of the BBWAA electorate.

21. The Last Worst MVP: The Future of the Award

Of the three macro trends shaping the future of the award, we can say with some confidence that an increasingly progressive BBWAA electorate will have the most impact. What this means for the future of the award remains to be seen, but the days of the one-dimensional slugger taking the prize over the all-around player appear to be as numbered as the days of the complete game.

As fans, we may need to find something else to argue about.

Appendix: The List, 1911–2015

Year	NL MVP	AL MVP	Addendum
2015	Bryce Harper WSH .330/.460/.639	Josh Donaldson TOR .297/.371/.568	Mike Trout (AL runner-up) finishes second for the third time in four years.
2014	Clayton Kershaw LAD 21–3, 1.77, 239 K	Mike Trout LAA .287/.377/561	Kershaw becomes the first NL pitcher since 1968 named MVP.
2013	Andrew McCutchen PIT .317/.404/.508	Miguel Cabrera DET .348/.442/.636	Cabrera's 2012 Triple Crown was probably his *worst season* from 2010 to 2013.
2012	Buster Posey SFG .336/.408/.549	Miguel Cabrera DET .330/.393/.606	2010: .328/.420/.622 38 HR 126 RBI 178 OPS+ 2011: .344/.448/.586 30 HR 105 RBI 179 OPS+
2011	Ryan Braun MIL .332/.397/.597	Justin Verlander DET 24–5, 2.40, 250 K	2012: .330/.393/.606 44 HR 139 RBI 164 OPS+ 2013: .348/.442/.636 44 HR 137 RBI 190 OPS+
2010	Joey Votto CIN .324/.424/.600	Josh Hamilton TEX .359/.411/.633	Votto takes the MVP in surprisingly dominant fashion (31 out of 32 votes) over Pujols, who was exactly as good.
2009	Albert Pujols STL .327/.443/.658	Joe Mauer MIN .365/.444/.587	2009: A record-breaking campaign for Mauer, who establishes the single-season mark for batting average for a catcher while claiming his third batting title (also a record for catchers).
2008	Albert Pujols STL .357/.462/.653	Dustin Pedroia BOS .326/.376/.493	
2007	Jimmy Rollins PHI .296/.344/.531	Alex Rodriguez NYY .314/.422/.645	With 54 HR in 2007, Rodriguez owns single-season records for HRs by a third baseman *and* a shortstop (57 in 2002). No other player at either position can claim more than 48 in a season.
2006	Ryan Howard PHI .313/.425/.659	Justin Morneau MIN .321/.375/.559	
2005	Albert Pujols STL .330/.430/.609	Alex Rodriguez NYY .321/.421/.610	AL vote *much* closer vote than it should have been. Boston DH David Ortiz was listed 1st on 11 ballots.
2004	Barry Bonds SFG .362/.609/.812	Vladimir Guerrero ANA .337/.391/.598	Most Walks in a Season Barry Bonds, 2004: 232
2003	Barry Bonds SFG .341/.529/.749	Alex Rodriguez TEX .298/.396/.600	Barry Bonds, 2002: 198 Barry Bonds, 2001: 177 Babe Ruth, 1923: 170
2002	Barry Bonds SFG .370/.582/.799	Miguel Tejada OAK .308/.354/.508	Ted Williams, 1947: 162 Mark McGwire, 1998: 162
2001	Barry Bonds SFG .328/.515/.863	Ichiro Suzuki SEA .350/.381/.457	Ichiro becomes the first (and to date, the only) Asian-born player named MVP.

Year	NL MVP	AL MVP	Addendum
2000	Jeff Kent SFG .334/.424/.596	Jason Giambi OAK .333/.476/.647	Giambi: 7.7 WAR .333/.476/.647 43 HR 137 RBI (bad 1B) A-Rod: 10.4 WAR .316/.420/.606 41 HR 132 RBI (great SS)
1999	Chipper Jones ATL .319/.441/.633	Ivan Rodriguez TEX .332/.356/.558	Rodriguez is first catcher in 23 seasons to be named most valuable.
1998	Sammy Sosa CHC .308/.377/.647	Juan Gonzalez TEX .318/.366/.630	The voters went 0-for-two. Sosa's MVP has a kernel of logic ... not so much for the Gonzalez vote.
1997	Larry Walker COL .366/.452/.720	Ken Griffey SEA .304/.382/.646	Griffey (56 HR, 147 RBI) was almost as good the following season, but was ignored by voters.
1996	Ken Caminiti SDP .326/.408/.621	Juan Gonzalez TEX .314/.368/.643	Gonzalez was probably the single worst pick in a decade of lousy picks.
1995	Barry Larkin CIN .319/.394/.492	Mo Vaughn BOS .300/.388/.575	Larkin had his career year the following season, but was basically ignored in the voting (finishing 12th).
1994	Jeff Bagwell HOU .368/.451/.750	Frank Thomas CHW .353/.487/.729	As you may have read elsewhere, Thomas and Bagwell are exactly the same age. Thomas was a slightly better hitter, Bagwell a better all-around player (pacing Thomas in career WAR 80 to 74). Thomas was inducted into the HOF in 2014; as of this writing, Bagwell still awaits his call from the Hall because ... he had muscles?
1993	Barry Bonds SFG .336/.458/.677	Frank Thomas CHW .317/.426/.607	
1992	Barry Bonds PIT .311/.456/.624	Dennis Eckersley OAK 1.91, 93 K 51 SV	
1991	Terry Pendleton ATL .319/.363/.517	Cal Ripken BAL .323/.374/.566	Ripken's 11.5 WAR is the highest in the AL over the last 48 (and counting) years.
1990	Barry Bonds PIT .301/.406/.565	Rickey Henderson OAK .325/.439/.577	Despite missing 37 games between them, Bonds and Rickey produced a combined 61 HR and 117 SB.
1989	Kevin Mitchell SFG .291/.388/.635	Robin Yount MIL .318/.384/.511	Now a centerfielder, former SS Yount is one of two players to claim MVPs at different positions (Alex Rodriguez).
1988	Kirk Gibson LAD .290/.377/.483	Jose Canseco OAK .307/.391/.569	1988: Canseco becomes the charter member of the "40-40" club (now at four members). "If I'd have known it was such a big deal, I would have done it," said Mickey Mantle.
1987	Andre Dawson CHC .287/.328/.568	George Bell TOR .308/.352/.605	
1986	Mike Schmidt PHI .290/.390/.547	Roger Clemens BOS 24-4, 2.48, 238 K	Apropos of nothing, the last three starting pitchers named AL MVP have won 24 games.
1985	Willie McGee STL .353/.384/.503	Don Mattingly NYY .324/.371/.567	See Chapter 15 for more on the 1985 MVP vote.
1984	Ryne Sandberg CHC .314/.367/.520	Guillermo Hernandez DET 1.92, 112 K, 32 SV	Sandberg is the last second baseman to claim MVP honors in the National League.
1983	Dale Murphy ATL .302/.393/.540	Cal Ripken BAL .318/.371/.517	1982–1983: The first of two trophies for Ripken and Yount. Twenty men have two MVP trophies on their mantle (or on the wall, or buried in the back of a closet). All but three are in the HOF: Murphy, Juan Gonzalez and Roger Maris (Miguel Cabrera—with two awards and counting—is still working on his HOF resume as of this writing).
1982	Dale Murphy ATL .281/.378/.507	Robin Yount MIL .331/.379/.578	
1981	Mike Schmidt PHI .316/.435/.644	Rollie Fingers MI 1.04, 61 K, 28 SV	
1980	Mike Schmidt PHI .286/.380/.624	George Brett KCR .390/.454/.664	Brett leads baseball in WAR (9.4) despite missing a *quarter* of the season. He sat at .400 as late as Sept. 19.
1979	Keith Hernandez STL .344/.417/.513 Willie Stargell PIT .281/.352/.552	Don Baylor CAL .296/.371/.530	The 1979 NL vote was a fractious affair, with eight players receiving first-place votes. The worst by far was the one given to Bill Madlock, who played but 85 games for the Pirates.

Year	NL MVP	AL MVP	Addendum
1978	Dave Parker PIT .334/.394/.585	Jim Rice BOS .315/.370/.600	Jim Rice's 1977–1979 peak, home—away OPS splits: 1977—H: 1.057 A: .880 1978—H: 1.165 A: .837 1979—H: 1.153 A: .809 Rice hit 124 HRs over these three seasons—82 (66%) of them at home. He might consider adding a relief of the Green Monster to his HOF plaque.
1977	George Foster CIN .320/.382/.631	Rod Carew MIN .388/.449/.570	
1976	Joe Morgan CIN .320/.444/.576	Thurman Munson NYY .302/.337/.432	
1975	Joe Morgan CIN .327/.466/.508	Fred Lynn BOS .331/.401/.566	
1974	Steve Garvey LAD .312/.342/.469	Jeff Burroughs TEX .301/.397/.504	*Combined*, Garvey (4.4 WAR) and Burroughs (3.8) weren't as valuable as Mike Schmidt (9.4), Joe Morgan (8.6) or Gaylord Perry (8.6).
1973	Pete Rose CIN .338/.401/.437	Reggie Jackson OAK .293/.383/.531	The press conference just wrapped (see, because Reggie and Rose could *talk* ... aw, you get it).
1972	Johnny Bench CIN .270/.379/.541	Dick Allen CHW .308/.420/.603	Johnny Bench owns three of the top-10 seasons by a catcher as ranked by WAR.
1971	Joe Torre STL .363/.421/.555	Vida Blue OAK 24–8, 1.82, 301 K	Torre was great; Fergie Jenkins, Tom Seaver, and Willie Stargell were better.
1970	Johnny Bench CIN .293/.345/.587	Boog Powell BAL .297/.412/.549	Powell had a good year for a great team; Yaz had a *great* year for a good team and should have won the AL MVP.
1969	Willie McCovey SFG .320/.453/.656	Harmon Killebrew MIN .276/.427/.584	Killebrew wasn't a great choice; Reggie was clearly the best player in the American League.
1968	Bob Gibson STL 22–9, 1.12, 268 K	Denny McLain DET 31–6, 1.96, 280 K	McLain didn't lead the AL in ERA. Boston's Louis Tiant (1.60) took honors.
1967	Orlando Cepeda STL .325/.399/.524	Carl Yastrzemski BOS .326/.418/.622	WAR (12.4) rates Yaz's 1967 Triple Crown as the best all-around season by a position player since 1927 (Ruth).
1966	Roberto Clemente PIT .317/.360/.536	Frank Robinson BAL .316/.410/.637	A Triple Crown effort for Robinson. He's the only man to claim the award in both leagues.
1965	Willie Mays SFG .317/.398/.645	Zoilo Versalles MIN .273/.319/.462	Mays captures only his second MVP award, and sets a record for most seasons between awards (11).
1964	Ken Boyer STL .295/.365/.489	Brooks Robinson BAL .317/.368/.521	Boyer's selection over Willie Mays stands among the worst of all time.
1963	Sandy Koufax LAD 25–5, 1.88, 306 K	Elston Howard NYY .287/.342/.528	The LA Dodgers can count three of the four NL MVPs given to a pitcher over the last 60 years.
1962	Maury Wills LAD .299/.347/.373	Mickey Mantle NYY .321/.486/.605	Mantle's last truly great season. As for Wills.... Mays was robbed.
1961	Frank Robinson CIN .323/.404/.611	Roger Maris NYY .269/.372/.620	Maris got the press, of course—but NL MVP Robinson had a better year. Neither was as good as Mantle.
1960	Dick Groat PIT .325/.371/.394	Roger Maris NYY .283/.371/.581	Groat's MVP is often considered the worst selection of all time; it wasn't good, but it wasn't *that* bad.
1959	Ernie Banks CHC .304/.374/.596	Nellie Fox CHW .306/.380/.389	Astonishingly, one voter in 1958 thought Bill Mazeroski (.275/.308/.439) more valuable than Banks. The two first-place votes given lumbering third baseman Frank Thomas (.281/.334/.528; 2.9 WAR) are even worse.
1958	Ernie Banks CHC .313/.366/.614	Jackie Jensen BOS .286/.396/.535	
1957	Hank Aaron MLN .322/.378/.600	Mickey Mantle NYY .365/.512/.665	Mantle *didn't* lead the league in BA, OBP or SLG. Williams hit .388/.526/.731.
1956	Don Newcombe BRO 27–7, 3.06, 139 K	Mickey Mantle NYY .353/.464/.705	In his Triple Crown season, the Mick establishes the record for most HRs (52) by a batting titlist.

Year	NL MVP	AL MVP	Addendum
1955	Roy Campanella BRO .318/.395/.583	Yogi Berra NYY .272/.349/.470	For the second time in five years, this pair of New York catchers sweeps the MVP award. Only one of them deserved it (Hint: You probably *can't* quote him).
1954	Willie Mays NYG .345/.411/.667	Yogi Berra NYY .307/.367/.488	Berra is in the midst of one of the greatest extended runs in the history of MVP voting.
1953	Roy Campanella BRO .312/.395/.611	Al Rosen CLE .336/.422/.613	Mickey Vernon denied Rosen the Triple Crown by outpointing him .337–.336.
1952	Hank Sauer CHC .270/.361/.531	Bobby Shantz PHA 24–7, 2.48, 152 K	See Chapter 10 for more on Sauer, Chapter 14 for more on Shantz.
1951	Roy Campanella BRO .325/.393/.590	Yogi Berra NYY .294/.350/.492	Who ya got? WAR totals, 1951–1955: Berra—25.1; Campanella—22.8.
1950	Jim Konstanty PHI 16–7, 2.66, 56 K	Phil Rizzuto NYY .324/.418/.439	Discuss: Does Rizzuto make the Hall of Fame without the 1950 MVP award on his resume?
1949	Jackie Robinson BRO .342/.432/.528	Ted Williams BOS .343/.490/.650	What Robinson accomplished in his time ... it seems impossible.
1948	Stan Musial STL .376/.450/.702	Lou Boudreau CLE .355/.453/.534	Despite being one of the slowest players in the league, Boudreau was the best defensive shortstop of his day.
1947	Bob Elliott BSN .317/.410/.517	Joe DiMaggio NYY .315/.391/.522	1947: Bob Elliott? Really? Bob Elliott: .317/.401/.517 92 R 22 HR 113 RBI
1946	Stan Musial STL .365/.434/.587	Ted Williams BOS .342/.497/.667	Ralph Kiner: .313/.417/.639 118 R 51 HR 127 RBI Johnny Mize: .302/.384/.614 137 R 51 HR 138 RBI
1945	Phil Cavarretta CHC .355/.449/.500	Hal Newhouser DET 25–9, 1.81, 212 K	1945: "[Cavarretta] is described by his teammates as a ballplayer's ballplayer, a strategist, a quick thinker and a sure and rangy fielder."—*United Press, 1945*
1944	Marty Marion STL .267/.324/.362	Hal Newhouser DET 29–9, 2.22, 187 K	
1943	Stan Musial STL .357/.425/.562	Spud Chandler NYY 20–4, 1.64, 134 K	1943: Chandler didn't get a chance to pitch in the majors until he was 29, and he was more than a war-time fluke: He won 20 again in 1946, led the league in ERA in his last season (1947), and has the highest career W% of any starter with at least 100 wins. He clinched the pennant for the '43 Yankees with a 14-inning, one-run effort, and followed that with two wins in the WS. He was as tough as advanced calculus, but also injury-prone. He *also* hit a game-winning HR off of Satchel Paige during a 1946 barnstorming tour.
1942	Mort Cooper STL 22–7, 1.78, 152 K	Joe Gordon NYY .322/.409/.491	
1941	Dolph Camilli BRO .285/.407/.556	Joe DiMaggio NYY .357/.440/.643	
1940	Frank McCormick CIN .309/.367/.482	Hank Greenberg DET .340/.433/.670	
1939	Bucky Walters CIN 27–11, 2.29, 137 K	Joe DiMaggio NYY .381/.448/.671	DiMaggio missed a quarter of the season and *still* led position players in WAR (8.1)
1938	Ernie Lombardi CIN .342/.391/.524	Jimmie Foxx BOS .349/.462/.704	Keys to a long life: Eat right. Don't smoke. Exercise daily. Don't pitch batting practice to Ernie Lombardi.
1937	Joe Medwick STL .374/.414/.641	Charlie Gehringer DET .371/.458/.520	Greenberg's 184 RBI aren't enough to capture the AL MVP.
1936	Carl Hubbell NYG 26–6, 2.31, 123 K	Lou Gehrig NYY .354/.478/.696	1936: "This husky Yankee player has already broken all records for consecutive games, and with his superb health there is nothing to stop him from playing the 2500 games that is his ambition."—*The Reading Eagle, 1937*
1935	Gabby Hartnett CHC .344/.404/.545	Hank Greenberg DET .328/.411/.628	
1934	Dizzy Dean STL 30–7, 2.66, 195 K	Mickey Cochrane DET .320/.428/.412	Dizzy's brother Paul was pretty good himself (19–11, 3.43, 150 K, 5.1 WAR).

Year	NL MVP	AL MVP	Addendum
1933	Carl Hubbell NYG 23–12, 1.66, 156 K	Jimmie Foxx PHA .356/.449/.703	Foxx was, of course, a great hitter. But he was helped tremendously by his home parks.
1932	Chuck Klein PHI .348/.404/.646	Jimmie Foxx PHA .364/.469/.749	1932: Klein's numbers are inflated to an absurd degree by his home park. H: .423/.464/.799 29 HR 97 RBI 1.263 OPS A: .266/.340/.481 9 HR 40 RBI .821 OPS
1931	Frankie Frisch STL .311/.368/.396	Lefty Grove PHA 31–4, 2.06, 175 K	
1929	Rogers Hornsby CHC .380/.459/.679	No Award	Hornsby: .380, with 39 HR and 149 RBI. And doesn't lead the league in any category. Welcome to 1920s baseball.
1928	Jim Bottomley STL .325/.402/.628	Mickey Cochrane PHA .293/.395/.464	1928: Bottomley and Cochrane were both poor choices. Cochrane might—*might*—be defensible by some measures. Not so for Bottomley. He simply didn't deserve the award over Dazzy Vance or Rogers Hornsby.
1927	Paul Waner PIT .380/.437/.549	Lou Gehrig NYY .373/.474/.765	
1926	Bob O'Farrell STL .293/.371/.433	George Burns CLE .358/.394/.494	Burns' record for doubles (64) is short-lived. Earl Webb smacks 67 five seasons later.
1925	Rogers Hornsby STL .403/.489/.756	Roger Peckinpaugh WSH .294/.367/.379	Hornsby's third .400 season in four years. His combined line for 1922–1925: .404/.479/.704.
1924	Dazzy Vance BRO 28–6, 2.16, 262 K	Walter Johnson WSH 23–7, 2.72, 158 K	1924: Dazzy's amazing season is often overlooked when ranking the best pitching performances of all-time. It belongs on any list. This isn't a misprint: Vance: 7.6 K/9; League: 2.8 K/9.
1923	No Award	Babe Ruth NYY .393/.545/.764	
1922	No Award	George Sisler SLB .420/.467/.594	From 1920–1922, Sisler hit .400/.443/.596, with 128 SB. He *averaged* 240 hits per season over this period.
1914	Johnny Evers BSN .279/.390/.338	Eddie Collins PHA .344/.452/.452	Second baseman sweep the award in 1914; voters won't be so kind to the keystone position over the next century.
1913	Jake Daubert BRO .350/.405/.423	Walter Johnson WSH 36–7, 1.14, 243 K	"Daubert's Maxims for the Base Stealer"[1] • Learn to slide from either side of the base. • Train for a steal as you would train for a short dash. • Never be afraid to hit the dirt. • Always watch the pitcher. • A good start is half.
1912	Larry Doyle NYG .330/.393/.471	Tris Speaker BOS .383/.464/.567	
1911	Frank Schulte CHC .300/.384/.534	Ty Cobb DET .420/.467/.621	

Chapter Notes

Chapter 1

1. This was at the dawn of the automotive industry, when cars were still replacing horses as the primary mode of transportation. Chalmers was content to leave the masses to Henry Ford and his Model T; his aim was to capture what automakers today call the "entry-level luxury market." In contemporary terms, Chalmers built cars for people who couldn't afford that high-end BMW, but didn't want to drive an entry-level Toyota.

2. Timing is everything: Honus Wagner took seven batting titles from 1900 to 1909; I don't know what he drove after 1910, but I'll bet it wasn't a Chalmers.

3. There's more—much more—to the story (gambling, game fixing, lies, damned lies, and statistics), and readers are encouraged to seek out some of the many resources available on the subject. Rick Huhn's book, The Chalmers Race: Ty Cobb, Napoleon Lajoie, and the Controversial 1910 Batting Title That Became a National Obsession, is recognized as a definitive recent account.

4. The batting title was officially awarded to Cobb (.385 to Lajoie's .384) when Hugh Fullerton, official scorer for the New York Highlanders, claimed he had failed to credit Cobb with a hit that had been changed from an error. However, that wasn't the end of the intrigue: Seventy years later, the Sporting News discovered that Cobb had been credited twice for a two-hit game. Removing the extra game from the ledger dropped Cobb one point behind Lajoie. Despite a 1981 commissioner's ruling that Cobb, despite this new evidence to the contrary, was still the batting champion, Lajoie is routinely recognized as the AL's leading hitter in 1910.

5. In the immediate aftermath of the scandal, Johnson declared that "from now on, no more individual contests for prizes will be allowed."

6. Despite some serious star power in the American League: Ty Cobb, Tris Speaker, Walter Johnson, and Eddie Collins each claimed a car. The NL roster of Schulte, Larry Doyle, Jake Daubert, and Johnny Evers was anemic in comparison.

7. Chalmers, ahead of his time in many ways, was never able to translate his marketing acumen into profits. After years of underwhelming sales, Chalmers Motor Company was eventually purchased by the Maxwell Motor Corporation (1924), which was in turn combined with several other manufacturers and renamed the Chrysler Corporation. Hugh Chalmers went on to head several other companies, including a defense contractor that manufactured anti-aircraft guns.

8. Which of the following is unlike the others? (A) Thomas Jefferson; (B) Abraham Lincoln; (C) Martin Luther King; (D) Rogers Hornsby. While the idea of a publicly funded baseball monument in the nation's capital today seems far-fetched, it gained a measure of traction in its day (speaking to the immense popularity of the sport during the 20s). The American League earmarked $100,000 for the project, and in 1923 the U.S. Senate drafted a joint resolution granting permission to begin construction (the House of Representatives later rejected the proposal). The scope and design of the monument was discussed and debated in the press ("Ruth or Cobb?"), but the initiative collapsed when the owners withdrew financial support in 1925.

9. There was also an element of self-interest

involved: Overseeing the annual award gave the BBWAA undeniable clout and cache within the game. And then there was the practical consideration that the MVP award gave baseball reporters something to write about—never underestimate the need to feed the beast.

10. We're applying hindsight here. At the time, the Frisch vote wasn't considered controversial (or even notable). Frisch's reward for being named MVP? The Cards asked him to take a pay cut after the season

11. There were three total MVPs awarded in 1979: Willie Stargell and Keith Hernandez tied for the NL vote. Percentages have been adjusted to account for the two 1979 NL awards.

12. He'd also love the fact that All-Star Game and World Series MVPs receive a car along with their trophy.

Chapter 2

1. Defensive statistics are not to be believed—certainly not if they're 100 years old. The best information we have, unfortunately, is anecdotal—but by reputation, Joe Tinker was a great shortstop.

2. Yet Christy Mathewson, of all people, called Tinker "the most dangerous hitter in the league." Mathewson had enormous respect for Tinker's bat control and ability to spoil great pitches.

3. The 1906–10 Cubs stand among baseball's greatest teams. Chance's club took four pennants in five years, winning two World Series. They averaged 106 wins per season, back when teams would play 150ish games a year. They own the best one, two-, three-, four-, and five-year winning percentages in history.

4. In a breathtaking display of chutzpah and cynicism, the Veterans Committee inducted Tinker, Evers, and Chance into the HOF in 1946 for no other reason, it seems, but the poem. There is simply no case to be made for Tinker and Evers. Chance, in his dual role as player-manager, was the only one of the three who deserved serious consideration.

5. Installing Evers as manager cost Murphy his shortstop, Joe Tinker. Tinker and Evers despised each other; when Evers was named Cubs manager (replacing the beloved Chance), Tinker demanded a trade. The Cubs shipped him to Cincinnati, where he was installed as player-manager for the Reds. He played well, but his team finished seventh in the standings. Tinker jumped to the newly formed Federal League the next year—the first true MLB star to make the move. As player-manager he led the Chicago Whales (who drew more fans than the Cubs) to the Federal pennant in 1915.

6. The Federal League comprised eight franchises in established major league cities. While the Federals successfully poached a few high-profile stars of the day, the quality of play was probably closer to "AAAA" then to the majors (Japan's major leagues today suggest a comparison). Given time, the level of play may have attained parity with the majors as the Federals were openly and aggressively recruiting talent away from the National and American Leagues.

7. The Federals didn't adopt MLB's onerous "reserve clause," which essentially bound a player to one team for the entirety of his career; with no reserve clause in place, players in the Federal League were essentially free agents—this was about as appealing as a tax audit to MLB owners. Legal and financial worries forced the Federals to cease operations after just two seasons.

8. It was James' one shot at glory: He injured his arm the next season, appearing in 14 games and pitching an ineffective 73 innings. Save for a one-game comeback attempt in 1919, his career was over at 23.

9. There is, of course, no shortage of intelligent players in today's game. Catchers and middle infielders are traditionally thought of as the most astute practitioners of the subtle and important elements of the game. For two decades, Derek Jeter set the most visible example for leadership, baseball intelligence, and rigid adherence to "playing the game the right way." Of course, Derek Jeter also hit like Derek Jeter.

Chapter 3

1. Babe Ruth holds the record for most 10+ WAR seasons with nine (Willie Mays and Rogers Hornsby trail with six apiece). Walter Johnson leads all pitchers with seven seasons of 10+ WAR; nobody else has more than three. Rickey Henderson (1985, 1990) and Bob Feller (1940, 1946) twice posted seasons of 9.9 WAR. Slackers.

2. AL teams scored 5.19 R/G in 1925, the 11th highest total in league history. The surge of offense in the 1920s can be traced to four overlapping and interconnected events: (1) the spitball (and other "alternative" deliveries) was banned after the 1919 season; (2) the leagues introduced a new ball in 1920, with pitchers complaining that the new construction—with

its less-pronounced seams—made it more difficult to grip the ball (and thus more difficult to rip off a breaking pitch); (3) beginning in 1921, umpires were required to place fresh, clean baseballs into play throughout the game; this rule, enacted in the aftermath of the fatal beaning of Ray Chapman in August 1920, had a significant impact on batting averages; (4) Babe Ruth's walloping ways rendered the hunt-and-peck approach of the Deadball era obsolete; it took a few years, but players began to realize it was ok to swing hard. As a result, offensive levels popped in 1920 (4.38 runs per game as compared with 3.88 R/G the season prior), exploded in 1921 (4.85 R/G), and basically stayed at stratospheric levels through the 1930s. Scoring peaked in 1930, at 5.55 R/G. The game wouldn't see this type of offense again until the 1990s.

3. From 1925 to 1924, Bucketfoot Al hit .359. One can quibble with Simmons' relative lack of patience, as he was never one to take a walk. But when you hit .380 four times, how many walks do you need? Simmons finished his career with a .334 BA. It should be noted, he was helped by his home parks. His career splits: H: .346/.397.560; A: 323/.364/.511

4. There's an element of bad luck at play: His two best chances for MVP were probably 1929–30, but the AL didn't offer the award those years. Simmons collected an ersatz MVP of sorts in 1929, when he topped an unofficial poll commissioned by The Sporting News.

5. Tris Speaker (.389/.479/.578) and Ty Cobb (.378/.468/.598) were even better, but injuries limited the playing of the two veteran superstars.

6. He fell four hits shy in 1921 and 1925; *one miserable little blooper in 1927.*

7. Johnson, having won MVP in 1924, wasn't eligible for the award in 1925. The rules of the time prohibited a player from being named MVP more than once.

8. Remarkably, despite being 35 years old, Sam Rice was only at the halfway point of his playing days. Rice followed one of the more unusual career arcs you'll ever encounter: He began his major league career—as a relief pitcher—at 25; caught on as a full-time outfielder at 27; and, after missing a season due to military service, began a 15-year run of excellence at 29. Rice finished his career at 44, just 13 hits shy of 3000.

9. Myer turned out to be a much better hitter than Peckinpaugh, peaking in 1936 when he led the league with a .349 average. He was never Peck's equal with the glove, but few players of the day were.

10. Chance helmed the Cubs from 1905 to 1912, but it is obviously their 1906–10 run that places them amongst the best teams of all time.

11. Caldwell would compile a 27–36 record while pitching to a sub-average ERA for the post–Chance Yankees. He was traded to the Red Sox after the 1918 season.

12. He would later manage the Cleveland Indians (1928–33; 1941). His long career in baseball also included a stint as Cleveland's General Manager.

13. This is a highly abridged version of player WAR. For a full explanation—which includes all of the math—visit Baseball-Reference. com's "Position Player WAR Calculations and Details": http://www.baseball-reference.com/about/war_explained_position.shtml.

14. Visit http://joeposnanski.com/explaining-cabrera-trout-and-war/ for more.

Chapter 4

1. This isn't hyperbole. A typical meal might involve several steaks and a platter of hot dogs washed down with gallons of beer. As for the women ... perhaps the less said, the better. Ruth's boundless indiscretions were rarely acknowledged in print; reporters of the age acted as stewards and protectors of the game's stars. Imagine Ruth in the age of viral videos and Twitter.

2. The true circumstances of Ruth's illness have never been confirmed. The Yankees—firsthand witnesses to Ruth's rolling carnival of debauchery—assumed it was a sexually transmitted infection.

3. At 5'6", 140 lbs., Huggins was known as "The Mighty Mite."

4. Gehrig, Goslin, Heilmann, Manush—take your pick. They were all great.

5. Ruth was most valuable in every way one could be valuable. Here are the Yankees attendance figures for 1924–26: 1924—1,053,533 (1st of 8); 1925—Ruth's lost season: 697,267 (5th of 8); 1926: 1,027,675 (1st of 8). Source: Baseball-Reference.com

6. Burns' record didn't last long: Earl Webb smacked 67 two-base hits in 1931, a record that still stands. It was the only time Webb ever exceeded 30 doubles in a season.

7. He would also be the second. Almost two years to the day, Ruth again victimized the Cardinals in Sportsman's Park. His three-HR game on October 9, 1928, sealed a World Series sweep for the Yankees.

8. This is probably the most famous at-bat

in baseball history—Alexander re-told the story countless times after he left baseball (it was his primary source of limited income). We won't do it justice here. Read Leigh Montville's account of the game in *The Big Bam*, his wonderful biography of Ruth.

9. Ruth's final WS line: .300/.548/.900, with four HR, five RBI, six R, and 11 BB.

10. Alexander was one of the few men in baseball who could drink with Ruth. Unlike Ruth, he wasn't the life of the party. Coming off three consecutive pitching Triple Crowns (1915–17), "Alex" in 1918 was drafted into military service. He fired mortar rounds for seven weeks on the front line, witnessing first-hand the particular horrors of World War I trench warfare. His service came at a terrible price: The war took his hearing, damaged his golden right arm, and nearly destroyed his psyche ("shell shock," or what we now refer to as PTSD). In addition to the toll of war, Alexander suffered from epileptic seizures his entire life (at the time untreatable). Alexander was a broken man, physically and mentally, and he tended his injuries with whiskey.

11. There is no disputing his defense, but O'Farrell was far from a power at the plate. He hit .304 for the series, but drove in only two runs while slugging an anemic .348. Cards shortstop Tommy Thevenow was their hitting star, with a .417/.440/.583 WS line (he also scored five runs and drove in four).

12. Hornsby led the NL with a 150 OPS+ in 1919; Snuffy Stirnweiss led the war-depleted AL with a 145 OPS+ in 1945.

13. And Walter Johnson was clearly superior to both.

14. And in a nice bit of baseball continuity, Greg Maddux started his career the year Seaver ended his run (1986).

15. Although ... shame on this author for including W% in the equation. Mathewson twice posted superb W-L records despite a sub-par performance. In 1906, "Big Six" went 22–12, but with an adjusted ERA 12% worse than the league average; he essentially repeated the trick in 1914, pitching to a 24–13 record while once again compiling an adjusted ERA 12% worse than league average (allowing more earned runs than any other pitcher in the league).

16. Ken Griffey, Jr., broke Seaver's long-standing HOF% standard with 99.3% of the vote in 2016.

17. If we include Seaver's AL tenure (three seasons), he leads the quartet in strikeouts and places second in career starts (656) and WAR (106).

18. Per Baseball Prospectus.com, FIP was developed by Tom Tango and Clay Dreslough, based on the work of Voros McCracken. You can read McCracken's groundbreaking work on pitching and defense at http://www.baseballprospectus.com/article.php?articleid=878.

19. Keeler hit .424 in 1897.

20. Of course, many of these pitchers were relievers, so Maddux wasn't competing against 300 other guys for the ERA title.

21. Earned Run Rate = Runs allowed per nine innings/earned run average * 100.

22. Pud Galvin holds the single-season record for WAR, with 20.5 in 1884. He pitched 636 innings, completing 71 of 72 starts. Needless to say, that WAR total is meaningless by today's standards.

23. Maddux, at his zenith during the strike-shortened 1994–95 seasons, loses several points of WAR due to his comparatively low innings totals.

Chapter 5

1. Gary Gillette and Pete Palmer, editors of the *Baseball Encyclopedia* (later known as *The ESPN Baseball Encyclopedia* and last published in 2008), listed their "Ex Post Facto" MVP Award winners all the way back to 1871. We reach many of the same conclusions for the 1901–30 time period, with the following exceptions: In the NL, Gillette and Palmer list Honus Wagner as their 1903 NL MVP (we choose McGinnity); 1910, Sherry Magee (Mathewson); 1919, Ed Rousch (Groh); 1920, Rogers Hornsby (Grimes).

Our AL lists are more dissimilar: 1903, Lajoie (our pick: Young); 1910, Jack Coombs (Cobb); 1916, Cobb (Ruth); 1918, Ruth (Johnson); 1919, Cicotte (Ruth). Gillette and Palmer stuck with the League Award winners from 1922 to 1928: 1924, Johnson (Ruth); 1925, Peckinpaugh (Goslin); 1926, Burns (Ruth); 1928, Cochrane (Ruth). In 1929, they choose Lou Fonseca (Simmons); 1930, Joe Cronin (Gehrig).

While our lists are similar (the *Baseball Encyclopedia* provides its picks without commentary), this author would not suggest his research approaches that of the *Baseball Encyclopedia*, which for a generation of fans stands as the greatest single-volume reference work ever produced about the game.

2. Wagner even contributed out of the bullpen (albeit in meaningless September game): Relieving beleaguered rookie Harvey Cushman, Wagner struck out five batters in 5.1 innings

(while giving up four hits, two walks, and two unearned runs).

3. The 2000 Seattle Mariners matched the Cubs with 116 wins (albeit it in 162 games). Like the Cubs, Seattle's amazing season ended in post-season disappointment.

4. There is no disputing that Chance was lionized by the media of the day. The question is, why? He was a borderline dirty player who incited fans, spiked opponents, and started countless brawls (the equivalent of a hockey enforcer, Chance had a reputation as the meanest fighter in the league). Ty Cobb, displaying the same personality deficiencies, was pilloried by the media; Chance was exalted.

5. In fairness, Laughing Larry was a pretty good hitter (.330/.393/.471, 132 OPS+), especially for a second baseman. But MVP? No way.

6. Years later, the Cactus was still pricked by the 1913 Chalmers vote. "I hit for .341," wrote Cravath in 1918 for *Baseball Magazine*. "I made more hits than any other batter. I was second in doubles, third in triples, first in home runs. I led the league by a wide margin in total bases. I drove in more runs than any other batter by a wide margin. Surely that record ought to have counted for something." He was right.

7. Vaughn, of course, is best known for his 1917 no-hit duel with Cincinnati's Fred Toney. After nine full innings, neither team had secured a tally. The Reds broke through in the top of the tenth; Toney held the Cubs hitless in the bottom of the inning for the Cincinnati win.

8. Here's a snippet of Dante's lost chapter: Bunt. Steal. Bunt. Spit. Argue with umpire. Sacrifice. Steal. Slash. Spit. Caught stealing. Bunt. Peck. Caught stealing. Argue with umpire. Passed ball. Steal. Swinging bunt. Sacrifice. HBP. Caught stealing. Spit. Steal. Bunt. Sacrifice. HBP. Spit. Passed ball. Sacrifice. Spit. Sacrifice. Steal. Peck. Opposite field single! Final score: 1–1 tie, game called due to darkness. This is the stuff of Hieronymus Bosch.

9. If remembered at all, this great Cincinnati team (96–44, for a .686 W%) is known as the opponent in the 1919 World Series.

10. And Waddell might have been more dominant in 1903: Despite missing the last six weeks of the season, Waddell led the league in strikeouts with 302; Detroit's Bill Donovan was next with 187. In late August, an exasperated Connie Mack—fed up with Waddell's unexplained absences (drinking binges)—suspended his star pitcher for the remainder of the season.

11. Waddell is usually painted as a charming man-child, a good-natured "rube" lacking in impulse control. He was charming, but there was a dark side to Waddell's "antics." He was suspended for five games in 1903 for assaulting a fan, and in 1905 was indicted on charges of assault with a deadly weapon—in a fit of drunken rage, Waddell allegedly beat his father-in-law over the head with a flat iron. He was locked up several times for non-payment of alimony/support to his three ex-wives. In addition to his heavy drinking, Waddell may very well have suffered from mental impairment or illness.

12. Cleveland named their franchise after Lajoie. You could say he was afforded a certain standing in the game.

13. Coombs was one of the best pitchers in baseball in 1910. He was the luckiest pitcher in baseball in 1911 (and maybe ever): Despite posting an era 11% worse than league average (3.53), surrendering more hits (360), and coughing up more earned runs (132) than any other pitcher in the league, Coombs went 28–12 for the mighty Athletics. Coombs finished his career with an excellent 158–110 record, for a .590 W%—but his career ERA+ (99) suggests he was a league-average pitcher.

14. Quite frankly, so is this author. But facts are facts.

15. Which is akin to gazing upon Mt. Rushmore and saying "I think there's a hair out of place on Roosevelt's head."

16. Speaker's contract squabbles with the club precipitated his departure. Recognizing his performance had slipped a bit, Speaker, who earned $18,000/year in 1914–15, offered to take a pay cut to $15,000/year for five years; Lannin low-balled him with an insulting one-year, $9,000 offer. The game's highest-paid stars were making north of $20,000.

17. It might come as a surprise to learn that Yankees Stadium hurt Gehrig over the course of his career: .329/.436/.620 at home vs. .351/.458/.644 on the road. Gehrig was probably the second greatest road hitter in baseball history (behind Ruth, of course).

Chapter 6

1. For many reasons—chief among them the fact that the MVP debate degenerated into a proxy battle between "old school" observers of the game, and a younger generation of writers and fans who used contemporary statistical analysis to evaluate player performance.

2. "Career" Triple Crowns: Ruth, Mays, Aaron, DiMaggio, Manny Ramirez, Johnny

Mize, Barry Bonds, Alex Rodriguez, Albert Pujols, and Andres Galarraga.

3. Based on OPS+, Cabrera had the "worst" Triple Crown season—he's the only player to lead the league in all three categories and fail to lead in adjusted production (Trout). He is also the only Triple Crown winner to post an OBP lower than .400. None of this denigrates an outstanding season.

4. Washington's Mickey Vernon outpointed Rosen .337-.336 for the batting title; Rosen comfortably led the league in HR (43) and RBI (145) and claimed MVP honors.

5. All of Cobb's HRs were of the inside-the-park variety, including two in one game (July 15, 1909). Source: *Baseball Almanac*

6. At a pre-season press conference announcing the terms of his 1947 contract ($60,000), Williams was uncharacteristically modest (or maybe just coy). "I just hope I can hit well enough to be worth the money they're paying me." Fair to say Williams lived up to his end of the deal.

7. Mike Trout, the best player in baseball, averaged 30 strikeouts a month in his 2014 MVP season. A different game.

8. Even wealthy team owners weren't immune to the effects of the Great Depression. Mack sold off his dynastic club for parts. Future HOFers Cochrane, Jimmy Foxx, Al Simmons, and Lefty Grove were all shipped as merchandise in 1932–33.

9. Shocked everyone but Mack, who in January of 1934 told the Associated Press "Detroit has a good chance to win the pennant.... I wouldn't be a bit surprised if they won it."

10. How then does one factor in managerial responsibilities when considering Cochrane's case for MVP? WAR doesn't account for bullpen management, on-field strategy, and, of course, the thankless and never-ending task of trying to run a clubhouse (which is like trying to manage a classroom of petulant teenagers, except these teenagers have money and fame and are of legal drinking age). Not only did Cochrane play the most difficult and demanding position on the field, he played it well—all the while coaching and leading a team. The Tigers were so pleased with his performance they awarded Cochrane a $10,000 bonus after the season ended—a fantastic sum during the depths of the Great Depression, and an act of ownership largesse simply unheard of in baseball. Still, the award is Most Valuable Player, not Most Valuable Person.

11. Brilliant again. Nicknamed "The Mechanical Man" for his consistent excellence, Gehringer is often forgotten when discussing the best second baseman of all time. He shouldn't be. A lifetime .320 hitter, he was a great player.

12. Let's call it Ruth, Williams, Bonds, Gehrig, Hornsby, in that order. Discuss.

13. Note: RBI didn't become an official statistic until 1920, so all Triple Crowns prior to then have been recognized retroactively.

14. When Gehrig died in 1941, a full-page obituary ran on the front page of just about every newspaper in America. If the phrase "triple Crown" was used, it remains lost to history.

15. Mantle, of course, did capture the Triple Crown in 1956. But he's obviously an exception to the rule, which states "predicting a triple crown in early May is ridiculous, but let's do it anyway."

Chapter 7

1. Simmons was traded to the Anaheim Angels after the 2015 season.

2. The official statistician of Major League Baseball.

3. But the time will soon be at hand. See Chapter 21, "The Last Worst MVP."

4. Scrappy. Adj. scrap·py \ˈskra-pē\: Player short in stature but long in "grit." Usually applies to middle infielders with little natural ability but dogged determination. No power, excellent bat control; willing and able to lay down a sacrifice bunt or chop the ball behind the runner; always covered in dirt, scabs, and bruises. Rarely a great player, but almost always a useful player.

5. "The reedy Marion stands out like a flagpole on a henhouse whenever he makes even a simple play," wrote the AP's Whitney Martin.

6. Some writers justified Marion's selection by citing his "numerous clutch hits" throughout the season. This was nonsense. The Cardinals were in first place from Opening Day, and didn't play a meaningful game after May. Marion's one "clutch hit" came July 2, when he singled to drive in Whitey Kurowski in the bottom of the 14th to tie the score against Brooklyn. St. Louis went on to win the game, extending their lead over the second-place Pirates to 9.5 games.

7. How quickly they forget. A more recent and apt comparison would have been Rabbit Maranville, another defensive specialist who couldn't hit. Maranville's glove kept him in the

majors for 23 seasons (1912–35), and eventually landed him in the Hall of Fame.

8. Only 30 men in the history of the game compiled a lower career OPS+ than Marion while playing in as many as 1500 games. As you might expect, all of these players were slick-defending shortstops, second basemen, and catchers. Tim Foley, with a career OPS+ of 64 (in more than 2000 games), sits at the bottom of this list. You have to be one hell of a glove man to last 2000 games in the majors with a career OBP of .283.

9. The Cards went 94–47 with Marion in the lineup, 11–2 without him.

10. And they did this despite losing their best pitcher, Red Munger, to military service in July (Munger on July 7 was 11–3 with a 1.34 ERA).

11. The 1906 Chicago Cubs own the record for best adjusted team ERA in history (151). They were nearly as good in 1905 (146 ERA+) and 1909 (147 ERA+).

12. In fairness, second baseman Emil Verban (a 28-year-old rookie) was even worse than Marion. A lot worse (.257/.287/.293, 62 OPS+). But no one was touting Verban as the best player since Wagner. Verban was an accomplished defender in his own right, and he managed to stay in the league for seven seasons (even making a pair of All-Star appearances). He couldn't hit at all.

13. In 1942, there were 31 official minor leagues; by 1944, there were only 10 leagues in operation.

14. Actually, we don't have to guess: Marion's post-war OPS+ was 75—meaning he was 25% less productive than a league-average hitter.

15. The Octopus couldn't grab everyone. "All this talk about Marion being Mr. Shortstop is a lot of idle blabbing," said Dodgers manager Leo Durocher in 1946. "Sure he makes plays, but there are other shortstops who make plays and who outhit Marion. He happened to be with a real good all-around ball club during the last few years."

16. The Emergency Stabilization act was enacted in 1942 as a hedge against inflation during the war; among other measures, it essentially froze wages and agricultural prices. Unable to offer workers salary increases (despite an acute war-time labor shortage), companies were forced to get creative with perks and benefits to attract and retain labor. It is during this period that the notion of widespread employer-sponsored health insurance is introduced to the U.S. populace. While it's certainly within the realm of possibility that the Cardinals were handcuffed by the rules regarding Wage Stabilization, only Sam Breadon knew for sure.

17. Unheralded, but not entirely unknown. Barrett's one claim to fame: On August 10, 1944, he threw a complete game shutout using only 58 pitches. The game lasted a scant 75 minutes.

18. They were right. Barrett never again approached his 1945 success.

19. His critics will characterize him as a few other things as well … we won't rehash or defend the complications and failings attendant to McGwire's career.

Chapter 8

1. Jimmy Foxx, Joe DiMaggio, Stan Musial, Yogi Berra, Mickey Mantle, Mike Schmidt, Alex Rodriguez, and Albert Pujols have three MVPs to their credit.

2. Honorable mention goes to Alex Rodriguez, who won three MVPs (2003, 2005, 2007) and should have won at least two others (1996, 2002).

3. Some ground rules: The MVP as we know it today was established in 1931, so this disqualifies players such as Honus Wagner, Walter Johnson, and, of course, Babe Ruth, who would have claimed eight or so MVPs had the award existed in its present form.

4. If we equate great seasons with great art, Williams would fill a wing at the Louvre. Only Babe Ruth and Barry Bonds at their very peak can claim seasons better than Williams' 1941. Between them, Williams, Ruth and Bonds own the 10 best hitting seasons in MLB history (as measured by OPS+).

5. For more than one reason: Two writers gave first-place votes to his Red Sox teammate Johnny Pesky. The rookie had himself a nice season, batting .331 and leading the league in hits—but it boggles the mind that anyone would think Pesky belonged anywhere near the top of the ballot. The same (and more) can be said for Vern Stephens (.294/.341/.433, 2.5 WAR), who somehow received a first-place vote.

6. We should clarify: Joost was hopeless with the bat through the first half of his career. Through 1947, he owned a career OPS+ of 77. But he was a downright productive hitter from 1948 to 1955 (113 OPS+), compiling massive walks totals and showing excellent power for a shortstop. The difference? Believe it or not, Joost was fitted for eyeglasses after the 1947

season. Now able to actually see the ball, he became a fantastic all-around player. Credit Rob Neyer (http://www.sbnation.com/2011/4/14/2111153/eddie-joosts-career-transformed-by-eyeglasses) for a nice bit of sleuthing.

7. The 1947 NL vote wasn't much better: An undeserving Bob Elliott took honors over Boston Braves teammate Warren Spahn. Johnny Mize and Ralph Kiner were also far better choices than Elliott.

8. This is not meant to diminish what DiMaggio accomplished. He played the entire season on bad legs, and bone chips in his elbow stabbed him every time he made a throw. There was no revisionist embellishment needed: The man played hurt, and had a good year. He was not in Williams' class.

9. That would be Jim Busby, he of a .262/.314/.360 career slash line. He hit a total of 48 HRs over an itinerant ML career.

10. Sniping aside, Griffith was well acquainted with Mantle's gifts as a player. It was against Griffith's Senators that Mantle launched his most famous HR. The astounding shot he hit off Chuck Stobb on April 17, 1953, was for decades considered the longest home run ever "measured" (in this case, by Yankees publicity director Arthur "Red" Patterson, who put the distance at 565 ft.). With no witnesses to corroborate his account, Patterson asked the press to take his word for it—and they did. As Mantle's legend grew, so did the mythology surrounding this HR. The number is pure fiction—at best, an embellished guess. That said, while the ball certainly didn't travel 565 ft., it was an astonishing blast: The only ball ever to carry the left field bleachers and exit Griffith Stadium.

11. Berra's post-baseball persona as a diminutive, cuddly fount of absurdist Zen koans bears no resemblance to the man in his playing days. He was revered by the writers (and his teammates) for his toughness, intelligence, and leadership on the field, and he dominated the MVP vote during his prime. His year-by-year MVP finishes, 1950–56: Third, **first**, fourth, second, **first**, **first**, second.

12. He "only" led the league in WAR, runs, home runs, walks, and adjusted production.

13. Somewhat lost to history is Norm Cash's amazing 1961. Second to Mantle in WAR (a superb 9.2), Cash produced an incredible line of .361/.487/.662 with 41 HR and 132 RBI. He later admitted to using a corked bat. It was the only season in his 17-year career that he hit over .300.

14. What is not understandable or forgivable is that five writers gave first-place votes to Baltimore's Jim Gentile (who had a great season, but c'mon).

15. It may come as a surprise to some that WAR rates Bonds as the second-best player of all time (although the difference in WAR between Bonds and Mays is negligible). Bonds didn't have the defensive gifts of Mays, but he was plenty good in leftfield. Mays gets the nod in base running, but again, Bonds was excellent. Bonds fills all gaps between them with his production as a hitter: While Mays was a great hitter, Bonds defers only to Ruth and Williams (and a case can be made that they defer to him).

16. Yes, it's a bit silly to call a decade and a half of playing time a "peak," when a typical peak is 5–7 years. But Mays never got the message that it was ok to have an off-year once in a while.

17. ESPN.com's talented and prolific Dave Schoenfield also looks at a decade's worth of Mays-related MVP voting at http://espn.go.com/blog/sweetspot/post/_/id/66606/why-did-willie-mays-win-just-two-mvp-awards-in-his-career.

18. Admittedly, this is like saying "Except for the singing, dancing, acting, and costumes, I loved the show." Stuart wasn't yet known by his famous nickname, "Dr. Strangeglove" (Kubrick's film wasn't released until 1964). In 1960, the hapless first baseman went by the less colorful—but no less accurate—"Stonefingers."

19. You might have a different perspective if you're a Phillies fan. They coughed up a 6.5 game lead with 12 left to play, the worst collapse in league history. The Phillies lost ten of their last dozen games (the 10 losses coming consecutively, Sept. 21–30). Pick up David Halberstam's *October 1964* for a wonderful account of a wonderful season.

Chapter 9

1. It must be said that there was an element of luck to Konstanty's 1950 season: He didn't strike anybody out, and his control wasn't anything special (he walked as many as he fanned: About three per nine IP). He pitched to a very high rate of contact, but sometimes the baseball gods bequeath gifts (and good defense). Opponents' batting average on balls in play (BABIP) was .207, which is unheard of (the league average in 1950 was .275; Konstanty's career BABIP was .266). At 3.77, his fielding-independent ERA (FIP) was more than a full run higher than his traditional ERA. All of this is to say that

Konstanty was helped a great deal by his defense.

2. In addition to his three MVP trophies, Stan the Man would place runner-up three straight seasons: 1949–51.

3. Robin Roberts was arguably the most valuable pitcher of the 1950s. WAR rates him just ahead of Warren Spahn as the decade's best. Roberts led the 1950s in starts, complete games, and strikeouts while averaging 20 wins/season.

Chapter 10

1. As noted elsewhere, Ernie Banks (1958–59), Andre Dawson (1987), Alex Rodriguez (2003), and Cal Ripken (1991) are also on this illustrious list. In 1913, Jake Daubert was voted the Chalmers prize despite toiling for the seventh-place Giants.

2. Although, by Wrigleyville standards, it should be said that this represented a significant improvement over the last-place finish of the season prior. It was the first time in five years the Cubs finished within 20 games of first place.

3. As a reward for his many Wrigley home runs.

4. Sauer is the only man in baseball history to twice hit three home runs in a game off the same pitcher. He victimized Curt Simmons on August 28, 1950, and again June 11, 1952.

5. Jose Bautista (2010), Matt Kemp (2011), and Chris Davis (2013) are recent examples.

6. What in the name of Joe McGinnity was Phillies Manager Steve O'Neill thinking? Sacrificing your ace in the first game of a meaningless doubleheader to save your bullpen for the second game of a meaningless doubleheader? Lunacy. Roberts, of course, wasn't the worse for wear: He completed his next five starts, all wins.

7. See Chapter 18, "Are MVP Voters Racist?"

8. A naturally quiet man, Roberts was called "aloof" in some quarters; might this perception have cost him the 1952 MVP? Only the writer who snubbed him knows for sure.

9. Of course, there is a long tradition of writers casting allegiance (and votes) to players on the teams they cover. A recent example are the two first-place votes afforded St. Louis catcher Yadier Molina in 2013. The votes cast by Rick Hummel and Derrick Goold, both of the *St. Louis Dispatch*, were the only two that didn't go to NL MVP Andrew McCutchen. Credit where credit is due: Goold provided a thoughtful, thorough explanation of his vote at http://www.stltoday.com/sports/baseball/professional/birdland/goold-why-i-voted-for-molina-as-nl-mvp/article_74ef3d15-1b7e-5f40-9048-dae5b58667bf.html.

10. Young's home-road splits: H: .357/.409/.453, 10 HR; R:.322/.377/.399, 1 HR.

11. About those teammates: Ian Kinsler (7.1 WAR) and Adrien Beltre (5.7) were much better than Young.

12. Later reduced to 12 teams for the 2013 and 2017 version of the tournament.

13. "Our club?" A quick check of the record confirms that beat writer Nichols was not part of the Minnesota roster. And Nichols had the gall to claim he wasn't a "homer," else he would have "voted for Killebrew."

14. The only real competition for worst vote of all time are the two first-place votes accorded Eddie Joost (.205 avg.) in 1947. See Chapter 8, "Sticking It to the Splinter."

15. Martin was really just trying to defend his player. Despite having nothing at all to do with the vote, Tovar received his fair share of ridicule.

16. Dark, known for his slow southern drawl and quick mind for the game, did have a nice season. He was recognized for his efforts with the Rookie of the Year Award (and a cool nickname: "The Swamp Fox.") He would later claim a World Series title as manager of the 1974 Oakland Athletics.

17. A 30-year-old rookie, Wilcy Moore did have a wonderful year, leading the league in actual and adjusted ERA over 213 innings (mostly out of the New York bullpen). He'd last another five (mostly mediocre) seasons in the majors.

18. It wasn't all cushy security details for Widmer in World War II; he was once shot in the hand by a Nazi sniper.

19. Turned into a 1930 rom-com starring Claudette Colbert and Ginger Rogers. Don't believe Vidmar was a singular personality? Ask yourself how many other reporters served as the inspiration for a romantic novel about a playboy sportswriter. Before you answer, keep in mind that "playboy sportswriter" is an oxymoron.

Chapter 11

1. The 1979 ballot was fractious and odd: Eight different players received first-place votes, none worse than the one wasted on Bill Madlock, who appeared in but 85 games for the Pirates after joining the team via midseason trade.

2. Hernandez was simply the best defensive first baseman to ever take the diamond. The quickest feet, the quickest mind, and those hands. Wayward throws were like plankton to a whale.

3. Stargell's feats of strength were legendary (source: Baseball-Almanac.com):
- He was the first player to hit a ball completely out of Dodgers Stadium (with Mark McGwire, Mike Piazza and Giancarlo Stanton the only other players to replicate the feat)—and he did it twice.
- The Pirates called Three Rivers Stadium home for 30 years. In that time, six home runs made the right field upper deck. Stargell launched four of them.
- In the 61-year history of Forbes Field, 18 baseballs cleared the roof. Stargell hit seven of them. No one else had more than one.
- He hit the longest home run ever recorded at Veterans Stadium in Philadelphia—nothing too unusual about that, as Stargell owned distance records all over the league. What is unusual is the fact that the Phillies commemorated the blast by marking the landing spot. Yep. Mike Schmidt's team commemorated a visiting player's home run.

4. Stargell at Forbes (496 G): .284/.347/.499/74 HR; Stargell at Three Rivers (682 G): .294/.389/.577/147 HR.

5. Stargell's dream season continued throughout the playoffs: He claimed NLCS MVP honors by hitting .455/.511/1.182 during the Pirates' three-game sweep of the Cincinnati Reds, and was named World Series MVP when he powered (.400/.375/.833, with three HR) the Bucs to a seven-game victory over the Baltimore Orioles.

6. How respected was Stargell in 1979? He was also named AP's Athlete of the Year, The Sporting News Man of the Year, and *Sports Illustrated*'s Man of the Year (with Pittsburgh Steelers quarterback Terry Bradshaw).

7. The best Angels player that year was probably a toss-up between Brian Downing and Bobby Grich.

8. Although ... it must be said that Lynn's home/road splits were extreme. In home games, he hit .386/.470/.798, vs. .276/.371/.461 on the road. He was Ted Williams at Fenway, Gerald Williams everywhere else. His MVP case is certainly compromised by his home park. So why doesn't it disqualify him outright? George Brett was also the beneficiary of home cooking that year, hitting .373/.423/.633 at Kauffman Stadium, and .283/.327/.492 on the road, for an OPS delta of more than 200 points. Not as quite extreme as Lynn, but more than significant.

9. This, it should be noted, isn't easy to do. There are exceptions of course (Carl Yastrzemski, Barry Bonds, Brett Gardner, etc.), but left field is where teams usually try to hide their worst outfielder.

Chapter 12

1. Owner of a .356 career BA (third best of all time), Jackson never won a batting title. He finished second to Cobb in three successive seasons (1911–13), despite hitting .408, .395, and .373.

2. Remember Robinson every time you hear a player or coach congratulate themselves for "overcoming adversity," which in today's parlance means coming from behind to win a game or series, or having to answer questions from the media about boorish, inappropriate, or illegal behavior. Getting trolled on Instagram isn't "adversity."

Chapter 13

1. The same "logic" is employed by the small percentage of Hall of Fame voters who simply refuse to give a vote to any player in their first year of eligibility, because "Ty Cobb wasn't unanimous, and Player X is no Ty Cobb." Thankfully, these small-minded members of the electorate seem to be ageing out of the process; we may get our first unanimous HOFer in the next few years.

2. There's also the small but inconvenient fact that hitters also have their own award: The Hank Aaron Award was launched in 1999 to recognize the top offensive player in the league, but it's never really caught on among fans (or the media). The MVP is still the one that matters.

3. Rich Gossage was even more dominant, but he threw only 46.2 innings (but what innings: 0.77 ERA, 0.77 WHIP, 9.3K/9).

4. An awful idea. There were 50 games left in the season when Kuhn made his decree—plenty of time for legitimate division races. The Yankees, having clinched a playoff spot as of June 12, mailed it in for the "second season," generally going through the motions. Playing to a .617 winning percentage in the first season, the Yankees were a sub-.500 club in the second half.

5. It begs the question: The league played two separate seasons, so why not award two MVPs? Teams weren't ranked on their entire body of work, so why were the players? Silly, right? Welcome to 1981.

6. Nobody can accuse Anderson of being disingenuous. Decades later he was still giving Hernandez the lion's share of the credit for the team's success. At a team function marking the 20th anniversary of the 1984 World Champion squad, Anderson said "Nobody could ever do what Hernandez did for us in '84, because that's as good as I have ever seen."

7. 1984: Ladies and gentleman of the jury, I give you the Game Winning RBI (look it up).

8. Toronto pitcher Doyle Alexander tied Ripken for 27th place.

9. It should be said that none of this is a knock on Eckersley, who was a wonderful pitcher. But the 1992 vote was terrible.

10. Jack Coombs in 1911 (28–12, 89 ERA+) owns what is probably the luckiest season ever for a pitcher. Filling out the rest of the luckiest staff ever: Lefty Gomez, 1932 (24–7, 97 ERA+); Christy Mathewson, 1914 (24–13, 88 ERA+); Storm Davis, 1989 (19–7, 85 ERA+); Roxy Lawson, 1931 (18–7, 89 ERA+). That's a combined 113–46, despite an ERA more than 10% worse than their respective leagues.

11. If one were to make the case for Clemens' value (aside from his league-leading WAR, ERA, adjusted ERA, WHIP, FIP, and K/W ratio), one could point to Boston's 21–11 team record (.656 W%) when Clemens took the mound, as compared with 52–78 (.400) when anybody else took the ball. But that's only if one wanted to make the case.

12. It also argues that Clemens should have won the Cy Young Award in a landslide. Eckersley's Cy Young is even more egregious than his MVP.

13. This was of course before those disturbing post-career allegations surfaced.

14. Joe Carter's third-place finish is due to the writers prostrating themselves to the RBI. Carter and his .309 on-base percentage don't really belong in this company.

15. Think of it another way: You have the first pick in the expansion draft. Baseball's best pitcher, best position player, and best closer are available. Who do you select? Hint: It's not the closer.

16. Of course, any decent pitcher is going to compile a great record when their team scores six or more runs behind them. The point here is that Newcombe was terrible in these games, but got the "win" 93% of the time.

Chapter 14

1. Of course it was. It was extraordinarily unlikely that anyone other than Sosa's partner in crime, Mark McGwire, would cross the 60-HR threshold. After launching 52, then 58 home runs the previous two seasons—many of them of the jaw-dropping, eye-widening, involuntary "whoaaaa" variety—it was almost a foregone conclusion that McGwire would seriously challenge Ruth and Maris. The expectations of McGwire were unrealistic and immense—and he exceeded them with room to spare. No matter how he got there, he got there.

2. Well ... it's more accurate to say that Ted Williams gave away his third Triple Crown. A 3-for-26 slump over his last six games dropped his average from .349 to .343.

3. And probably the most polite word.

4. A July 14, 1952, article by the Associated Press is representative of the type of coverage Shantz inspired: It leads with "Bobby Shantz, midget southpaw of the Philadelphia Athletics, can become the biggest winner in Philadelphia's American League history."

5. On the season, Shantz went the distance 27 times in 33 starts (no other Athletics starter completed more than 15 games). There's no disputing that Philadelphia's bullpen was terrible—17–26, with a composite 5.57 ERA—but it was unfair to have Shantz shoulder (no pun intended) such a heavy burden.

6. And for what? The Athletics were clearly going nowhere.

7. Casey Stengel was a fan of Shantz. In 1952 he called him "not only the best pitcher in the league, but a player who could be the only left-handed shortstop in baseball." This was Stengel's way of saying Shantz was good at covering bunts. Actually, he was very good: Shantz was awarded eight consecutive gold gloves from 1957 to 1964.

8. Then again.... Bill James, in his eponymous *New Historical Baseball Abstract*, lists Mitchell's 1989 season as the top "fluke" season of all time (eh, what does he know, anyway?).

9. Mitchell grew up in a violent, drug-infested San Diego neighborhood in the 1970s. Running with gangs, he was shot at on multiple occasions and engaged in countless fights. Years after his retirement, he acknowledged he was unable to leave his old life behind once he established himself as a major league star.

10. Older and wiser, Mitchell apologized to Rosen at a 20-year reunion of the pennant-winning 1989 club.

11. Lost seasons, all. Mitchell suited up for 135 total games from 1996 to 1998.

Chapter 15

1. The St. Louis Cardinals are the MVP standard-bearers in the National League: Fifteen players have captured 19 awards.

2. No pitcher born in the 20th century—Gibson, Pedro, Maddux, Clemens, Seaver, Kershaw, Koufax—can claim a season as good. One needs to look to Walter Johnson's 1912-13 peak to find a performance demonstrably better than Doc Gooden in 1985.

3. Is any baseball player as closely associated with a year as Dwight Gooden, 1985? McGwire/Sosa in 1998 comes to mind, but that season bares an obvious stain. Gibson in 1968? Mantle/Maris in 1961? DiMaggio/Williams 1941? Ruth/Gehrig 1927?

4. Why is Gooden's 1985 better than 1994-95 Greg Maddux or 1999-2000 Pedro Martinez? Because Gooden threw about 70 additional innings, or almost a third of a season in today's game. Pedro and Maddux may have been better on an inning-by-inning basis, but they can't close the gap on total body of work. Gooden also helped his cause with modest contributions at the plate.

5. Robert Adair's classic *The Physics of Baseball* explains in fascinating detail how a curveball works. There is nothing supernatural about it—it's a simple combination of mechanics and physics. But tell that to the hitters who dubbed Gooden's curveball "Lord Charles." The classic sobriquet for a curve—"Uncle Charley"—was deemed inadequate.

6. A word about John Tudor. If there was no 1985 Dwight Gooden, the world would be talking about 1985 John Tudor. At the end of May, Tudor's record stood at 1–7, with an unsightly-for-the-time ERA of 3.74. A lost season? Hardly. From that point on, he went 20-1 with a 1.37 ERA. Clutch? You could say that. In two September starts against the arch-rival Mets, Tudor threw 10 innings of shutout ball. That's not a combined total—he threw 10 scoreless innings in each start.

7. Johnson's teammate Curt Schilling finished ahead of the Big Unit on the 2001 MVP ballot (10th place for Schilling, 11th for Johnson)—yet Johnson was the overwhelming choice for the Cy Young award. Go figure.

8. Gonzalez never hit more than 31 HR in any other season, but did hit 354 over the course of his career.

9. As most fans remember, the Expos were cruising to a division title in 1994. They had the best record in baseball when MLB owners decided to abort the season. It would be the closest the Expos ever came to true success. The powerhouse 1994 club was sold for parts over the next couple of seasons.

10. OK, it wasn't shapeless. It was a flying saucer placed underneath a giant, cantilevered guitar neck. In addition to its dreary, multi-functional stadium, the "Big O" also features the Montreal Tower, rising 574 ft.—on an incline—above the stadium. Someone thought it a sound idea to lean a 50-story building over a sports arena (luckily, the Stadium was always empty, so the risk of casualties was low).

11. Olympic Stadium was literally crumbling. Portions of the tower collapsed in 1986; in 1991, a 55-ton support beam crashed to earth. Thankfully, nobody was injured in either incident.

Chapter 16

1. Davis would never play close to a full season. The 474 AB he registered in 1987—at 25 years old– would be his career high.

2. Compounding Davis' misery were the unprotected outfield walls. Citing cost, Cincinnati owner Marge Schott refused to cover the outfield walls with padding. Her penurious ways were the least of it: *Sports Illustrated*'s Jay Jaffe provides a glimpse into this sad, eccentric character at http://www.si.com/mlb/strike-zone/2014/04/29/donald-sterling-marge-schott-mlb-reds-clippers-suspend-nba.

3. How good was Davis in 1987? "It's an honor to be compared to Eric Davis," said Willie Mays.

4. He was almost as spectacular in 1986, when he hit 27 HR and stole 80 bases in only 132 games. Davis and Rickey are the only two players in history with 25 HR/80 SB in a season.

5. An incomplete list includes a lacerated kidney (famously suffered in game four of the 1990 World Series; he would spend more than a week in the intensive care unit), herniated discs in his neck (causing him to sit out the 1995 season), and ongoing and assorted problems with his knees, hips, and shoulders (Davis would have eight surgeries during his playing days). He missed most of 1997 battling colon cancer, and came back in 1998 to have one of his best years. Davis' body often betrayed him, but his iron will never flagged. It's somewhat

remarkable that he was able to play as much as he did. Credit to Craig Fehrman's essay on Davis in "The Hall of Nearly Great" for background on Davis' injury history.

6. Alex Rodriguez (2003) has since replicated the feat.

7. Writers used the binary argument to deny an MVP to the dynastic Yankees teams of 1996–2001. "How valuable could [Derek Jeter/ Bernie Williams/Jorge Posada] be? The Yankees would have finished first without him."

8. Dawson was a truly great outfielder with the Expos. Superb range and instincts ('The Hawk'), and one of the best arms in the league. Years of pounding Olympic Stadium's artificial turf wrecked his knees, and by the time he signed with the Cubs in 1987, he was a ghost of his former defensive self. His reputation, however, carried with him for years.

9. And far and away the most important part of any lineup in baseball. The 1987 Cardinals hit 94 HRs; Clark owned 35 of them (Terry Pendleton was next on the team with 12). No other player on any team was as vital to an offense.

10. No relation to the Genie.

11. Numerous theories have been put forth to explain the one-season spike in offense (especially those HR totals). Most can be summed up in two words: "Juiced ball" (but there's no definitive proof).

Chapter 17

1. Gonzalez 1996 home-away splits: .333/ .408/.717 (H) vs. .299/.335/.589 (A).

2. When tracking fly balls, Gonzalez showed the judgment of a teenager on prom night.

3. To see how it works, visit http://www.baseball-reference.com/about/equiv_stats.shtml. Warning: You will lose many hours of your life to this fascinating tool.

4. And underscore the greatness of Hank Aaron. That said, Aaron in 1971 was also the beneficiary of home park largesse. Atlanta Fulton County Stadium was a hitter's paradise, and Aaron hit .346/.411/.786, with 31 HRs in 66 home games. Aaron still rates as the best hitter in the league after factoring in his home park.

5. AL records that stood until 2000, when 23 players crossed the 30-HR threshold, and 31 players cracked 100 RBI.

6. Two Seattle writers listed Griffey Jr., ahead of Rodriguez on the ballot. It caused a bit of a media stir at the time, but in hindsight, this is certainly understandable. Both would have been a fine choice for the award that year.

7. Which led to juiced attendance figures that led to juiced revenues that fed the juiced egos (and coffers) of players, owners, and MLB.

8. A rhetorical question. We know why Thomas was named MVP: His White Sox took their division by eight games over the second-place Rangers.

9. Paul Molitor, DH for the Blue Jays, was runner-up to Thomas in the vote. Griffey Jr., gold glove centerfielder with 45 HRs, placed fifth.

10. Well, if "superior" is the right word in describing Belle's defense. His glove was the lesser of two evils.

11. Guess who led AL position players in WAR in 1995. Go on. Guess. Nope. Guess again. C'mon. Once more. Guess. Nope. It was John Valentine, catcher for the Red Sox.

12. We have to say something. He played leftfield with the same speed and grace Peter Boyle brought to the monster in "Young Frankenstein."

13. "Ill-bestowed MVP gains" is the more accurate description.

14. The coolest stat from this season? Pedro struck out 100 more batters than innings pitched (313Ks in 213 IP). Randy Johnson (2001) and Nolan Ryan (1973–74) are the only other pitchers to turn the trick. Pedro did it in far fewer innings.

15. The sting of the 1999 vote hasn't abated for Martinez, who in his 2015 autobiography openly wondered if racial bias played a part in the MVP vote. See Chapter 18 for more on race and the MVP.

16. There is the not-insignificant matter of why Neal was even allowed to vote on the award. In the wake of the 1986 AL vote that saw Roger Clemens claim the award over Don Mattingly, BBWAA Secretary-Treasurer Jack Lang offered a stern rebuke to those who would suggest a pitcher should never win the award. "The rules that are sent out to the voters on the [MVP] committee state: 'Keep in mind that all players are eligible. That includes pitchers.' Anybody that cannot vote for a pitcher, we replace them." Clearly, there was a disconnect between Neal and the BBWAA—he should not have had a vote in 1999. This wasn't the last MVP controversy generated by Neal. Days before the 2012 AL MVP ballots were due (again, Neal is on the record as saying he won't vote for a pitcher; why does he receive a ballot?), Neal published a column with the headline "Angels' Trout is the Right Pick for AL MVP."

It was later revealed that Neal gave his first-place vote to Miguel Cabrera. Neal was elected president of the BBWAA in 2013.

17. King's perfectly reasonable 1999 first-place vote went to the Yankees' Derek Jeter, who rated as the league's best position player.

18. Through 1995, over the course of nearly a century of what we recognized as major league baseball, 11 men had cleared 50 HR in a season. Since 1995–20 years—16 men have accomplished the trick. In all, 27 men have hit 50 or more HRs a total of 43 times—24 times since 1995.

19. In addition to swagger, flair, and showmanship.

20. Ok, it is done. Just not very often:
- Eric Davis came very close. In 1987, Davis stole 50 bases while slugging .593.
- In his 1990 MVP season, Barry Bonds stole 52 bases while leading the league in slugging at .565.
- While he never slugged near .577 (basically impossible in the Deadball era), Honus Wagner was one of a select few to lead the league in slugging and stolen bases in the same season. Hans accomplished this rare "double double" four times.
- Willie Mays holds the record for highest slugging while leading the league in stolen bases: .624 in 1957 (with 38 SB). He also holds the single-season record for most HRs by a player who led the league in stolen bases (1956, when he posted 40 SBs and 36 HRs). He was pretty good.
- And then there's Ty Cobb, who in his 1911 MVP season outdid Rickey by slugging .621 while leading the league with 83 SB. Oh, he also hit .420 and led the league in runs, hits, doubles, triples, and RBI. In 1917, Cobb slugged .570 while leading the league in stolen bases and hitting .383. Cobb (1909) is one of two players to lead his league in stolen bases (76) and home runs (9) in the same season (Chuck Klein, in 1932, is the other).

Chapter 18

1. Clemente would capture the award in 1966.

2. Not even the MVP trophy could lessen the toll paid by Robinson. He openly contemplated retirement when learning of his award. "The sooner I can get out of baseball, the better," he said in 1949. "The strain of the last three or four years has done something to me."

3. It's more accurate to say they loved New York catchers: Campanella and Berra captured six awards between them from 1951 to 1955.

4. In response to those sobering statistics, then–Commissioner Bud Selig convened a task force charged with stemming the continued decline in the numbers of African American players. According to the *New York Times*, the task force since 2014 has focused efforts on expanding baseball's urban leagues and academies; improving and modernizing coaching (which suggests a connection between coaching and the ability to attract young black athletes), and aggressively marketing black players. It's a complex issue, with no easy solution. The most promising and accomplished young athletes choose football and basketball over baseball, and elite college programs gear their scholarships as such. As Tyler Kepner of the *New York Times* wrote, "There may be only so much baseball can do."

5. Gonzalez, of course, was a terrible pick both years; Tejada's award was questionable; Ivan Rodriguez was a borderline pick, while Guerrero was … defensible.

Chapter 19

1. *The Sporting Life* of October 22, 1898, ran a lead story detailing a throwing exhibition won by the then-unknown Wagner, who set a record for longest recorded throw. "[Wagner] … made a wonderful throw, the measurers of the distance announcing that it was 134 yards 1 foot 8 inches [403 feet 8 inches]." This is equivalent to throwing a ball over a major league centerfield wall from home plate.

2. Crawford was a wonderful player over 19 seasons, most with the Detroit Tigers. He was the first player to lead each league in home runs, and at various times led the AL in runs, RBI (three times), total bases (twice) and triples (six times). Crawford is the all-time leader in three-base hits with 309—a mark that will likely stand forever.

3. Decades after he retired, Wagner was asked about his approach to hitting. "Well, my theory was always just to get a solid smash at the ball. I figured if I hit enough of them hard enough a good percentage of them would go safe." Keep it simple, stupid.

4. Or "The Big Train Award." Now that would be a great-looking trophy (although one must acknowledge the creepy, gothic charm of today's "disembodied-hand-gripping-baseball" Cy Young plaque).

5. Cleveland's Joe Sewell averaged 63 at-bats per strikeout for his career. In four separate seasons, he came to the plate more than 500 times and struck out four times or less. He walked nearly eight times for every strikeout. His "worst" year in terms of contact hitting was 1922, when he whiffed 20 times and drew 73 walks.

6. Wasting his talent for the International League Baltimore Orioles, Grove went 111–39 over five minor-league seasons. By 1923, he was the most coveted property in baseball. Baltimore owner Jack Dunn simply refused to sell Grove to a big league team until he got his price. Connie Mack eventually landed the star pitcher in 1925 for $100,000.

7. Gehrig would play eight games in 1939 before taking himself out of the lineup.

8. Boudreau was named Cleveland manager in 1942—at the age of 24. He would later manage the Red Sox and the Athletics.

9. Joe D. was great in his limited playing time, compiling a .325/.404/.568 line in 925 games. But his 44 total WAR places him fifth for the decade.

10. How many times in baseball history has the game's most powerful hitter also been its fastest runner? Mickey Mantle and Bo Jackson are the only two that come to mind. Despite being a much larger man, Jackson was even faster than the Mick.

11. There's more to the story, of course: Mantle had been sprinting after a long fly, only to pull up at the last possible instant to avoid colliding with Joe DiMaggio, who had camped under the ball. As he came to an abrupt stop, Mantle caught his spikes on a drain covering and collapsed in agony. That fly ball was hit by.... Willie Mays.

12. Mantle's Yankees played in seven World Series during the 50s, winning five of them. Mantle contributed 10 HR.

13. Well ... except Stan Musial, who led the decade in batting average (.330) and doubles, and placed second to Mantle in on-base, slugging and adjusted production. It's unfair to leave him out of this comparison, but then I wouldn't have been able to use "Willie, Mickey, and the Duke" in the "contenders" line.

14. As measured by WAR (11.2 and 11.3, respectively), Mantle's 1956-57 were the two best seasons of the decade. Carl Yastrzemski (12.2 WAR in his 1967 Triple Crown season), Barry Bonds (11.9 in 2001, 11.8 in 2002), and Cal Ripken, Jr. (11.5 in 1991) are only position players to better the mark since.

15. With a career line of .182/.323/.348 in 50 games, Morgan inexplicably disappeared during the post-season. He had the World Series of his life in 1976, but his efforts are largely forgotten because WS MVP Johnny Bench was a destroyer, batting .533 with two home runs and six RBI.

16. That would be Doug Flynn, Pat Zachary, Steve Henderson and Dan Norman.

17. Seaver took another Cy Young trophy in 1969.

18. I confess, this came as a surprise. My money was on Schmidt.

19. How good was 2001–2004 Bonds? His average OPS+ (256) over those four seasons is better than the single best seasons of Babe Ruth (255 OPS+ in 1920) and Ted Williams (235 OPS+ in 1941).

20. More accurately, he wasn't able to land a job after posting a .480 OBP, a .565 SLG, hitting 28 HRs, and publicly offering to play for the league minimum. Bonds and the MLB player's union later filed a grievance against MLB alleging collusion on the part of the owners. An arbitrator ruled against Bonds in the summer of 2015.

21. There are a number of very smart people working to quantify the cost in dollars of acquiring an added win on the free agent market. For our purposes, we referred to Matt Schwartz's conclusions as explained at HardballTimes.com.

22. Here's the list: Honus Wagner.

Chapter 20

1. Yankees fans should have been more upset at the four first-place votes afforded Jim Rice, who finished a whisker behind Mattingly on the ballot. That anybody would consider Rice (.324/.384/.490, 5.6 WAR) more valuable than Clemens or Mattingly is mystifying.

2. And sure, WAR rates Clemens significantly better than Mattingly. Despite his numbers, WAR doesn't rate Clemens as the best player in the league in 1986. That would be Milwaukee's Teddy Higuera.

3. In the end, the voters got it right with the 1986 Clemens pick. The 1978 vote was more problematic.

4. And five other excellent books, and scores of columns and stories for the likes of *Sports Illustrated*, *NBC Sports*, and his wonderful blog, JoePosnanski.com.

5. Except, of course, when a great hitter and great pitcher jostle at the top of the ballot.

6. Burroughs was a poor choice for the

award, but how do you begrudge a 23-year-old kid who displays such gratitude and enthusiasm?

7. Farrell was right: Ruth was selfish. But his personal failures didn't impact the team's on-field success. The Yankees still managed to claim the AL pennant (losing to the cross-town rival Giants in the World Series).

Chapter 21

1. Twins ace Johan Santana was the league's most valuable commodity, but, well ... pitchers.

2. *The New York Post* gleefully framed the 2006 vote as a conspiracy designed to thwart a certain Yankees shortstop. Headlines include: "Why We Snubbed Jeter: Writers Defend Their MVP Votes" and "Oh Morneau! Bronx Bias Strikes Jeter."

3. "Strong production"—look, we're not damning Morneau with faint praise here. He was very good—you hit .362 with a 1.023 OPS and you're having a nice run. But we're still in the throes of the Selig era here: Everybody was hitting (and everybody, except the Twins, was hitting home runs by the bushel). AL teams averaged nearly 5 R/G, and teams as a whole averaged more than a HR/G. In this context, Morneau was very good, but not outstanding. Santana, for example, went 15–2 over the same time period, basically leading the world in every important pitching category.

4. And he was no Fenway Park construct: Ortiz hit an incredible 32 HR on the road.

5. But only one bad one: On May 17, 2014, the Arizona Diamondbacks torched Kershaw for seven runs in 1.2 innings. It was the only time Kershaw surrendered more than 3 runs in a game the entire season.

6. Of course, this assumes that technology will underscore the value of defense—there's also the possibility that technology will reveal that the voters had it right all along: In today's game, defense is overrated—that the delta between an elite centerfielder and an average centerfielder just isn't that great, and that teams are better off going with the slightly better hitter.

7. Gagne, the 2003 Cy Young winner, finished higher than any other pitcher on the MVP ballot. The Cubs' Mark Prior was robbed in both instances. The Cy Young snub is particularly acute when one considers Prior was bedeviled by a series of debilitating injuries beginning the following season. Prior, the most promising young prospect since Dwight Gooden, was out of the major leagues at the age of 25.

8. Which is not out of the realm of possibility. Given the small sample sizes attendant to relief work, it's not inconceivable that closer could ride a 45-inning scoreless streak to a major award. It isn't very likely, but it's the most likely of the three scenarios presented above.

9. Trout has led position players in WAR four consecutive seasons (2012–15, with only one MVP to show for it). An extraordinary feat—but he's only halfway to the record. Honus Wagner did it eight consecutive years (1902–09). Ruth had a six-season streak (1926–31). Mantle (1955–59) and Mays (1962–66) both had a five-season streak, while Bonds has two separate four-year streaks (1990–93; 2001–04).

10. I might be exaggerating. But not by much.

Appendix

1. It should be noted, Daubert was a lousy base stealer. In his 1913 MVP season, he stole 25 bases, but was caught stealing 21 times.

Bibliography

Aaron, Hank, and Willie Mays. Interview by Bob Costas, *Costas Now*. First aired 30 Sept. 2008 (HBO).

"AL Most Valuable: Guidry, Rice Only Choices." Associated Press, 7 Nov. 1978.

"Al Rosen Hopes to Hit Triple Crown Jackpot." *The Sunday Herald* (Bridgeport, CT), 15 June 1952.

"American League Will Meet Today." Associated Press, 26 July 1922.

Anderson, Dave. "Nellie Foxx Made It Easier for Joe Morgan." *New York Times* News Service, 7 Dec. 1975.

Anderson, R.J. "With Big Data, Moneyball Will Be on Steroids." *Newsweek*, 24 July 2014. Web.

Anthony, Ted. "Captain Willie was Pittsburgh Icon." *Pittsburgh Post-Gazette*, 9 Apr. 2001.

Appel, Marty. "Roger Peckinpaugh." The National Pastime Museum. Web.

Baer, Bill. "Scoring Change Shaves 16 points off of Felix Hernandez's ERA." *Hardball Talk*, NBCSports.com, 27 Sept. 2014.

Bailey, Judson. "Joe DiMaggio Out to Shoot for Baseball triple Batting Title Crown." Associated Press, 3 July 1941.

Bailey, Judson. "NY Writers to Recognize Ted Williams as Player of the Year." Associated Press, 18 Jan. 1943.

"Ban Johnson Visits Capital." *Reading Eagle*, 10 Jan. 1924.

Bang, Ed. "Chance a Failure." *Sporting Life*, 28 Nov. 1914, p. 5.

Barra, Allen. *Clearing the Bases: The Greatest Baseball Debates of the Last Century*. New York: Thomas Dunne Books, 2002.

Basco, Dan, and Jeff Zimmerman. "Measuring Defense: Entering the Zones of Fielding Statistics." *The Baseball Research Journal* 39, no. 1 (Summer 2010).

"A Baseball Monument." *The Reading Eagle*, 3 July 1923.

Beane, Billy. "Billy Beane on the Future of Sports: A Tech-Driven Revolution." *Wall Street Journal*, 7 July 2014.

Bell, Floyd L. "Rogers Hornsby Is Modest, Unassuming and Regular Fellow." *Sarasota Herald-Tribune*, 27 Feb. 1927, Section 2, p. 2.

Benson, John, and Tony Blengino. *Baseball's Top-100: The Best Individual Seasons of All Time*. Wilton, CT: Diamond Library, 1995.

Berger, Ken. "Indians' Curtis Injures Thumb in Scuffle with Mitchell." Associated Press, 22 May 1997.

Berkow, Ira. "Will Denny McLain Ever Hear the Cheers Again?" Newspaper Enterprise Association, 7 July 1971.

Beschloss, Michael. "Clemente, the Double Outsider." *New York Times*, 19 June 2015.

"Betrayed Matt Kemp: Ryan Braun Should Lose 2011 MVP." Associated Press, 23 July 2013.

"Bitsy Bobby Shatz Throws Big Win Number 20 for 1952." Associated Press, 6 Aug. 1952.

Blum, Ronald. "Gonzalez Clears AL Obstacles." Associated Press, 15 Nov. 1996.

"Bobby Shantz Is Retiring from Baseball." Associated Press, 11 Dec. 1964.

"Bobby Shantz Is Sidelined with Injured Shoulder." United Press, 22 May 1953.

Bock, Hal. "10 Better Than Stargell?" Associated Press, 15 Nov. 1979.

Borell, Brendan. "Are Octopuses Smart?" ScientificAmerican.com, 27 Feb. 2009.

"Boston's Jim Rice Gets Nod as AL Most Valuable Player." Associated Press, 8 Nov. 1978.

Boswell, Thomas. *The Heart of the Order*. New York: Doubleday, 1989.

Boyle, Havey J. "Mirrors of Sport: About Catchers." *Pittsburgh Post-Gazette*, 30 Sept. 1943, p. 14.

Bradlee, Ben. *The Kid: The Immortal Life of Ted Williams*. New York: Little, Brown, 2013.

Bradley, Michael. "WAR in MLB: The Rise and Importance of Advanced Statistical Metrics." *The Sporting News*, 25 March 2013. Web.

"Brock Bitter About Exclusion from Award." *New York Times*, 14 Nov. 1974, p. 65.

Broeg, Bob. "Big Year for Ted Williams." Wide World Features, 21 July 1942.

Brown, Hugh. "Homesick Hurler." *Milwaukee Sentinel*, 7 Sept. 1952.

Burke, Don. "Power and Speed." *The Milwaukee Journal*, 20 May 1987. Sports/Business, p. 1.

"Burroughs American League's MVP." *New York Times*, 21 Nov. 1974, pp. 61, 67.

"Calvin Griffith Says Mantle Doesn't Compare to Busby." Associated Press, 7 April 1954.

"Cards Settle Case of Mort Cooper, Trading Him to Boston Braves." Associated Press, 24 May 1945.

"Cars for Players Done." *Sporting Life*, 2 Jan. 1915, p. 25.

Carver, Lawton. "Durocher Disputes Title of Mr. Shortstop for Marion." International News Service, 28 March 1946.

Casella, Paul. "How Far Will Statcast's Reach Extend?" MLB.com, 5 May 2015.

Casselberry, Ian. "Miguel Cabrera Gets One MVP Vote." SBNation.com, 23 Nov. 2009.

Chadwick, George. "Valuable Player Award Near Finish." *The Sunday Star* (Wilmington, DE), 11 May 1930, p. 30.

"Chalmers Give Out Cars." *Milwaukee Sentinel*, 13 Oct. 1912, Part III, p. 5.

"Chalmers Talks About Salesmanship." *Pittsburgh Press*, 24 Sept., 1911, Editorial Section, p. 8.

Chalmers, Hugh. "Motor Races Increase." *Indianapolis Star*, 4 Apr. 1909.

Chalmers, Hugh. "Auto Advertising and Salesmanship." *New York Times*, 27 Feb. 1910, p. S4.

Chamberlain, Charles. "Ted Williams, Yanks, Pace Assault on Major League Records in 1947." Associated Press, 27 Dec. 1947.

"Chance Paid Off, Leaves the Yankees." *New York Times*, 16 Sept. 1914, p. 9.

"Charlie Gehringer and Joe Medwick Win Batting Honors." United Press, 5 Oct. 1937.

"Clemens Choice Stirs Controversy." Associated Press, 20 Nov. 1986.

"Clemens Is Eighth to Sweep MVP and Cy Young Prizes." Associated Press, 19 Nov. 1986.

"Cleveland Infielder Is Headed for Triple Crown." Associated Press, 24 Aug. 1953.

"Cleveland, In Master-Stroke Gets Speaker." *Sporting Life* 67, no. 7 (15 April 1916), p. 8.

Collier, Gene. "Obituary: Willie Stargell: Numbers Couldn't Measure the Man." *Pittsburgh Post-Gazette*, 10 Apr. 2001.

Constans, L. H. "Honus Wagner." *Baseball Magazine* XI, no. 4 (Aug. 1913), pp. 95–96.

Costello, Rory. SABR Bio Project: Cesar Tovar. SABR.org.

Crasnick, Jerry. "Agent: Little Chance Bonds will Play in Majors This Season." ESPN.com, 14 July 2008.

Crasnick, Jerry. "Andrelton Simmons Is a Hard-Working Human Highlight Reel." ESPN.com, 27 April 2015.

Crasnick, Jerry. "Sign Stealing Enters Information Age." ESPN.com, 16 June 2015.

Cravath, Gavvy. "What the Batting Records Have Cost Me." *Baseball Magazine* XXI, no. 3 (July 1918), pp. 281–282, 298.

Cronin, Brian. "Sports Legends Revealed: Did Ted Williams Lose an MVP Award Because a Boston Writer Left Him off the Ballot?" *Los Angeles Times*, 21 Sept. 2010.

"Cubs Slugger, Hank Sauer, Most Valuable in National." Associated Press, 20 Nov. 1952.

Cuddy, Jack. "Cavarretta, Mayo Candidates for 'Most Valuable' Awards." United Press, 18 Sept. 1945.

Daley, Arthur. "Gordon Tops Williams for Award as American League's Most Valuable Player." *New York Times*, 4 Nov. 1942, p. 31.

Daley, Arthur. "How Valuable Is Most Valuable?" *New York Times*, 30 Oct. 1949, p. 37.

Daley, Arthur. "Mark of Excellence." *The Day* (New London, CT), 29 Oct. 1971.

Daley, Arthur. "Sports of the Times: A Question of Value." *New York Times*, 26 Nov. 1952. P. 30.

Daley, Arthur. "Sports of the Times: The Story of Mr. Shortstop." *New York Times*, 24 July 1944. P. 20.

Davis, Sydney. SABR BIO Project: Red Barrett. SABR.org.

Deane, Bill. "Who Was Really the 1979 NL MVP?" BaseballAnalysts.com, 4 May 2006.

"Denny McLain Is Not Ted Williams Admirer." United Press International, 29 March 1972.

"Denny McLain Suspended from Baseball Until July 1." Associated Press, 2 Apr. 1970.

Derespina, Cody. "It's Time for a New Triple Crown." *Newsday*, 20 Sept. 2013.

"Dethroning of Giants Big Upset of Baseball Season." *The Evening Independent* (St. Petersburg), 26 Dec. 1925, p. 15.

Domowitch, Paul. "Davis 2 HRs Help Reds Beat Phils." *Philadelphia Daily News*, 2 May 1987.

Dow, Bill. "Darrell Evans, Willie Hernandez Were the Key Acquisitions for 1984 Tigers." 24 July 2009.

Down, Fred. "Jackie Robinson Lauded as Most Valuable Player." United Press, 25 Jan. 1950.

"The Downfall of Denny McLain." Baseball-Prospectus.com, 28 Feb. 2003.

Drebinger, John. "Dodgers' Robinson Most Valuable National League Player." *New York Times*, 19 Nov. 1949, p. 14.

Drebinger, John. "Rizzuto Named Player of the Year by Writers." *New York Times*, 16 Dec. 1949, p. 40.

Drebinger, John. "Sauer Chose Over Roberts and Black as Most Valuable." *New York Times*, 21 Nov. 1952, p. 30.

Dufresne, Chris. "Denny McLain: Things are Afoul for Yesterday's Hero." *Los Angeles Times Service*, 24 Dec. 1984.

Eck, Frank. "Kellner Sees Bobby Shanz as NY Starter." Associated Press, 20 Apr. 1957.

Edes, Gordon. "Ortiz Raps MVP Voting." *Boston Globe*, 11 Sept. 2006.

Edes, Gordon. "Pendleton is MVP on ... Personality?" *Miami Sun-Sentinel*, 21 Nov. 1991.

"Eric Davis Proving the Scouts Correct." Associated Press, 4 May, 1987.

"Ernie Lombardi, 69, a Catcher; Batted .306 in 17-Year Career." *New York Times*, 28 Sept. 1977, p. 35.

Farrell, Henry L. "Peck the Goat of Big Series." United Press, 31 Oct. 1925.

Farrell, Henry L. "Stars Are Not Always Most Valued Players." United Press, 21 Feb. 1922.

"FBI Investigates Cardinals for Hacking into Astros' Database." ESPN.com, 16 June 2015.

"Federal League Secures Stars from Americans and Nationals." *The Miami News*, 18 Apr. 1914, p. 10.

"Federal League Stands Pat." *Boston Evening Transcript*, 22 Jan. 1914, p. 8.

"Fight for Batting Prize Is Attracting Fans Attention." *Milwaukee Journal*, 25. Aug. 1910.

"Former MVP Kevin Mitchell Latest to Grab Ball, Bat and Head to Japan." Associated Press, 13 Feb. 1995.

Foster, John B. *Spalding's Official Baseball Guide 1921*. New York: American Sports Publishing Company, 1921.

Foster, John. "Most Valuable Player Stunt Due to Be Junked." *Milwaukee Journal*, 18 March 1929.

"Frank Frisch, Cards' Captain, Named Most Valuable Player." *Schenectady Gazette*, 21 Oct. 1931.

"Frisch Chosen Most Valuable." Associated Press, 31 Oct. 1931.

"Frisch, Cards' Star, Among the Hold Outs." *New York Times*, 18 Feb. 1932, p. 29.

Futterman, Mathew. "Has Baseball's Moment Passed?" *Wall Street Journal*, 31 March 2011.

"George Burns, Veteran First Sacker with Cleveland, Most Valuable American Leaguer." Associated Press, 13 Oct. 1926.

"George Sisler Most Valuable Player in Major League." Associated Press, 22 Sept. 1922.

Getty, Frank. "Cracking Yankees Go Down in Sensational Defeat." United News, 11 Oct. 1926.

"Giants Slugger Mitchell Traded to Seattle Mariners." Associated Press, 11 Dec. 1991.

"Gibson 'Stunned' by Most Valuable Award." Associated Press, 14 Nov. 1968.

Gillette, Gary, and Pete Palmer, eds. *The ESPN Baseball Encyclopedia, Fourth Edition*. New York: Sterling Publishing Co., 2007.

Goldstein, Richard. "Hank Sauer, MVP in 1952 and Mayor of Wrigley Field." *New York Times*, 27 Aug. 2001.

Goodmen, Mark. "Willie Stargell: He's Tops (and "Pops") to His Teammates and His Kids." *Family Weekly*, 6 April 6, pp. 6–7.

Goold, Derrick. "Why I Voted for Molina as NL MVP." *St. Louis Post-Dispatch*, 15 Nov. 2013.

"Gordon Named Most Valuable." Associated Press, 4 Nov. 1942.

Gould, Alan. "Lew Fonseca Judged Best in American." Associated Press, 16 Oct. 1929.

Gould, Alan. "Rogers Hornsby Voted Most Valuable Player in National League." Associated Press, 7 Dec. 1929.

Gould, Stephen Jay. "The Extinction of the .400 Hitter." *The Armchair Book of Baseball*. New York: Collier Books, 1985.

Grant, Evan. "Why I Gave Michael Young his only First Place Vote." *Dallas Morning News*, 21 Nov. 2011.

"Greenwell Makes Case for '88 MVP." ESPN.com, 17 Feb. 2005.

"Grover Alexander Joins Hall of Fame." Associated Press, 19 Jan. 1938.

"Grover Cleveland Alexander Remembers: 1926 World Series, Game 7." Our Game, 18 Dec. 2012.

Grow, Nathaniel. "*Judge Landis, the Federal League, and Baseball's First Anti-Trust Trial*." *Hardball Times*, 2 Feb. 2015.

Halberstam, David. *October 1964*. New York: Villard Books, 1994.

"Hall Inductees an Unusual Mix." Associated Press, 2 Aug. 1986.

Hand, Jack. "Marty Marion Most Valuable in Ball Loop." Associated Press, 22 Nov. 1944.
Harrison, James. "Record Vote Rates O'Farrell on Top." *New York Times*, 6 Dec. 1926, p. 6.
Hart, Harold, and Ralph Tolleris. *Big-Time Baseball*. New York: Hart Publishing Co., 1950.
Heyman, Jon. "MLB Prevails Over Barry Bonds in Collusion Case Over His Career Ending." CBSSports.com, 27 Aug. 2015.
Holtzman, Jerome, ed. *No Cheering in the Press Box*. New York: Henry Holt & Co., 1995.
Holtzman, Jerome. "A Lesson in Triple Crown History." *Chicago Tribune*, 8 Sept. 1991, p. 11C.
Holtzman, Jerome. "MVP Stir Recalls Rice vs Guidry." *Chicago Tribune*, 23 Nov. 1986.
Holtzman, Jerome. "Replacements During WWII Was One Thing…" *Chicago Tribune*, 20 Feb. 1995, p. 3B.
Honig, Donald. *Baseball America*. New York: Galahad Books, 1985.
"Hugh Chalmers Dies at 58 Years." *Montreal Gazette*, 3 June 1932.
Huhn, Rick. *The Chalmers Race: Ty Cobb, Napoleon Lajoie, and the Controversial 1910 Batting Title That Became a National Obsession*. Lincoln: University of Nebraska Press, 2012.
"Infield Stars Rated as Best in 1944 Races." Associated Press, 29 Aug. 1944.
"Infielders Win 1944 Star Awards." Associated Press, 11 Oct. 1944.
"It's Willie and Keith as Co-MVPs." Associated Press, 14 Nov. 1979.
"Jackie Robinson Most Valuable, May Retire at the End of Next Year." *Pittsburgh Post-Gazette*, 19 Nov. 1949, p. 12.
Jacobsen, Lenny. SABR Bio Project: Joe Tinker. SABR.org
Jaffe, Jay. "Controversy Over NBA's Sterling Recalls Twice-Suspended Late Reds Owner Schott." *Sports Illustrated* (SI.com), 29 April 2014.
Jaffe, Jay. "MLB Unveils Revolutionary, Next-Level Tracking Technology on Defense." SI.com, 3 March 2014.
Jairo, Ramos. "Baseball's Demographic Shifts Bring Cultural Complexities." *Code Switch*, 18 April 2014.
James Bill. *The New Bill James Historical Baseball Abstract*. New York: Simon & Schuster, 2001.
James, Bill, and Rob Neyer. *The Neyer/James Guide to Pitchers*. New York: Fireside, 2004.
Jenkins, Bruce. "Giants Say Mitchell Not Worth Trouble." *San Francisco Chronicle*, 18 Dec. 1991.

"Jim Konstanty Becomes Joe Page of 1950 Season." Associated Press, 7 July 1950.
"Jim Konstanty Is Phil Factor." Associated Press, 10 Aug. 1950.
"Jim Konstanty Stacks Up as Best Fireman in Game." *The Sunday Star* (Wilmington, DE), 3 Sept. 1950.
"Jim Konstanty, Phils' Reliefer, Uses New 'Palm' Ball to Success." *The Sunday Star*, (Wilmington, DE), 2 July 1950.
"Jimmy Foxx Named Most Valuable." Associated Press, 12 Oct. 1933.
"Joe Medwick Is Best National Outfielder." Associated Press, 24 Dec. 1937.
"Just What's an MVP?" Associated Press, 23 Nov. 1991.
Kain, Ida Jean. "Gehrig Breaks Record in Health and Baseball." *The Reading Eagle*, 17 May 1937. P.11.
Kalkman, Sky, and Marc Normandin. *The Hall of Nearly Great*. Skymark Ventures LLC, 2012. eBook.
Kaufman, Ira. "Rice Is AL Most Valuable Player." United Press International, 8 Nov. 1978.
Keegan, Tom. "King Denies Pedro Crown: Post Writer Blew It by Omitting Martinez." *New York Post*, 19 Nov. 1999.
Kepner, Tyler. "M.L.B. Report Highlights Sobering Number of Black Players." *New York Times*, 9 April 2014.
Kepner, Tyler. "Belatedly, Voter Explains Why He Chose Cabrera Over Mauer for MVP." *New York Times*, 3 March 2010.
Kepner, Tyler. "Morneau Wins MVP Over Jeter in Close Race." *New York Times*, 21 Nov. 2006.
Kepner, Tyler. "When Gamesmanship Crosses the Line." *New York Times*, 16 June 2014.
Keri, Jonah, ed. *Baseball Between the Numbers*. New York: Basic Books, 2007.
Kieran, John. "Sports of the Times: Clear-Sighted Like Moles." *New York Times*, 21 May 1929. P.46.
Kieran, John. "Sports of the Times: Preparedness. Naming Names. Defensive Tactics, Double Play Technique." *New York Times*, 20 Aug. 1929, p. 34.
Kieran, John. "Sports of the Times." *The New York Times*, 9 June, 1929. P. S2
King, George A. "Why We Snubbed Jeter For Award: Writers Defend Their AL MVP Votes." *New York Post*, 22 Nov. 2006.
King, George III. "Why I Left Pedro Off My MVP Ballot; MVP Voting Isn't Life and Death Issue." *New York Post*, 24 Nov. 1999.
King, Steven A. "The Strangest Month in the

Strange Career of Rube Waddell." The National Pastime 2013, SABR.org.

"Klein and Foxx Named Big League Stick Champs." Associated Press, 2 Oct. 1933.

Krogstad, Jens Manuel. "67 Years After Jackie Robinson Broke the Color Barrier, Major League Baseball Looks Very Different." Pew Research Center, 16 Apr. 2014.

Lacy, Sam. "Morgan's 'Double' Adds Up to 18 of Last 30 National League MVPs." *Baltimore Afro-American*, 30 Nov. 1976, p. 15.

"Lajoie's Case." *Sporting Life*, 22 Oct., 1910, p. 8.

Lane, F. C. "Jake Daubert, the Hal Chase of the National League." *Baseball Magazine* IX, no. 3 (July 1912), pp. 43–50.

Lane, F. C. "The Sensational Evers Deal." *Baseball Magazine* XIII, no. 4 (Aug. 1914), pp. 27–32, 98, 100, passim.

Lane, F.C. "Editorials." *Baseball Magazine* XV, no. 6 (Oct. 1915), pp. 17–18.

Lane, F.C. "Jake Daubert, a Self-Made Success." *Baseball Magazine* XII, no. 4 (Feb. 1914), pp. 33–46.

Lane, F.C. "The Secret of Christy Mathewson's Success." *Baseball Magazine* XVII, no. 6 (Oct. 1916), pp. 65–70.

Leach, Matthew. "Statcast Greatly Expanding in 2015." MLB.com, 28 Feb. 2015.

Leavy, Jane. *The Last Boy: Mickey Mantle and the Loss of America's Childhood*. New York: Harper Books, 2010.

Lebman, Bennett. "Origins of Triple Crown." *New York Times*, 24 Apr. 2008.

Leerhsen, Charles. *Ty Cobb: A Terrible Beauty*. New York: Simon & Schuster, 2015.

Lieb, Fred. "Hornsby ('24), Ryan ('73) Share Injustice of Voters." *St. Petersburg Times*, 24 Jan. 1974, p. 5C.

Lieb, Fred. "Once Most Valuable Tag Was Worth Sack of Gold." *St. Petersburg Times*, 9 Jan. 1963.

"Long Wait Over Now for Robin." Associated Press, 24 Jan. 1976

"Lost & Found: Ty Cobb's Chalmers." *Hemmings Daily*, 5 Oct. 2010.

"Louis Aparicio's Sticky Glove May Make Him Most Valuable." United Press International, 3 Aug. 1959.

Macht, Norman L. "Does Baseball Deserve This Black Eye?" *The Baseball Research Journal* 38, no. 1 (Summer 2009), pp. 5–9.

Mack, Connie. "Reminiscence of Rube Waddell." *Baseball Magazine* VIII, no. 4 (Feb. 1912), p. 73.

Malcolm, Don. "RBIs and MVP." *Hardball Times*, 19 Dec. 2008.

"Mantle Finds Ted Threatening His Triple Crown Claim." Associated Press, 14 June 1957.

"Mantle Selected as Loop's Most Valuable." Associated Press, 13 Nov. 1956.

Maraniss, Dave. "The Last Hero." *Washington Post*, 2 April 2006.

Marine Review 46 (Aug. 1916), p. 70.

Martin, Whitney. "No Sense Comparing Marion and Wagner." Associated Press, 14 Oct. 1944.

Martinez, Pedro, with Michael Silverman. *Pedro*. New York: Houghton Mifflin Harcourt, 2015.

"Master Cars for Master Men" [advertisement]. *Sporting Life* 63, no. 12 (23 May 1914), p. 19.

Mathewson, Christy. *Pitching in a Pinch: Or, Baseball from the Inside*. 1912.

"May Erect Baseball Monument in Capital." *The Lewiston Daily Sun*, 1 March 1923.

McCarron, Anthony. "Former Mets Slugger Kevin Mitchell Now Fighting the Good Fight." *New York Daily News*, 25 July 2009.

McCracken, Voros. "Pitching and Defense: How Much Control Does a Pitcher Have?" *Baseball Prospectus* (www.baseball prospectus.com), 23 Jan. 2001.

McDonald, Anna. "The MVP Voting: What Are the Standards?" HardballTimeswww, 19 Nov. 2010.

McFarlane, John P. "The Sports Front." *Pittsburgh Post-Gazette*, 25 Sept. 1942, p. 16.

McHugh, Roy. "Zoilo Shows He's Best." *The Pittsburgh Press*, 7 Oct. 1965, p. 55.

Mell, Randall. "Weight of the World." *Sun Sentinel*, 11 March 1993.

Menke, Frank. "Federal League Worries Futz." *The Independent* (St. Petersburg), 27 Feb. 1914.

Mihoces, Gary. "Clemente Was Often Complex." Associated Press, 3 Jan. 1973.

"Mickey Mantle Heading for Triple Crown?" Associated Press, 7 May 1956.

Miller, Stuart. "M.L.B.'s Triple Crown, Polished for the Present." *New York Times*, 26 Sept. 2009.

"Mitchell Accused of Assaulting Girlfriend." Associated press, 9 Sept. 1989.

"Mitchell Arrest Puts Giants in Limbo." Associated Press, 4 Dec. 1991.

Mockler, Stan. "Marion, Sewell Get 1944 Awards." United Press, 27 Dec. 1944.

Montville, Leigh, *The Big Bam: The Life and Times of Babe Ruth*. New York: Broadway Books, 2006.

"Mort Cooper Gives Up Even Beer in His Effort to Make a Comeback." Associated Press, 15 March 1949.

"Mort Cooper, Poor Guy, May Need a Tag Day Yet." Associated Press, 31 Dec. 1947.

"Mort Cooper's Epitaph Six Little Words." United Press, 11 Aug. 1948.

"Most Valuable to Get Diploma." *Spartanburg Herald Journal*, 6 Feb. 1924.

Mulford, Ren. "The Chalmers Baseball Trophy." *Baseball Magazine* XII, no. 6 (April 1914), pp. 79–82.

Murray, Jim. "Grover Cleveland Alexander: He Still Can't Be Beat." *Herald-Tribune*, 24 Apr. 1974.

"National League Batting Records." *New York Times*, 28 Oct. 1907, p. 14.

Neal, LaVelle E., III. "Angels' Trout Right Pick for AL MVP." *Minneapolis Star-Tribune*, 30 Sept. 2012.

Nevius, C.W. "Canseco Makes Perfect Target." *Spokesman-Review*, 2 Sept. 1992, p. C2.

"New Generation of Negro Stars Have Deep Respect for Robinson." United Press, 8 Apr. 1971.

"New MLB Technology Shows How Absurdly Talented Players Are." *New York Post*, 13 June 2014.

"Newcombe Given Another Honor." Associated Press, 29 Nov. 1956.

Newhouse, Dave. "Aftershocks of Kevin Mitchell Trade Still Felt." *Lodi News-Sentinel*, 19 Dec. 1991.

Newman, Mark. "MLBAM Introduces New Way to Analyze Every Play." MLB.com, 1 Mar. 2014.

"Newspaper Ads Are Best Says Hugh Chalmers." *Pittsburgh Gazette*, 17 May 1914, Editorial Section, p. 6.

Neyer, Rob, and Eddie Epstein. *Baseball Dynasties*. New York: W.W. Norton, 2000.

Neyer, Rob. "Baseball and World War II." The National Pastime Museum.

Neyer, Rob. "Eddie Joost's Career Transformed by Eyeglasses." SBNation.com, 14 Apr. 2011.

Neyer, Rob. "Was the Federal League Really a Major League?" The National Pastime Museum.

"Not How Large But How Good" [advertisement]. *Nashua Telegraph*, 21 Oct. 1910, p. 1.

Nuwer, Rachel. "Ten Curious Facts About Octopuses." Smithsonian.com, 31 Oct. 2013.

O'Keeffe, Michael, and Teri Thompson. *The Card: Collectors, Con Men and the True Story of History's Most Desired Baseball Card.* New York: Harper, 2008.

"Old Pete Alexander Works for Flea Circus." Associated Press, 20 Jan. 1939.

Orr, William, ed. *Public Speaking: Instructor's Manual (YMCA).* New York: Association Press, 1920.

Pattison, Mark, and David Raglin, eds. *Detroit Tigers 1984: What a Start! What a Finish!* SABR, 2012.

Pearlman, Jeff. *The Bad Guys Won.* New York: HarperCollins, 2004.

"Peckinpaugh and Ruel to be Benched for Pair of Youngsters, Says Griffith." *New York Times*, 20 Jan. 1926, p. 18

"Peckinpaugh Signs to Manage Cleveland Club Again in 1931." *New York Times*, 1 Aug. 1930, p. 24.

"Pennock and O'Farrell in Line for 'Most Valuable Player' of Major Leagues." Associated Press, 8 Oct. 1926.

Phelon, William A. "Reminiscences of Christy Mathewson." *Baseball Magazine* XIV, no. 2 (Dec. 1914), pp. 45–48.

"Phillies Trade Klein to Cubs for $65,000 and Three Players." Associated Press, 22 Nov. 1933.

"Phils Turned Down on Marion, Kurowski." Associated Press, 4 June 1945.

Pollis, Lewie. "How Much Does a Win Really Cost?" SBNation.com, 15 Oct. 2013.

Posnanski, Joe. "Explaining Cabrera, Trout and WAR." joeposnanski.com, 12 Aug. 2012.

Posnanski, Joe. "Setting the Record Straight." NBCSports.com, 23 Dec. 2015.

Posnanski, Joe. "Top-100 Players of All-Time: No. 40: Eddie Collins." Joe Posnanski.com, 5 Mar. 2015.

Rankin, C.T. "Anecdotes of Rube Waddell." *Baseball Magazine* IX, no. 1 (May 1912), pp. 31–32.

Ray, James Lincoln. SABR Bio Project: Chuck Klein. SABR.org.

"Reds' Davis Shrugs Off Glowing Reviews from Media." Associated Press, 3 Feb. 1987.

Reichler, Joe. "Rosen Guns for Triple Crown Despite Big Flop by Cleveland." Associated Press, 24 Aug. 1953.

Reichler, Joe. "Target of 30 Wins in 1952 is Big Mark." Associated Press, 14 July 1952.

Reichler, Joe. *"Vote Newcombe Most Valuable."* Associated Press, 21 Nov. 1956.

"Reminiscences of Rube Waddell." *Baseball Magazine* XII, no. 3 (Jan. 1914), pp. 43–45.

Rice, Grantland. "Grantland Rice Says...." *Pittsburgh Press*, 15 Aug. 1949, p. 19.

Rice, Grantland. "The Sportlight: Marion Keeps Moving." *Harrisburg Telegraph*, 11 Oct. 1944.

Rice, Grantland. "The Sportlight: An Old Argument." *The Reading Eagle*, 2 Dec. 1952, p. 22.

"Richards Vidmer Biography." The Bill Shannon Biographical Dictionary of New York Sports, New York Historical Society Museum and Library (http://sports.nyhistory.org/).

Richter, Francis C., ed. *The Reach Official American League Baseball Guide for 1912*. Philadelphia: A.J. Reach Company, 1912.

Richter, Francis. "Murray's Case." *Sporting Life*, 7 May 1910, p. 5.

Ritter, Lawrence S. *The Glory of Their Times*. New York: Quill, 1984.

"Rival Stars in World's Series Are Named as Greatest Players in the Game." *Milwaukee Journal*, 4 Oct. 1912, p. 16.

Rogers, Phil. "Rodriguez Wins AL MVP in a Debatable Decision." *Chicago Tribune*, 19 Nov. 1999.

Russell, Thomas Herbert, ed. *Advertising Methods and Mediums*. Washington Institute, 1910.

Ryhal, Gregory. SABR Bio Project: Frank Chance. SABR.org

Sandoval, Jim. SABR Bio: Jake Daubert. SABR.org.

Schoenfeld, Dave. "Chris Archer: Cy Young and MVP Candidate." ESPN.com, 24 June 2015.

Schoenfield, Dave. "How Come Derek Jeter Never Won the MVP?" ESPN.com, 26 Sept. 2014.

Schreiber, Jay, and Elena Gustines. "Mets Hope Harvey Can Lift Attendance as Gooden Did." *New York Times*, 14 Apr. 2015.

Sedeno, David. "Mitchell May Have to Undergo Counseling." Associated Press, 9 Sept. 1989.

Shaiklin, Bill. "Barry Bonds Loses Collusion Case Against MLB." *Los Angeles Times*, 27 Aug. 2015.

Sheldon, Mark. "Votto Wins NL MVP by Overwhelming Margin." MLB.com, 22 Nov. 2010.

Sherman, Ed. "Getting in the Way of the Story." *Chicago Tribune*, 26 Nov. 1999.

Shiner, David. SABR Bio Project: Johnny Evers. SABR.org.

"Should Most Valuable Player Award Become Player of the Year?" United Press International, 19 Apr. 1963.

"Simmons Is Choice in Baseball Poll." *New York Times*, 25 Dec. 1929, p. 33.

Skipper, John C. *Wicked Curve: The Life and Troubled Times of Grover Cleveland Alexander*. Jefferson, NC: McFarland, 2006.

Smith, Claire. "Bonds Is Voted MVP in a Landslide." *New York Times*, 20 Nov. 1990.

"Sorry Result." *Sporting Life*, 15 Oct. 1910, p. 2.

Spander, Art. "Giants' Kevin Mitchell Has Come a Long Way." *Chicago Tribune*, 26 July 1987.

Sports Reference, LLC. "Baseball-Reference.com WAR Explained." Baseball-Reference.com, Major League Statistics and Information. http://www.baseball-reference.com/. 2014–2015.

Sports Reference, LLC. "Position Player WAR Calculations and Details." Baseball-Reference.com. Major League Statistics and Information. http://www.baseball-reference.com/. 2014–2015.

"Spring Series Off in Future, Magnates Say." *St. Petersburg Times*, 11 Feb. 1925.

"St. Louis Writers Question Award to Vance; Want Details of Vote Which Beat Hornsby." *New York Times*, 7 Dec. 1924, p. 120.

Stack, C.P. "Evers and the Umpires." *Baseball Magazine* XII, no. 3 (Jan. 1914), pp. 71–73.

"Starting in 2013, Players Banned From Awards if They Have Bonus Clauses." Associated Press, 5 Dec. 2012.

Stewart, Mark. SABR Bio Project: Spud Chandler. SABR.org.

Super, Henry. "Medwick Named Nationals Most Valuable Player." United Press, 10 Nov. 1937.

"Supreme Court." *Sporting Life*, 5 Mar. 1910, p. 2.

Svrluga, Barry, and Ellen Nakashima. "FBI Investigation of Cardinals Could Signify New Era of Cheating in Sports." *Washington Post*, 17 June 2014.

"Team Stunned as Mitchell Leaves Japan." Associated Press, 27 May 1995.

"Ted Williams Is 1942 AL Batting Champion." Associated Press, 21 Dec. 1942.

"Ted Williams Makes Good in Navy as He Did on Diamond." *Wilmington Sunday Star*, 12 Dec., 1943.

"Ted Williams Signs, Salary Reported to Be $60,000." United Press, 3 Feb., 1947.

Thesier, Kelly. "Morneau Upsets Field in MVP Race." MLB.com, 21 Nov. 2006.

Thorn, John, ed. *The Armchair Book of Baseball*. New York: Collier Books, 1985.

"Thumbnail Sketches of Players in Series." *Schenectady Gazette*, 30 Sept. 1925, p. 18.

"Tigers Look to Trammell for Leadership." Associated Press, 20 Jan. 1988.

"Toronto's Bell Wins AL MVP Award." Associated Press, 17 Nov. 1987.

"Tovar Doesn't Like to Create Trouble." United Press International, 2 April 1968.

"Troubles of Managers." *Sporting Life*, 19 Sept. 1914, p. 3.

U.S. Census Bureau. "Definition of Hispanic Origin." www.census.gov.

"Valuable Player Award is Stopped by American Loop." *The Pittsburgh Press*, 7 May 1929.

"Valuable Player Sorry Simmons Didn't Get Coveted Honor." Associated Press, 24 Sept. 1925.

"Vaughn Edges Belle for AL Most Valuable." Associated Press, 17 Nov. 1995.

Vidmar, Richards. "Picking Best Yank Is Latest Problem." *New York Times*, 3 Aug. 1927, p. 17.

"Vote Cronin, Terry Most Valuable Men." United Press, 26 Nov. 1930.

"Waddell's Youth." *Sporting Life*, 27 July 1907, p. 15.

Wagner, Honus. "Hail! Pirates of 1902! " *Pittsburgh Press*, 6 May 1937, p. 37.

"Wagner's Big Feat." *Sporting Life* 32, no. 5 (22 Oct. 1898), p. 4.

Warner, Bill. "Old Argument Over Pitcher's Right to Become MVP Surfaces Again." *Bangor Daily News*, 20 Nov. 1986, p. 13.

"What's Behind This Year's HR Derby?" Associated Press, 24 May 1987.

"When Evers Criticises." *Baseball Magazine* 19, no. 4 (Aug. 1917), 426.

"Where's Kevin? Mitchell No-Show at Giants Practice, Will Get Heavy Fine." Associated Press, 12 Oct. 1989.

"White Sox' Nellie Fox Named Most Valuable During 1959." Associated Press, 12 Nov. 1959.

Whiting, Robert. *The Meaning of Ichiro: The New Wave from Japan and the Transformation of Our National Pastime*. New York: Hatchett Book Group, 2009.

"Why Boston Sold Tris Speaker." *Sporting Life* 67, no. 8 (22 April 1916), p. 5.

Wiley, Ralph. "These Are Red Letter Days." *Sports Illustrated*, 25 May 1987.

Wilgus, Horace LaFayette. "The Standard Oil Fine." *Michigan Law Review* 6 (1907): 118–35.

"Will Choose Most Valuable Player in American League." *New York Times*, 3 May 1922, p. 27.

"Writers Honor Joe Medwick." United Press, 10 Nov. 1937.

"Yankee Pitcher Bobby Shantz Called AL Comeback of the Year." Associated Press, 29 Oct. 29 1957.

Yankees 1986 Official Year Book.

Index

Aaron, Henry 100, 102, 120, 165, 174–175, 185, 191, 195–196
Adair, Robert 226ch15n5
Adams, Franklin Pierce 16
added win, cost of 189
adjusted ERA 3
adjusted production *see* OPS+
African-American players, decline in number 176–177, 226n4
Alexander, Doyle 225ch13n8
Alexander, Grover Cleveland 20, 21, 38–39, 41–49, 58, 60, 73, 181; life after baseball 218n10; military service 218n10
Allen, Dick 18, 175
Alomar, Roberto 138
Anderson, Brady 141
Anderson, Sparky 133, 134, 146, 225ch13n6
Aparicio, Luis 145, 146
Appel, Marty 30
Arizona Diamondbacks 150, 154–155
Armour, Mark 177
Atherton, Keith 133
Atlanta Braves 148, 167
Atlanta Fulton County Stadium 227ch17n4

Bagwell, Jeff 168, 222
Baker Bowl 3, 78
Baltimore Orioles 117, 168
Banks, Ernie 86, 100, 102, 134, 174–175, 177
Barnum, P.T. 7
Barrett, Red 90–92, 221n17
Bartell, Dick 116
base running runs 31
Baseball Encyclopedia 218ch5n1
Baseball Magazine 18, 55, 57, 64, 219n3
Baseball Prospectus.com 218ch5n1
Baseball-Referencewww 2, 4, 24, 31, 159, 165, 189, 196

Baseball Writers Association of America *see* BBWAA
baseballs, dead 46
Baseball's Sad Lexicon 16
bat control 22, 216ch2n2, 220ch7n4
batting average on balls in play 206
batting runs 31
Bautista, Jose 111, 204
Baylor, Don 122–123
BBWAA 13–15, 50, 72, 106, 119, 131, 145, 193, 205–207, 215n9
Beane, Billy 202
Belanger, Mark 16
Bell, Buddy 132
Bell, George 134, 162
Belle, Albert 148, 166, 168
Beltre, Adrien 223n11
Bench, Johnny 121, 149, 175, 186
Bender, Chief 66
Beniquez, Juan 134
Berra, Yogi 98, 175, 221ch8n1, 222n11, 228ch18n3
best pitching seasons, 1987 to 2014 204
Bichette, Dante 169; defensive abilities 227ch17n12
The Big Bam 218n8
big data 202
"The Big Red Machine" 120–121
Bill James New Historical Baseball Abstract 225n8
Black, Joe 108–109
Blue, Vida 129, 131, 146
Blyleven, Bert 132, 186
Boggs, Wade 53, 162, 186–187
Bonds, Barry 93, 94, 99, 101–102, 115–116, 128, 148, 151, 153–155, 167, 169, 176–178, 187–189, 228n20, 229n19, 229n20
Bonilla, Bobby 115, 116
Bosch, Hieronymus 219n8

239

Index

Boston Braves 18, 57, 90, 113
Boston Red Sox 58, 62, 66–70, 95, 99, 113, 123, 136, 148, 191–192, 197
Bottomley, Jim 61
Boudreau, Lou 85, 86, 97, 142, 183, 184
Boyer, Ken 101, 175
Boyle, Peter 227*ch*17*n*12
Bradshaw, Terry 224*n*6
Braun, Ryan 176, 178
Braves, Milwaukee 109
Breadon, Sam 5, 6, 90, 92
Brett, George 112, 122, 128, 186, 200
Brock, Lou 101, 194
Brooklyn Dodgers 100, 105, 108, 109
Brooklyn Robins 12, 60
Brooklyn Superbas 51, 53, 57
Brown, Kevin 169
Brown, Mordecai 52–54, 56
Buffalo Blues 29
bullpen specialist 203
Bumgarner, Madison 52
Burgess, Smokey 101
Burkett, Jesse 51
Burks, Ellis 2, 3
Burns, George 21, 22, 37, 59, 199, 217*ch*4*n*6
Burroughs, Jeff 34, 175–176, 194
Busby, Jim 98

Cabrera, Miguel 32, 75–76, 82, 111–112, 176, 178, 200, 206; 2012 MVP debate 74, 205
Cain, Lorenzo 202
Caldwell, Ray 29, 217*n*11
California Angels 122, 224*ch*11*n*7
Camacho, Ernie 133
Caminiti, Ken 2, 3, 148, 153, 169, 170
Campanella, Roy 100, 174–175, 177
Canseco, Jose 194
Carew, Rod 75, 175
Carlson, Hal 41
Carlton, Steve 43, 130, 149
Carter, Gary 156, 157
Carter, Joe 225*ch*13*n*14
Cash, Norm 222*n*13
Casuga, Dr. Sheryll 194–195
catcher, greatest seasons 149
Cerone, Rick 112
Cerv, Bob 99
Cespedes, Yoenis 202
Chalmers, Hugh 4–5, 9–11, 15, 20, 41, 56, 67, 125–126, 189; 215*n*1, 215*n*7; Chalmers-Detroit Model-30 8, 189, 215*n*2; origins of auto company 7–8
Chalmers Award (trophy) 8, 11, 56, 57, 66–67
Chance, Frank 16, 17, 24, 29–30, 52–54, 125; reputation as dirty player 219*n*4
Chapman, Ray 216–217*n*2

Chase, Hal 57
Chesbro, Jack 63
Chicago Cubs 16, 19, 29, 51, 52, 55–56, 58, 61, 77–78, 86, 91, 104, 107–109, 116, 126, 152, 160
Chicago Whales 216*n*3
Chicago White Sox 3, 65, 68–69, 125, 137
Chrysler Corporation 215*n*7
Cicotte, Eddie 69
Cincinnati Reds 59, 93, 101, 117, 127, 147–148, 159, 186
Clark, Jack 160, 161
Clemens, Roger 129, 131, 136–137, 139, 166, 172, 191, 192, 204, 225*ch*13*n*11–12, 226*ch*15*n*2, 227*n*16, 229*ch*20*n*1, 229*ch*20*n*2, 229*ch*20*n*3
Clemente, Roberto 100, 128, 173, 175, 228*ch*18*n*1
Cleveland Indians 13, 20, 37, 38, 41, 43, 58, 68–69, 76, 82, 99, 132–133, 142, 168, 183
Cleveland Naps 8–9, 64
closer (relief pitcher) 134, 136, 225*n*15, 230*n*8
Coakley, Andy 64
Cobb, Ty 8–10, 55–56, 65–69, 73, 76, 77, 81, 122, 125, 127, 153, 180–182, 199, 228*n*20
Cochrane, Mickey 78–80, 107, 135; managerial responsibilities 220*n*10
Colavito, Rocky 99
Colbert, Claudette 223*n*19
Collins, Eddie 10, 65–69
Colorado Rockies 153
Comeback Player of the Year 145
Connolly, Joe 22
contact rate 87
Coombs, Jack 66; *see also* luckiest seasons; pitchers
Cooper, Mort 88, 90–92
Cooper, Walker 90
Coors Field 3, 111, 153, 169
Corriden, Red 9–10
Covaleski, Stan 28
Crasnick, Jerry 193, 195, 196
Cravath, Gavvy 21, 22, 57, 59, 219*n*6
Crawford, Sam 180
Cronin, Joe 12–13, 218*ch*5*n*1
Cushman, Harvey 218*ch*5*n*2
Cy Young award, impact on MVP vote 130

Daiei Hawks 147
Daley, Arthur 87, 110, 143
Danning, Harry 116, 117
Dante's *Inferno* 59
Dark, Alvin 113, 116, 223*ch*10*n*16
Darling, Ron 192
Daubert, Jake 34, 57, 223*ch*10*n*1; "basestealing maxims" 213

Davis, Eric 159–161, 226*ch*16*n*1–5, 228*n*20
Davis, Storm 225*ch*13*n*10
Dawson, Andre 156–157, 160–162, 186, 199
Deadball era 46, 52, 54, 59, 120
"Death Valley" 95
defense: best defensive seasons by MVP 85; how to value 84–87; impact on 1944 MVP vote 87; reliability of statistics 33, 216*ch*2*n*1; shifts 87
demographic shifts in electorate 205
designated hitter 111, 198–199, 209
Detroit Tigers 27, 64–65, 68–69, 79, 80, 112, 118, 133, 146, 162, 163, 171
Devery, Bill 30
Devlin, Art 52
DiMaggio, Joe 77, 82, 86, 94–98, 104, 109, 135, 184, 194, 196, 199
Doby, Larry 175
"Dr. Strangeglove" 126, 222*n*18
Dodgers Stadium 3, 153, 169, 224*ch*11*n*3
Donaldson, Josh 176, 178, 200
Donovan, Bill 219*n*10
Doyle, Larry 56
Dreslough, Clay 218*n*18
Dressen, Charlie 110
Dunn, James C. 68
Durocher, Leo 221*n*15
Dykes, Jimmy 144

earned run rate 46–47, 54, 218*n*21
Eckersley, Dennis 34, 126, 131, 135–139, 167, 172, 203
Edes, Gordon 197
Eldred, Cal 137
Elias Sports Bureau 85
Elliott, Bob 184, 214*n*7
Ellsbury, Jacoby 111, 204
Emergency Stabilization Act 221*n*16
Ennis, Del 106
ERA+ *see* adjusted era
ERR *see* earned run rate
Evans, Dwight 132
Evers, John 10, 16–23, 52, 55, 57, 125–126, 215*n*6, 216*n*4, 216*n*5

FanGraphs.com 206
Farrell, Henry 195
Federal League 19, 29, 216*n*5, 216*n*6, 216*n*7
Feller, Bob 216*ch*3*n*1
Fenway Park 3–4, 182
Fielder, Cecil 171
fielding independent pitching 44, 53–54, 63, 218*n*18
fielding runs 31
Fingers, Rollie 131–132, 136, 139
FIP *see* fielding independent pitching

first-step acceleration 202
fluke seasons 141–149
Foley Tim 221*n*8
Fonseca Lou 218*ch*5*n*1
football 194
Forbes Field 120
Ford, Henry 7, 215*n*1
Ford, Whitey 145
Foster, George 171, 175
Fox, Nellie 86, 175, 224
Foxx, Jimmy 71–72, 74, 76, 81, 93, 183
Frisch, Frankie 13, 34, 40, 85, 108, 216*ch*1*n*10
Fullerton, Hugh 215*n*4

Gagne, Eric 203
Galvin, Pud 218*n*22
game-winning RBI (official statistic) 225*n*
Garciaparra, Nomar 166
Garver, Ned 143
Garvey, Steve 34, 175, 176, 194
"The Gashouse Gang" 80
Gehrig, Lou 27, 36, 37, 71–73, 76, 78–81, 98, 107–109, 114, 116, 135, 182–183, 196
Gehringer Charlie 78–80
The Genie 158
Gentile, Jim 222*n*14
George Washington University 115
Getty, Frank 39
Giambi, Jason 126, 176, 222
Gibson, Bob 4, 43, 52, 101–102, 130, 139, 174, 175
Gillette, Gary 218*ch*5*n*1
Glavine, Tom 91, 130, 167
The Glory of Their Times 39, 70
Goldschmidt, Paul 155
Gomez, Lefty 79
Gonzalez, Juan 34, 126, 164–166, 168–170, 176, 178, 228*ch*18*n*5; defensive abilities 227*ch*17*n*2
Gonzalez, Luis 155
Gooden, Dwight 130–131, 133, 150–152, 226*ch*15*n*2, 226*ch*15*n*3, 226*ch*15*n*4, 226*ch*15*n*5
Goold, Derrick 223*n*9
Gordon, Joe 77, 95, 225
Goslin, Goose 28, 36, 37, 71, 80
Gossage, Rich "Goose" 224*ch*13*n*3
Gould, Stephen Jay 45
Grant, Evan 111, 118
The Great Depression 220*ch*6*n*8, 220*ch*6*n*10
Greenberg, Hank 79–80
Greenwell, Mike 194
Greinke, Zack 149, 204
Grich, Bobby 132
Griffey, Ken, Jr. 166, 168, 174, 176, 187, 218*ch*4*n*16, 227*ch*17*n*6

Griffith, Clark 28, 98, 222n10
Grimes, Burleigh 60–61
Groat, Dick 86, 92, 100–101, 173, 175
Groh, Heinie 59
Grove, Lefty 13, 182–183
Guerrero, Pedro 152
Guerrero, Vladimir 156, 178
Guidry, Ron 192
Gwynn, Tony 160–161

Hafey, Chick 13
Haines, Jesse 39
Halberstam, David 222n19
Hall of Fame Veterans Committee 216n4
The Hall of Nearly Great 226ch16n5
Hamilton, Josh 200
Hamner, Granny 106
The Hank Aaron Award 224ch13n2
Harper, Bryce 155, 176, 178
Hartnett, Gabby 116, 126, 200
Hedges, Robert Lee 10
Heilmann, Harry 27, 36, 37, 71
Henderson, Rickey 101, 127, 132, 167, 171, 187, 228n19, 228n20
Henrich, Tommy 143
The Herald Tribune 115
Hernandez, Felix 3
Hernandez, Guillermo 133–134, 139, 146
Hernandez, Keith 119, 121
Hernandez, Roberto 137
Heyward, Jason 202
Higuera, Teddy 229ch20n2
Hispanic players, MVP vote 174
Hoak, Ralph 100–101, 173
Hofman, Solly 56
Hoiles, Chris 168
Holtzman, Jerome 115
Hooper, Harry 70
Hornsby, Rogers 5–6, 12, 38, 39, 59–61, 73–74, 76–77, 81, 182, 216ch3n1
Howard, Elston 174
Howard, Ryan 178, 200
Howell, Harry 9; see also 1910 AL Batting Race
Hubbell, Carl 77, 116, 183
Huggins, Miller 35–36
Huhn, Rick 215n3
Hummel, Rick 223n9

"intangibles" 30, 126, 184, 195–196, 200
intentional walks, record 128
International League 229n6

Jackson, Bo 229n10
Jackson, Joe 125
Jackson, Reggie 175, 187, 194
Jaffe, Jay 226n2

James, Bill 125, 206
James, Bill (pitcher) 20, 216ch2n8
Jay, Joey 117
Jenkins, Ferguson 130, 223
Jensen, Jackie 99, 175, 224
Jeter, Derek 117–118, 134, 166, 197–199, 216ch2n9
Johnson, Ban 9, 11, 29, 30, 215n5
Johnson, Randy 63, 130, 154, 168, 204, 227n14
Johnson, Walter 28, 56, 67–68, 70–71, 73, 125, 136, 181–182, 215n6, 216ch3n1
Jones, Chipper 143, 169, 176, 178
Joost, Eddie 96, 97, 221ch8n6
juiced ball 167, 222n11

Kansas City Athletics 99
Kansas City Royals 133, 149
Kauffman Stadium 224n8
Keeler, Willie 45
Kell, George 143
Keller, Charlie 95
Kemp, Matt 178
Kent, Jeff 153–154, 176, 222
Kepner, Tyler 228ch18n4
Kershaw, Clayton 129–131, 139, 140, 154, 176, 178, 200, 203–204
Kieran, John 12
Killebrew, Harmon 75, 175
Kiner, Ralph 93, 108
King, George 170, 227n17
Kingman, Dave 134
Kinsler, Ian 223n11
Klein, Chuck 3, 13, 76–78, 81, 116
Kluszewski, Ted 116
Koenig, Mark 38
Konishi, Keizo 112
Konstanty, Jim 103–106, 109, 143, 175, 222ch9n1
Koufax, Sandy 42, 52, 100, 102, 130, 139, 140, 175, 195
Kremer, Ray 41
Kubrick, Stanley 222ch8n18
Kuhn, Bowie 132, 224ch13n4
Kurowski, Whitey 92

Lajoie, Napolean 8–10, 62, 64–66, 76, 80, 181
Landis, Kenesaw Mountain 13, 195
Lang, Jack 227n16
Lannin, JJ 68
Larkin, Barry 153, 168, 169
La Russa, Tony 133
Latino player population 177; see also Hispanic players; MVP vote
Lawson, Roxy 225ch13n10
Lazzeri, Tony 36–38, 39, 41, 49, 71, 114

Leach, Terry 137
Leach, Tommy 181
Levitt, Daniel R. 177
Lewis, Michael 206
Lieb, Fred 5
Lofton, Kenny 53
Lombardi, Ernie 127, 225
Longoria, Evan 155
Lopez, Aurelio 133
"Lord Charles" 226ch15n5
Los Angeles Angels of Anaheim 6, 220ch7n1, 227n16
Los Angeles Dodgers 139–140, 152–153, 171, 178, 184
luckiest seasons, pitchers 225n10
Luque, Dolph 60
Lynn, Fred 122, 123, 175, 224n8

Mack, Connie 64, 79, 86, 219n10, 220ch6n8, 220ch6n9, 229ch19n6
Maddux, Greg 43–49, 130–131, 153, 169, 204, 218n20, 218n23, 226ch15n4
Magee, Sheree 21, 22
Maisel, Fritz 68
Manager of the Year award 14
Mancuso, Gus 117
Mantle, Mickey 76, 82, 94, 102, 117, 127, 151, 171, 175, 194–195, 229n14; knee injury 184, 227n11; "longest" HR 222n10; MVP snubs 98–99
Manush, Heinie 36, 37
Maranville, Rabbit 20, 220ch7n7
Marichal, Juan 43, 130
Marion, Marty 85–90, 92, 126, 201, 220ch7n5, 221n8, 221n9, 221n14, 221n15
Maris, Roger 99, 117, 121, 145, 175, 200
Martin, Billy 113, 223n15
Martinez, Edgar 168
Martinez, Pedro 3, 169–170, 183, 194, 204
Mathews, Eddie 93
Mathewson, Christy 41–49, 51–52, 55–56, 64, 67, 73, 216ch2n2, 218n15, 218ch5n1, 225ch13n10
Mattingly, Don 129, 134, 162, 191–192, 195, 227n16, 229ch20n1, 229ch20n2
Mauer, Joe 112, 149, 176, 197–200
Maxwell Corporation 215n7
Mays, Carl 59
Mays, Willie 2, 59, 66, 85–86, 94, 105, 107, 116, 151, 166, 171, 174–175, 177, 184–185, 196, 216ch3n1, 228n20; MVP snubs 99–102
Mazeroski, Bill 101
McCatty, Steve 132
McCormick, Frank 93
McCovey, Willie 3, 152, 174–175
McCracken, Voros 218n8

McCutchen, Andrew 84, 85, 155, 176, 178, 200
McGee, Willie 152
McGinnity, Joe 51, 223ch10n6
McGraw, John 153, 180
McGwire, Mark 92–93, 138, 162, 166, 169, 221n19, 224ch11n3, 225ch14n1, 226ch15n3
McLain, Denny 128, 131, 139, 175, 200
McQuinn, George 96
McReynolds, Kevin 152
Medwick, Joe 76, 81, 82, 116, 141, 142
Meusel, Bob 38, 39
Miami Marlins 150, 154, 204
Milwaukee Brewers 91, 132, 137
Minnesota Twins 75, 112–113, 117, 138, 197
"The Miracle Braves" 20
Mitchell, Kevin 146–148, 225ch14n8, 225ch14n9, 225ch14n10
Mize, Johnny 92, 93, 109, 222n7
MLBwww 2
Model T 227, 215n1
Molina, Yadier 178
Moneyball 206
Montgomery, Jeff 137
Montreal Expos 120, 155–157, 226ch15n9
The Montreal Tower 226ch15n10
Montville, Leigh 218n8
Moore, Wilcy 114
Morgan, Cy 66
Morgan, Joe 125, 175, 177, 185, 186
Morneau, Justin 117, 118, 176, 178, 197–199
Morris, Jack 137
Most Valuable Player Award: history 7–15; list of winners 209–213; pitchers 138–140; trends 199; voting rules 14
Mt. Rushmore 219n15
Mulford, Ren 56
Murphy, Charles 19, 216ch2n5
Murphy, Dale 156, 186
Musial, Stan 89, 105, 108–109, 113, 126, 183–184, 195, 223ch9n2, 229n13
Mussina, Mike 136
MVP monument, Washington D.C. 215n8
Myer, Buddy 28, 217ch3n9
Myers, Hi 59

National Cash Register Company 7
Neal, La Velle E. III 170; voting irregularities 227n16
neutralized batting 165
New York Giants 29, 51–53, 56, 105
New York Mets 43, 147, 150, 151–153, 185, 186, 191, 192
New York Yankees 6, 22, 27, 29, 30, 35, 36–39, 55, 68, 70, 72–73, 79, 95–99, 104–105, 112, 114–115, 118, 128, 132, 143–146, 150,

152, 167, 170, 174, 185–186, 191–192, 195, 197–199
Newcombe, Don 100, 130, 139, 140, 175, 225*ch*13*n*16
Neyer, Rob 221–222*ch*8*n*6
Nichols, Max 113
Nicholson, Bill 86, 89
1910 AL batting race 8, 215*n*4, 215*n*5
1926 World Series 37
1930 scoring levels 61–62, 164, 217*ch*3*n*2
1981 player's strike 132, 224*ch*13*n*4, 224*ch*13*n*5
1994 player's Strike 168
Norman, Dan 229*n*16

Oakland Athletics 132–133, 136, 138, 148, 171–172, 202
O'Connell, Jack 14
O'Connor, Jack 9
October 1964 222*n*19
O'Farrell, Bob 34, 38–41, 61, 124
Olerud, John 168
Oliva, Tony 86
Olympic Stadium 226*ch*15*n*10, 226*ch*15*n*11, 227*ch*16*n*8
O'Neill, Steve 223*ch*10*n*6
OPS+ 2; record for lowest, career 221*n*8
Ortiz, David 197–199
osteomyelitis 184
O'Toole, Jim 117

Page, Joe 96, 143
Palmer, Jim 186
Palmer, Pete 218*ch*5*n*1
Parker, Dave 120, 152, 175
Parrish, Lance 134
Patterson, Arthur "Red" 222*n*9
Peckinpaugh, Roger 24–25, 28, 30–34, 71, 85, 88–89, 92, 135–136, 199, 217*ch*3*n*9
Pendleton, Terry 92, 148, 167, 227*ch*16*n*9
Pennock, Herb 38, 92
Pesky, Johnny 221*ch*8*n*5
Pew Research Center 177
Philadelphia Athletics 20, 25, 36, 62, 63, 65, 67, 72, 96, 144
Philadelphia Phillies 58, 60, 78, 92, 101, 103, 104, 105, 109, 151
Phillippe, Deacon 54
The Physics of Baseball see Adair, Robert
Piazza, Mike 149, 153–154, 169, 224*ch*11*n*3
pitcher usage patterns 203
pitcher vs every day player MVP debate 191, 192
pitcher WAR *see* Wins Above Replacement
Pittsburgh Pirates 28, 41, 51, 55, 61–62, 78, 84, 85, 100–101, 115, 119–122, 152, 155, 173, 178, 181

Plank, Eddie 66
player population demographics 176
positional adjustment runs 31
Posnanski, Joe 31, 193, 194, 202
PTSD 60, 218*ch*4*n*10
Puckett, Kirby 138
Pujols, Albert 126, 154, 174, 176–178, 188–190

"Quadruple Crown" 65
Quinn, John 91
Quisenberry, Dan 133

racial demographics, MLB 177
racism, MVP vote 173–179; 227*ch*17*n*15
Ramirez, Hanley 154
Ramirez, Manny 93, 166
Raschi, Vic 105
Reese, Pee Wee 127
relief pitchers, MVP vote 106, 108–109, 130–138, 200, 203; *see also* closer (relief pitcher)
replacement-level player 1
replacement-level runs 31
reserve clause 216*n*7
Rice, Grantland 110
Rice, Jim 187, 192, 194, 229*ch*20*n*1
Rice, Sam 28, 217*n*8
Ripken, Cal 16, 86, 125, 134–135, 167, 186
Ritter, Lawrence 39
Rizzuto, Phil 92, 142, 143, 175, 224
Roberts, Robin 105–106, 108–110, 112
Robinson, Brooks 16, 145
Robinson, Frank 100, 102, 117, 174
Robinson, Jackie 14, 105, 109, 128, 174–175, 224*ch*12*n*2; 1949 MVP 228*ch*18*n*2
Rodriguez, Alex 134, 164, 166, 170, 176–178, 188–189, 199–200, 220*ch*6*n*2, 221*ch*8*n*1, 221*ch*8*n*2, 223*ch*10*n*1, 227*ch*16*n*6, 227*ch*17*n*6
Rodriguez, Ivan 169, 178, 200
Rogell, Billy 80
Rogers, Ginger 223*n*19
Rollins, Jimmy 129
Rookie of the Year award 14–15, 134
Roosevelt, Eleanor 115
Rose, Pete 121, 175, 186
Rosen, Al 76, 82, 147, 175, 225*ch*14*n*8
rosin 46
Roush, Edd 59
Rudolph, Dick 21
rule changes to game 216*n*2
runs above average 33
runs allowed per nine innings 46
Ruth, Babe 11, 27, 35–41, 50, 59, 61, 68–73, 80, 98–99, 108, 113, 114, 117, 121, 151, 171, 182–183, 195, 196, 216*ch*3*n*1, 229*n*19;

"bellyache heard round the world" 35; extra-curricular activities 217*ch*4*n*1, 217*ch*4*n*2
Ryder, Jack 12

Safeco Field 3
Sain, Johnny 113–114
St. Louis Browns 9, 36, 71, 96, 143
St. Louis Cardinals 5, 6, 12, 38, 39, 60–61, 80, 86–93, 101, 104, 113, 116, 119, 124, 128, 130, 151, 152, 178, 194
Sale, Chris 3
saliva 22
San Diego, California 3, 225*n*9
San Francisco Giant 6, 29, 51, 52, 55–56, 60, 67, 77, 82, 101, 116–117, 147, 185
Santana, Johan 117–118, 150, 199
Sauer, Hank 107–109, 110, 175
Schilling, Curt 226*ch*15*n*7
Schmidt, Mike 156, 186, 187, 191
Schoenfield, Dave 203, 222*n*17
Schott, Marge 226*n*2
Schulte, Frank 56
Schwartz, Matt 229*n*21
scrappy 220*ch*7*n*4
Seattle Mariners 3, 21, 147
Seaver, Tom 43–49, 130, 152, 185, 186
Selig, Bud 155, 162, 228*ch*18*n*4
Sewell, Joe 182, 229*ch*19*n*5
Shantz, Bobby 125, 143–145, 175, 225*ch*14*n*4, 225*ch*14*n*5, 225*ch*14*n*6
Shea Stadium 153
Sheffield, Gary 169
Shibe Park 73, 182
short-relievers, MVP vote 203
Simmons, Al 12, 25, 36, 71–73, 217*ch*3*n*3, 217*ch*3*n*4
Simmons, Andrelton 84, 85
Simmons, Curt 223*ch*10*n*4
Singleton, Ken 122
Sisler, George 71
slash-line triple crown 75
Smith, Earl 28
Smith, Ozzie 16, 160–161
Smith, Sean 1
Smithsonian Institute 11
Smoltz, John 169
Snider, Duke 100, 140, 184, 185
Sosa, Sammy 93, 141, 169, 176, 177
The Soul of Baseball 193
Southworth, Billy 59, 87
Spahn, Warren 42, 117
Speaker, Tris 56, 66–69, 122
spin rate 201
spitball 59
The Sporting News most valuable players 12

Sportsman's Park 38, 217*n*7
Stade Olympique 156; *see also* Olympic Stadium
The Stadium at Arlington 111
Stallings, George 19
Stanky, Eddie 105
Stanley, Bob 133
Stanton, Giancarlo 154, 204
Stargell, Willie 24, 31–34, 89, 107, 119–122, 136, 175–176, 224*ch*11*n*3, 224*ch*11*n*4, 224*ch*11*n*5, 224*ch*11*n*6
StatCast 201, 202
Stengel, Casey 22, 98, 144–145, 184
Stephens, Vern 221*ch*8*n*5
Stewart, Dave 172
Stieb, Dave 132
Strawberry, Daryl 152
Stuart, Dick 101
Suzuki, Ichiro 176, 178, 200

Tampa Bay Rays 150, 155, 203
Tango, Tom 218*n*18
Tayler, Jack 51
Tejada, Miguel 178
Terry, Bill 12, 13, 62, 148, 167
Texas Rangers 111, 118, 164, 166
Thevenow, Tommy 38, 218*n*11
Thomas, Frank 125–126, 138, 166–168, 177, 198
Thompson, Milt 161
Three Rivers Stadium 121, 224*ch*11*n*3
Tinker, Joe 16, 17, 19, 77, 125, 216*ch*2*n*1, 216*ch*2*n*2, 216*ch*2*n*3, 216*ch*2*n*4, 216*ch*2*n*5
tobacco spit 46
Toney, Fred 219*n*7
Toronto Blue Jays 132, 135–136, 138, 162–163, 168, 171
Tovar, Cesar 113
Trammell, Alan 85, 133–134, 162–163
Triple Crown (hitting) 8, 27, 36, 61, 71, 74–83, 95–96, 98, 107, 109, 113, 116–117, 142–143, 151, 167, 200–201, 205–206; pitching 44, 60, 70, 183
Trout, Mike 32, 176, 178, 200, 205; 2012 MVP debate 74, 206
Tudor, John 151, 226*ch*15*n*6
Tulowitzki, Troy 134

Upshaw, Willie 134
U.S. Cellular Field 3
Utley, Chase 178

Valenzuela, Fernando 151
Vance, Dazzy 5–6, 12, 60, 61
Vaughn, Hippo 58, 219*n*7
Vaughn, Mo 107, 168, 174
Verban, Emil 221*n*12

Index

Verlander, Justin 111, 130–131, 139, 176, 178, 203–204
Versalles, Zoilo 86, 92, 124, 141, 145, 175
Veterans Stadium 224*ch*11*n*3
Vidmer, Richards 114–115, 223*n*18, 223*n*19
Waddell, Rube 63, 64, 219*ch*5*n*10, 219*ch*5*n*11

wage stabilization *see* Emergency Stabilization Act
Wagner, Honus 16, 25, 51, 52, 55–56, 62, 64, 73, 77, 86–87, 135, 142, 167, 180–181, 228*n*20, 229*n*22; throwing record 228*ch*19*n*1
Walker, Larry 153, 156
Walsh, Ed 65, 67
Walters, Bucky 91
Waner, Paul 40, 61
Waner, Paul 40, 61, 225
WAR *see* wins above replacement
Ward, Duane 135
Washington Nationals 155
Washington Senators 11–12, 24, 32, 41, 67, 71, 79, 98, 145, 156
Webb, Earl 141, 217*ch*4*n*6
Welch, Bob 139, 172
"The Whiz Kids" 105
Wilks, Ted 88
Williams, Ken 36
Williams, Ted 2, 74, 76–77, 82, 86, 102, 109, 116, 142, 143, 151, 165, 170, 175, 183–184, 194, 196, 225*ch*14*n*2, 229*n*19; MVP snubs 94–97
Wills, Maury 92, 101, 107, 175, 199
Wilson, Hack 13, 40, 61–62
Win Shares 1
Winfield, Dave 138
wins above replacement (WAR): components 31; definition 1, 2, 5, 217*n*13; lowest WAR in an MVP Season 34; for pitchers 1; scale 24; use in player comparison 32, 33
Wood, "Smoky" Joe 67
World Baseball Classic 112
World War II 88, 89, 93
Wright, David 178
Wrigley Field 108, 223*ch*10*n*2, 223*ch*10*n*3

Yankees Stadium 73, 95
Yastrzemski, Carl 74, 113, 167, 175
Young, Cy (player) 62, 181
Young, Michael 111, 223*ch*10*n*10
Young Frankenstein 227*ch*17*n*12
Young Man of Manhattan 115, 223*n*19
Yount, Robin 186

Zachary, Pat 229*n*16
Zimmerman, Heinie 75, 77
Zobrist, Ben 155, 202
Zone Rating 85